The Republicans

The Republicans

A History of the Grand Old Party

LEWIS L. GOULD

OXFORD
UNIVERSITY PRESS

OXFORD
UNIVERSITY PRESS

Oxford University Press is a department of the
University of Oxford. It furthers the University's objective
of excellence in research, scholarship, and education
by publishing worldwide.

Oxford   New York

Auckland   Cape Town   Dar es Salaam   Hong Kong   Karachi
Kuala Lumpur   Madrid   Melbourne   Mexico City   Nairobi
New Delhi   Shanghai   Taipei   Toronto

With offices in

Argentina   Austria   Brazil   Chile   Czech Republic   France   Greece
Guatemala   Hungary   Italy   Japan   Poland   Portugal   Singapore
South Korea   Switzerland   Thailand   Turkey   Ukraine   Vietnam

Oxford is a registered trade mark of Oxford University Press
in the UK and certain other countries.

Published in the United States of America by
Oxford University Press
198 Madison Avenue, New York, NY 10016

Library of Congress Cataloging-in-Publication Data
Gould, Lewis L.
The Republicans : a history of the grand old party / Lewis L. Gould.
      pages   cm
Includes bibliographical references and index.
ISBN 978-0-19-993662-5 (alk. paper)
1. Republican Party (U.S. : 1854-)—History.   I. Title.
JK2356G69   2014
324.273409—dc23
2014004065

1 3 5 7 9 8 6 4 2

Printed in the United States of America
on acid-free paper

Contents

The Republicans

Introduction

A VISITOR TO THE WEBSITE of the modern Republican Party finds there a restatement of familiar themes. The Republicans are "the party of freedom, the party of prosperity, and the party of vision." The Democrats, on the other hand, represent a "fundamentally different" manner of governance. The historical record shows that through more than a century and a half of its existence, the Republican Party has viewed the world of American politics as an arena in which it is entitled to govern against a partisan rival that has always been out of the national mainstream. Thus, for the Republican Party, the issue of legitimacy is not some arcane political science term. Republicans have always believed that they have an inalienable right to hold power because of their record and their values. They see themselves holding firm against the Other: Democrats—potentially if not actually disloyal, influenced by non-American ideas, and never to be trusted. The unfolding of Republican history has been the working out in practice of these fundamental beliefs.

This perspective on American politics arose in the first decade of the existence of the Republican Party. Established to block the spread of slavery and to in time roll back bondage, the party under the leadership of Abraham Lincoln found itself in 1861 in a struggle to preserve the Union against a proslavery, Confederate rebellion. Many Democrats supported the war effort, but others did not. Some in the hierarchy of the Democratic Party wanted a negotiated peace, accepted the disruption of the Union, and would have tolerated the continued presence of slavery in the South. Imagining the consequences of these policies, Republicans concluded that the Democrats had not just flirted with treason: they had consorted with the enemy. Their hearts were prone to treason.

The trauma of the war and the huge casualty lists seared into the minds of the Republicans at all levels that the Democrats lacked true allegiance to the United States. These passions burned bright for a decade or so. As the nation debated industrialism, grew accustomed to racial segregation in the South, and left the Civil War behind, the Republicans regarded the Democrats with bemused contempt as ineffectual representatives of a failed ideology. Leaders might argue about the protective tariff (a key Republican doctrine) or the gold standard, but these questions could be worked out without putting the assumptions of democracy under assault. For the most part they were resolved in a normal fashion. The two parties differed over government regulation of the economy, but that debate did not become charged with allegations of disloyalty to the nation and its values.

The onset of another war in 1914, however, introduced what would be the second of three tests of Republican toleration of the existence of the Democrats. As Bolshevism and other radical ideologies arose in Europe and Asia, Republicans saw Democratic programs under Woodrow Wilson as offshoots of these noxious systems. In 1920, addressing the Republican convention, Henry Cabot Lodge said: "Mr. Wilson stands for a theory of administration and government which is not American."[1]

The questioning of Democratic loyalty returned and became more intense during the New Deal of Franklin D. Roosevelt. Voices on the right asserted that the entire administration of FDR was controlled by the Kremlin. The existence of Soviet espionage rings in the United States validated for Republicans the presumption of a treasonous mindset among Democrats at all levels. Republicans became convinced, as a recent book affirms, that FDR and his party had given away Eastern Europe to Joseph Stalin and his tyranny.[2]

In the decades after World War II, Republicans also sought ways to break up the Democratic electoral coalition of southern whites and northern minorities. As Harry Truman and John F. Kennedy pursued, with varying degrees of enthusiasm, civil rights legislation and social change, Republicans sensed a bounty of white votes in the states of the old Confederacy. Under Dwight D. Eisenhower and then Richard Nixon, Republicans reaped a rich harvest of white support, and the party dominated the presidency in the 1970s and 1980s. In the minds of Republicans, race became the third test the Democrats failed, as they became outspoken and illegitimate enemies of white ascendancy.

The accession of former southern Democrats into the Republican Party produced changes in the way the Grand Old Party thought and operated. Under leaders like William Jennings Bryan, the Democrats had emphasized the virtues of emotion over reason, conversion over persuasion, religion over science. To win the allegiance of southerners, the Republicans became more in tune with these attitudes. Where once between 1865 and 1940 the Republicans had been the organization of intellectuals and the well educated (alongside the rank and file, of course), after 1970 a greater premium went to spontaneity, authenticity, and intuition. If the choice was between the doctrine of evolution or the creed of creationism, Republican politicians soon learned where they had the most safety among their voters. Science was not a process that affirmed physical truths about the universe. It was an ideology that was no better and likely worse than the doctrines that seemed so identified with common sense and personal values.

These developments occurred within a nation still struggling with the most explosive human predicament—the question of race. Republicans took justified pride in their record in the nineteenth century of freeing the slaves and enacting the Reconstruction amendments to the Constitution. Democrats had taken an unduly long time to discard their racist past. In the 1960s and 1970s, however, the parties passed each other in opposite directions. The party of Kennedy and Lyndon Johnson became as identified with the aspirations of African Americans as previous members of their party had been with keeping alive segregation and discrimination. Republicans, for their part, found reasons to champion the cause of white southerners and like-minded northerners in the service of victory at the polls and the opportunity to hold power.

In this first edition of this study, the narrative ended with some forebodings of difficulties to come in the wake of the disputed election of 2000. The tragic consequences of the terrorist attacks on 9/11 destabilized American politics and gave the Republicans a chance to show how they would handle national power once again. By 2008, with war in Iraq and a near collapse of a wounded economy, the country was ready for a change. When the change proved to be a first-term Illinois senator who was an African American with a foreign-sounding name, the Republicans found their worst fears confirmed about the future of the nation and the lack of true legitimacy. Some saw Barack Obama as a Socialist usurper. Others concluded that he was not even a citizen but rather a kind of Manchurian candidate out to destroy everything good in America.

Republicans decided that in the profound national crisis brought on by the election of Obama the rules of American political life no longer applied. The party had long believed that the positive workings of such customs were theirs by right and a matter of grace for the Democrats. But in 2008–2009, with the very future of American democracy under assault, the rulebook was tossed aside. Any means—pervasive filibusters in the Senate to block nominations, state legislation to cut back or bar minorities from the polls, changes in constitutional law to enhance the power of corporate money—should be followed to the desired end of a Republican president and a Congress with GOP majorities in both houses. That strategy went into effect once President Obama was in office. Its end is not yet in sight.

American politics can be dramatic, but it is not a melodrama with heroes and villains. Throughout their history, Republicans have pursued policies that seemed plausible and appropriate at the time they were adopted and implemented. It was right to end slavery and defend the Union. Apprehensions about the menace of Communism and internal espionage reflected real dangers from a nation that meant the United States no good. As for race, it is arrogant to sit in judgment of fellow citizens who encountered a volatile set of circumstances with imperfect knowledge, immediate fears, and human frailties. Yet the shift from the aspirations of Lincoln to the chauvinism of electoral restrictions and the denial of minority opportunities is a transition to ponder with sadness.

It is not the task of the historian to propose future answers to historical dilemmas. After studying the Republicans for half a century and writing books about three of their presidents, the subject remains fascinating. There is also a tragic sense that the implanting of doubts about Democratic legitimacy during the Civil War introduced a fault line into national politics that has yet to be remedied. Like a hidden crack in a piece of machinery, this core Republican conviction became so ingrained that party members did not perceive its existence. The press, the public, even the Democrats themselves operated under the assumption that a natural ability to govern was inherent in the DNA of the Grand Old Party. For the most part these elements of society still believe that to be the case. They have failed to notice that one major party has decided that democratic procedures should no longer constrain its behavior. Thus a major breakdown in how American politics works has gone unremarked. The purpose of this book is to address how the history of a major political party led to this situation. If the narrative about the Republicans provokes discussion and (surely) dissent, it will have achieved its goal.

The Party of Lincoln, 1854–1865

CHICAGO HAD NEVER SEEN anything like it. Ten thousand Republicans had crammed themselves into a pine-board frame building called the Wigwam to nominate a candidate for president in mid-May 1860. After two days of deliberation about the platform, the enthusiastic delegates turned to the key business of nominations on Friday, May 18. Everyone knew who the front runners were: William H. Seward of New York and Abraham Lincoln of Illinois. Two or three dark horses were also in the mix. The Illinois crowd clamored for Lincoln; some timely printing of bogus ticket helped inflate the crowd with supporters of "Honest Abe." After Lincoln's name was placed in nomination, the arena exploded with noise. "No language can describe it," said one observer. "A thousand steam whistles, ten acres of hotel gongs, a tribe of Comanches, headed by a choice vanguard from pandemonium, might have mingled in the scene unnoticed."[1]

In the balloting that followed, Seward led Lincoln on the first tally, but neither had the 233 votes needed for nomination. The second ballot produced a big gain for Lincoln. Seward's lead was a scant three votes. When it became evident on the third ballot that Seward could not win, Lincoln moved toward a majority as the other contenders fell away. When Lincoln reached 231½ votes, four Ohio delegates switched their votes, and Lincoln was then the nominee of the Republican Party. Another tumultuous celebration ensued, while back in Lincoln's hometown of Springfield congratulatory telegrams poured in. The Republicans had become the party of Lincoln.

What made the moment surprising was the rapid rise of both the nominee and his party to political prominence. Six and a half years earlier, in January 1854, the Republican Party did not exist, and Abraham Lincoln was a successful but politically obscure attorney in Springfield. If anyone in Illinois that winter seemed likely to become president, it was the state's Democratic senator Stephen A. Douglas. Yet with a speed that in retrospect seems incredible and almost preordained, the new party became one of the two major political organizations in the United States.

To Americans in the 1850s the chain of events that led to the rise of the Republicans and the Lincoln presidency grew out of the crisis over human slavery that convulsed the nation. Twists and turns, unexpected episodes, and some plain historical luck enabled the Republicans to survive the turbulent circumstances of their early years and put Lincoln in the White House in 1860. Once in power the party that had been founded in an effort to restrict the further expansion of slavery found itself in a major war that required an unprecedented expansion of governmental power for victory. At the same time, the struggle with the South posed the problem of how to structure a multiracial society after the fighting ended. That dilemma would divide the country and shape the destiny of the Republicans for the next century and a half.

The Republican Party emerged in a United States that was still an agricultural and rural nation. Census takers counted twenty-three million people in 1850; the figure rose to twenty-six million four years later. There were thirty-one states, with California on the West Coast as the most recent addition. The majority of the population lived east of the Mississippi River, and most Americans still made their living off the land through farming or raising livestock. Industrialization and urbanization had made beginnings in the North, and these forces accelerated during the 1850s. In Lincoln's Illinois, for example, the 110 miles of railroad track in the early 1850s expanded to nearly two thousand miles by the end of the decade.

Economic times were good. The discovery of gold in California in 1848 and an influx of British investment into the United States fueled a robust economic expansion. Railroad building surged as money poured into the new industry. With immigration climbing as well, the country had a growing, hard-working labor force in the North. So dramatic was this rise in prosperity that some commentators predicted an end to the partisan issues that had shaped national politics for two decades: the wisdom of having a national bank, the merits of a protective tariff, and the constitutionality of internal improvements such as canals, wagon roads, and railroads.

Yet Americans knew that beneath the surface the United States was a troubled land. The tide of immigration in the 1850s intensified social tensions. In 1853, 369,000 people arrived from overseas. Almost half were newcomers from Ireland, another 141,000 were of German origin, Immigration peaked in 1854 with 427,000 individuals entering the country. The Irish, because of their Roman Catholic faith, and many of the Germans, also Catholics, aroused fears among native-born Protestants who remembered the Reformation, disapproved of the elaborate rituals, and worried about the fealty of devoted

Catholics to the papacy. These new Americans usually aligned themselves with the Democrats, who were seen as more culturally tolerant than their major rivals, the Whigs.

In the 1850s, religious beliefs and national origin often shaped voting decisions as much as economic class and social status did. These ethnocultural pressures showed themselves in the reaction against the tide of immigrants. So large had been the arrival of newcomers and so powerful was their impact on local and state politics in New York, Pennsylvania, and Massachusetts, for example, that native voters reacted against the immigrant presence with laws to mandate the teaching of English in public schools, the closing of saloons on Sundays, and the prohibition of alcohol. The vehicle for their antiforeign impulses became a new political party that emphasized secrecy in its opposition to both immigrant and Catholic influence. When asked about their organization, members were told to say, "I know nothing," a phrase that gave the movement its name. Know-Nothings, or the Native Americans, as they were sometimes called, picked up followers during the first half of the 1850s at a rate that stunned politicians. "At the bottom of all this," remarked a Pennsylvania Democrat, "is a deep-seated religious question—prejudice if you please, which nothing can withstand." Many public figures hoped or feared that the Know-Nothings might replace the embattled Whigs as the primary alternative to the Democrats.[2]

Even more troubling to many people in the North was the presence of slavery in the South. There were 3.2 million men, women, and children in bondage in the South in 1850, and the "peculiar institution," as the South called slavery, dominated every aspect of life in the fifteen slave states stretching from Maryland and Delaware to Texas. Law, customs, and the Constitution meant that slavery also wove its way through American government and daily life. Northerners understood that by law they must help return fugitive slaves to their owners and that slavery could not be eliminated without changing the Constitution. Though the issue had quieted since the approval of the Compromise of 1850, feelings remained volatile. Harriet Beecher Stowe's novel *Uncle Tom's Cabin* became an instant best-seller in 1852 in the North for its depiction of the cruelties of slavery and their impact on a mother and her family.

The South saw slavery not as a moral burden on the nation or an evil to be expunged but more and more as a positive good for both master and slave. "Slavery has not been a crime," wrote a Texas judge in 1860, "but has resulted in positive blessings, both to the negro and his master." If left alone and "not tampered with by misguided white men the slave is for the most part contented and happy."[3] Believing this, many leading southerners contended that they should have the right to take their human property wherever they wished. Efforts to restrict slavery or limit its expansion would justify secession from the Union.

The North was more divided. Slavery had receded from the region by 1853, but northerners did not have a coherent view of the institution's future. Radical abolitionists, a definite minority, opposed slavery on moral grounds. Others disliked slavery because its spread might bring blacks into the North and West as competitive cheap labor. In 1848, northern opponents of slavery established a Free Soil Party that sought to block the spread of slavery in the West. Still others, driven by racist impulses, wanted African Americans to stay in the South or be returned to Africa. Whatever their attitudes toward slavery, residents of the North often resented the South's political power and regarded the land below the Mason-Dixon line as backward, out of step with progressive currents of the nineteenth century. An uneasy sectional peace, based on the Missouri Compromise of 1820 and the Compromise of 1850, existed as 1854 began.

These two historical sectional bargains defined the way in which Americans viewed the politics of slavery as the 1850s began. In 1820, Congress had decided, after heated debates, to admit the new state of Missouri as one where slavery existed, and Maine as one where it did not. In the rest of the territory gained from the Louisiana Purchase of 1803, slavery would be barred north of a line running along the latitude 36°30′ north. Conscious of themselves as sections divided by slavery, North and South accepted this arrangement for three decades. But in the wake of the Mexican War, another crisis threatened over the fate of the western land obtained from the victory in that conflict. Lawmakers decided to let California enter the Union as a free state, to leave the fate of slavery in the rest of the new territory in limbo for the time being, and to strengthen the right of the South to capture and return fugitive slaves from the North. The settlement did not satisfy either side, but most moderate Americans agreed that the Compromise of 1850 maintained the sectional balance and extended the principles of the Missouri Compromise. Undoing these compromises would plunge the nation into renewed turmoil.

American politics responded to these conflicting pressures. At the time and for much of the rest of the nineteenth century, partisan warfare occupied much more of the nation's attention than would be true a century and a half later. Frequent elections kept voters attuned to the fortunes of their party. Allegiance to a party defined the lives of most white male voters; independents represented only a small fraction of the electorate. The voters did not scorn parties as corrupt institutions but valued them for their role in democracy. "Party is the great engine of human progress," said one northern Democrat in 1852. Loyalty to a party was essential and, as a result, "to forsake a party is regarded as an act of greatest dishonour."[4]

Interest in elections and press coverage of politics was intense. Newspapers did not pretend to be objective dispensers of information. Owned by partisans, they slanted reporting and editorials to advance party fortunes. Yet overall coverage of conventions, rallies, and speeches was far more detailed and elaborate than now. The hundreds of partisan newspapers kept voters up to date on the latest successes or failures of each party.

Meanwhile, voters and their families attended "mass meetings" and political rallies where speakers might go on for an hour or two. Such events often lasted all day and into the night, with meal breaks. Audiences knew the issues and expected a sophisticated treatment of contemporary concerns. Orators had to have command of the complexities of their subject, whether it was slavery in the territories, the merits of a protective tariff, or the constitutionality of a national bank. No one used speech writers, and an orator's thoughts on the stump were very much his own.

On the surface, the United States had a working two-party system in 1854 with the Democrats in power and the Whigs as their main opposition. The Democrats in the mid-nineteenth century were the party of small, limited government and of white supremacy. They did not believe that the national government should be in the business of sponsoring economic growth through canal construction, railroad building, or railroad promotion. Accordingly, their platform in 1852 opposed "a general system of internal improvements," promised "the most rigid economy in conducting our public affairs," and asserted that Congress had no power to interfere with slavery in the South. Well established in the North and strong in the South, the Democrats (or "the Democracy" as they were sometimes called) had the stronger national base of the two parties. However, sectional divisions within the Democracy over slavery meant there were in the North among unhappy Democrats potential recruits for an antislavery party. The Democrats were more fragile than they seemed after the landslide election of Franklin Pierce in 1852.[5]

The Whigs, meanwhile, had fallen into disarray after 1852. The party had originated in the turbulent politics of the Jacksonian era when opponents of Andrew Jackson adopted the term "Whig" to evoke memories of the anti-monarchical party in England. "King Andrew" united many men against his strong presidential leadership between 1829 and 1837. Democrats applauded what Jackson had done with his authority to prevent government excesses. As a result, suspicion of executive power was one Whig tradition that carried over to the Republicans.

So, too, were the Whig economic policies associated with the "American System" of Henry Clay of Kentucky. His program advocated the use of government power to promote the growth of enterprise through a protective tariff, a national bank, sale of public lands, and internal improvements. Whigs stressed the common interests of society and contended that their policies helped all classes. Yet the identification of the Whigs with business and commercial interest led the Democrats to accuse them of being the party of the rich. But throughout the 1830s and 1840s the Whigs were credible rivals to the Democrats in both the North and the South.

As the slavery issue came more to the fore, the Whigs found themselves increasingly divided between their northern and southern wings. Their platform in 1852 labeled slavery a dangerous issue in 1852 but said little more than that the sectional compromise should be maintained. The decisive defeat of the Whig nominee in 1852 raised serious doubts about whether the Whigs could survive. That candidate had been Winfield Scott, a Mexican War hero, but unlike William Henry Harrison in 1840 and Zachary Taylor in 1848, he had endured a stunning defeat in the electoral vote, with 254 electoral votes for Pierce and 42 for Scott. Scott had done better in the popular vote, running two hundred thousand ballots behind Pierce, but the Whig fortunes were on the decline. In fact, the whole party system seemed antiquated and out of touch with the concerns of average Americans.

On January 4, 1854, however, American politics took a dramatic turn that eradicated the Whig Party, split the Democrats, and enabled the Republicans to come into being. The clamor over the Kansas-Nebraska Act thrust the slavery question to the forefront of the national debate. Senator Stephen A. Douglas, an Illinois Democrat, reported out of his committee a bill in Congress to organize the western territory of Nebraska. The measure soon became legislation to create the territories of Kansas and Nebraska. What made it so explosive was the attitude of Congress and Douglas toward the future of slavery in the area and therefore in the nation as a whole.

The Missouri Compromise of 1820 specified that slavery would be outlawed north of the line of 36°30′ north. Although Missouri was admitted to the Union as a slave state, the territory west and north of its southern border was closed to bondage. The firm dividing line between slave and nonslave territory that the Compromise established was popular in the North. As time passed, more and more southerners regarded the restriction of slavery on the basis of a geographic line as an unfair limit on their ability to take their property wherever slavery might prosper.

The Compromise of 1850, in addition to admitting California as a free state and toughening the law on the return of fugitive slaves, dealt with the question of how the territory acquired from Mexico after the war should be organized into territories and states. The Compromise legislation stated, "When admitted as a State, the said Territory, or any portion of the same, shall be received into the Union with or without slavery, as their Constitution may prescribe at the time of their admission." Since much of the Mexican cession lay below the Missouri Compromise line in areas where the growth of plantation slavery seemed difficult, this approach did not unduly rile northern feelings. In addition, because of Mexican law, the territory did not have slavery.[6]

But in the case of Kansas and Nebraska the situation was much different. The proposed territories were above the Missouri Compromise line, and when Douglas used the language of the Compromise of 1850 in his legislation, he was in effect abrogating the 1820 settlement and opening these areas to slavery. To make this point explicit, Douglas was forced to add wording which stated that the Missouri Compromise restriction was "hereby declared null and void."[7] As a northern Democrat who believed that climate made slavery ill-suited to the western plains, Douglas saw the bill as a way to conciliate the South without giving up anything of real substance. The people of the new territories themselves would decide whether to have slavery or not, a doctrine that was known as "popular sovereignty." Douglas did not like slavery as such, but he saw no moral issue involved, since in his mind African Americans were a lesser order of human beings with few of the rights of their white counterparts.

Because it subverted the Missouri Compromise, which many in the North regarded as a solemn sectional bargain and a way of confining slavery to the South, the Kansas-Nebraska Act ignited a firestorm of criticism in the North during the first half of 1854. By the time the southern Democrats and allies of Douglas enacted the Kansas-Nebraska measure into law on May 30, 1854, protest meetings and political upheaval had convulsed the North.

In two states, protesting citizens from both the Democratic and Whig parties, outraged at the implications of what Douglas was proposing about slavery in the territories, began to shape a new political party almost at once. Antislavery sentiment was strong in Wisconsin and Michigan, while nativist prejudices were not as powerful. At Ripon, Wisconsin, on February 28, a coalition of dissident Democrats, Whigs, and members of the Free Soil Party

vowed to create a new "Republican" party if the Kansas-Nebraska Act became law. This action represented one of the earliest uses of the name Republican for a political organization. Their second meeting, on March 20, 1854, is
often called the birth of the Republican Party. Michigan's claims to primacy
as the Republican birthplace rest on a state convention in Jackson, Michigan,
that gathered on July 6, 1854, nominated candidates for state office, and wrote
a platform for the campaign.[8]

Why did the name Republican gain such favor? Simply as a title it connected voters with the original political organization of Thomas Jefferson
in the 1790s, the Democratic-Republican Party. Tying the new name to the
framer of the Declaration of Independence underlined the commitment of
northerners to doctrines of political equality and expanding economic opportunity. In a broader context, "Republicanism" tapped into a rich historical
tradition dating back to the Italian renaissance and the English revolution
that saw republics as embodying public-spirited citizens acting in the political
sphere to preserve civic virtue and the welfare of all. There was a strong ethical
strain in Republicanism that accorded well with attacks on slavery as both
unjust and menacing to free labor in the North.

The problem for antislavery northerners in 1854 and 1855 was not how to
create a new party in an institutional sense. Most men knew from their own
experience as Democrats or Whigs how a party was organized. They key was
a system of conventions at all levels where white male voters took part in elections. In a precinct or election district, partisans assembled in a convenient
meeting place where they picked candidates, created platforms, and debated
issues. Their most important function was choosing delegates to a convention
at the next level of the congressional or judicial district. At the top was the
state convention that set policy for the party until the next election or the
next convention.

Every four years the process culminated in a national convention to select
a presidential candidate. These gatherings did not simply ratify a selection
already made in preferential primaries (which did not exist as such in the
1850s) but selected a nominee for the party after a series of ballots. Convention
strategies evolved based on what delegates from around the nation would do
on a second, third, or fourth ballot. Republicans never adopted the Democratic
rule that a winning candidate had to receive the ballots of two-thirds of the
delegates.

Putting a party organization together was simple once a sufficient number
of like-minded men agreed to act in concert. The problem for those who
wanted a northern party devoted to curbing slavery in 1854–1855 was the

Know-Nothings. They provided an alluring alternative for voters who were unhappy with the Democrats and their policies, and they attracted those dissidents that the new Republicans needed to become a viable national party. The Know-Nothings (or the Americans, as they now called themselves) asserted that the menace of immigrant voters loyal to the Roman Catholic Church and antagonistic to American values posed a greater danger to the nation than slavery or southern aggression. Before the Republicans could become a credible rival to the Democrats, they had to extinguish the hopes of the Know-Nothings.

The Republicans accomplished that goal in 1855–1856, thanks in part to Know-Nothing divisions over slavery and better leadership that outfought their adversaries in key northern states. Nonetheless, the success of the new party was not guaranteed. The fragility of the Republicans was one reason that a man such as Abraham Lincoln did not enlist in their ranks in 1854. Other antislavery parties had flourished and then died. Until Lincoln and men like him were sure that the Whigs were indeed doomed, they kept their options open.

The political tide in 1854 ran against the Democrats. Lincoln spoke out against Douglas and the Kansas-Nebraska Act on October 16, 1854, at Peoria, Illinois. He objected to the new law "because it assumes that there can be *moral right* in the enslaving of one man by another." Lincoln conceded that public opinion and his own views would not allow for freeing the slaves and making them, "politically and socially, our equals." But he believed that what Douglas had done went against the promise of the Declaration of Independence. "Our republican robe is soiled, and trailed in the dust," he concluded. "Let us repurify it. Let us turn and wash it white, in the spirit, if not the blood of the Revolution."[9]

The elections showed that the Whigs were all but dead. Their candidates failed, and the Republicans received much of the antislavery protest vote. But it was not yet clear that the Republicans could surpass the Know-Nothings in the North. Indeed, events in 1855 seemed to indicate that the Know-Nothings might have an edge. Although Republicans joined with Know-Nothings in Ohio to achieve victory, elsewhere, running on their own, the Republican suffered defeats. As one disgruntled Massachusetts Republican remarked in November 1855, anti-Irish and anti-Catholic voters in his state "want a Paddy hunt & on a Paddy hunt they will go."[10]

These comments attested to the problem that the Republicans faced in overcoming the desire of many northerners to pursue ethnic goals rather than antislavery ends. The animus against Irish immigrants permeated a nation where social and economic change seemed to threaten Protestant values. Many nativists saw these newcomers as unwilling to adapt to American political customs. "It is the prevailing and besetting sin of Irishmen when they come to America that they will not become *Americans*, but persist in remaining *Irishmen*, with all the crochets and absurdities which their national education has given them," said the *Chicago Tribune*, an opponent of Irish immigration. The ease with which immigrants could vote raised the prospect of undue influence at the polling place as well. The Catholic Church appeared to large numbers of voters as a menace at least as potent as the South and slavery.[11]

Republican fortunes improved during the first half of 1856. The party elected Nathaniel Banks, a former Know-Nothing, as Speaker of the national House of Representatives by combining with the Know-Nothings and thus established their first national base. In May, incidents in Kansas and the United States Senate further boosted the Republicans. On May 21, a proslavery mob attacked the town of Lawrence, Kansas, a center of sentiment to make Kansas a free state, in what the Republicans called the "sack of Lawrence." The next day a more celebrated episode rocked the Senate. Charles Sumner, a Massachusetts Republican and passionate foe of slavery, had denounced, in personal terms, a senator from South Carolina during debate. A relative of the southern solon, Congressman Preston Brooks, attacked Sumner with a heavy rubberlike cane and beat him badly. The assault outraged moderate northern opinion as an example of southern aggression. "*Brooks* has knocked the scales from the eyes of the blind, and they now see!" observed a Vermont Republican.[12]

Coming only a month before the Republicans held their first national convention in Philadelphia, these traumatic events offered encouragement to the young party about potential victory in the fall. The Republicans nominated the popular western explorer John C. Fremont as their presidential candidate and hoped to ride his celebrity into the White House. Their platform was explicit about their efforts to curb slavery. The delegates denied the right of Congress to sanction slavery in the territories. Instead, it was the "imperative duty" of Congress to "prohibit in the Territories those twin relics of barbarism—Polygamy and Slavery." The Mormons in Utah practiced multiple marriages, to the dismay of Republicans. The main thrust of the convention was indicated in the party's new slogan: "Free Speech, Free Press, Free Men, Free Labor, Free Territory, and Fremont."[13]

To win the contest the Republicans confronted a problem about electoral votes that would recur over the next century. With 296 electoral votes in contention, the Democrats had a virtual lock on the slave South and could thus rely on 112 electoral votes before any ballots were tallied. Republicans had to find their majority of the electoral college from the remaining 184 votes among northern states. Pennsylvania, with 27 electoral votes, thus became a key battleground between the parties.

Fremont and his party did well in 1856, but the Democratic nominee, James Buchanan, carried Pennsylvania, New Jersey, and several other northern states to amass 174 electoral votes to 114 for Fremont. Millard Fillmore, a former president and the candidate of the Know-Nothings, won Maryland's 8 electoral votes. The Know-Nothing Party faded from the political scene after 1856, although the voters it had enlisted remained important in Republican calculations. They had lost the presidency, but the Republicans were pleased with their strong showing in the North. They looked forward to 1860. As one Maine Republican commented: "We are beaten, but we have frightened the rascals awfully."[14]

The Republicans now faced the question of how to win the next presidential election. Opposition to slavery had built a strong foundation for their new organization, but would it be enough to win the next election? Republican efforts to broaden the party's base has aroused some of the most intense historical criticism of any aspect of the Republican record. In attempting to secure support through economic appeals such as the protective tariff, for example, were the Republicans demonstrating that they were more interested in power than the moral issues that had brought the party into being? The question of Republican attitudes toward race and Republicans' capacity to measure up to standards of justice and equity has been a point of contention since the late 1850s.

The underlying problem of Republican sincerity and morality on racial issues goes even deeper. Democrats at the time and historians since have questioned whether the Republicans in the 1850s were sincere opponents of slavery, whether their underlying motives were genuine and based on an honest belief in equality, and whether the civil war that broke out in 1861 was worth the blood and sacrifice that ensued. The even larger question turns on the issue of race, a problem that runs through the record of the major political parties for their entire histories. In the case of the Republicans, the test has been whether their opposition to human bondage looked forward to the racial egalitarianism of the twenty-first century. A fair answer must be "Yes and no," depending on which Republicans are examined for the 1850s and 1860s. While even in the nineteenth century it was correct to call the Republicans "the party of freedom," the label requires some clearer definition in light of the racial attitudes of that period.

The United States in the 1850s was a nation where color and ethnic prejudices ran deep. Belief in the concept of the common humanity of all people
did not yet exist. Instead, white Americans thought that nature had made
them superior to blacks, Native Americans, Mexicans, and Asians. Racial stereotypes, crude jokes, and insulting images pervaded the culture. Those who
dared to think that all human beings ought to have political and legal rights
were a small minority in the North.

As a result, expressions of racial prejudice show up in the private and public statements of Republicans. "I want to have nothing to do with the free
negro or the slave negro," contended Lyman Trumbull, a Republican senator
from Illinois. Another party leader said in 1858 that "it is certainly the wish of
every patriot that all within the limits of our Union should be homogeneous
in race and of our own blood." The most famous such statement, of course,
was that of Abraham Lincoln in his fourth debate with Stephen A. Douglas
on September 18, 1858: "I am not nor ever have been in favor of making voters
or juror of negroes, nor of qualifying them to hold office, nor to intermarry
with white people; and I will say in addition to this that there is a physical difference between the white and black races which I believe will forever forbid
the two races living together on terms of social and political equality."[15]

Southerners and Democrats in the 1850s, and many historians since, have
used such statements either to indict the Republicans for insincerity and hypocrisy or to accuse them of having other motives for their opposition to
slavery. These goals allegedly include a desire to keep blacks in the South as
slaves or wage laborers and thus advance capitalism. More powerful has been
the charge that simple antisouthernism fueled the Republican dislike for
slavery. The new party is said to have exploited conspiracy fears in the North
and thus transformed the South into a proslavery monolith that never existed.
The Republicans could then evoke the menace of an internal threat to
American liberties for their own purposes. The Slave Power, wrote the *New
York Times*, "will stop at no extremity of violence in order to subdue the people of the Free States and force them into tame subservience to its own
domination."[16]

To judge Republican views on race without including the views of either
northern Democrats or southerners leaves the misleading impression that
if only Republicans had adopted egalitarian positions their political success
would have been secure. The opposite is in fact the case. One constant that
Republicans confronted was the intensity of northern prejudice against
blacks, which Democrats exploited repeatedly. Stephen A. Douglas said in
1858, for example: "I do not question Mr. Lincoln's conscientious belief

that the negro was made his equal and hence is his brother, but for my own part, I do not regard the negro as my equal and positively deny that he is my brother or any kin to me whatever." No Democrat ever received a rebuke from his party leaders for taking bigotry too far. The South was even less restrained.[17]

The Republicans were opposing majority opinion in the North when they asserted that slavery needed to be restricted and that the fate of slaves affected the nature of the Union. When a leader such as Lincoln made the case that free blacks in the North were human beings who were entitled to the opportunities of the Declaration of Independence, his opinions represented a significant advance in the understanding of what society ought to do for African Americans in terms of legal rights. Republicans still contended that blacks should not be allowed to vote or hold office, but in the exercise of other political and legal rights they should be treated as all other citizens were. Such a stance might seem modest by today's standards, but in the context of the mid-nineteenth century it represented a significant potential change in the nation's racial practices.

Two other issues have clouded the reputation of the Republicans during this period of their history. If slavery was on the decline as an unprofitable institution and would have disappeared in due course, then Republican attempts to restrict it were not needed and made the situation worse, or so runs the argument. To the contrary, Republicans believed that slavery was dynamic and expanding, and much modern scholarship bears out their claim. While hypothetical scenarios cannot be proved, there is strong evidence from the economic behavior of slaveholders that if the Civil War had not intervened, bondage could have prospered and adapted to industrial conditions, which would have kept it going for many decades.

The second problem relates to Republican fears about the "Slave Power" in the South and whether southern politicians were as determined to protect slavery and imperil the Union as many northerners believed. That there was not a vast web of conspiracy across the South is, of course, correct. But there was a consensus among southern political leaders and their constituents that slavery deserved the right to become a nationwide institution. Accordingly, politicians from Dixie acted in concerted ways, both in an out of Congress, to ensure that law and custom protected the peculiar institution. As this regional agenda developed after 1854, the North saw in operation a troubling southern attitude. The North would have to defer to slavery and allow it to exist, expand, and in the end become established everywhere. As Abraham Lincoln said of the South in 1860, "Holding, as they do, that slavery is morally right, and socially elevating, they cannot cease to demand a full national recognition of it, as a legal right, and a social blessing."[18]

A judgment on Republican ideology on the slavery question turns in the end on whether the Civil War was justified as a means of preserving the Union and abolishing slavery. It is easy to assert that some way of ending slavery and avoiding disunion that did not entail the death of six hundred thousand soldiers in combat should have occurred. Critics of the Republicans in this regard do not face the question of why black Americans should have been asked to endure more decades of bondage and its cruelties as their contribution to the preservation of the Union in 1860–1865. On this issue, for all their lapses into racial prejudice, political equivocation, and poor judgment on specific aspects of the sectional crisis, the Republican Party was on the right side of the historical argument in the 1850s and its opponents were not. Modern Republicans who find appeal in the neo-Confederate arguments for state rights and limited government separate themselves from the founding traditions and moral high ground of their party.

In 1857, a series of striking events boosted Republican fortunes. The Supreme Court on March 6, 1857, decided in the Dred Scott case that Congress lacked the power to keep slavery out of the territories. The ruling intensified Republican fears that the "Slave Power" might, through a court ruling, validate slavery nationwide. The ongoing struggle over Kansas as a free or slave state split the Democrats between the forces of Douglas and President Buchanan. The new administration favored generally the claims of southerners to take their slaves into Kansas and establish the institution there. Moreover, Republicans saw in the efforts of the Buchanan administration and the South to make Kansas a slave state further evidence of the existence of a conspiracy to nationalize bondage. When a severe economic downturn began in October 1857, it triggered a depression that lasted for four years and added to the woes of the Democrats.

As a result, Republicans looked forward to the 1858 elections with confidence. To capitalize on the discontent with hard times, the new party advocated a protective tariff and homestead legislation to encourage western settlement. With the tide of events running their way, the Republicans made important gains. They did well in Pennsylvania, an important state in the 1860 contest, and also won victories in such crucial states as New York and Ohio. Overall, conservative voters in the North rallied to the Republican banner.

The election of 1858 produced one of its most important results in Illinois, where Abraham Lincoln ran against Stephen A. Douglas for the United

States Senate. The seven debates that the two men conducted have become legendary. For the Republicans, the confrontation was decisive because it thrust their greatest leader and most potent political symbol onto the national stage and on his way to the presidency in 1860.

Abraham Lincoln was forty-nine and at the beginning of 1858 would have seemed an improbable presidential candidate. After an impoverished youth, he had made his way as a lawyer in Springfield, Illinois, and gained a reputation as a dedicated member of the Whig Party in the 1830s and 1840s. Following a single congressional term in 1847–1849, he had returned to Springfield, where he prospered and, with his wife, Mary Todd Lincoln, raised their three sons. Lincoln had sought a Senate seat in 1855, but had lost in the balloting in the Illinois legislature.

Though his record as an officeholder was sparse, Lincoln became recognized during the 1850s as a compelling champion of the policy of restricting slavery in the territories. He hated slavery as an institution but accepted that Congress lacked the power to abolish its existence in the South. Believing that slavery contradicted the promises of the Declaration of Independence, Lincoln contended that both North and South should agree to place it "in the course of ultimate extinction." To that end, Lincoln favored schemes to relocate former slaves to Africa. At this stage of his life, Lincoln did not see a viable future for blacks in the United States, but neither did he have any practical answers for their situation when and if slavery ended.[19]

For the moment, Lincoln's sights were set on his own political future and the defeat of Senator Douglas. As the Illinois lawmaker broke with President Buchanan, some eastern Republicans, such as the editor of the *New York Tribune*, Horace Greeley, looked to a possible alliance with Douglas and a union of Republicans and antislavery Democrats. In Lincoln's mind, Douglas' moral indifference to the evils of slavery disqualified him for such a political partnership. The two men agreed to a series of seven debates, and Lincoln sought to draw a bright line between himself and Douglas even before the confrontations commenced. His famous "house divided" speech of June 16, 1858, launched his Senate campaign with the statement that "a house divided against itself cannot stand." Lincoln continued: "I believe that this government cannot endure permanently half *slave* and half *free*." Either slavery would be put on the road to extinction "or its *advocates* will push it forward till it shall become lawful in *all* the States, old as well as *new—North* as well as South."[20]

Lincoln pressed the argument during the debates that slavery presented a moral issue for the United States that could not be evaded. If the institution

This photograph of Abraham Lincoln, taken in 1864, shows the first Republican president amid the challenges of the Civil War. Library of Congress, LC-USZ62–984.

was not restricted, it would expand. As the primary social evil in the nation, it must be confined and in time eliminated. When Douglas labeled him an advocate of social and political equality with blacks, Lincoln responded with language that his critics have often identified as racist. Yet, had Lincoln espoused broader rights for African Americans in the United States of 1858, he would have had no political future. The difference between Lincoln and Douglas was that the Republican senatorial candidate did not rule out that black people should have the opportunity to better themselves through their own effort. "I agree with Judge Douglas he [a black man] is not my equal— certainly not in color, perhaps not in moral or intellectual endowment. But in the right to the bread, without leave of anybody else, which his own hand earns, *he is my equal and the equal of Judge Douglas and the equal of every living man.*"[21]

Although Lincoln lost the senatorial election to Douglas, his performance in the debates stimulated talk of a presidential candidacy throughout 1859. The apparent front runner for the nomination, William H. Seward of New York, was identified with the antislavery cause in the popular mind. In a famous speech, Seward had predicted an "irrepressible conflict" between North and South. Yet Seward was weak where Lincoln was strong. The New Yorker had denounced nativism, which did not sit well with former Know-Nothings. Republicans grumbled that Seward could not win in the five northern states that had gone for Buchanan and the Democrats in 1856 and were essential for Republican victory in 1860.

Lincoln, on the other hand, while opposed to the Know-Nothings, had not said much to alienate them. He could carry Illinois and perhaps Pennsylvania where Seward could not. Lincoln appeared sound on slavery without the appearance of radicalism that dogged Seward. By the spring of 1860, the Republicans sought a candidate with broad appeal. In the wake of John Brown's unsuccessful raid on Harper's Ferry, Virginia, in late 1859 in an attempt to trigger a slave insurrection, antislavery passions had been muted. Since the Democrats had split at their convention and the northern wing of the party had nominated Douglas, Lincoln more and more seemed the best choice to carry the Republicans to victory against Douglas, John Bell of the Constitutional Union Party, and John C. Breckinridge, the candidate of the southern Democrats.

The convention that nominated Lincoln at Chicago in May 1860 also adopted a platform that took into account popular fears about the new party in control of the White House. The delegates affirmed that slavery in the South would not be harmed, and they denounced "the lawless invasion by armed force" of any state or territory as John Brown had done. But the Republicans also asserted that "the normal condition of all the territory of the United States is that of freedom," and they criticized southern calls to reopen the slave trade and any idea that slavery in the territories might be legal.[22]

At the end of the platform, the delegates called for a protective tariff, a homestead law, internal improvements, and construction of a Pacific railroad. By these planks the Republicans sought to assemble a majority coalition to win a presidential contest. They thus went beyond an appeal grounded only on their opposition to slavery. For the party to follow such a course was hardly surprising. Political parties grow by winning elections rather than suffering defeats based on perceived moral purity. Yet in 1860 and in historical accounts, Republicans were criticized both for risking the Union because of their antislavery position and for hypocrisy when they muted their opposition to slavery to attract potential voters.

With victory certain if the Democratic split persisted, the Republicans concentrated on keeping enthusiasm high and getting their voters out to the polls. Their style of campaigning, which featured marching units of "Wide Awake" societies, became a characteristic trademark of subsequent campaigns for more than three decades. Meanwhile, Lincoln remained in Illinois and said almost nothing in public. By long-standing tradition, presidential candidates did not make a personal appeal for votes.

When the ballots were tallied, Lincoln was a sectional and minority president with less than 40 percent of the popular vote. He won all of the northern states except New Jersey, which he split with Douglas. As a result, Lincoln had 180 electoral votes to the combined total of 123 votes for his three opponents. Even if the votes of Douglas and Bell in the North had been lumped together, Lincoln would still have won. The Republicans were well aware that they had not received a popular majority and feared what would happen if the Democrats, North and South, ever reunited.

After the election of Lincoln, southern states seceded from the Union, forming the Confederate States of America, and the Civil War began. For the Republicans, the experience of the conflict transformed their party. During the four years from 1861 to 1865, the nation, under their leadership, achieved the destruction of slavery and the preservation of the Union, in which the power of the South was now much reduced. The war and Reconstruction that followed also created real political rights for African Americans in the United States for the first time. By 1865 the antislavery agenda of the Republicans had been realized in full.

In the effort to win the war, however, the Republicans expanded the power of the national government in the economic sphere. They established a national banking system, imposed an income tax, created a system for dispersing public land in the West, and started a transcontinental railroad. The role of the national government in promoting economic growth went beyond even what the Whigs had contemplated. A corollary was an increasing identification of the Republicans with the ambitions and power of the business community in the North and Midwest. A party that began in an attack on the existing political order became an organization that believed in an identity of interests of capitalists, workers, and farmers. Over time, the commitment to business outweighed the concern for other elements in the economy.

These accomplishments occurred despite the continuation of the partisan struggle with the Democrats throughout the conflict. While many loyal Democrats in the North supported the war and the preservation of the Union, there was less agreement on how the South should be subdued and, more important, on how black Americans should be treated during and after the fighting. The Democratic identification with white supremacy had wide appeal in sections of the North, and Republicans remained a minority party in a significant number of states. In the congressional elections of 1862, the Democrats made gains in the House and Senate. Even in the 1864 election, when Lincoln defeated George B. McClellan as the Union military triumphs crested, the Democrats still polled 45 percent of the popular vote.

The war shaped a distinctive Republican view of the Democrats that cast a long shadow into the future. While the majority of northern Democrats supported the war effort and, with somewhat less enthusiasm, the Lincoln administration, a substantial minority of the opposition wanted a negotiated peace with the Confederacy even at the price of perpetuating slavery. At the fringes of the party, some Democrats, notably Clement Vallandigham of Ohio, did more to give aid and comfort to the South. Fairly or unfairly, the Democrats gained a reputation in the minds of Republicans as a party that had trifled with treason. In the presidential campaign of 1864, the party's speakers and newspapers assailed the Democrats for their alleged disloyalty. The opposition, said the *New York Tribune*, was "ready to barter the integrity of the Union for the sake of political power." The term "copperhead," meaning a southern sympathizer, became identified with the peace wing of the Democrats.[23]

At some instinctive level, Republicans were convinced that their political opposition was less patriotic, even less American, than Republicans in the nation's greatest crisis. As a result, while they did not question in principle the right of the Democrats to hold power, throughout the years in the minds of Republicans a Democratic president lacked legitimacy, especially if the chief executive had come to office with less than a majority of the popular vote. These attitudes originated during the Civil War when, as one writer noted in 1864, the Democratic Party gained "the taint of disloyalty, which whether true or false, will cling to it, like the poisoned shirt of Nessus, for a century."[24]

The requirements of winning the Civil War led Republicans to champion the biggest expansion of the role of the government in the economy up to that point in the nation's history. Since the Republicans have been the perceived advocates of limited government into the twenty-first century, their record as the party of expanded government in the nineteenth century may seem improbable. The evidence shows them to be the supporters of a large federal role in the wartime emergency, including a strong commitment to income taxes. As one Republican leader in the Senate, John Sherman of Ohio, put it in 1863, "All private interests, all local interests, all banking interests, the interests of individuals, everything, should be subordinate now to the interests of the government."[25]

The measures enacted from 1861 to 1863 in the Thirty-seventh Congress included the issuance and sale through popular subscription of bonds to finance the Union cause. The government also issued paper money (called "greenbacks" because of the color of the paper) to pay for the armies and their supplies. The government's debt rose dramatically because of these moves, but Republican editors contended that there was little risk to such a financial policy. Better a national debt owed to Americans than to foreign bondholders. "*What is owed to our own people is no loss*, the nation is no poorer for it."[26]

In 1863, Congress created the National Banking System. Since Andrew Jackson had destroyed the Second Bank of the United States in the 1830s, the country had not had any kind of organized banking structure. The National Banking System established a kind of national currency supported by government bonds that enabled banknotes to circulate. In the process a market for government bonds was initiated. The measure reduced the power of state banks and concentrated financial power in Washington. The bill became law in February 1863. In an amended statute, passed a year later, Congress imposed a tax on state banknotes to reduce the power of these state institutions. John Sherman captured the centralizing philosophy of wartime Republicans: "The power of taxation cannot be more wisely exercised than in harmonizing and placing on the secure basis of national credit all the money of the country."[27]

Financing the war required that the Republican Congress impose higher tariff duties and an income tax. In the case of the Morrill Tariff of 1861, Congress imposed duties on more than just manufactures. It sought to protect from foreign competition a wide range of agricultural items and useful minerals. Republicans contended that such policies would help farmers and free laborers as well as business owners. The new law became the basis for Republican tariff legislation for the rest of the nineteenth century.

Even higher tariffs did not bring in enough revenue to sustain the Union cause. The desperate need for more funds led to the adoption of an income tax. The Republicans adopted versions of the income levy in the various revenue laws enacted to pay for the war in 1861, 1862, and 1864. During the congressional debates, Republicans contended that "a tax properly levied upon incomes...is an equitable and just tax." Some party members favored making the tax system graduated so the burden fell more heavily on the wealthy. After much discussion, Congress accepted such a proposal in the tax bill of 1864. Individuals with incomes over $10,000 would pay 10 percent in taxes. The citizens of the North tolerated most of the revenue legislation as a necessary war measure for ultimate victory. After the war, in 1872, the income tax lapsed. Nonetheless, the Democrats labeled the Republicans the party of high taxes and big government for decades.[28]

Efforts to promote agricultural settlement on the western plains also embodied the Republican commitment to government activism. The party's ideology favored providing the free laborer with easy access to land for farming. The Homestead Act of 1862–1863 granted 160 acres of land from the public domain to actual settlers. As the proponents of the measure argued, the establishment of a prosperous nation of independent farmers was a worthy goal. "What is beneficial to the people cannot be detrimental to the Government; for in this country the interests of both are identical," remarked a Republican member of the House.[29]

A similar spirit led to the creation of the Department of Agriculture and the establishment of a system of land-grant colleges to diffuse education among the children of farmers. A key element in Republican thinking, adopted from the Whigs, was the belief in an identity of interests among all the producing elements of society. Accordingly, the federal government should encourage and promote the diverse classes of the economy, and all would profit together.

A railroad to the West Coast would further knit the nation together and hold California and the Pacific Northwest within the Union. The presence of cheap, efficient transportation would also stimulate the development of the agricultural sector. The advocates of the railroad project believed that honest entrepreneurs, acting in the national interest, would build a rail line at a reasonable profit for themselves. As it turned out, the increasing complexity of an industrializing economy brought into the projects capitalists who pursued profit over efficiency. The resulting scandals in the 1870s involving the Crédit Mobilier Company suggested that the Republican faith in a congruence of private and public interest was less certain than many party members believed. The Republicans did not want government regulation of the economy, preferring to allow the workings of the marketplace to correct inequities. Promotion without regulation was viable in the 1860s and helped win the Civil War. How it would fare in peacetime in an industrial nation remained an issue for the future.

The war proved a powerful engine of economic prosperity for the North. Even though there were several hundred thousand Union dead and many more wounded, the population expanded as immigrants came to fight and work. Such industries as railroading, clothing manufacturing, and meatpacking expanded to meet wartime demands. Young capitalists—such as Andrew Carnegie and John D. Rockefeller—laid the foundations for their businesses and fortunes. Many unskilled workers did not share in the good times as inflation rose and real wages declined, but skilled workers did well. Overall, the perception that Republican economic policies had promoted prosperity even in the midst of a devastating civil war created an association between the party and the nation's economic health that endured until the Great Depression of the 1930s.

The Republicans and President Lincoln wielded the power of the government in other ways. The right of habeas corpus was suspended. A draft was instituted after volunteering for the military ebbed. Press censorship of dissenting newspapers occurred and some instances of political arrests took place as well. Despite Democratic protests and the opposition of parts of the judiciary, the federal government sought to punish disloyalty and prevent the undermining of the Union cause with its greatly expanded powers. On the other hand, relatively few dissidents were punished. Amid all of this turmoil, political battles raged and elections took place on schedule.

The Republicans revealed important internal divisions during the first half of the 1860s. The main point of contention was the issue of race and the party's position on the future of black Americans. Those Republicans who favored the expansion of rights for blacks and a stringent policy toward the South became known as "Radicals." A middle ground of the party styled themselves as "Moderates," while those who wanted to win the war but not to do much for freed slaves were labeled "Conservatives." Lincoln acted as a conciliator among these divergent parts of the party. The size and strength of these factions shifted with specific issues and problems as Republican policy toward slavery and then Reconstruction emerged.

Among the Radicals, the most famous members in Congress in historical terms were Charles Sumner, the Massachusetts senator, and Thaddeus Stevens, a House member from Pennsylvania. While both men had influence, neither of them dominated his colleagues in Congress in the manner that Democratic critics alleged. Radicalism was a more wide-ranging movement within Republican ranks and not the brainchild of two leaders.

In the first half of the twentieth century, the Radicals came under fire as militants who sought to impose racial egalitarianism on the South despite evidence that white southerners did not want such social change. Critics also asserted that African Americans were not ready for self-government during the Reconstruction years. The critique of the Radicals, racist in its essential elements, held sway until the end of World War II.

After 1945 and with rising intensity during the civil rights movement of the 1960s, the Radicals were rehabilitated. In a time such as the 1860s, when racism dominated the United States, the Radicals seemed at least a vanguard for a more just and equitable nation. Yet the Radicals did not always embody modern ideals, and their performance often fell short of their proclaimed goals. Historians suggested that the Radicals had not been militant enough.

Instead of seeking social change in race relations with vigor, they had settled for half a loaf. As a result, when Reconstruction faltered and the white South regained control over blacks in the 1870s, segregation closed in and the Radical program became a dead letter. After generations of criticism for having done too much, the Radicals are now indicted for having done too little for African Americans.

From 1861 to 1865, in the midst of the Civil War, the Republican Party wrestled with the issue of what the political role of black Americans should be and what legislative and constitutional means could best achieve these aims. The debate on the Republicans and blacks during the war has centered on Abraham Lincoln. His assassination in April 1865 left forever unsolved the mystery of what he would have done with the defeated South. Historians have gone over and over his record in the White House searching for clues. Was Lincoln close to the Radicals or distant from their program? Was he moving toward the idea of votes for some blacks when he was killed? How would he have dealt with the southern states once the fighting stopped? It is well known what happened when Andrew Johnson became president. Was he carrying on Lincoln's plan (as he said he was), or did Johnson's accession mark a major change in policy toward the South and African Americans? These questions have dogged debate about the nature of the Republican Party during the 1860s.

During the Civil War, Republicans endorsed striking changes in the status of African Americans. At the start of the conflict, President Lincoln recognized the strategic importance of the border states, Maryland, Kentucky, Delaware, and Missouri, to the Union cause. If those states joined the Confederacy, defeating the rebellion would become almost impossible. Accordingly, the president resisted efforts in 1861 and 1862 to make emancipation of the slaves Union policy. As the corrosive effects of the war on the institution of slavery became more apparent, Lincoln concluded that freeing the slaves would strengthen the Union cause with European nations that otherwise might be tempted, for economic or diplomatic reasons, to recognize the Confederacy as an independent state. Freeing the slaves also undermined the economic base of the South as those the military advance released from bondage left their homes.

The Emancipation Proclamation of 1862–1863 was not in itself an inspiring document. It did not free any slaves beyond Union control. It did put the North on a course of changing the situation of African Americans in the United States that would be difficult to reverse. A return to slavery became impossible. Black males who joined the army could provide vital manpower for the North. As blacks performed well in combat and supplied resources to defeat the Confederacy, it became harder to contend that they were not human beings entitled to some degree of political rights.

Abraham Lincoln pushed northern war aims a step further toward a broader affirmation of political liberty in the Gettysburg Address of November 19, 1863. When he spoke of "these honored dead" who had fought for "a new birth of freedom," he indicated that the larger purpose of the conflict was to achieve freedom for all Americans, black and white. The leader of the Republican Party thus identified himself with the aspiration of African Americans to a better life after the fighting ended, but he did so within the limits of a nation where currents of racism persisted.[30]

In 1864–1865, the Republicans looked more and more to a constitutional amendment outlawing slavery as a means of putting the issue beyond the reach of a temporary majority should the South rejoin the Union or the Democrats regain power in the presidential election of 1864. In the Republican senate, the measure sailed through. The amendment fell short of the necessary two-thirds vote in the House on June 15, 1864, with a very solid Democratic vote against it. Once the National Union Party (as the Republicans styled themselves in 1864) had won the election and Lincoln received a second term, the House approved the antislavery amendment on January 31, 1865. Lincoln himself signed the amendment, although he did not have to do so.

The question of what to do with the South once the war was over competed for attention with the issue of the fate of African Americans during the fighting. Although Reconstruction (as the process was known at the time) seemed to have commenced once the hostilities ended, Lincoln and his administration had been grappling with the problem for several years. The president had hoped to use the possibility of amnesty and leniency to pull southerners away from the Confederacy. Like many in the North, Lincoln believed that loyal southerners, their pro-Union views repressed by the Confederates, were ready, with the proper inducements, to support his side of the conflict. In December 1863, Lincoln put forward a plan that allowed southern men who had taken the oath of loyalty to the Union to create state governments in the South based on as little as 10 percent of the white population. Freed slaves would not be allowed to vote. The plan did not attract many southerners, yet it seemed inadequate and much too lenient to Radical Republicans.

Their answer was embodied in a bill that Republicans Benjamin F. Wade and Henry Winter Davis of Maryland introduced in 1864. This measure imposed much more stringent requirements on the South. Confederate veterans would be barred from holding office, and a majority of white male citizens in each southern state would have to endorse a constitutional convention to establish

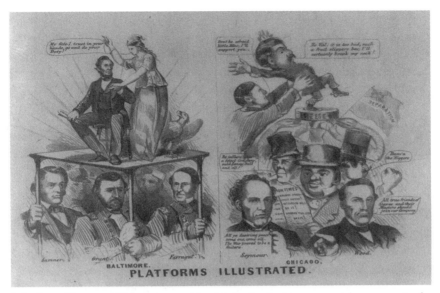

"Platforms Illustrated." The 1864 presidential election had intense racial overtones in the midst of the Civil War. This Republican cartoon contrasts Liberty endorsing Lincoln on a platform upheld by U. S. Grant and other Union stalwarts with the racist rhetoric of the Democrats. Library of Congress, LC-USZ62–7176.

a new state government. The Wade-Davis Bill looked to reshape southern society to ensure black freedom and to give the Republicans a chance to be competitive in the region. Although the Wade-Davis Bill passed both houses, Lincoln used a pocket veto to prevent it from becoming law. The president did not want Congress to tie his hands in reconstructing the South.

For the 1864 presidential election, the Republicans nominated Lincoln for a second term at their Baltimore convention in June of that year. The delegates adopted the name of the National Union Party in an effort to make it easier for pro-war Democrats to support Lincoln. Some Republicans believed that the party had achieved so many of its goals from the 1850s that it was time to break with the abolitionist past of the Republicans and find a label more appealing to a broad spectrum of voters. For all of their success, the Republicans understood that they had not yet become the majority party in the North. In any case, the "National Union" tag seemed reasonable at a time when the military progress of the North was still stalemated in the bitter fighting between Ulysses S. Grant and his Army of the Potomac and the Confederates under Robert E. Lee.

The desire to present a broad front against the Democrats and their probable candidate, former general George B. McClellan, led to one fateful decision in the convention. Lincoln's vice president was Hannibal Hamlin of Maine, a state the party was sure to carry. In the historical tradition of balancing the ticket, the delegates dumped Hamlin and selected Andrew Johnson from Tennessee to run with Lincoln. Johnson was a war Democrat who had served as military governor of his state. As American politicians have always done, the Republicans assumed that Johnson would perform the routine duties of the vice president and stay out of Lincoln's way. No one inquired about Johnson's views of African Americans, his possible style as president, or his character as a politician.

The National Union strategy worked in the short run. Lincoln gained from Union Army victories during the fall of 1864, the support of the soldiers who voted for him in large numbers, and the ineptitude of the Democrats. While Lincoln won all but three states, he received just 55 percent of the popular vote, attesting to the residual strength of anti-Republican sentiment. The Republicans understood that Democratic assaults on them as champions of black equality provoked a strong response among a sizable minority of the northern electorate.

Union victory arrived in April 1865 when Lee surrendered at Appomattox. The outcome made the Civil War a struggle that the Republican Party had fought and won despite all the internal disagreements and temporary setbacks of those painful four years. The preservation of the Union and the end of slavery imparted a sense that the Republicans and the United States were identical entities. In a profound sense, that perception of themselves as the only natural and legitimate governing party has never left the Republicans' ethos.

As April 1865 unfolded, Republicans turned to the task of fulfilling their promise to make the country a more prosperous and just society. Much remained to be done with the defeated South, but with the wise, war-tested Lincoln in the White House, all things seemed possible for a party that had not existed even a dozen years earlier.

The last thing that Americans expected after four bitter years of war was that the president would be assassinated. Angry over Lincoln's commitment to black rights and determined to avenge the defeat of the South, John Wilkes Booth murdered Lincoln on the evening of April 14, 1865, at Ford's Theater in Washington, D.C. The nation was plunged into mourning. A president who had been the subject of vicious attacks just months earlier became a martyred hero to a grieving nation. As Lincoln was almost deified, the party he had led embraced him as their transcendent political symbol. Republicans boasted that they and they alone were "the party of Lincoln."

They had reason to be proud of their fallen leader. In the crisis of the Civil War, Lincoln had shown himself to be a masterful wartime president and an eloquent advocate for the Union cause. Although he never adopted the agenda of the Radical wing of the party, Lincoln had come a long way from the views of blacks that he had expressed in his debates with Stephen A. Douglas. In his own person, he had little of the color prejudice that so many white Americans displayed. By the end of his life, Lincoln endorsed a limited form of suffrage for blacks. Whether he would have gone further with the Republicans toward the Fourteenth Amendment granting the vote to black males is unknowable. It seems improbable that Lincoln would have moved toward the Democrats and away from his own party as he implemented Reconstruction.

But Lincoln was now dead, and a southern Democrat, Andrew Johnson, sat in the White House. The new president hated the Confederacy and its leaders and spoke in harsh terms about those who had waged the rebellion. Yet he really did not oppose slavery as such. Perhaps Johnson would prove to be a wise choice for vice president. As April 1865 brought the first peacetime spring in Washington in four years, Republicans waited to see where President Johnson would lead them.

2

The Republicans and Reconstruction, *1865–1877*

THE LINES OF MARCHING MEN stretched for miles down Pennsylvania Avenue. On May 23 and 24, 1865, the Union veterans made their way from the Capitol to the White House in review. Crowds cheered and waved handkerchiefs, and the bands played "The Battle Hymn of the Republic" and "Marching through Georgia" as the armies paraded one last time before the grateful residents of the nation's capital. The conflict that dominated several generations of American history and shaped national politics for decades was over. The leadership of the country had already turned to the vexing issues of Reconstruction—the return of the South to the Union and the place of newly freed African Americans in postwar society.

A burst of exuberant nationalism followed. The population soared from nearly thirty-six million people in 1865 to more than forty-six million eleven years later on the nation's centennial. New states, Nebraska in 1867 and Colorado in 1876, swelled the total to thirty-six. The purchase of Alaska from Russia added another vast expanse to the continental territory. Railroads penetrated the West as a transcontinental line was completed in 1869. On the frontier, the new territory of Wyoming instituted woman suffrage as a way of attracting immigrants to its arid spaces. Above all, there was a strong sense that the Civil War had marked a turning point in American history. The older society had been remade in the crucible of the bloody conflict. A historian concluded in 1869 that a "great gulf" existed "between what had happened before it in our century and what has happened since, or what is likely to happen hereafter." He added: "It does not seem to me as if I were living in the country in which I was born."[1]

Although the Republicans came out of the war with the luster of victory and an indelible link to the memory of the martyred Abraham Lincoln, the dozen years from 1865 to 1877 proved fateful for the party. Their policies on Reconstruction left permanent changes in the Constitution as the Fourteenth and Fifteenth Amendments joined the Thirteenth in defining the rights of the former slaves under the law. However, the effort to create a viable Republican Party in the South, despite some initial success, proved to be a transitory one. By 1877 the white Democratic South was on its way toward dominance in the region and the establishment of a one-party structure that would remain in place for seventy-five years.

The other development that affects the historical reputation of the Republicans stemmed from its increasing identification with the business community and rapid economic growth. In the wake of the war, ethical standards collapsed; a series of scandals in the federal government touched many Republican officials and imparted a sense of pervasive corruption to the period. The labels of the misdeeds tell the story: the Gold Corner, the Whiskey Ring, the Crédit Mobilier, and the Salary Grab. As a result, the Republicans in power found themselves the object of popular derision. In fact, neither party had a monopoly on virtue, but the Republicans sometimes acted as though they did. The 1870s showed the error of that presumption.

Reconstruction became intertwined with scandal. Democrats used examples of malfeasance to undercut the racial policies of their opponents. As the pressures of war subsided, moreover, the traditional American suspicion of government resurfaced along with the racial prejudices that persisted throughout the fighting. Since they were perceived as the party of black rights and stronger government, the Republicans suffered the most as these forces emerged. By 1877 the natural partisan balances of American politics had reasserted themselves. Any hope that the Republicans could become the nation's majority party seemed illusory. Perhaps the Civil War had not transformed politics after all.

The murder of Abraham Lincoln and the accession of Andrew Johnson to the presidency proved a permanent disruption for Republican policy on Reconstruction. While Lincoln's policies before his death were ambiguous as to how the South would be brought back into its proper relationship with the rest of the Union, the slain president had recognized that freed slaves would have to play some part in the government of the South. In his last speech, on April 11, 1865, Lincoln said about black suffrage, "I myself would prefer that it were now conferred on the very intelligent, and on those who serve our cause as soldiers." At the very least that would have meant enfranchising several hundred thousand black men. The president had earlier endorsed the Bureau of Refugees, Freedmen, and Abandoned Lands that Congress had created on March 3, 1865, to assist the transition from slavery to freedom.[2]

Having been a member of the Republican Party since 1855 and then its first president, Lincoln saw his political future in his second term as linked to the party. While he was not a Radical by any means, neither was it likely that, if confronted with an intransigent South after the war, Lincoln would have moved toward the Democrats. Whatever his differences with men such as Thaddeus Stevens and Charles Sumner, they all spoke the same partisan language and saw the world in the same terms.

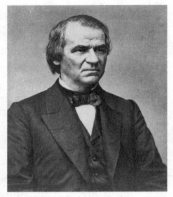

This was not the case with President Andrew Johnson. The nominal leader of the Republicans was born in 1808 and had risen to prominence in Tennessee as a Democrat. He had stayed with the Union when the war began, and Lincoln rewarded his loyalty with an appointment as military governor of Tennessee in 1862. His strong performance in that role led in turn to his nomi-

Elected on the Union ticket with Lincoln, Andrew Johnson proved more of an enemy to the Republicans than their leader during Reconstruction. Library of Congress, LC-USZ62–13017.

nation for the vice presidency on the National Union ticket. During the war and before he became president, Johnson denounced the white leadership of the South for secession and advocated harsh treatment for their "treason." When Johnson was inaugurated on March 4, 1865, he had taken some brandy for a cold, made a slurred and rambling speech, and embarrassed himself in the process. But politicians hoped Johnson would be sympathetic to the Republican view of how the South should be handled.[3]

Once the South had been defeated, though, Johnson's belief in white supremacy and his personal racism conflicted with mainstream Republican thought. "This is a country for white men," Johnson said, "and by God, as long as I am President, it shall be a government for white men." The president believed in the easy readmission of the southern states to the Union and expected white southerners to resume their historic dominance over blacks. After all, in his mind, African Americans were an inferior race and not fit to govern themselves.[4]

So in May 1865, Johnson set in motion a process that provided swift amnesty for most whites in the South. He did ask the political leaders of the region to ratify the Thirteenth Amendment, repudiate the secession ordinances of 1860–1861, and agree that their states would not seek payment for the debts of the Confederacy. But he ignored any provision for black suffrage, even along the lines Lincoln had indicated.

The question of blacks voting was a divisive one in the victorious North. Voters in Connecticut defeated an amendment to the state's constitution that would have given the two thousand African Americans residing there the right to vote. Two other northern states rejected similar proposal during the fall of 1865. Johnson calculated that northern prejudices would outweigh wartime idealism and produce a political alliance of northern and southern Democrats, along with conservative Republicans from the North, that could allow Johnson to win the presidency on his own in 1868.

During the second half of 1865, the intransigent position of the defeated South emerged. Though they had lost the conflict on the battlefield, southerners believed their antiblack ideology would prevail in the long run. A Texas newspaper on June 30, 1865, proclaimed that "the only hope of permanent free government is to be found in the maintenance of the principles of State rights and the view that has hitherto prevailed as to the status of the negro."[5] If the North expected contrition and regret for the war from their beaten enemies, they were disappointed.

The posture of Andrew Johnson encouraged the South to believe that lenient treatment and a quick return to normal would occur. No real change in the status of black southerners would be required as the constitutional conventions set about writing new fundamental documents. Often the delegates said nothing about Confederate debts or secession. To recapture the privileges for whites of the time of slavery, these conventions and state legislatures enacted "Black Codes" that limited in severe ways the economic rights of African Americans. While many Republicans had gone along with Johnson's program, they did so on the assumption that the South had accepted its defeat, would show a submissive spirit, and would provide some economic and political future for former slaves.

As Republicans looked on with dismay, the southern states seemed anything but contrite. In Louisiana and other states, blacks and Unionists found themselves under political assault and even the threat of renewed violence. A Republican editor wrote of the South: "We conclude (from every source of information within our reach) that public sentiment is still as bitter and unloyal as in 1861."[6] When they elected senators and representatives to return to Congress, southern white voters sent former Confederate offices who were disqualified to take an oath of allegiance to the United States. The South seemed to be pretending that the war had never happened. Republicans wondered if their recent victory had been real or just a passing illusion.

With the president casting his lot with the South, Republicans looked to the session of Congress that assembled in December 1865 to straighten out the confusion and show the former Confederates their real position. The Republican majority decided not to seat the newly elected members from the South. Had they done so, the future of any Reconstruction policy would have been compromised by the presence of southern lawmakers. In the winter of 1866, Republican legislators sought to frame laws that would protect the freed slaves and give their party a chance to gain a foothold in the South.

Three measures defined the emerging struggle between the Republican Congress and Andrew Johnson. The Freedmen's Bureau, which Congress had established in early 1865, before Lincoln's death, was by modern standards a small federal agency. It deployed some nine hundred agents across the South, and they set about creating procedures for contracts between and rules for white landowners and their black workers. Scheduled to exist for only one year after the war, the bureau was up for renewal in January 1866. The bill, adopted at once, was not a revolutionary measure. It made white discrimination against blacks more difficult. The Republicans expected the president to endorse it.

Yet President Johnson vetoed the Freedmen's Bureau Bill on February 19, 1866. He argued that Congress lacked the power to enact such a law now that the war had ended. In addition, the South was not represented in Congress and therefore should not be subject to such legislation. A day later, Johnson lashed out at his enemies in an intemperate speech. Despite unhappiness in Congress with Johnson's position, enough Republicans still supported the president that his veto was sustained.

The Republican majority pressed forward with a bill to safeguard the rights of freed slaves. It declared that African Americans were citizens of the United States and entitled to all the rights and privileges of that status. The bill did not provide voting rights to black men, and the political rights accorded to the freed slaves were minimal. Nonetheless, Johnson vetoed the civil rights measure on the grounds that it moved "toward centralization and the concentration of all legislative power in the National Government." The president also contended that the bill would allow Congress to void state laws prohibiting racial intermarriage. This appeal to racism irritated congressional Republicans.[7]

The Republicans overrode Johnson's veto and made the Civil Rights Act of 1866 law. It was clear, however, that a future Democratic Congress could repeal the legislation and would do so if the Democrats triumphed in the fall elections. As a result, the majority party coalesced around a new principle: there must be a separate amendment to the Constitution that inscribed the principles of civil rights into the fundamental law of the nation. In what became, in effect, the peace terms of the Civil War, the amendment established the concept of national citizenship for everyone born or naturalized in the

United States. It became illegal for any state to deprive any person "of life, liberty, or property without due process of law."[8] The amendment did not mandate black suffrage, but included language penalizing the southern states if they excluded African Americans from political life.

The Fourteenth Amendment has sparked many interpretations since 1866, but it remains one of the most important historical legacies of the Republican Party. The amendment could only have been approved in the postwar context and in response to the obstructive behavior of President Johnson. Later the amendment's language served other purposes. In the years after it was adopted, corporate lawyers and the United States Supreme Court used the "due process" clause to block state regulation of business. During the twentieth century, the amendment became a means of extending the rights of citizens beyond even what its framers had envisioned. During the early twenty-first century, Republicans talked about repealing the amendment as a way of preventing the children of illegal immigrants from becoming citizens. Few amendments to the Constitution after the first ten have had the enduring impact of the Fourteenth.

President Johnson denounced the amendment and urged the southern states to oppose ratification, which they did. Johnson hoped to unite the South, northern Democrats, and Conservative Republicans into a political coalition that would keep him in the White House. His plan included a meeting of Unionists in August 1866 that supported his program. He also allocated federal patronage to line up supporters in each state. The midterm elections of 1866 provided a key test of Johnson's approach to Reconstruction.

Johnson had misread northern sentiment. While the Republicans disagreed among themselves on a number of economic issues such as the protective tariff, the proper amount of currency in circulation, and the role of banks, they shared a common distaste for the South and a suspicion of what would happen to free slaves if white southerners regained power. When Johnson made an issue of the Reconstruction question, he had picked a topic on which most Republicans agreed.

Then the president took an unprecedented political step: he launched a personal campaign to sway voters to his position. For a president to make a speaking tour, or a "Swing Around the Circle," as it became known, on behalf of congressional candidates was regarded as undignified. As with most presidential innovations, the trip would have won praise had it been successful. The president was out of touch with northern attitudes. He castigated Radicals in speech after speech, comparing himself to the martyred Lincoln, and asked if his opponents wanted his blood too. As the president's rhetoric became more ill-tempered, as well as coarse, audiences booed him, and Johnson yelled back at hecklers. By the time Election Day neared, it was clear that Johnson's initiative had flopped. He had once said, "I care not for dignity." To most northern Republicans, Johnson's disastrous tour underlined the accuracy of this remark.[9]

Adding to the Republican indignation was southern brutality toward black Americans. Race riots in Memphis in May and in New Orleans in late July confirmed southern intransigence. Republicans contended that only the election of a Congress with enough opponents of Johnson to make a veto-proof majority would safeguard northern rights. Voters gave the Republicans the mandate they sought. In both houses of Congress the party had enough members to override a Johnson veto. "The people expect a bold and independent course with regard to the President," said Benjamin F. Wade, one of the leading Radicals.[10]

The Republicans and President Johnson continued their struggle in the short session of Congress that ended on March 4, 1867. The majority in Congress decided that the unrepentant South should be subject to military rule. The Reconstruction Act, passed on March 2, 1867, divided the South into five military districts and provided a process by which the southern states could regain power. They were required to convene constitutional conventions to write new fundamental documents. These bodies in turn had to approve the Fourteenth Amendment and allow all men to vote. Once the new constitutions had been written, a majority of the citizens of the state and Congress needed to approve them. Only after all these steps had been followed would the individual southern states be readmitted to the Union. The process would secure the ratification of the Fourteenth Amendment and place the civil rights of blacks beyond the reach of any temporary Democratic majority in Congress.

Passing this act produced the results that the Republicans wanted. One by one the southern states approved the Fourteenth Amendment. The coercive nature of the process made the Republicans vulnerable to later charges that they had imposed "Radical Reconstruction" on the South, and indeed they had, as victors in civil wars usually do to their defeated enemies. Southerners who had been eager to leave the Constitution behind in 1861 now assailed the Republicans for amending it.

The ensuing Reconstruction in the South received negative historical evaluations until the 1960s when the emergence of the civil rights movement caused scholars to reexamine the effort to reshape the South between 1865 and 1877. Previous historians had criticized the Republicans for going too far in their approach to the South; now the conclusion became that the party, hampered by its own racist views, had done too little to ensure the rights of black Americans. The allegation had some merit, but it also overlooked the forces working against progress both in southern race relations and in the nation at large.

The way in which the Republican Congress had shaped Reconstruction policy laid rough hands on the states of the former Confederacy, but there was no inclination to abolish these states within the Union and start anew. Nor was there among a majority of Republicans in the North a disposition to overturn property rights in the South by redistributing land to the freed slaves. That action would have demanded an expansion of government power beyond what had been contemplated during the war and would also have been an implicit threat to property rights in the North.

Remaking the South was therefore left to an alliance of newly enfranchised African Americans and whites who supported Republican policies. During the early years of Reconstruction, there was also the threat of military force from the Army. These elements proved to be more fragile than Republicans had anticipated. Terrorist groups such as the Ku Klux Klan intimidated black voters. Whites who endorsed the Republicans faced economic and cultural pressure, along with the threat of violence, to remain in the Democratic column. As the size of the postwar army dwindled over time, its ability to support Republican parties in the South waned. The case for using the military to sustain unpopular governments became hard to make, especially as northern interest in changing the South dissipated during the 1870s.

The Reconstruction experiment did produce positive results during its brief existence. Blacks voted and held office in the South, though the number of elected African Americans did not match their proportion of the population. White and black Republicans, using the power of state governments, addressed long-deferred issues such as public education and economic development. The governments that Republicans formed had some corrupt elements, to be sure, but so did the Democratic administrations that "redeemed" the South when white Democratic rule triumphed. Southern Republicans were not saints, but their days in power offered a better chance for the region than the ideology of the Democratic Party at that time. Because southern Democrats wrote the history of Reconstruction, Republicans of both races were usually maligned in the accounts of Reconstruction that appeared between 1877 and 1965. In many parts of the South, and among modern Republicans, these stereotypes about corruption and black dominance persist, and the constructive achievements of the Republicans in the region have been forgotten.

Another challenge that the Republicans faced in the late 1860s was the effort to drive Andrew Johnson from office through impeachment and conviction. Until the possible impeachment of Richard Nixon in 1973–1974 revived interest in the earlier episode, the impeachment and trial of Johnson was depicted as a vindictive step of Radical Republicans to complete their takeover of the government.

The reappraisal of Johnson as a racist who frustrated Republican endeavors to accord blacks political rights caused historians in the 1970s to look again at this first case of presidential impeachment. While scholars did not find that Johnson had committed indictable offenses such as the ones alleged against Richard M. Nixon, they did decide that the president had used all the powers at his command to block the Reconstruction policies of the Republican Congress in 1867–1868. This continuing resistance to legislative initiatives finally led to efforts to remove Johnson from office.

The president's obstructionism took many forms. He removed army generals in the South who were sympathetic to Congress and its policies. Despite the Tenure of Office Act, which required Senate approval for the ouster of cabinet officers, Johnson removed Secretary of War Edwin M. Stanton early in 1868. For these and other violations of the edicts of Congress, the House impeached Johnson on February 24, 1868. His trial began on March 30 and ran for more than five weeks. As the proceedings went on, Johnson bent in his opposition to Reconstruction to stave off conviction. In the end, Johnson was acquitted when the Senate fell one vote short of the two-thirds needed for conviction.

A number of elements produced this result. The case against the president was political, not criminal, and even on that score the evidence was ambiguous. Ousting Johnson would have made the president pro tem of the Senate, Benjamin F. Wade, the next president, and he was too radical for most members of Congress since he favored woman suffrage. The biggest point in favor of leaving Johnson in office was that his term would end in only nine more months. The senators who voted to acquit, while not profiles in courage, did not think it was worth disturbing the constitutional system to remove Johnson. Neither were those Republicans who voted to acquit Johnson driven out of the party or forced into political oblivion. They supported U. S. Grant in the fall election.

Andrew Johnson proved a major disruptive force in the history of the Republican Party. As president he made the least of the historical opportunity afforded to him, and his racism has tainted his reputation. For the Republicans the need to fight Johnson and his obstructive policies prevented them from forming a consistent and clear policy toward the South in 1865 that might have gained acceptance from the defeated rebels. Johnson encouraged the South to believe that it could escape the consequences of the war. In so doing, the president made the task Reconstruction divisive and bitter. The nation and the Republican Party would long feel the effects of the decision to put Andrew Johnson on the party's ticket in 1864.

By the summer of 1868, the Republicans thought that they had a presidential candidate who could lead them to victory in the fall and, more important, end all the wrangling with Congress over the proper policy to pursue toward the South. The hero of the Union, Ulysses S. Grant, was the unanimous choice when the Republicans gathered in convention on May 20, 1868, just four days after Johnson was acquitted. There were no candidates other than Grant, and the Speaker of the House, Schuyler Colfax, became his running mate. The sentiment of the party, said John Sherman of Ohio, was "that our candidate should be so independent of party politics as to be a guarantee of peace and quiet."[11]

The election of 1868 is usually described using the phrase with which Grant closed his formal letter accepting the Republican nomination: "Let us have peace." In fact, the presidential contest that year illustrated the extent to which the race issue affected American politics after the Civil War. It also emphasized the perilous electoral position of the Republicans with regard to the voters. There had been strong signs in 1867 that northern voters did not endorse Republican efforts to achieve suffrage for blacks in the South. Suspicion persisted regarding the full extent of the legislative aspects of Radical Reconstruction. The Democrats won state elections in Connecticut because Republicans there had pushed for black voting. Similar results occurred in September in Maine and California. A month later, Democrats carried Pennsylvania, and a suffrage amendment went down to stinging defeat in Ohio. In the Buckeye State, a Democrat said that Ohio must be spared "the thralldom of niggerism." Overall, the Democrats had bounced back from their 1866 defeats. The lesson that many Republicans took from the election results was that racial issues must be downplayed. "The Negro will be less prominent for some time to come," said one Ohio operative. These events formed the political context in which Grant ran for president.[12]

The Republican presidential candidate did not campaign and only issued a public letter or two on specific question in dispute during the contest. Tradition held that presidential hopefuls did not seek the office in an active way. However, other Republicans had to meet the spirited challenge from the resurgent Democrats, who played the race card for all that it was worth in a manner that was vicious even for the nineteen century. They promised to rid the nation of "an irresponsible oligarchy upheld by a standing army and negro votes."[13]

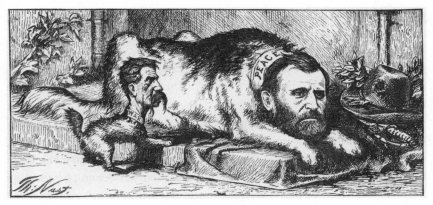

"War and Peace." This Thomas Nast cartoon from *Harper's Weekly* shows the Democratic vice presidential candidate in 1868 Frank Blair as a little dog "War" snapping at the dignified watchdog of "Peace," the Republican candidate for president, Ulysses S. Grant.

To oppose Grant, the Democrats nominated Horatio Seymour, the former governor of New York, and Frank Blair of Missouri as his running mate. Their platform pledged to abolish the Freedmen's Bureau "and all political instrumentalities designed to secure negro supremacy." Meanwhile, they accused the Republicans of subjecting the southern states, "in time of profound peace, to military despotism and negro supremacy." In the campaign the Democrats asserted that they were the defenders of Stephen A. Douglas, who had proclaimed "ten years ago, a government by white men, of white men, and for white men."[14]

The Republicans countered with charges that their opponents wanted a return of the South's power and reversal of the outcome of the war. Their platform endorsed the principle of "equal suffrage to all loyal men of the South" but added that "the question of suffrage properly belongs to the people of those States." Backing away from support of black suffrage nationwide defused Democratic attempts to capitalize on racial prejudice in the North, but it also undercut the general moral standing of the Republicans. By 1868 the postwar zeal of the North to remake the South had waned.[15]

Reviving the lingering animosity about southern loyalty remained a winning tactic for the Republicans. On one occasion a party orator held up a bloodstained tunic of a Union veteran and urged the crowd to vote the way they had shot in the war. The moment was immortalized in the phrase "waving the bloody shirt," which became a coded slogan for Republican emphasis on the passion of the war over more reasoned and presumably more important issues.

Examples of "bloody shirt" oratory abound. In these speeches the treasonous and illegitimate character of the Democrats as a party received particular stress. One of the most succinct expressions of the device came in a speech by Oliver P. Morton of Indiana in 1866:

> Every man who labored for the rebellion in the field, who murdered Union prisoners by cruelty and starvation, who conspired to bring about civil war in the loyal states, who invented dangerous compounds to burn steamboats and Northern cities, who contrived hellish schemes to introduce into Northern cities the wasting pestilence of yellow fever, calls himself a Democrat. Every dishonest contractor who has been convicted of defrauding the government, every dishonest paymaster or disbursing officer who has been convicted of squandering the public money at the gaming table or in gold gambling operations, every officer in the army who was dismissed for cowardice or disloyalty, calls himself a Democrat. Every wolf in sheep's clothing, who pretends to preach the gospel but proclaims the righteousness of man-selling and slavery; every one who shoots down negroes in the streets; burns negro school-houses and meeting-houses, and murders women and children by the light of their own flaming dwellings calls himself a Democrat.

Morton then ended his tirade with a flourish:

> In short, the Democratic party may be described as a common sewer and loathsome receptacle, in which is emptied every element of treason North and South, and every element of inhumanity which has dishonored the age.[16]

That Republicans such as Morton used the Civil War for partisan purposes is clear. But critics of the party do not add that the Democrats in the South used memories of the war too. Some were still invoking the luster of the Confederacy as late as 1920.

Grant defeated Seymour and the Democrats in 1868, but the results fell well short of a popular landslide. Grant and the Republicans won twenty-five states with 214 electoral votes to eight for the Democrats with 80 electoral votes. Grant received just under 53 percent of the popular vote, while Seymour garnered just over 47 percent of the ballots. In the South, where the Republicans had readmitted seven states during 1867–1868, Grant won 41 electoral votes in six states that were more likely to be Democratic in future elections. Three other states, Texas, Virginia, and Mississippi, were not yet back in the Union, and they, too, would be Democratic in future contests.

From the Republican point of view, the most telling result was that Seymour and Blair won a majority of the white vote. New black voters put Grant over the top or enabled him to do well in southern states where former Confederates were still barred from voting. Nonetheless, southern Republicans and blacks faced terror tactics in the 1868 contest. To many Republicans the outcome underlined the dangers of pressing forward with more vigorous Reconstruction policies in the South.

Before Grant was inaugurated, the Republicans in Congress adopted another constitutional amendment on February 26, 1869. The Fifteenth Amendment guaranteed universal manhood suffrage for all races (but did not include Indians). Such a change in the Constitution would finesse the problem of a lack of white support for unlimited male suffrage in the North and would also build a Republican base in the South. President Grant endorsed the amendment in his inaugural address. A year later the amendment had been adopted. The Republicans believed that they had ensured political rights for the freed slaves with the Fourteenth and Fifteenth Amendments. They were mistaken, as southern ingenuity in thwarting these documents would soon prove.

When Grant was elected, the *New York Tribune* announced that the nation "may now look forward to a long era of peace and prosperity." In the history of the Republicans, few predictions have proved more inaccurate.[17] A great general in the Civil War, Grant has come down in American history as a weak president who tolerated corruption in his administration. Along with Warren G. Harding, Grant usually ranks among the presidential failures. Much of Grant's sour reputation in the White House arose from pro-southern scholars who painted his tenure as one of unalloyed failure and weakness. More recent investigation of his eight years provides a more balanced portrait of his presidency.

Often criticized as a weak president, Ulysses S. Grant has been gaining ground among historians in recent years for his defense of blacks in the South. Library of Congress, LC-USZ62–13018.

Grant faced a daunting set of circumstances in the South as Democratic resistance to blacks in politics hardened during the 1870s. By modern standards, Grant's policies fell well short of protecting African Americans from Democratic terror tactics and consistent intimidation. There was only so much the president and the remaining Radicals in Congress could do to stem the shift of national attention away from the issues of Reconstruction and toward the emerging questions of an industrial society.

The new president was a month and a half short of his forty-seventh birthday when he took the oath of office on March 4, 1869. Nine years earlier, as the Civil War neared, Grant was an obscure West Point graduate who had left the army during the 1850s and, after a string of failures, was working for his father in the tanning business. The outbreak of the war brought Grant back into the army. From there his prowess as a commander led him to victory, national fame, and ultimately the presidency. Grant did not look imposing, but, as his Confederate enemies had discovered, the future president was a determined individual who would approach his White House duties with a similarly strong sense of personal resolve and purpose.

But the Republican Party that he now led was far from a united and cohesive political organization. Within each state, competing factions sought advantage. Beyond that customary state of affairs, some party members, many of them younger Republicans, hoped to address newer issues of economic development through the protective tariff and government subsidies for business enterprise. In the East, advocates of deflation endorsed a currency policy that would back every dollar in circulation with an equal amount of gold. Western party members were less certain of the benefits of higher tariffs, and, as representatives of a developing area, they hoped for easier credit that put more money in circulation.

While suspicion of the South and dislike of the Democrats united Republicans, the question of what to do about the future of black Americans produced different answers in 1869. By now all but three southern states were back in the Union and entitled to conduct their own political affairs. The dilemma for Republicans was acute. If the federal government let southern Republicans fend for themselves, these fragile organizations would be vulnerable to Democratic pressure, intimidation, and violence. If the army were sent in to preserve order and repress terror tactics, the Republicans would be admitting that their southern colleagues lacked genuine popular backing. Reliance on the military in peacetime also conflicted with the principles of the Constitution.

These and other problems taxed Grant's political skills at the outset. Not a strong partisan at the beginning of his administration, he hoped to govern with only modest deference to Republican leaders in Congress. Yet the experience of resisting Andrew Johnson made congressional Republicans skeptical about the exertion of presidential power even from a chief executive of their own party. The ingrained Republican belief that Congress was the preeminent branch of government shaped the party's internal history during the Grant years.

The new president got off to a shaky start because of his cabinet. He did not give much heed to party leaders and selected men whom he had known before or who impressed him as cautious and efficient. In the case of his secretary of the Treasury nominee, Alexander T. Stewart, a prominent Manhattan merchant, Grant ran afoul of the law that had created the Treasury Department in 1789. That statute barred those involved in trade from holding the post. The Senate refused to make an exception for the new president, and Grant suffered embarrassment.

Other problems plagued Grant's first year. In the summer, two New York speculators, Jay Gould and Jim Fisk, sought high profits by manipulating the market in gold to achieve a "corner" (a monopoly of the available supply). The price of gold rose, and by September 24, 1869, investors who had agreed to sell their gold at lower prices faced ruin. The administration foiled the scheme by selling some of its gold from government vaults. The furor over the episode embarrassed the White House when it was revealed that members of Grant's family had aided Gould and Fisk. The president was in no way involved, but this scandal was the first of many that would mar his presidency.

The administration also embarked on an ill-fated venture to annex the Dominican Republic, then known as Santo Domingo. The diplomatic initiative aroused suspicion in the Senate, particularly from Charles Sumner of Massachusetts, who remained committed to the idea of prewar abolitionism and civil rights. The debate over the annexation treaty produced a break between the Massachusetts Radical and the president. The treaty itself failed during the summer of 1870. The incident contributed to a popular impression of a president in over his head and a government in disarray,

Reconstruction policy provided Grant with his biggest challenge. In his first year, the president saw Republicans lose ground in the South as Democrats intimidated both black and white Republicans. The following year a new phenomenon appeared. Republicans who sought an end to Reconstruction aligned themselves with Democrats in what were called Liberal Republican alliances in states such as West Virginia and Missouri.

One hundred and forty years later, the words "liberal" and "Republican" would not coexist in the same sentence, but during the 1870s "liberal" connoted a set of political values entirely different from what it does now. At the start of the Grant presidency, the term meant a dislike of the growth in the size of government, disapproval of the protective tariff, and opposition to the continuation of Reconstruction. Another reform that Liberals endorsed was the introduction of a nonpartisan civil service to staff the government. At a time when political patronage determined who got jobs in the federal service, civil service reform hit at the source of strength of politicians and promised an objective, nonpolitical standard for government employment. Among the leaders of the Liberal Republicans were Carl Schurz, a German American from Missouri, Charles Francis Adams of Massachusetts, and Horace Greeley, the editor of the *New York Tribune.*

Some of the attacks Liberal Republicans made on the excesses of politicians had merit. However, they had a large blind spot when it came to race. Their discontent with their party often reflected an ample amount of bigotry. The prospect of blacks involved in politics disturbed them almost as much as the sight of immigrants voting in the large cities where many of the Liberals lived. Liberals led the way toward the Republican abandonment of civil rights in the South and in time pulled the rest of the party along with them.

President Grant resolved not to give in to the pleas of his Liberal critics. The Democrats could always placate dissidents more than he could, and wavering would only alienate his base with the Republican regulars. So the president turned to those in his party who offered loyalty to the White House. One leading exponent of the president's faction was the colorful and controversial Senator Roscoe Conkling of New York.

Conkling was forty years old when Grant took office. He had served six years in the House representing Utica, New York, before his election to the Senate in 1867. In the upper house, Conkling cut quite a figure. His dress often included green trousers and yellow shoes. Well groomed with a prominent "Hyperion curl" that fell just above his handsome face, Conkling dazzled women in Washington. There were rumors of a long-standing affair with Kate Chase Sprague, the wife of the senator from Rhode Island. The senator had built a political organization to control the faction-ridden New York Republicans, and party regularity formed the guiding principle of his career. Real and fancied slights aroused instant resentment. As one observer put it, he "seemed to consider all men who differed with him as enemies of the human race."[18]

One enemy whom Conkling never forgave was a magnetic fellow Republican from Maine, James G. Blaine. The two men disliked each other from the start. During a debate in the House in 1866, Blaine twitted his colleague about his "haughty disdain, his grandiloquent swell," and "his majestic, super-eminent, over-powering, turkey-gobbler strut." Blaine was ready to apologize and let the incident pass as one of those moments that occur among politicians. Conkling, who had been depicted as a turkey in cartoons, nursed his resentment and determined to have his revenge in the future.[19]

The emergence of an individual such as Conkling among Republicans reflected the shift in the party that marked the late 1860s. The earlier generation that had opposed slavery and fought the Civil War was giving way to professional politicians who approached their calling with less concern for ideology and more for their continued electoral survival. Economic issues such as the currency and the protective tariff meant more to these men than did the fate of African Americans in the South. As long as voters in the North responded to Civil War issues, these regulars would endorse protection for blacks, but it was not a high priority. Their interests and those of the Grant administration ran together in the early 1870s, since neither group wanted to see the Liberal Republicans gain power with the cooperation of the Democrats.

The 1870 congressional elections were a setback for Grant and his party. With the South fully restored to national politics, the Democrats picked up forty-one seats in the House and narrowed the Republican majority to thirty seats. The Democrats added another six seats in the Senate as well. Many Republicans contended that the results confirmed the need to abandon harsh Reconstruction policies and be more conciliatory toward the South. After all, the party had freed the slaves and given them a chance in life. That was all that black Americans could expect. As a Boston newspaper with leanings toward the Radicals observed in 1870, "A party cannot be maintained on past traditions. It must move on to new conquests."[20]

Before the party turned to these newer issues, however, it faced one more challenge from the white South that could not be ignored. During the 1870 elections and afterward, reports of violence against blacks in the South multiplied. The Ku Klux Klan, founded in 1869 as a paramilitary terror organization, depended on intimidation and murder to keep African Americans from voting. Blacks who ran for office were told, as one Republican in Tennessee put it after the Klan beat him, "that they didn't dispute I was a very good fellow...but they did not intend any nigger to hold office in the United States." Republican campaign rallies were often broken up. The outright killing of blacks became known as a "negro chase." A North Carolina Republican leader warned President Grant: "An organized conspiracy is in existence in every County in the State, and its aim is to control the government."[21]

While not all Republicans believed that the threat of the Klan demanded action, most did in 1870–1871. "If the Federal Government cannot pass the laws to protect the rights, liberty, and lives of the citizens of the United States in the States," asked Benjamin Butler of Massachusetts, "why are the guarantees of those fundamental rights put in the Constitution at all?" Congress enacted laws to counter fraud and coercion in state elections. The lawmakers went even further in the Ku Klux Klan Act of 1871. That measure made it a crime to deprive voters of their civil rights and to prevent qualified citizens from holding office. The government was given greater power to use district attorneys and military force to curb the Klan. The Democrats denounced these laws as unconstitutional, but Republicans such as George Frisbie Hoar of Massachusetts replied that "it was the great and leading purpose of the framers of our Constitution to place the fundamental civil rights of the people under the protection of the strongest and supremest power known to our laws, the power of the General Government."[22]

Under the leadership of Attorney General Amos T. Akerman (who had fought for the Confederacy) and the new Department of Justice created in 1870, the government went after the Klan in 1871, resulting in hundreds of trials and the conviction of some of the key leaders in states such as North Carolina and South Carolina. This kind of federal resolve drove the Klan back into the shadows of southern society and helped restore the political morale of Republicans in the region. The need to subdue the Klan, according to Akerman, "revealed a perversion of moral sentiment among the Southern whites which bodes ill to that part of the country for this generation." The suppression of the Klan was one of the notable achievements of Grant's presidency.[23]

As the 1872 election approached, Grant's popularity with the average Republican voter remained high despite some of the more awkward episodes of his administration. Grant was the strongest candidate the party could nominate. But for the Liberal Republicans another term for the president would be intolerable. They recoiled from the perceived failures of Reconstruction and the increase in governmental power that had accompanied it. The alleged corruption of southern Republican governments and their reliance on the votes of poorly educated African Americans offended the aristocratic sensibility of these upper-class reformers. They wanted to leave the issues of the Civil War behind as well as those who benefitted as a result of that conflict. "Reconstruction and slavery we have done with," wrote the editor of *The Nation*, a periodical friendly to the Liberal cause, "for administrative and revenue reform we are eager."[24]

Choosing a popular and likely candidate to run against Grant on the Liberal Republican ticket was another matter. Most of the disaffected Republicans in the Liberal camp were disappointed candidates or losers in factional struggles with men such as Roscoe Conkling, Simon Cameron in Pennsylvania, or Zachariah Chandler in Michigan. None of them seemed much like presidential timber, although that did not stop seven or eight of them from dreaming of the prize. His birth in Germany disqualified Carl Schurz, and a lack of real popular appeal stalled the aspirations of Charles Francis Adams, the son of former President John Quincy Adams. These Republican rebels gathered in Cincinnati in May 1872 to unite on a single candidate.

Out of their tangled deliberations came the odd choice of the editor of the *New York Tribune*, Horace Greeley. In his long career as a journalist, Greeley had opposed most of the issues that had brought the Liberals together in the first place. They supported lower tariffs; Greeley was a protectionist. Civil service reform was a major issue to the Liberals, but a matter of indifference to a New Yorker. Moreover, Greeley had endorsed prohibition, vegetarianism, spiritualism, and the use of human manure to improve agricultural productivity. Mainline politicians found Greeley's views odd. The one issue on which the Liberals and Greeley concurred was lenience toward the South and an end to efforts to help black Americans.

The Democrats saw Greeley as their best chance to defeat Grant, and they, too, nominated him as their candidate. Both parties adopted identical platforms that asked "for the Nation a return to the methods of peace and the constitutional limitations of power." But the journalist proved to be an inept candidate who made a speaking tour in defiance of the conventional approach that an aspirant for the presidency let others make the case for him. If Greeley had been a compelling speaker, the innovation might have worked, but his appearances produced few converts. "That Grant is an Ass no man can deny," concluded a Liberal Republican in Ohio, "but better an Ass than a mischievous Idiot."[25]

To counter the Liberal Republican–Democratic campaign and keep potential defectors in the party, the Republican Congress reduced tariff duties and extended amnesty to those former rebels who had not yet had their political rights restored. Grant did not campaign, but the Republican leadership turned out for him. The prospect of a Democratic victory galvanized African American voters. Frederick Douglass, the most famous black politician of the day, summed up the views of most African Americans two years later: "The Republican party is the ship and all else is the sea." That view largely prevailed for the six decades that followed.[26]

The collapse of Greeley's political fortunes produced a decisive victory for Grant and the Republicans. It was the last such solid triumph for more than twenty years in presidential contests. Greeley carried only six states, three in the South plus the border states of Kentucky, Tennessee, and Missouri. Everywhere else Grant prevailed with 56 percent of the vote and a margin of three-quarters of a million ballots. The Liberal Republican vote fizzled out, and the Democrats also seemed repudiated. The election in the South had been relatively fair, featuring fewer acts of violence, which enabled the Republicans to rebound in the region.

But these results proved only temporary. While the Liberal Republicans and the Democrats lost the electoral war of 1872, they won the battle of ideas. The Liberal critique of Reconstruction as costly and corrupt impressed many in the North who nevertheless voted for Grant and his party. Civil service reform and the attacks on politicians it engendered resonated with voters who read about Democratic leader "Boss" William M. Tweed's corrupt political machine in New York City in their daily newspapers. In the future, Democrats played down their overt identification with racist ideas and pro-southern policies. They assailed the Republicans for their ties to business, their spending of government funds, and their activism on social issues involving religion and alcohol. Because of these changes in tone, the Democrats were well positioned when the economy faltered in late 1873.

As the Civil War faded into patriotic memory, the Republican commitment to changing the South and assisting the freed slaves also waned. The South seemed of less concern than the economic depression and social unrest that emerged in the mid-1870s. In this setting, black Republicans were increasingly on their own. Northerners read partisan tracts about wrongdoing in southern state governments and concluded that African American incapacity explained the failures of Republicanism in the region. Meanwhile, the powerful forces of racism within both major parties reasserted themselves after the brief heyday of egalitarianism during Reconstruction.

A flurry of political scandals enhanced the impression that corruption had stained American politics. Just before the 1872 election, the Crédit Mobilier scandal came to light, cresting at the start of 1873. The firm at the heart of the scandal, named for a French business, had been set up by investors in the Union Pacific Company and provided with government contracts to build the transcontinental rail line during the 1860s. Shares in the company were given to key members of Congress who voted on subsidies for the rail construction. Their votes increased the value of the securities that they owned. The public discovery of this scheme compromised the reputation of Schuyler Colfax, Grant's first vice president; Henry Wilson, Grant's running mate in 1872; and other notable congressional figures, including the future president James A. Garfield.

While the Crédit Mobilier scandal was becoming public, Congress voted itself a 40 percent retroactive pay raise as the lame-duck session wound down in early March 1873. The press dubbed the measure "The Salary Grab Act," and critics pelted the lawmakers for their greed. While the Democrats had been part of the legislation, the onus for the move fell on the majority Republicans.

Not since 1857 had the nation experienced a severe economic downturn. The Panic of 1873, which began with the failure of the banking firm of Jay Cooke and Company on September 18 of that year, scrambled American politics for the remainder of the decade. As other banks failed and businesses laid off workers, the economy collapsed. Overexpansion of railroad construction following the Civil War led to a boom in the stock market premised on the idea of ever-greater returns from the profitable transportation sector. When the traffic from these new rail lines did not sustain profits, the bubble burst, the lienholders went bankrupt, and investors lost large amounts in the ensuing slump.

The 1870s produced a transformation in the American economy. Increased production from industrialization drove down prices and began a period of sustained deflation that lasted for over twenty years. Businesses in such key areas as steel and oil consolidated under the leadership of Andrew Carnegie (steel) and John D. Rockefeller (oil). Reliance on machinery and relentless cost-cutting produced greater profits and efficiency, but also led to unemployment for many skilled workers. As a result, strikes and labor unrest spread.

Republicans had preached and believed in the harmony of workers and capitalists in a society of small farmers and businesses of modest size. Through tariffs and other subsidies, the government could encourage all segments of society to prosper together. But as Republican policies promoted economic growth during the 1860s, they replaced this version of an interdependent society with an economic order where divisions between capital and labor widened and social conflict became more of a fact of life. The party and its defenders did not forsake their original ideology, but their identification with American business strengthened as the late nineteenth century unfolded.

In the short run, the Republicans, as the party in power, suffered the political repercussions of the events of 1873. This kind of periodic crisis was called a "panic" because of the hysteria it evoked. The twentieth century would replace that loaded term with the more reassuring label of "depression." When Congress assembled in December 1873, the question for Republican leaders was what, if anything, should be done about the spreading hard times and the irate voters they produced. The Democrats were ready to ride the issue into the 1874 congressional elections.

Economic orthodoxy in the nineteenth century provided few options for the government in the face of a slump in the business cycle. Neither the

Republicans nor the Democrats envisioned any kind of large-scale government intervention to lessen the direct effects of hard times. Grant floated the idea of the national government generating jobs through public works, but his congressional advisers and cabinet members told him, in the words of one of them, "It is no part of the business of government to find employment for people." When midwestern Republicans supported a bill to increase the amount of money in circulation as a way of easing the crisis, the president, following the advice of counselors who favored hard money and deflation, vetoed the measure. Divisions over currency policy among Republicans would persist for two decades.[27]

The congressional elections of 1874 delivered a strong political rebuke to the Republicans. They lost eighty-five seats in the House as the Democrats regained control for the first time since before the Civil War. The Democrats also gained ten seats in the Senate. In New York, Samuel J. Tilden led the state Democratic Party to a triumph that endangered Republican prospects of carrying that crucial state in 1876. With Grant not able to run again because of the two-term tradition, Republican chances of holding the White House now seemed in doubt.

In the wake of their electoral defeat, the lame-duck Republican Congress enacted one more civil rights measure in early 1875, which provided rights of public accommodation for blacks in theaters, on railroads, and in hotels. The statute did not include any enforcement mechanism beyond suits by individuals in response to discrimination that they had experienced. In 1883 the Supreme Court declared the law unconstitutional as an infringement on the rights of the states. No other civil rights law would pass Congress for eighty-two years.

During 1875, the Republicans moved away from Reconstruction and toward an emphasis on issues of finance and trade. President Grant used the army to avert a Democratic threat to Republican state government in Louisiana, an action that drew criticism from even northern Republicans. Democrats regained control of state politics in Mississippi when the administration and congressional Republicans concluded that they could no longer sustain their southern counterparts with military intervention.

More scandals plagued the Grant White House in 1875. The president's secretary, Orville E. Babcock, was linked to the infamous Whiskey Ring, in which officials received kickbacks for not collecting federal excise taxes on the beverage. Babcock was acquitted, but his difficulties embarrassed the administration. The secretary of war, W. W. Belknap, had taken cash gifts from a man who sold supplies to Indian tribes. Belknap resigned rather than face impeachment. Though none of these or other episodes ever touched Grant himself, the Republicans faced a record of misdeed on which the Democrats intended to capitalize. By 1876 the party sought ways to escape further connection with Grant's political baggage.

As the election neared, the Democrats united around Governor Tilden, who was dubbed "Whispering Sammy" for his soft-voiced approach to politics and "the Great Forecloser" for his stern approach to business affairs. He had gained a reputation as a reformer when he supported the campaign that overthrew Boss Tweed in New York City. The Democratic platform denounced "the rapacity of carpet-bag tyrannies" in the South and charged the Republicans with having "infected States and municipalities with the contagion of misrule, and locked fast the prosperity of an industrious people in the paralysis of hard times." Promising reform, attacking corruption, and downplaying their racial views, the Democrats hoped that Tilden could lead them back to the White House.[28]

The Republicans seemed to have one leading contender in the person of James G. Blaine, a popular orator and former Speaker of the House of Representatives. Blaine had cemented his standing among Republicans when he led the fight to prevent the Democratic majority in the House from providing amnesty to Jefferson Davis and other high-ranking Confederates earlier in 1876. "The Man from Maine" appeared to be on the verge of leading the Republicans. But days before the national convention opened in Cincinnati, questions about Blaine's financial relations with an Arkansas railroad surfaced in the newspapers. Blaine responded with a vigorous, if somewhat misleading, rebuttal to the charges in the House. Six days later, he suffered an apparent physical collapse. With controversy swirling around him, Blaine remained the front runner, but many in the party hoped to select an unblemished candidate as an alternative.

The national convention well illustrated some of the unique features of the Republican Party in the late nineteenth century. While religious piety underlay much of the appeal of the party, the Republicans also had room for unorthodox opinions. Robert G. Ingersoll placed Blaine's name in nomination. One of the most famous Republican orators of the period, Ingersoll was also noted for his passionate belief in atheism, a commitment that did not prevent him from addressing the party faithful. He gave one of the great speeches of the era, which had the delegates enthralled. In his peroration, he alluded to Blaine's opposition to Democratic attempts to provide amnesty for Jefferson Davis and other former Confederate leaders. "Like an armed warrior, like a plumed knight, James G. Blaine marched down the halls of the American

Congress and threw his shining lance full and fair against the brazen foreheads of the defamers of his country and the maligners of his honor."[29]

It was a superb piece of oratory that provided indelible imagery about Blaine for the rest of his career. But as good as Ingersoll was, he could not make up for Blaine's liabilities. Nominating him would hand the Democrats the issue of ethics and make the party defend its nominee's misdeeds. After six ballots, the anti-Blaine Republicans united behind Governor Rutherford B. Hayes of Ohio. A Civil War veteran and former member of Congress with no hint of scandal in his record, Hayes could carry his home state and would not alienate former Liberal Republicans as Blaine would have done. Although he favored temperance and respected the religious beliefs of others, Hayes did not belong to a church himself. Such a status was not a bar to the presidency in this period. Hayes stood for civil service reform and, most of all, would be conciliatory toward the South. The convention then selected William A. Wheeler of New York to balance the ticket with someone from the East who could help in Tilden's home state.

The platform asserted that "the United States is a nation, not a league," and the Democratic Party was "the same in character and spirit as when it sympathized with treason." In their control of the House of Representatives, the Democrats were also guilty of "reasserting and applauding in the national capitol the sentiments of unrepentant rebellion." Republicans promised to protect all citizens in the South "in the free enjoyment of all their rights," endorsed the civil service, and approved "the substantial advances recently made toward the establishment of equal rights for women."[30]

The Republicans knew that they were in for a hard battle to get Hayes elected. If Tilden carried New York, New Jersey, and Indiana and swept the South, he would be over the total of 185 electoral votes needed to win. The Republicans had an outside chance in a few southern states if the black vote was not suppressed, but the odds seemed to favor Tilden and his resurgent party. The Republicans rested their campaign on the issue of the war but did not stress black rights in their appeal to northern voters. Money was tight during the depression, and the Republicans concentrated their limited funds on the states that Hayes had to carry. The candidate himself observed the custom of not campaigning. In the South, Democrats kept black votes well below the levels of 1872 through a combination of coercion and violence.

For the northern electorate, military-style campaigning was the order of the day as the "Boys in Blue" marched through the streets of cities and towns. These Republican clubs and marching societies staged flag and banner raisings to stir partisan enthusiasm. Campaign songs based on familiar melodies filled the night air with the pledge "We will not vote for Tilden." The crowd listened to men such as Robert Ingersoll denounce the Democrats: "Soldiers, every scar you have on your bodies was given to you by a Democrat." Hayes endorsed the bloody-shirt strategy because, he said, "It leads people away from hard times, which is our deadliest foe."[31]

On election night, the early returns forecast an apparent Tilden triumph. The Democrat had carried Indiana, Connecticut, New Jersey, and New York, with their 75 electoral votes, and was running well in the South. His popular vote total was well ahead of Hayes's. As the night wore on, Tilden had 184 electoral votes from sixteen states in his column and was one short of victory. Hayes had 165 electoral votes from the eighteen states he had carried. The Republican managers noted that Hayes could still win. If he triumphed in the remaining southern states of Florida, Louisiana, and South Carolina, their electoral votes would give him the White House.

The Republicans had a tenuous hold on the governments of those three states. The directors of the Hayes effort on the Republican National Committee fired off telegrams to local officials asked them to "hold your state." The chairman of the committee, Senator Zachariah Chandler of Michigan, told reporters the next day that "Hayes has 185 electoral votes and is elected." Soon the state election boards in the three states declared Hayes entitled to their electoral votes. The Democrats countered with their own returns from the three states and dispatched their electoral returns to Washington for Tilden. Lawmakers were confronted with two sets of votes from the three states in dispute. It would be up to Congress to decide who was the winner of the 1876 election.[32]

The Constitution did not provide a clear prescription for how to resolve such a dispute. If a challenge was made to a state's electoral vote when the Congress tabulated the returns, then stalemate would likely occur, because the Senate was Republican and the House Democratic. Neither chamber could settle the crisis without the endorsement of the other. To bring the disputed election to a conclusion, Congress created an electoral commission with fifteen members, ten from Congress and five from the Supreme Court. The panel was to contain seven Republicans and seven Democrats, with one independent member, the Supreme Court justice David Davis of Illinois. It was presumed that Davis would cast an unbiased vote to break a tie. Then Davis was elected to the United States Senate when Democrats in the Illinois legislature gave him their votes to oust the Republican incumbent. Davis left the commission, and a Republican justice took his place. In a series of eight-to-seven votes, the commission accepted the Republican electors from the three southern states, and Hayes was declared the winner with 185 electoral votes to 184 for Tilden.

Who, in fact, did win the election of 1876? Tilden led in the popular vote with a majority of 264,000, and he had gained a majority of the white vote in South Carolina, Louisiana, and Florida. In those states, however, black voters had been terrorized. As an African American from South Carolina reported, "They have killed col'd men in every precinct."[33] What an honest vote in these states would have shown can never be determined, but on the merits, the Republicans had as good a claim to these electoral votes as the Democrats did.

The decision of the electoral commission still had to receive congressional approval, especially from House Democrats. They began a filibuster to pressure negotiators for the two parties. As the inauguration date of March 4, 1877, approached, intense bargaining ensued. Southern Democrats sought railroad subsidies and other economic concessions in return for the acceptance of Hayes as president. But both parties realized that the larger issue was the end of Reconstruction. Hayes made it clear that he would not continue to support Republican regimes in the South using military power. As he told Carl Schurz, "There is to be an end of all that, except in emergencies which I do not think of as possible again."[34]

The practical effect of the outcome of the election of 1876 and the compromise that settled the dispute was a turning away from the goals of Reconstruction. The House Democrats abandoned their filibuster, and Hayes became president on March 4, 1877. Once in office, the new chief executive took federal troops out of politics in Louisiana and South Carolina (but not out of the states themselves), indicating that Reconstruction was over. Black Americans were now on their own, and commentators predicted that their fate would cease to be a factor in national politics.

On a basic level, the Republicans simply refused to concede defeat during the crisis of 1876–1877. From the night of the election onward, they maintained that Hayes had been elected and was entitled to the presidency. Tilden and the Democrats had a failure of nerve. They seemed to have decided from the outset of the controversy that they could not win the White House, and the best they could do was to force some concessions from the Republicans. They also hoped that anger over the election tactics of the Republicans would provide a campaign issue for 1880. When the Democrats investigated the disputed vote after 1877, it turned out that they had been as opportunistic and underhanded in the South as their opponents. In this election, the core Republican conviction that they were the nation's only legitimate party worked in the party's favor.

Although the outcome in 1877 did not signify complete Republican abandonment of black Americans, it did mark an important turning point in the nation's approach to race. Over the next quarter of a century, the South became less Republican and more segregated. Civil rights would not return to the region for seventy-five years. In the America of 1877, there was probably little that Republicans could have done to avert this result. After a generation of trying to build a freer and more open society for all of its citizens, the United States lapsed back into the customs and prejudices of old.

Nevertheless, the Republicans had reason to be proud of what they had done during the Civil War and Reconstruction. The Thirteenth, Fourteenth, and Fifteenth Amendments were building blocks on which racial justice could later rest. Republicans had done their best between 1865 and 1877 make Reconstruction achieve its goals in the face of intense Democratic opposition. But when all the justifiable historical reasons for the Republican abandonment of black Americans have been recalled, there remains the hard truth that a party committed in its origins to human freedom came up short on that issue at a crucial moment in its history.

3

Republicans in the Gilded Age,
1877–1893

ELECTION DAY, NOVEMBER 4, 1884, climaxed a long and bitter presidential campaign between Republican candidate James G. Blaine and his Democratic rival, Grover Cleveland. For months personal scandals over the alleged moral depravity of each candidate regaled the nation. Had Cleveland fathered a child out of wedlock? Was Blaine's marriage legitimate? Was the Republican nominee a lackey of big business and anti-Catholic as well? Had Cleveland failed the test of patriotism when he hired a substitute to serve for him during the Civil War? Were these two men the best the nation could offer in its political leadership?

Bands of marching men, clad in gaudy uniforms and moving with military precision, sounded these issues as they tramped through the streets of cities and towns large and small throughout the autumn. The Democratic supporters chanted:

> Blaine, Blaine, James G. Blaine
> Continental liar from the State of Maine!
> Burn this letter!

Republicans countered with marchers who pushed baby carriages, symbolizing Cleveland's purported illegitimate child, asking:

> Ma, Ma, where's my pa?[1]

In the militarized ballyhoo and spectacular hoopla that marked the politics of the late nineteenth century, the election of 1884 had it all: controversial candidates, sizable doses of scandal, and a close contest. A mere thousand votes swung the key state of New York into Cleveland's column, providing enough electoral votes for him to win the presidency. Observers argued about the factors large and small that won the election for Cleveland and brought the Democrats back into national power after twenty-four years in the minority. Everyone understood that the 1884 race would live in memory. After all, so much was at stake and the results were so close. No one would ever forget such excitement.

More than a century later, the 1884 election and the intense politics of that gaslight era seem remote and antiquated. Did groups of marching men fill the streets for their candidate? How quaint. Did newspapers print column after column filled with speeches pro and con about the protective tariff? How distant from the era of sound bites and photo opportunities. Did those Americans who were eligible go to the polls at much higher rates than now? How odd and partisan. When thinking about late-nineteenth-century politics at all, modern writers pigeonhole both the Republicans and Democrats as irrelevant to the real needs of the society that was undergoing industrialism, labor unrest, and constant change. Many historians say that James Bryce, the British commentator who wrote at the end of the 1880s, had it right at the time when he decided that "neither party has any principles, distinctive tenets." His conclusion remains part of the conventional wisdom about political parties in this period. "All has been lost, except office or the hope of it."[2]

The Republicans have suffered the most in historical terms from this negative interpretation of the late nineteenth century. Up until 1877, the Grand Old Party, as it now called itself, at least stood in theory for the rights of black Americans against the racist Democrats. But with the Compromise of 1877 and the end of Reconstruction, the Republicans are said to have revealed their true colors. As the party of big business, special privilege, and corporate America, they forfeited most of their claims to historical respect. This harsh verdict, though undermined by several generations of historical research, has proven long-lasting and powerful. The real story of Republicanism during the last quarter of the nineteenth century is more complex and more interesting than these historical clichés suggest.

Mark Twain and Charles Dudley Warner gave this period an enduring label when they titled their 1873 novel *The Gilded Age*. Its main character, Colonel Beriah Sellers, became a symbol of the expansive, often fraudulent style of boosterism and pretense that was associated with the economy's explosive growth. The words themselves suggested an era when surface opulence hid the truth depths of economic inequality, business avarice, and corporate power. An unregulated economy had little room for the rights of the needy and less powerful.

The late nineteenth century had all these problems and more. Yet it was also a time when Americans struggled to make sense of changes that were occurring at a dizzying rate. Inventions crowded in to transform daily life: the telephone, the phonograph, the motion picture, and, at the end of the period, the automobile. Cities exploded in size, railroads crisscrossed the landscape, and laboring men and women stirred with resentment and aspiration as big business grew. The Indian wars sputtered to an end after three centuries, and the frontier no longer existed as a recognizable line of settlement by the time of the 1890 census. While many Americans cursed the changes that industrialism brought, others found the quickened pace of life exhilarating.

In 1870, the national income stood at $7 billion. When the century closed, the figure had reached $17 billion. The spread of railroads, the rise of oil and steel as major industries, the creation of a national market—these developments put telephones in one million homes and four thousand automobiles on the road by 1900. Big business and its bureaucratic style of management shaped the working experience of more and more Americans. The entrepreneurs who made this happen—Andrew Carnegie, John D. Rockefeller, James J. Hill—became national celebrities as symbols of the rapid growth of large enterprises. Some called them "robber barons." They preferred to see themselves as industrial statesmen bringing new products and services to millions. How their behavior should be regulated, if at all, was one of the nascent concerns of the late nineteenth century. Neither the Republicans nor the Democrats had ever faced the problem of governmental power quite this way in the past.

The dilemma of how to deal with the upsurge of industrialism arose because the growth of big business had not been borne on a wave of national prosperity and steady economic growth. Instead, a long period of deflation followed the Panic of 1873 and lasted until the late 1890s. Cost-cutting in major industries, combined with the productivity of American workers, brought prices down and sparked industrial expansion. The burden of falling prices weighed on farmers, whose income diminished. Unskilled workers, whose incomes often receded in the periodic recessions of the 1880s and the depression of the 1890s, suffered in the knowledge that their employers might terminate them at will without cause.

Adding to the economic turbulence of the period was the increase in immigration that marked the postwar era. During the two decades after 1870, nearly seven and a half million immigrants swelled the national population. "New immigrants" from southern and eastern Europe settled in the large cities of the East Coast and the Middle West. The lifestyles of Poles, Italians,

Hungarians, and Eastern European Jews mixed uneasily with the already established cultural patterns of earlier immigrants and native-born Americans. Often the Democrats proved more adept at recruiting these newcomers. The Protestant moralism of many Republicans, who emphasized temperance in the consumption of alcohol, insisted on the use of English in public schools, and demanded strict observance of the Sabbath, did not sit well with many Catholic and Jewish immigrants. If a newly emigrated workingman wanted to watch baseball with his children on a Sunday afternoon, have a beer in the park, or go to a dance, why should the local Republican government tell him he could not because of a Sunday closing law?

In a volatile economic and cultural climate, the underlying political issue for both parties became how best to spur the growth of the industrial sector while addressing the plight of farmers, workers, and small business. The idea that the national government might regulate the economy to lessen the negative impact of industrialism was advanced only on the fringes of the political spectrum in the 1870s and into the 1880s. The parties did not reflect their modern alignments on the role of government. The Democrats in this period contended that government should be small, with limited taxation, frugal government expenditures, and a reliance on states' rights. The last principle dominated in the southern base of the Democrats, because greater governmental power might mean more rights for African Americans.

The Republicans, on the other hand, were the party of governmental activism and economic nationalism. As they did during the Civil War, the Republicans insisted that the broad powers of the national government should be used to distribute public lands, promote the expansion of railroads and other enterprises, and encourage the growth of industry through high customs duties on goods imported from overseas. "Protecting" American capitalists from foreign competition seemed a wise use of national power. The party envisioned the national economy as a "vast cooperative productive enterprise in which the social or the public economic interest was promoted by energetic and promiscuous stimulation of productive agencies in private hands." This sense of innate social harmony as the central fact of American political and economic life remains a key element in Republican thought and is revealed in Republicans' frequent criticism of the Democrats for engaging in "class warfare."[3]

Since the Republicans controlled the presidency for all but four years between 1876 and 1892, they should have been well positioned to enact their philosophy into public law, but politics in the Gilded Age was not that simple. What might appear at first glance a period of Republican supremacy was anything but. A closer look at the electoral situation reveals not Republican dominance but sixteen years of political stalemate. The Republicans took the White House by narrow margins time after time. Although the Compromise of 1877 put him into office, Rutherford B. Hayes lost the popular vote to Samuel J. Tilden. Four years later James A. Garfield had a plurality over his Democratic rival of just nine thousand votes. In 1888, Benjamin Harrison also lost the popular vote to Grover Cleveland by more than eighty-nine thousand ballots but triumphed in the electoral college. When the Democrats won in 1884, Cleveland outpolled James G. Blaine by just under thirty thousand votes. Only in 1892, in his second race against Harrison, did Cleveland achieve a 372,000-vote margin over his Republican opponent. Landslides and big swings of voter sentiment from one party to another did not exist during the Gilded Age.

The balance of power in Congress presented a similar picture. The Republicans controlled both houses of Congress in 1881–1883 and again from 1889 to 1891. The Democrats enjoyed one brief period of control of both houses, from 1879 to 1881. Otherwise, the Democrats usually won the House of Representatives, in part because of their strength in the South. The Republicans kept a majority in the Senate, whose members were still chosen by state legislatures, because of their strength in many northern states. In this closely balanced setting, getting any legislation through Congress was a real accomplishment.

During this period when every vote counted, most white male voters belonged to one of the two major parties. Independents made up at most about 5 percent of the electorate. Belonging to a political party was a civic duty. Voting was expected, and so voters in the northern states would regularly turn out for elections at rates of 70 to 80 percent, twenty or thirty points above what became common in the late twentieth century and the first decade of the twenty-first century. As an up and coming young Iowa Republican, Jonathan P. Dolliver, said in 1884: "The man who, having the right to vote, is too lazy or high-toned to mingle with his fellow citizens at the polls, is the merest ape and echo of a citizen."[4]

Americans obtained their information about politics from the daily and weekly newspapers, which covered the partisan debates with an intensity that resembles modern attention to professional sports. Each party had its own newspapers to advance the cause, and no pretense of objectivity stood in the way of reporting the news. A Democratic paper might describe a party convention as enthusiastic and optimistic The Republican counterpart in the same town would call the gathering poorly attended and demoralized.

Newspapers did carry the full text of speeches, reported on local and state conventions in copious detail, and dissected party machinations of the other party in their editorials at length. The debates in Congress and the progress of bills were followed in rich detail, often with elaborate discussion of what one faction or the other was doing. The political universe of the Gilded Age pervaded American life.

Despite their apparent dominance of American politics since 1860, the Republican's hold on power was precarious. They still faced a daunting electoral arithmetic when their candidate sought the presidency. Because of their unbreakable grip on the South, the Democrats could count on about 135 electoral votes from that region and the border states no matter who their presidential candidate might be. If the Democrats could then add New York and Indiana to their total, they would be very near the 185–190 electoral votes needed to win. The doctrines of limited government and states' rights gave the Democrats a powerful national base in a country where suspicion of the federal government and its power still prevailed.

The position of the Republicans was much less secure. The party's strength was rooted in the Northeast and Middle West, but only in the states of upper New England, such as Maine, Vermont, and New Hampshire, was victory assured. There the Democratic Party was weak, and Republican loyalties, formed during the 1850s and deepened during the Civil War, remained strong. Middle western states such as Indiana, Ohio, and Illinois were disputed battlegrounds where Democrats were a significant presence. The Middle Atlantic states, New York, New Jersey, and Pennsylvania, also were in play because of their diverse populations. The Republicans had to win almost every one of these key states to have any chance at the presidency. For them, unlike the Democrats, there was no margin for error in a race for the White House.

The Republicans confronted difficult choices during the late 1870s and into the 1880s. Reconstruction seemed to have failed, and the fate of African Americans, while useful as a campaign rallying cry, did not sway voters who were not already fierce partisans. Republicans complained with much justification that African Americans ought to have the right to vote in the South and were blocked from doing so by the extralegal tactics and outright violence of the Democrats. But what was to be done? Military government could not be restored, and expensive government programs to help the former slaves ran up against a national feeling that a large federal government initiative was dangerous. Whenever the Republicans took even small steps in this direction, Democrats denounced them in racist terms for their friendship with black Americans.

Cultural issues did much to divide the party. Republicans with strong Protestant leanings wanted local, state, and national governments to promote a more godly society by prohibiting the sale of alcohol, requiring a strict observance of the Sabbath, and mandating that public schools teach their courses in English rather than the languages of the immigrants. These ethnocultural arguments galvanized Republicans in the Middle West, but they also aroused strong feelings among immigrant groups who saw these policies as discriminatory against Catholicism and restrictive toward personal liberties. Party leaders asked if the pursuit of these ideals cost as many votes as they gained for Republican candidates.

The legacy of corruption from the 1860s and early 1870s continued to be a problem for the party. Since Republicans believed they were morally superior to the Democrats, the scandals of the Grant years had been embarrassing. The Whiskey Ring, the Salary Grab, the Crédit Mobilier—all these and other examples of wrongdoing compromised the portrait of the Republicans as the party of virtue and honesty.

On an ideological level, the Republicans were also a tough sell for prospective voters. A leader like Thomas B. Reed of Maine claimed: "The Republican party does things, the Democratic party criticizes; the Republican party achieves, the Democratic party finds fault."[5] However, many Americans in the late nineteenth century still looked with suspicion on a government that taxed imported goods, used grants and subsidies to stimulate corporate expansion, and poked into local affairs on behalf of African Americans or militant Protestantism. Americans liked the benefits that came from Republican policies—railroads, military bases, and land distribution. At the same time, average citizens retained a fondness for the Democratic argument that emphasized "the master wisdom of governing little and leaving as much as possible to localities and individuals." Some Republicans, as the 1870s ended, believed the party "must have a broadened base and reinforcements, or it is gone, and the Democratic party will come into power for a generation."[6]

Predictions of an imminent Republican demise would appear at other times in the party's history. Then, as in the 1870s, they would be overstated. Because of the Civil War, the Republicans were associated with preserving the Union and ensuring the survival of the American experiment in self-government. The patriotic link remained strong across the North in such powerful pressure groups as the Grand Army of the Republic, an alliance of Union veterans. As the wife of an Ohio senator wrote many years later in describing Gilded Age attitudes: "The Republican party had saved the Union. It was the Union." Men who had fought in the conflict forged an emotional attachment to Republicanism that endured for decades and was passed on to their children. Growing up in Ohio in this period, the novelist and diplomat Brand Whitlock recalled the Republican Party as "a synonym for patriotism, another name for the nation." To Whitlock's family and friends, "it was inconceivable that any self-respecting person could be a Democrat."[7]

The belief that the Democrats were proponents of disloyalty and disunion still permeated the Republican Party. After Grover Cleveland brought his party back into power in 1884, a New York Republican wrote: "I think of our condition under democratic rule as like that of the Jews in captivity."[8] New York Republicans in 1876 alleged that the Democratic Party was "the same in character and spirit as when it sympathized with treason."[9]

Contempt and derision toward the Democrats affected Republican views about the illegitimacy of their partisan opponents. Jokes abounded about Democratic ineptitude. It was said that the Democratic Party was like alcohol: it killed everything that was alive and preserved everything that was dead. The *New York Tribune*, in those days a leading Republican newspaper, editorialized in July 1882 that "to join the Democratic party is to go down among the dead men at once, and to chain one's self to the dead past forever."[10]

The disdain of Republicans for their political rivals went beyond bemusement at the follies of their opposition. The Democrats were simply unworthy to govern and incapable of doing so. Senator George Frisbie Hoar of Massachusetts articulated feelings of many of his party in 1889:[11]

> The men who do the work of piety and charity in our churches; the men who administer our school systems; the men who own and till their own farms; the men who perform skilled labor in the shops; the soldiers, the men who went to war and stayed all through; the men who paid the debt and kept the currency sound, and saved the nation's honor; the men who saved the country in war, and have made it worth living in peace, commonly, and as a rule, by the natural law of their being, find their place in the Republican party; while the old slave-owner and slave-driver, the saloon-keeper, the ballot-box stuffer, the Kuklux, the criminal class of the great cities, the men who cannot read and write, commonly, and as a rule, by the natural law of their being, find their congenial place in the Democratic party.

The Republicans during the Gilded Age possessed a higher degree of internal unity than the Democrats. Despite the intraparty feuds that often marked campaigns and conventions, the Republicans displayed a cohesion and common purpose that more often eluded the Democrats. The reigning belief in the Grand Old Party was that no single party member was more important than the fate of the Republicans as a whole. Nowhere was their unity more evident than in the Republican conviction that the protective tariff ought to be the driving force in national economic policy.

One issue on which most Republicans agreed during the Gilded Age was the protective tariff. The doctrine stood at the heart of Republican thinking about the economy. More than a century later the Republicans are now, at least in their rhetoric, the party of free trade and open markets. The evolution of the GOP from protectionism to free trade took decades. In the years after the Civil War the tariff became "the sacred temple of the Republican party." For several generations a test of Republican orthodoxy was devotion to the tariff and the ideology of nationalistic government that it represented.[12]

In the years before the income tax was adopted, two main sources provided revenue to the federal government. The levies on the sale of alcohol and other domestic luxuries provided internal revenues. Taxes imposed on imported goods brought the remainder of government funds. In 1881, for example, internal revenues accounted for more than $135 million. Customs revenues totaled some $198 million. From 1866 to 1893, the government ran surpluses as tariff revenues from the growing international trade swelled the nation's coffers.

While the Democrats believed that tariffs should be set low and the amount of revenue available to the government be kept small, Republicans argued that a tariff policy that raised rates on foreign imports brought a number of positive results. First and foremost, it provided security for American manufacturing firms against competition from overseas. Tariff rates, said GOP members, should be "so levied as to give full and adequate protection to the laborer, the producer, and the industries of the United States." A related protariff argument contended that such an approach also safeguarded the jobs of American workers who bore the brunt of job losses when cheap imported goods flooded the domestic market. Although Democrats said that protection served only the interest of employers and industrialists, the doctrine appealed to skilled workers who connected retention of their jobs to the higher tariff in what protectionists called "the home market."[13]

Protection was more than just an economic policy. In the hands of the Republicans, it also connoted nationalism and patriotic pride. James G. Blaine and later William McKinley were Republican leaders who were adept at making this link. "Vote the Republican ticket," said McKinley in 1886, "stand by the protective policy, stand by American industry, stand by that

STRANGER THINGS HAVE HAPPENED.
HOLD ON, AND YOU MAY WALK OVER THE SLUGGISH ANIMAL UP THERE YET.

The cartoonist Thomas Nast created the Democratic donkey and the Republican elephant in this 1879 cartoon from *Harper's Weekly*.

policy which believes in American work for American workmen, that believes in American wages for American laborers, that believes in American homes for American citizens." Since the major free trade nation of the world was Great Britain, which imposed no protective tariffs on goods that it imported, tariff protection tapped into anti-British feelings in a manner that strengthened the Republican appeal to ethnic groups, such as the Irish, who were otherwise loyal to the Democrats.[14]

Drawing on ideas that had their origins in the Whig Party, Republicans contended that American society was a network of interdependent producers. As a result, the tariff did not favor a single class but spread its benefits across all levels of society by ensuring markets and jobs for all Americans. Since there was a natural harmony of interests throughout the nation, it was wrong to claim that the tariff favored the wealthy or the privileged few, as the Democrats often did. To use such rhetoric in campaigns, said Republicans, pitted one class against another in conflicts that were more characteristic of European socialism than the United States.

Objective circumstances made the tariff an urgent matter in this period. Foreign competition reached across many areas of the economy. Farmers and ranchers who raised beef and produced cattle hides faced rivals in Argentina. American lumber and coal vied with the products of Canadian forests and mines. Cheaper British, German, and French goods like clothes, eyeglasses, agricultural machinery, and jewelry came into the country to challenge the dominance of American manufacturers.

While the tariff in the main succeeded for the Republicans as a political creed, there were negatives as well. Higher customs duties raised prices for consumers of protected goods, a point that Democrats stressed when they accused their rivals of pushing high taxation on the American people. The financial and ideological links between the Republicans and large segments of the business community made the party vulnerable to charges that the protective tariff was simply payback for the support of industrialists and corporations. There was an identity of interest between the Republicans and the groups their policies favored, but the advocates of the tariff believed in their doctrine with as much firmness and conviction as their modern Republican counterparts believe in free trade.

As the size of business grew in the 1880s, many Americans worried about the emergence of the "trust" as a form of corporate organization. The many state laws that barred a corporation in one state from doing business in another led lawyers to devise the "trust" concept. Shareholders in oil companies in several states turned their shares over to the trustees of the Standard Oil

Trust and received trust certificates in return. The trustees then used their control of the various companies to establish a national strategy for dominating the oil business. The Democrats charged that the protective tariff, by encouraging the rise of big business, also spurred the establishment of these trusts—or, as they put it, the tariff was "the mother of all trusts." Moreover, said the Democrats, the economic size of the trusts made them a threat to small business everywhere. Republicans countered these arguments by claiming that the tariff fostered prosperity while the low-tariff, or "free trade," policy of the Democrats led to hard times. During the 1880s, the issue became a significant dividing line between the two parties.[15]

When Republicans and historians look back on the late nineteenth century, what is most significant about Rutherford B. Hayes, James A. Garfield, Chester Alan Arthur, and Benjamin Harrison is that these presidents have fallen into an obscurity that makes them almost indistinguishable to modern readers. The novelist Thomas Wolfe captured this view when he wrote some years later of these presidents as "The Four Lost Men":

> For who was Garfield, martyred man, and who had seen him in the streets of life? Who could believe his footfalls ever sounded on a lonely pavement? Who had heard the casual and familiar tones of Chester Arthur? And where was Harrison? Where was Hayes? Which had the whiskers, which the burnsides; which was which?
>
> And were they not lost?[16]

If the Republican presidents of the Gilded Age have slipped into historical limbo, they at least are counted among the list of American chief executives. The place of the most exciting, controversial, and interesting Republican of the period, James G. Blaine, on the roster of important members of the Grand Old Party has been forgotten, except among a few specialists. More than any other Republican of his time, Blaine shaped the destiny of the party for two decades, while making the tariff the centerpiece of Republican thinking. Born in 1830, he grew up in Pennsylvania, taught school in Kentucky and his home state, and then moved to Maine in the mid-1850s as a journalist. Soon his oratorical talents, encyclopedic memory, and personal magnetism led him into politics. After service in the Maine legislature, he was elected to the national House of Representatives in 1863 and became Speaker in 1869. From the beginning of his political life, Blaine inspired strong feelings. The saying in Washington was that he caused men to go crazy over him in pairs, one for and one against. The most dedicated of his followers called themselves "Blainiacs."[17]

Blaine was one of those politicians, like Franklin D. Roosevelt, John F. Kennedy, Richard Nixon, and Bill Clinton, whose mastery of American politics extended to the smallest detail. Ask Blaine about an obscure county in the Midwest, and he could provide an accurate summary of its politics and election returns. He never forgot a face and could recall in an instant a conversation with someone he had met years before. No public figure of the Gilded Age was better at articulating Republican doctrine and making its appeal clear to the electorate.

The tariff was an issue that Blaine had mastered. He saw it as a topic that could move the Republicans into the next phase of their history. In his mind, the effective use of national power would promote industrial growth and spread economic benefits. The war had persuaded him that "every thing which may be done by either Nation or State may be better or more securely done by the Nation."[18] For Blaine this philosophy involved sharing government revenues with the states to assist their educational programs and, in foreign affairs, a system of reciprocal trade treaties to open up foreign markets to American goods.

For all of his political talents and wide support among Republicans, Blaine had personal problems with corruption that made him controversial and in some ways a political liability.

While he was Speaker of the House, he had pushed through legislation in 1869 helpful to the owners of a railroad in Arkansas. He wrote some indiscreet letters in the process. When the episode came to light in 1876, he explained away how he later sold stock for the railroad, but this excuse did not satisfy his critics. Blaine was one of the earliest examples of the truism that the cover-up may be worse than the crime itself.

To prove his case he recovered from a clerk named Mulligan some of the damaging letters he had written, and he read portions of these missives on the House floor. His performance stilled doubts for a few days. Then when his critics read the full text of the letters in the newspapers, they claimed that Blaine had lied to protect himself. Since he had written at the bottom of one of the letters "Burn this letter when you have read it," he had provided damning evidence for his enemies to use against him.[19]

The most popular Republican politician of the late nineteenth century, James G. Blaine defined party policy on the protective tariff. Library of Congress, LC-USZ62-8753.

Blaine gave his opponents plenty of ammunition in other respects. He and his family lived well, and he refused to discuss the source of his income. There was always a sense that Blaine lived on the ethical edge. The Gilded Age did not have conflict-of-interest laws, and political morality was not as well defined as it would be a century later. Blaine was probably no better and no worse than most of his contemporaries in his financial transactions. Because he was so charismatic, he attracted more attention and coverage. In significant ways, Blaine anticipated the celebrity political culture of the century to come.

Blaine's spectacular feud with Roscoe Conkling, which arose in the "turkey gobbler strut" episode during the 1860s, defined Republican politics in the 1880s. Distinct factions emerged around the two men. The "Stalwarts," led by Conkling and his New York machine allies, clung to the issues of Reconstruction and believed that sectional appeals were still viable. Blaine and the men who followed him were known as "Half Breeds" because of their willingness to depart from Stalwart orthodoxy. They shared the disappointment that the Republicans had been shut out of southern politics, but they were also convinced that the Republican Party could only grow if it addressed some of the issues posed by industrialism. That did not mean government regulation of business. Half Breeds endorsed instead a protective tariff, revenue sharing with the states, and federal assistance for educating both blacks and whites in the South.

During the one-term administration of Rutherford B. Hayes, the Stalwarts fought the president's efforts to assert executive authority over the system of patronage and appointments that dominated national politics. Hayes favored civil service reform, the idea that nominees for federal positions should be qualified for selection by more than just their political connections. He believed that selecting officials because of their partisan loyalty led to the graft and scandals that embarrassed the party.

These ideas led the president into a confrontation with Conkling, who expected to control the federal offices in the city and state of New York. The key point was the customs house in New York City, through which flowed much of the nation's trade. The collector of customs received a percentage of the customs duties instead of a fixed salary. As a result, the position was one of the most lucrative jobs in the federal service. Hayes nominated two men to fill vacancies, but Conkling persuaded his fellow senators to block their confirmation. A year later Hayes ousted Conkling's friends and won Senate confirmation of his own choices. The episode received national coverage and was interpreted as a victory for presidential power and a defeat for senators who opposed civil service procedures.

These frequent disputes between presidents and influential senators explain why the issue of civil service reform became so central to Gilded Age politics. As it showed, powerful lawmakers who controlled government offices in their states and localities limited the power of the executive to improve the quality of government employees. Professionalizing the government service appealed to those who wanted trained experts to replace political amateurs. It also curbed the capacity of the state party leader relative to the national government. Some advocates also saw it as a means of limiting the power of the average citizen to play a role in politics, since expertise, rather than just political loyalty, would be needed. The civil service question was a constant source of contention within the Republican Party.

After winning the disputed election of 1876, Rutherford B. Hayes provided a single term that restored some confidence among Republicans. Library of Congress, LC-USZ62-13019.

In the eight years after the disputed election of 1876, three Republican presidents—Hayes, Garfield, and Arthur—held office. Each in his way sought to increase presidential power and authority, but circumstances made their efforts less than successful. Rutherford B. Hayes had a creditable single term. Garfield's bright promise fell victim to an assassin's bullet, and Arthur turned out to be a decent caretaker of his political inheritance. None of them were able to move the Republicans toward the status of majority party that so many coveted.

During his four years, Hayes sought to conciliate the South as he had promised during the disputed election, but the Democrats in Dixie rejected his overtures. Building a viable Republican Party around African Americans and whites attracted to GOP economic views proved untenable. The race issue dominated and the Democrats surged back into a clear ascendancy of southern politics between 1877 and 1881. The Republicans experienced much internal rancor during the process, but there was little support for a return to Reconstruction. Absent that, a reduction in Republican influence in the South was inevitable.

In other areas, Hayes saw his party become more intertwined with the interests of the industrial sector. The nationwide railroad strike of 1877, arising from pay cuts to workers during the persistent depression, brought walkouts and the threat of violence. Governors called out their state militias, but some units declined to fire on strikers whom they knew from their own communities. As the crisis worsened, Hayes dispatched army units to keep the peace. Middle-class Americans applauded the president's actions. Unhappy workers blamed the Republicans for the defeat of the strike.

With hard times lingering from the Panic of 1873, Democrats and some western Republicans wanted to move away from the policy that every dollar in circulation was backed by an equal amount of gold in the government's vaults. Using silver, which was more plentiful than gold, would lead to some inflation and a rise in prices for farmers. In 1878, the Bland-Allison Act was passed over the veto of President Hayes, who deemed the measure inflationary. It provided for the government to buy a fixed amount of silver each month, which did little to inflate the currency. Hayes's action pleased business interests, who favored a stable currency, but unhappy farmers would raise the issue of lifting crop prices again in the decade ahead.

Hayes had promised to serve only one term, and in 1880 the Republicans looked again for a winning candidate. Conkling and the Stalwarts pushed for a third term for Ulysses S. Grant who, after eight years in office and four touring the world, was now deemed ready to be president again. Blaine was the Half Breed hopeful, but the stigma of his ethical lapses lingered. The party turned to James A. Garfield, an Ohio congressman with the requisite Civil War record who had Blaine's appeal without his liabilities. To run with Garfield, the national convention selected Chester Alan Arthur, a New Yorker and friend of Conkling, to balance the ticket as the vice presidential candidate.

The Republicans emphasized the tariff issue in 1880, and Garfield eked out a narrow victory over the Democratic nominee, Winfield Scott Hancock. Garfield's majority was a scant nine thousand votes over his rival in the popular balloting, but he had a 214–155 lead in the electoral tally. In his brief presidency, Garfield faced down Roscoe Conkling over appointments in New York State and seemed to have established the authority of the president over that of powerful senators. With Blaine as his secretary of state, Garfield looked forward to expanding the nation's economic presence in Latin America and uniting the Republicans behind a program of tariff protection and economic nationalism. On July 2, 1881, while waiting at a Washington train station to leave on a vacation from the stifling heat of the capital, Garfield was assassinated by Charles J. Guiteau, an insane man who believed that he was entitled to a federal job. Guiteau shouted, "I am a Stalwart and Arthur is President" as police took him away.[20] Garfield died of his wounds in mid-September, and Chester Alan Arthur succeeded him.

JAMES A. GARFIELD
REPUBLICAN CANDIDATE FOR PRESIDENT

CHESTER A. ARTHUR
REPUBLICAN CANDIDATE FOR VICE PRESIDENT

The ill-fated James A. Garfield and his successor, Chester Arthur, were the last Republican presidents in the sequence that began with Abraham Lincoln. Library of Congress, LC-DIG-pga-02734.

Although he had been a Conkling ally, Arthur proved to be his own man as president. He dropped Blaine as secretary of state and took charge of his own administration. Congress enacted a civil service law to end some of the abuses of the patronage system. The lawmakers also passed the Chinese Exclusion Law to limit the number of immigrants from that country, in response to the persistent suspicion of newcomers from Asia. Finally, the enactment of a tariff law in 1883 did not satisfy either side in the debate over protection. The measure was such an awkward compromise that it became known as the Mongrel Tariff.

Arthur wanted the Republican nomination in 1884. Poor health and a lack of real support within the party doomed his candidacy. Blaine's turn at the nomination had come. His liabilities persisted. So many questions remained about his finances that some Republicans in the Northeast threatened to bolt the party if he was selected. These vocal proponents of civil service reform, political ethics, and smaller government had become known as "Mugwumps" (an Algonquian word meaning "important person"). They made up for in noise what they lacked in numbers, and they hated Blaine. One of their leaders, Carl Schurz, proclaimed that Blaine had "wallowed in the spoils like a rhinoceros in an African pool."[21]

The Republican convention nominated Blaine and his running mate, John "Black Jack" Logan of Illinois, and the Mugwumps bolted to the Democrats. Two young Republicans, Theodore Roosevelt and Henry Cabot Lodge, stayed with the party, thereby preserving their political futures. Blaine wanted to run on the tariff, and he went out on a speaking tour to rouse Republican enthusiasm. The candidate knew it would be a tough year for the party since the Republican vote had been in a slight decline nationally. Moreover, the Democrats had rallied behind their choice, the governor of New York, Grover Cleveland.

The 1884 campaign soon degenerated into one of the noisiest and dirtiest races in American history. Rumors of scandals in Cleveland's past had circulated for some time, and they broke open when he admitted that he had been sexually involved with a woman named Maria Halpin. Cleveland did not know for certain that he was the father of Halpin's child, but he accepted responsibility and paid for the young boy's education. Republicans jumped on these revelations to embarrass their rivals. The Democrats responded with charges that Blaine and his wife had been married only three months when their first child was born. Blaine replied that the couple had married in secret two years earlier. Charges and countercharges about these indiscretions filled the newspapers. Cities and towns echoed with the slogans of the rival candidates as military-style campaigners marched in huge rallies.

The most sensational event of the campaign occurred just before the voting. On October 29 Blaine attended a reception for predominantly Protestant clergy in New York City. Presiding over the meeting was Reverend Samuel D. Burchard of a Methodist church in the Murray Hill section of the city. Addressing Blaine, he said, "We are Republicans and don't propose to leave our party and identify ourselves with a party whose antecedents have been 'rum, Romanism, and rebellion.'" Blaine did not disavow the anti-Catholic slur on the spot or later, and within a few days controversy raged over the episode. Since New York went for Cleveland and cost Blaine the election, the Burchard remark has often been labeled as a slip that denied the Republican candidate the White House, and so it has passed into the folklore of American politics.[22]

On the night of Burchard's remark, Blaine addressed a fundraising dinner with an audience of business leaders and corporate executives at Delmonico's restaurant. The Democrats called it "Belshazzar Blaine and the Money Kings" in their cartoon (after the biblical king who saw his doom in the writing on the wall). The contrast between the opulence of the dinner and the plight of the working poor gave the Cleveland forces a theme for their campaign literature.

When the votes were tallied, Cleveland had won New York State by just over one thousand votes, but that was enough to give him the state and the election. The Democrat won 219 electoral votes to 182 for Blaine. The twenty-four-year Republican control of the White House had ended. In retrospect, neither the Burchard remark nor the Delmonico's dinner cost Blaine the election. He had run better than any other candidate would have for the Republicans. The Republican share of the national total fell from 48.3 percent in 1880 to 48.2 percent four years later, while the Democratic share rose 2 percent over what they had achieved in 1880. The election of 1884 was one of those close Gilded Age contests where the result could have gone either way based on a host of causes in specific states. Blaine had rallied the Republican base and enabled the party to stay cohesive for another winning race four years later.

If the Republicans hoped that Grover Cleveland would be a political failure and validate their belief in Democratic incompetence to govern, they were disappointed. While the president did not inspire enthusiasm within his own party, where his patronage policies irritated the faithful, he was a hard worker who performed his duties in an honest and efficient manner. The Republicans achieved some gains in the 1886 congressional elections, and observers expected another close and hard-fought election two years later.

During Cleveland's presidency, currents of social change intensified in both industrial and rural regions to challenge both parties. In May 1886, for example, working people in Chicago staged a rally to protest the role of police in breaking a strike against the McCormick Harvesting Machine Company. When the police tried to break up the gathering, a bomb exploded, killing one police officer. His comrades fired into the crowd, and a riot ensued. Eight alleged participants in a bombing conspiracy were tried and convicted, and four were executed. The Haymarket incident (named for the square in Chicago where the violence took place) seemed to signal to the middle and upper classes that social revolution could occur.

The growing presence of immigrants from southern and eastern Europe created additional unrest. The American Protective Association, an anti-Catholic organization with ties to Republicans in some Midwestern communities, sought to limit the role of immigrants in national politics with restrictive legislation. Local politics in the major cities saw urban political machines arise. These institutions, run by a city boss and based on a network of operatives in local wards of such places as New York, Chicago, and

Philadelphia, were most often Democratic in character. Relying as they did on the votes of immigrants and ethnic minorities, they pitted genteel, "respectable" Republicans, usually from the middle and upper classes, against the power of the bosses who ran the organizations.

At the same time, conditions in rural America worsened. The expansion of agriculture brought bumper crops of wheat and cotton during the 1880s. Farm prices sagged. On the Plains and in the South, unhappy agrarians joined the Farmers Alliance, seeking ways to raise prices and reduce the burden of debt that plagued farmers. Many settlers had bought lands at high interest rates earlier in the decade. In the South, the Alliance spelled trouble for the Democrats. In Kansas, Nebraska, Minnesota, and the soon-to-be states of North and South Dakota, Republicans felt the sting of farm protest. Among the ideas being promulgated was to increase the supply of available currency by abandoning the gold standard and coining silver, which was in ample supply. With an increase in the amount of money in circulation, debts would be easier to pay and the prices for commodities would rise. Republicans in the Northeast scorned such schemes, fearing that inflation would erode the value of the dollar and promote economic instability.

During the 1880s the trust problem moved to the center of political debate. Both parties soon felt the wave of public unease about what corporate giants might do to smaller entrepreneurs, but the issue hurt the Republicans more because of their strong base in the business community. The anger against railroads had resulted in the enactment of the Interstate Commerce Act in 1887 and the creation of the Interstate Commerce Commission through bipartisan legislation. Now the Democrats charged that big business and its impact was thwarting competition, and they blamed the Republicans for the threat that trusts posed to the traditional values of small business, individual enterprise, and economic freedom.

The presidential election of 1888 offered another opportunity for the two parties to present their competing visions of what constituted a good society. In December 1887, the president decided to devote his entire annual message to Congress to a single subject: the need for reform in the tariff system through a reduction of duties. Republicans leaped to the challenge with evident eagerness. They believed that a presidential race focused on the tariff would enable them to maximize their strength at the polls. The day after Cleveland delivered his written message to Congress, James G. Blaine, on vacation in Paris, shared his reaction with a reporter for the *New York Tribune*. Blaine maintained that a low tariff policy would produce instability for American business, lower wages for workers, and force companies to confront devastating competition from Great Britain and other European countries. In short, said Blaine, "The Democratic party in power is a standing menace to the prosperity of the country."[23]

The Republicans could have nominated Blaine to make the case for tariff protection, but the party realized that his candidacy would only dredge up the issues of 1884. Benjamin Harrison of Indiana had been a Civil War general, a one-term senator, and a successful attorney. Small in stature, "Little Ben" was effective on the campaign trail. His logical, well-delivered speeches appealed to large audiences. His personal integrity seemed impeccable. In 1888, Harrison could make the tariff case, carry Indiana, and give the Republicans a chance to win.[24]

The resulting election proved to be significant in several respects. The success of the Republican campaign for the protective tariff confirmed the perception that the party's interests ran with those of business. To help finance the canvass, department store owner John Wanamaker embarked on a systematic effort to raise money from big corporations through a businessman's committee. Other Republicans with ties to business did likewise. The technique became known as "frying the fat" out of corporations.

The money paid for the torrent of protariff literature that the party poured out. Meanwhile, Harrison stayed home and spoke to delegations that came to visit him. He made eighty speeches to more than three hundred thousand guests, articulating the Republican message in a crisp manner.[25]

The election ended in a Harrison victory, the Republican candidate winning 233 electoral votes to Cleveland's 168. In the popular vote, Cleveland had an eighty-nine thousand vote majority, largely based on the Democratic vote in the South, where black Americans were increasingly

The diminutive Benjamin Harrison won a close election in 1888 and then encountered troubles that led him to serve just one term. Library of Congress, LC-USZ62-7611.

excluded from politics. The Republicans had control of the House of Representatives by a margin of 166 to 159, and they held a two-vote majority in the Senate. The postelection consensus was that the protective tariff had played a major part and the Republicans had outworked and outfought their Democratic rivals. Now they had control of the legislative and executive branches of the government. It remained to be seen what they would do with their narrow but important victory.

Despite their narrow seven-vote margin in the House, the Republicans hoped to enact an ambitious agenda in the Fifty-First Congress that convened a year after the presidential election in December 1889. President Harrison wanted action to raise tariff rates and legislation to safeguard the voting rights of black Americans in the South. Democratic efforts to strip the franchise from African Americans had made the Republican presence in the South more fragile as the years passed. Mindful of the 1890 elections, some Republican lawmakers wanted to address the trust issue with laws curbing the expansion of monopolies. Responding to the growing discontent in the farm belt, Republicans from that area hoped to enact measures to inflate the currency through coining more silver.

Democratic obstructionism in the House of Representatives proved an immediate obstacle. For years attempts to enact legislation had run up against what was known as the "disappearing quorum." Democrats in the chamber sat silent when the clerk called their names for the purpose of establishing a quorum (the minimum number of members who had to be present for the House to take any legislative action). A determined minority could thus thwart the progress of any bill. Eager to defeat Republican initiatives, the minority party found this delaying tactic quite to their liking.

In December 1889, the Republican majority selected Thomas B. Reed of Maine as the new Speaker of the House. A giant of a man at three hundred pounds, Reed had a sarcastic wit that served him well in debate. When a Democrat boasted, echoing Henry Clay, that he would rather be right than president, Reed answered, "The gentleman need not be disturbed. He will never be either." Once he spoke to an audience that included many Democrats and claimed that a photograph taken of their party would reveal that they were doing some "mean, low-lived and contemptible thing." The crowd jeered and howled. Reed smiled and said, "There, I told you so."[26]

Beyond his sardonic demeanor, Reed believed that the Republican majority ought to be able to pass bills. In late January 1890, Reed ruled that members who were present but refused to vote could be counted for a quorum.

The Democrats complained and sought to block any further business through obstructive tactics. Reed also contended that the majority had the power to disallow motions that were designed to prevent legislation from going forward. The Speaker believed that an important principle was in the balance. "The danger in a free country," he wrote, "is not that power will be exercised too freely, but that it will be exercised too sparingly." The Democrats gave in and the House was able to move forward with the Republican program.[27]

The Congress that followed during the remainder of 1890 enacted laws that reflected the activism of the Republican majority. The McKinley Tariff (named after the chair of the House Ways and Means Committee, William McKinley of Ohio) raised rates on industrial products and initiated a system of reciprocal trade treaties with Latin American nations. The Republicans also adopted the Sherman Antitrust Act, which declared monopolies and combinations that were in restraint of trade illegal. The language was aimed at monopolies, but the definitions remained vague, as generations of antitrust lawyers could attest. The measure was not enforced much during its first decade, but it became the basis for subsequent prosecutions under Theodore Roosevelt after 1901.

The surge in protest from the farm sector that had begun during the late 1880s persuaded Republicans that they needed to make at least a symbolic gesture to placate agrarian unrest. While they drew back from coining silver into money without limits, they did try to assist the expansion of the currency by having the government buy a fixed amount of the metal each month. The mint could then coin it into money or not as it saw fit. Called the Sherman Silver Purchase Act (after Senator John Sherman of Ohio), it was a mild compromise, but in the minds of some eastern Republicans and their Democratic counterparts, it was a long and dangerous step toward the abandonment of the gold standard.

The major Republican disappointment occurred on the issue of voting rights for blacks. Representative Henry Cabot Lodge introduced an elections bill that would have given the federal courts the right to name bipartisan panels to regulate voter registration and administer elections. The judges could also name investigators to examine complaints of voting discrimination. The South erupted in protest at what was soon dubbed "the Force Bill" because it would compel their states to allow black Americans to vote. Grover Cleveland called it "a dark blow to the freedom of the ballot," and an Alabama newspaper said it would "deluge the South in blood." The bill passed the House on a party-line vote of 155 to 149 and then went on to the Senate. There it lingered until after the election of 1890, when the Democrats and some western

Republicans killed it. These Republican dissenters were more interested in inflationary solutions such as free silver than the rights of African Americans. With the bill's defeat went the last meaningful civil rights legislation for almost three-quarters of a century. As had happened so often in the past, mild Republican steps in the direction of political equality ran into unyielding Democratic opposition.[28]

As 1890 proceeded, Republicans sensed that their activism and policy agenda were meeting resistance from voters. Confident of the rightness of their cause, they pressed ahead. On the local level in the Middle West, other Republicans sought to implement their own programs in ways that compounded the party's problems. Since legislation could produce a more godly and pious society, party activists in states such as Wisconsin, Illinois, and Iowa pushed for laws to close sporting events and taverns on Sunday, to mandate that public schools receiving state support teach their classes in English (usually instead of German or Polish), and to impose stronger controls on alcohol. These measures alienated Irish Catholic and German Lutheran voters, who made up important swing blocs in key states. To many it seemed as if the Republicans wanted bigger and more intrusive governments at all levels. The Democrats saw their opportunity.

To make the case that the McKinley Tariff raised prices, the Democrats sent out peddlers to visit homes and tell residents that their goods now cost more because of the tariff. One Democratic speaker told a crowd in Detroit: "The McKinley Bill is with us always, at the table, at the bedside, in the kitchen, in the barn, in the churches and to the cemetery." The Democratic contention that the Republicans were the party of higher taxes and excessive government spending caught on with the voters. After all, the Fifty-first Congress had been the first to appropriate one billion dollars. That made a terrific negative slogan for the Democrats—the Billion Dollar Congress. Tom Reed countered that the United States was a "billion dollar country," but few voters bought that argument.[29]

Adding to the Republican problems in 1890 was the arrival on the political scene of the agrarian discontent that had been mounting since the mid-1880s. With farm prices falling, usually reliable Republican supporters in the Middle West listened as the new Farmers Alliance and their party, People's Party (or Populists), declared that the old ways of political life no longer suited the needs of the depressed farm sector. It was time for a party that would inflate the currency, raise prices, and make debts easier to pay. The angry agrarians had, said one New York newspaper, "caused almost a panic in the Democratic party of the South and the Republican party of the West."[30]

The election of 1890 was a Republican disaster. In one of the worst defeats in its history, the party dropped seventy-eight seats in the House and would have only eighty-eight members in the next session. The Republicans who went under in the Democratic tide represented both the party's past and future. Joseph G. Cannon, a future Speaker; Robert M. La Follette of Wisconsin; and William McKinley all saw their seats turned over to the Democrats. Surveying the wreckage, McKinley told his friend Joe Cannon that perhaps the setback was for the best. He would have time for a well-earned rest and the chance to make some money with his law business in Canton, Ohio. Cannon was more realistic. "That's what I tell the boys, but, Mack, don't let's lie to one another."[31]

In Republican strongholds such as Massachusetts, Illinois, Iowa, and Ohio, Republican House seats had become Democratic. Meanwhile, the Populists had made striking gains and elected nearly forty House members who were either outright Farmers Alliance men or sympathetic to the agrarian cause. The next two years would determine whether a farm-based party might actually supplant the Republicans in the American political system.

Gilded Age Republicans felt the pain of the 1890 defeat. They believed that they had offered the voters a moderate, reasonable program of economic and political growth. But the public had not liked the higher tariffs, the federal elections bill, and the increased spending that went along with Republican initiatives. With there being no apparent need for bigger government, the Republicans had been rebuked for their presumption. The defeat of the federal elections bill represented an especially painful setback because it had been a partial attempt to make southern politics more equitable. As Henry Cabot Lodge noted in his diary, "The sting of the present defeat lies in the fact that the Republican party never since the war deserved so well."[32]

The run of bad luck continued for the Republicans. The 1890 defeat signaled that President Harrison would have a difficult time winning another term, but there were equal dangers in rejecting an incumbent president. Harrison had named Blaine his secretary of state, and the two men collaborated during the initial stages of the administration. By 1891, tension between them had increased, and some Republicans looked to the possibility of a Blaine candidacy to bail the party out. Blaine was only sixty-one, but he was already an old man, with chronic illnesses and a sense of melancholy stemming from deaths in his family. Still, leaders who did not like the cold and aloof Harrison warmed to the thought of a Blaine candidacy and the chance to recapture the excitement the Plumed Knight had once evoked.

By the late spring of 1892, Blaine had left the Harrison administration and launched a last-minute bid for the Republican nomination. At the national convention in Minneapolis, the party decided not to ditch Harrison. Blaine's last foray in Republican politics failed. Harrison's chances of winning in the fall against Grover Cleveland, nominated a third time by the Democrats, were not much better. Disenchanted with Harrison's leadership, the Republicans prepared themselves for a likely defeat and looked ahead to 1896.

Social turmoil erupted during the 1892 election and foreshadowed the un-rest to come. In June 1892 the Carnegie Steel Company lowered wages in its Homestead Steel Works outside Pittsburgh. A violent strike followed as union members battled with strike breakers and Pinkerton detectives. Since Andrew Carnegie and Henry Clay Frick were notable Republican business leaders, the Democrats made much of what the tariff and big business had meant to the average worker in 1892. Other strikes dotted the United States. Labor militance that aroused antipathy against big business and the Republican Party helped the Democrats as the election neared.

The nature of elections themselves were changing. The days of marching men and spectacular rallies were yielding to what were now called "campaigns of education." Parties reached voters with pamphlets, newspaper advertising, and magazine articles. The glory days of eloquent stump speakers were sliding into the past. This new approach was costly, and the parties turned to corpo-rations for the funds to pay for campaign literature and ads. The Democrats adjusted to this kind of politics in 1892 better than their rivals did, and Cleveland had a well-funded campaign, while Harrison, whose defeat seemed certain, did not.

The presidential election of 1892 was a three-cornered race. The People's Party put a national ticket in the field with James B. Weaver as its candi-date. The Democrats and Populists were energetic and enthusiastic. The Republicans went through the motions. Cleveland won, Harrison was rejected, and the Populists achieved a mixed result. Cleveland carved out a popular margin of almost four hundred thousand votes, the most decisive result since Ulysses S. Grant defeated Horace Greeley in 1872. The Democrats won 277 electoral votes to 145 for Harrison and 22 for Weaver, who car-ried four western states. The Democrats also controlled both houses of Congress.

In the aftermath of the election, the Republicans seemed adrift and at a loss about their future. Both Rutherford B. Hayes and James G. Blaine died in January 1893. Their passing seemed to mark the end of Republican hopes to become the majority party. A young college professor named Woodrow

Wilson wrote in a magazine article, "The Republican party is going, or at any rate may presently go to pieces."[33] Few Republicans anticipated that a looming economic crisis would divide the Democrats, restore the Republicans to national power, and begin a long period in which the Grand Old Party would shape the nation's political destiny.

4

McKinley to Roosevelt, 1893–1904

DURING THE SUMMER AND FALL of 1896, people came to Canton, Ohio, from all over the North and the Middle West. In addition to their regular service, railroads scheduled special trains to convey Republicans of every stripe to William McKinley's hometown. The McKinley Escort Troop of forty-six men brought the delegations to McKinley's house on North Market Street, where he and his wife, Ida, had lived when they were married a quarter of a century earlier. After noon each day, the delegations assembled. McKinley mounted a chair, a box, and eventually a special stand, and then the Republican presidential candidate addressed them. Some 750,000 Americans, voters and nonvoters, journeyed to Canton during the campaign of 1896 for what became the high point of the "front-porch campaign" style of electioneering.

The people gathered at Canton sought relief from the hard times of the Cleveland administration. The economy had been depressed since 1893, and the angry electorate had defeated congressional Democrats in great numbers in the 1894 elections. McKinley was running against William Jennings Bryan and those Democrats who favored inflation of the currency as a way of promoting a return to prosperity. In contrast, McKinley stressed the need to maintain the dollar at its current value relative to gold bullion and to return to the policy of tariff protection. The crowd cheered his remarks as the bands pounded out such election anthems as "The Honest Little Dollar's Come to Stay." There was the feeling that it was a Republican year, and the people in Canton sensed that McKinley would soon be president. The political winds that had brought the Democrats into office four years earlier now blew in the direction of the Grand Old Party. The change signaled a transformation in American politics; it was the beginning of an era of Republican dominance.[1]

For years the Republicans had warned the American public that Democratic low-tariff policies would put an end to economic prosperity and plunge the nation into prolonged hard times. In the spring of 1893, these predictions began to come true. Another panic erupted in April as hundreds of railroads, banking houses, and industrial enterprises failed. As the economy went into a prolonged downturn, unemployment rose, despair spread, and optimism about the future disappeared. The crisis was not the fault of President Grover Cleveland and his new administration, but his record in office would be judged by how well he met the economic challenge.

Cleveland chose to blame the entire economic problem on the Sherman Silver Purchase Act of 1890 that had the government purchase a fixed amount of silver each month. Believing that the law hurt business confidence and undermined the gold standard, he summoned Congress to special session in August to repeal the offending law. The Democrats were divided. Their eastern, urban, commercial wing supported gold and sound money. Western and southern Democrats, predominantly rural, wanted inflation and an easing of their debts. Faced with Cleveland's support of gold, the Democrats broke into competing factions. In the 1892 election, Cleveland and his party had promised to reform the tariff, but that would have to wait until the Sherman Act was repealed.

While the economy foundered, the political situation for the Republicans brightened during the rest of 1893. Most of their members of Congress stood behind Cleveland in the fight to repeal the Sherman Act, though silver sentiment ran high among Republicans from the plains and mountain states. Whatever tensions might have existed within the GOP over silver, there was a powerful consensus that higher tariff rates were the key to fighting the depression. For many Republicans, using the power of the national government to relieve the suffering of the unemployed made sense. As Benjamin Harrison observed, "The Republican theory has been all along that it was right to so legislate as to provide work, employment, comfort to the American workingman. We believe that the National Government has a duty in this respect, as well as the city council and the board of county commissioners." This position stood in marked contrast to the unwillingness of the Cleveland administration to take any direct steps to ease the effects of hard times, to put people back to work, or even to understand the plight of those unemployed. Democratic orthodoxy, as Cleveland understood it, meant that "while the people should patriotically and cheerfully support their government, its functions do not include support of the people."[2]

Throughout 1893 and into 1894, the political situation of the Democrats deteriorated. The Cleveland administration blundered its way through a campaign to produce tariff reform. Because their control of the Senate was so narrow, the Democrats wrote a revenue bill that conciliated various interests within their party. As a result, what came out of the House as a measure to lower the tariff turned into more of a protectionist hodgepodge in the Senate.

There, the Democratic leader, Arthur Pue Gorman of Maryland, tried to assemble enough votes to pass some sort of tariff.

The resulting Wilson-Gorman Tariff, passed in August 1894, raised rates on some industrial products but was a travesty of the promised tariff reform. President Cleveland let the bill become law without his signature. "The distrust caused by the Democratic threats of a tariff revolution has produced its bitter fruits," said Nelson Dingley, a GOP House member from Maine, "and the end is not yet."[3]

The popular discontent that the depression produced only made things worse for the Democrats. The army of the unemployed, led by Jacob S. Coxey, had come to Washington in the spring of 1894 and were turned away by police before their petitions could be heard. Later that summer, a strike begun in Chicago against the Pullman Palace Car Company exploded into a national railroad walkout led by Eugene V. Debs and the American Railway Union. Meanwhile, the president seemed insensitive to the plight of the average American when he refused to use government power to aid those out of work.

The protest vote was up for grabs between the Populists, with their commitment to inflation in the form of free silver, and the Republicans, who emphasized the tariff. While an expanded currency appealed to debt-ridden farmers in the South and West, it had less relevance for industrial workers on a fixed income. The Populists sought to transcend their sectional appeal in 1894, but they were not able to outdo the Republicans in the crucial states of the Middle West and Northeast.

The 1894 campaign saw a united Republican Party making its case for a national majority against divided and dispirited Democrats. "The drift is all our way," exclaimed Theodore Roosevelt in September 1894. To ensure Republican success, such popular leaders as Representative Tom Reed and the governor of Ohio, William McKinley, took to the campaign trail and pounded the Democrats for their errors in policy. "Prosperity does not perch upon uncertainty," said Reed. "It can never ripen fruit as long as these noisy boys are shaking and clubbing the tree." McKinley gave 371 speeches in sixteen states during the canvass, and he came out of the election as one of the most likely candidates for the party's nomination in 1896.[4]

Before the votes were cast in 1894, Reed predicted that "the Democratic mortality will be so great next fall that their dead will be buried in trenches and marked 'unknown.'" If anything, Reed was too cautious. The magnitude of the party's victory surprised even the hardened professionals. On the eve of the election, the Republicans held 127 seats in the House. After the results came in, they had 244 seats. The Democratic loss of 113 seats marked the greatest transfer of strength from one party to another in the nation's history. Though they gained five seats in the Senate, the Republicans did not quite achieve control there, but the trend was clear.[5]

The outcome in 1894 transformed the electoral landscape for a generation and more. The stalemated politics of the Gilded Age had ended and an era of Republican dominance of Congress had begun. The GOP would not relinquish control of the House for sixteen years until the progressive-conservative split of 1910. After the Woodrow Wilson era from 1912 to 1918, the Republicans would again control the House from 1918 to 1930. This congressional election was one of the most important in the nation's history because it laid the foundation for a long period of Republican ascendancy.[6]

The Republicans had gained from the disarray of the Democrats. The timing of the Panic of 1893 and the inept performance of Cleveland had provided the Republicans with a chance to establish control. Yet, with the Populists in the field, angry voters could have rejected the GOP as well. For the middle-class electorate of the Northeast and Middle West, the Republican program of tariff protection, promotion of enterprise, and assertion of national authority seemed a wise answer to the depression. Industrial workers and others on a fixed income agreed that the tariff and a sound currency were more attuned to their specific needs than the inflationary policies of the People's Party.

Even a decisive victory in the off-year elections does not necessarily presage success in the presidential contest (for two recent examples, consider the elections of 1994/96 and 2010/12). Much depended on the candidate that the Republicans selected in 1896. As the party prepared to look at presidential hopefuls in 1895, a number of credible aspirants hoped to win the prize and capitalize on the Republican triumph that now seemed so certain. Tom Reed was the candidate of the forces within the party, largely in the Northeast, who wanted to make an unequivocal commitment to the gold standard and against inflation. However, Reed's sarcasm had made him as many enemies as friends. From the Middle West, William Boyd Allison of Iowa hoped to be a compromise choice if the convention deadlocked. Yet the cautious Allison seemed an unlikely prospect. More and more, as 1895 progressed, the front runner for the nomination was the former House member and governor of Ohio William McKinley.

In the annals of the Republican Party, William McKinley occupies an important place, but one that has become obscure as his presidency recedes in history. He had the bad fortune to serve before Theodore Roosevelt, and McKinley's reputation has never escaped from the shadow of Roosevelt's energetic tenure in the White House. Another drawback for McKinley's historical standing was his involvement with the Spanish-American War and the Philippine Insurrection, regarded as misguided imperialistic ventures. When his contributions as a president and a Republican are put in proper context, however, his central place in the history of the GOP in the 1890s is clear.

William McKinley was fifty-three years old in 1896. After a Civil War career in which he rose to the rank of major (and was known by that title to his friends thereafter), McKinley practiced law in Canton, Ohio, before his election to Congress in 1876. He served there for the next fourteen years. From the outset of his legislative career he steeped himself in the complexities of the protective tariff and succeeded James G. Blaine as the embodiment of its appeal to the Republican rank and file. In 1890, he helped shape the McKinley Tariff as chair of the House Ways and Means Committee.[7]

William McKinley was the first modern president who led the nation during the war with Spain and pursued policies of overseas expansion. Library of Congress, LC-USZ62-116008.

Defeated in his bid for reelection in the Democratic sweep of 1890, McKinley won the governorship of Ohio in 1891 and was reelected in 1893. His ability to carry that key Midwestern state, along with his popularity as an orator, made him a likely choice for the nomination in 1896. His labors for the party in 1894, along with his many friendships across the country, created a groundswell of support for him that none of his rivals could match. A Republican senator observed in 1896, "McKinley is in it with the masses in nearly every state in the Union, from New Hampshire to Wyoming, and from Minnesota to the Gulf." If the party faithful could speak, McKinley would be "the choice of at least seventy-five percent of the entire Republican voters in the Union."[8]

McKinley was a short man at five feet six, and he dressed to make himself seem taller than he was. A British reporter who visited him in 1896 described the candidate's "strong, clean-shaven face" with its "clear eyes, wide nose, full lips," concluding, "All his features suggest dominant will and energy rather than subtlety of mind or emotion." McKinley smoked cigars but was careful not to be photographed with one. Later, when he was president, a diplomat told a French reporter who came to interview McKinley, "You are going to see the Emperor in a dress suit." Because he listened more than he talked and displayed few emotions, McKinley was a hard man to know and an easy person to underestimate.[9]

McKinley has been a mystery for historians because of his reluctance to commit his private thoughts to paper. On the surface, his letters are terse and unrevealing. His invalid wife and his own discretion cordoned off his family affairs from public scrutiny. Few men, even those closest to him, really understood McKinley, and his skill and determination as a politician have not been recognized. Underneath his genial exterior was a cold, resourceful mind.

McKinley also had the unstinting aid of a prominent Ohio industrialist, Marcus Alonzo "Mark" Hanna. Their friendship has often been caricatured and usually misunderstood. McKinley, not Hanna, was the dominant figure in the relationship between the two men. Hanna supplied access to the business community, but he neither made the key decisions nor set the overall strategy.

Nonetheless, Hanna became one of the important figures in the history of the Republicans because of his friendship with McKinley. The Ohio business executive proved to be a favorite target for cartoonists, who depicted him as the stereotypical example of the excesses of big business. The notion that Hanna steered McKinley's fortunes translated into the perception that big business gave the orders and Republicans jumped to obey. The reality was more complex than that, but the image endured.

Marcus A. Hanna, an Ohio industrialist, shown here walking with Theodore Roosevelt after the death of McKinley, helped bring the Republicans into the new industrial order. Library of Congress, LC-USZ62-96530.

Hanna did assist McKinley and his finances at one key moment. During the Panic of 1893, a friend for whom McKinley had cosigned some debts went bankrupt. McKinley faced financial ruin. Hanna led the effort to raise funds for his friends to pay off his debts. This campaign, carried out in the public view, did not hurt McKinley with the voters. It made him seem more human during economic hard times.

The key to McKinley's appeal in 1896 was his identification with the tariff and his broad popularity within the party. To demonstrate his strength he campaigned as "the Advance Agent of Prosperity" and styled his canvass as "the People Against the Bosses." Republican leaders in the East tried to block his nomination by supporting Tom Reed or various other favorite sons in the hope that a compromise candidate might surface. Instead, McKinley went to the Republican National Convention in Saint Louis with a first-ballot victory in sight.

The question of the gold standard dominated the GOP deliberations. Against a Democratic Party within which inflation gained daily support, many Republicans, especially from the industrial East, wanted to proclaim an unequivocal endorsement of gold. Western Republicans, from states where free silver was strong, hoped for more conciliatory language. McKinley and Hanna, who was managing his candidate's fortunes at the convention, agreed with the platform's declaration that the party was "unreservedly" for sound money. The platform then added: "We are therefore opposed to the free coinage of silver, except by international agreement with the leading commercial nations of the earth, which agreement we pledge ourselves to promote." The wording sought to indicate to the westerners that McKinley, while backing the gold standard, left some room for compromise. A number of western Republicans bolted the party, despite the "international agreement" phrasing. The upshot of the convention was the fixed impression that the Republican Party had become the unwavering champion of the gold standard.[10]

As anticipated, McKinley achieved his first-ballot victory, and the party selected Garret A. Hobart of New Jersey to balance its Middle Western presidential candidate with an eastern vice president. The Republicans expected an easy time in the Northeast; the battleground of the election became the large states of the nation's heartland. If the Democrats picked anyone identified with the Cleveland administration and its problems, a landslide Republican victory seemed in the offing.

The Democrats then did the unexpected. They chose William Jennings Bryan as their nominee. Bryan was a two-term former House member from Nebraska who had established himself as the champion of free silver and rural values. His famous "Cross of Gold" speech at the Democratic convention in Chicago had electrified the nation with the line "You shall not crucify mankind upon a cross of gold." The People's Party also nominated Bryan. He could count on the Solid South and much of the far West. During the summer, the dynamic, youthful (he was only thirty-six) Bryan seemed the popular favorite to win the election, unless the Republicans could counter his charismatic style. Bryan soon was out on the stump attracting large audiences and building momentum.[11]

The Republicans responded with what became known as a "campaign of education." First, the GOP raised impressive amounts of money, probably between $3.5 and $4 million from eastern Republicans and corporate leaders fearful of a Bryan victory. In history, this large amount of cash has often been described as a slush fund used to buy voters and coerce industrial workers. The reality was more prosaic. The money went toward advertising and pamphlets.[12]

McKinley struck the keynote: "This is a year for press and pen." The Republicans used their money to pay for some two hundred million pamphlets and a torrent of newspaper advertising. Special inserts appeared each week in small-town papers about McKinley, his wife, and his family. In many languages, the stories described the virtues of both the candidate and a sound dollar. McKinley allowed himself to be filmed, and the party employed the crude movie in the campaign. Hanna watched over all these activities with his shrewd organizational sense.[13]

The candidate himself did the bulk of the actual campaigning from his front porch in Canton. The candidate coordinated his speeches in advance with visiting delegations to avoid any gaffes. Each day McKinley reiterated the keynotes of his campaign, and each day the nation's newspapers reported what he said. The Republican candidate seemed calmer and more states-manlike in this domestic setting. Thus, McKinley controlled the agenda of the election and blended an allegiance to sound money with an affirmation of the virtues of tariff protection.

Bryan's initial surge faltered as the autumn of 1896 approached. His party was split, with a Gold Democrat ticket in the field. The public's initial fasci-nation with free silver ebbed away, and the one-dimensional aspect of Bryan's appeal became evident. Bryan called the East "the enemy's country" and made a disastrous appearance in New York City, and his monetary doctrines did not resonate with the workingmen and small business owners of the Middle West.

As the election neared, the Republicans cast their campaign as a patriotic endeavor, and American flags became a feature of their rallies. The identifica-tion of their party with the nation and the suggestion that the Democrats were less committed to the cause of the country and its honor were too tempting for the Republicans to ignore. In the East, attacks on Bryan and his supporters as anarchists and revolutionaries spoke once again of Republican doubts about Democratic legitimacy. Theodore Roosevelt reflected this spirit when he told an English friend in October, "All the men who pray for anarchy or who believe in socialism, and all the much larger number who have not formulated their thoughts sufficiently to believe in either; but who want to strike down the well-to-do, and who have been inflamed against the rich until they feel that they are willing to sacrifice their own welfare, if only they can make others less happy, are banded against us."[14]

To counter the Republican surge, the Democrats pounded away at McKinley's alleged subservience to Mark Hanna. Cartoons depicted "Dollar Mark" with a little McKinley strapped to his waist. Democrats alleged that major corporations and businesses coerced their workers to make them vote for McKinley. No doubt some of McKinley's more impassioned supporters in the business community did try to strong-arm their employees, but laboring men on fixed incomes had good reason to dislike inflation and the economic uncertainty that would have accompanied a Bryan victory.

The outcome of the election of 1896 was a thorough Republican triumph. McKinley won 271 electoral votes to Bryan's 176, and received 7,035,638 popular votes to 6,467,945 for the Democratic-Populist ticket. The Republicans held on to control of the House with a large majority. Their grasp on the Senate was more tenuous.

The election galvanized voter interest. In the North more than 78 percent of the eligible voters went to the polls. These totals would not be repeated during the entire twentieth century. McKinley's victory assembled an enduring coalition of voters—urban dwellers in the North, prosperous farmers, and large segments of industrial workers. The Republican appeal reached into most ethnic groups, with the exception of the Irish. The election of 1896 solidified the result in 1894 and meant that the Republicans were the majority party of the nation everywhere but in the Solid South.

McKinley's election turned on domestic issues; the keynote of his administration became overseas expansion. The Cuban revolt against the rule of Spain, which had begun in 1895, emerged two years later as the leading foreign policy question. A significant sentiment in both parties sought American intervention to stop the conflict that was devastating the nearby island. Because this action culminated in the Spanish-American War and led to American intervention in the Philippines, McKinley's leadership in 1898 and beyond has become one of the most controversial parts of the Republican record in the 1890s.

During his first year in office, McKinley began the revival of the presidency, following the low point it had reached during the Cleveland years. He cultivated good relations with the press and brought the newsmen into the White House by setting up tables for them on the second floor. The new president traveled and used these junkets to push his programs with the electorate. Relations with Congress also improved as McKinley listened to what lawmakers of both parties had to say about the nation's future course.

On the domestic side, the new administration saw a protective tariff through Congress. The Dingley Tariff (named after Nelson Dingley, then chair of the Ways and Means Committee) raised rates on industrial goods. The law also contained language allowing the president to negotiate reciprocal trade agreements with other countries, a program that McKinley pushed hard during his tenure. After seeking a wider use of silver through international talks in 1897–1898 without success, the administration endorsed the Gold Standard Act of 1900, which put the nation behind a single standard of value for the currency.

The uprising of the Cubans against Spanish rule dominated the first year of McKinley's presidency. Unlike Grover Cleveland, who had sympathized with the Spanish and let them try to subdue the revolt, McKinley made it clear that his administration disapproved of continued turmoil and wanted the rebels and the Spanish to talk about a settlement. He insisted that any agreement be acceptable to the Cubans, which meant the ouster of Spain and independence for the island. During 1897 and into 1898, McKinley struggled to find a peaceful solution on the basis of these principles. Since Spain believed that Cuba was part of their sovereign Spanish territory and nation and would not surrender it without a fight, a solution remained elusive.

The Republicans in general favored intervention to end the fighting in Cuba, as did the Democrats. In early 1898 a crisis erupted. The administration had sent the battleship *Maine* to Havana harbor as a goodwill gesture. When the ship exploded in February, killing more than 250 sailors, Americans believed that Spain was responsible. Diplomatic relations with Madrid worsened, and Congress pressed for war. Despite these moves, the president, who hoped to achieve Cuban independence without violence, delayed as long as he could to find a way out of the crisis. In the end, since neither Spain nor the United States would yield, war came in late April. Contrary to the historical canards about his performance, McKinley had worked hard for peace until war became inevitable. Once the fighting broke out, he used his power as president to bring the conflict to a speedy and victorious resolution.[15]

The rapid series of American victories on land and water in the summer of 1898 enhanced McKinley's prestige and identified the Republicans with another national triumph. The president pursued the war in a nonpartisan fashion, allocating military commissions to Republicans and Democrats in equal measure. When the fighting ended in August and it came time to send commissioners to Paris to negotiate a peace treaty, he dispatched a panel that included members of both parties, several of them senators who would vote on any pact that resulted from the talks.[16]

While most Americans applauded the eviction of Spain from Cuba, there was less consensus on the fate of the Philippine Islands. The United States sent naval vessels to that Asian possession of Spain as part of a war plan to pressure Madrid to seek peace terms. The victory of Commodore George Dewey at Manila Bay on May 1, 1898, had given the United States a strong claim on the archipelago. As the summer progressed, the McKinley administration became more identified with an imperialistic policy that sought to establish an American presence in Asia. Democrats in the main dissented from these developments, and an anti-imperialist wing of the opposition party emerged during the last months of 1898.

The Republicans faced the congressional elections in 1898 as the party associated with victory over Spain. They still anticipated the losses that the incumbent party usually suffers two years after a presidential election. President McKinley capitalized on the opportunity that celebrations of the American triumph provided to make a speaking tour of the Middle West in October 1898. No chief executive had gone on such a journey during an off-year election since Andrew Johnson's disastrous "Swing Around the Circle" in 1866.[17]

While McKinley did not ask the voters to elect Republicans, he sounded notes of expansionism and made the case for retaining the Philippines. He also asserted that prosperity was returning. "Business looks hopeful and assuring everywhere, and our credit balances show the progress which the country is making." What the president said, and the crowds he attracted, helped hold down Republican losses in the House of Representatives. The GOP lost nineteen seats, while the Democrats gained fifty seats, many of those from the Populists. The Republicans added six seats in the Senate, thus putting the party in control of both houses.[18]

These majority Republicans would not take office until December 1899 under the system of congressional sessions that operated in the late nineteenth century. The Treaty of Paris now became the focus of partisan conflict. Signed in December 1898 between the United States and Spain, it removed the Philippine Islands from Spanish control and awarded possession to the United States. The treaty would be debated in the lame-duck session of the Senate that ran from December 1898 to March 1899. The Democrats in that chamber saw an opportunity to embarrass the administration by defeating the pact.

McKinley wielded the power of his office to achieve ratification. He spoke in the South on behalf of sectional harmony and thus pressured southern Democratic senators. The White House used patronage, backroom deals, and the leadership of key Senate Republicans on behalf of the document. William Jennings Bryan also helped when he advocated approving the treaty and fighting the issue in the 1900 elections. The Senate approved the treaty on February 6, 1899, with one vote more than the two-thirds necessary for ratification.[19]

On the same day the treaty went through, an insurrection in the Philippines erupted against American rule. Further challenges to the administration emerged in governing Cuba and Puerto Rico through the military. The president handled these crises by using his power as commander in chief to create military governments without congressional oversight. McKinley's speaking tours in 1899 stilled popular doubts over possible imperialism. Meanwhile, the Republicans proclaimed that prosperity had returned. When the GOP achieved success in the 1899 state elections, a Republican told McKinley that the campaign "has settled the issues and the candidates for the presidential election in 1900."[20]

Two issues promised future trouble for the Republicans. An upsurge in racial violence occurred as southerners imposed segregation on the black population. A white riot in Wilmington, North Carolina, for example, left at least fourteen blacks dead. McKinley said little about such events, as the party seemed to have lost much of its earlier commitment to protecting black rights. Black leaders fumed about the president's position. He was, said T. Thomas Fortune, "a man of jelly who would turn us loose to the mob and not say a word."[21]

McKinley's record was better than that, but only just. Like many white Americans, he and his party had concluded that efforts to pursue racial justice in the South were doomed to failure. The most that black Republicans could hope for was patronage positions and a role in furnishing delegates from Dixie at the national conventions. Compared to the Democrats, that was enough to retain the loyalties of those few African Americans who still managed to vote in the South. Nonetheless, the party had sacrificed a portion of its original purpose, one that proved hard to recapture.[22]

More pressing was the Republican attitude toward the burgeoning number of large businesses popularly known as "trusts." In the wake of prosperity, corporations had absorbed competitors at a dizzying pace. During 1899 some twelve hundred companies were bought out or taken over. Newspapers were filled with stories about the wave of corporate mergers. Just what the Republicans planned to do about these developments was not clear. "Jamming a stick into the machinery will only throw us back," said one Republican. Many party members shared the view of Senator Mark Hanna (who had been appointed to the upper house in 1897 and elected in 1898) that "a man had a right to do what he pleased with his own."[23]

The McKinley administration responded to these concerns with speeches that laid the groundwork for federal action in the second term. McKinley did not authorize the use of the Sherman Antitrust Act against the large corporations. Like other Republicans he favored publicity about corporate actions as a remedy for their excesses. The president sensed danger in a simple continuation of high protective tariffs. The Democrats were arguing that elevated rates promoted the growth of trusts. As a counter, McKinley pushed for reciprocal trade treaties as a way of defusing the tariff issue without destroying the protective system. Protectionists within the party disagreed, and reciprocity seemed fated to be a contentious issue once the president was reelected.

The impression that the Republicans were the party of big business was solidifying. Their senators were identified with corporate affairs. The party's original emphasis on the unity of capital and labor was giving way to a sympathy with business at the expense of other segments of society. As Americans thought of themselves more and more as consumers, Democratic charges that big business meant higher prices eroded support for Republicans among middle-class voters. As a journalist noted in 1900, "The Republican party may suffer innocently from a bad name, but I do not believe that one voter in ten in the United States honestly thinks that, if continued in power, it will wage successful war upon the trusts."[24]

As the election of 1900 neared, the most pressing business for the party was the choice of a new running mate for President McKinley. Vice President Hobart had succumbed to heart disease in November 1899, and the national convention would pick his successor. Talk swirled around the new governor of New York, Theodore Roosevelt, but neither McKinley nor Senator Hanna liked that option. The administration sought a more reliable, predictable vice presidential choice.

Keeping Theodore Roosevelt out of the roster was not easy. He was forty-one in 1899 and had been a celebrity since his first days in politics in the New York Assembly in the early 1880s. Following the death of his first wife in 1884, Roosevelt raised cattle in the West, where his reputation as a two-fisted hero spread. After six years on the Civil Service Commission from 1889 to 1895, he served on the board of police commissioners in New York City, was the assistant secretary of the Navy under McKinley, and left for the war with Spain as an officer in a volunteer regiment in April 1898. The unit became known as "Roosevelt's Rough Riders," and its spectacular charge up Kettle Hill in Cuba on July 1, 1898, made Roosevelt a national hero. Winning a tough race for governor of the Empire State in the fall of 1898 precipitated talk about his aspirations for higher office. Hobart's death turned the possibility of his aspirations into a reality.[25]

While Roosevelt enjoyed immense popularity, he made old-line Republicans uneasy. Part of why he provoked such qualms among his fellow Republicans was his hesitancy to embrace the protective tariff. He had flirted with free trade in his youth, and many proponents of protection sensed with good reason that Roosevelt found the subject boring. His aristocratic disdain for business enterprise was another element in the equation. Finally, the young Roosevelt seemed impetuous and erratic. As McKinley put it, "Roosevelt is always in such a state of mind."[26]

On the other hand, he was very popular, especially among younger party members in the West. Although he hated the name and no one who knew him well ever called him "Teddy," the nation styled him "Teddy" Roosevelt and followed his large family, his public exploits, and his vivid personality. He would bring excitement and energy to the ticket. The sticking point for those promoting Roosevelt was the candidate's own wavering in early 1900. Seeing 1904 as his best chance to run for the Republican nomination, he knew that if he ran for another two-year term as governor, he would be out of office in 1903 without a secure political base. Roosevelt thought that a cabinet post or a stint as governor general of the Philippines might round out his credentials as a presidential contender, but none of these options appealed to the White House. Within New York, the boss of the state party's organization, Senator Thomas Collier Platt, wanted Roosevelt out of the state. The governor had been too eager to publicize corporate abuses, and his activism ill suited the Republican hierarchy. So Platt encouraged Roosevelt's vice presidential hopes.

In the end the administration could not find a credible alternative to Roosevelt. The Republican convention met in Philadelphia, where Roosevelt showed up on the floor wearing the Rough Rider headgear that had become his trademark. "That's an acceptance hat," noted one observer, and so it proved. McKinley gave way to the inevitable. Senator Hanna fumed: "Don't you know there's only one life between that madman and the Presidency?" But the tide was too strong and Roosevelt was swept onto the ticket. The GOP went into the campaign brimming with confidence. A magazine editor, Albert Shaw, himself a Republican, sounded a cautionary note amid the self-congratulation. "The Republican party was never outwardly so harmonious as it is now since it was organized half a century ago, and apparently it was never as strong as it is now. But it is a little too fat and sleek and prosperous and its moral tone is not quite what it ought to be. It looks back with pride rather than forward with aspiration."[27]

McKinley observed the custom among incumbent presidents of not campaigning for reelection, so the bulk of the work fell to Roosevelt and Republican surrogates. The Democrats nominated Bryan for a second time. At first, the Democrat tried to make imperialism the key issue of the campaign, but McKinley defused the matter in his speech and letter of acceptance. Colonial government in the Philippines, the president argued, was preferable to Bryan's proposal for independence and a trusteeship status for the islands. Bryan then switched his emphasis to the trust question and then back to free silver. The Democrats never found a consistent theme for their campaign, nor did they offer a reason to turn McKinley out of office.

The result was a decisive McKinley triumph. The president won 292 electoral votes to 155 for his rival. The Republican ticket garnered 51.7 percent of the vote to Bryan's 45.5 percent. McKinley increased his popular-vote major-ity over Bryan by two hundred thousand votes. The Republicans also enjoyed a forty-six-seat majority in the House and had a twenty-four-seat edge in the Senate. McKinley told friends, "I am now President of the whole people."[28]

During the first half of 1901, McKinley made it clear that he intended to push for revision of the tariff through ratification of reciprocity treaties with Argentina and France. In June, he stated that he would not be a candidate for a third term in 1904. Noting the continued growth of trusts, the president discussed with aides what might be done in the way of revitalizing the Sherman Antitrust Act. In September, McKinley fulfilled a commitment to visit the Pan-American Exposition in Buffalo, New York. In a speech on September 5, he told the crowd: "The period of exclusiveness is past. The ex-pansion of our trade and commerce is the pressing problem. Commercial wars are unprofitable. A policy of goodwill and friendly trade relations will prevent reprisals. Reciprocity treaties are in harmony with the spirit of the times; measures of retaliation are not."[29]

McKinley understood that the tariff issue, long a source of Republican strength, was becoming a political liability. As prosperity returned, prices rose and industrial trusts and corporations spread. Discontent with protection appeared in key states such as Iowa, where farmers resented the increasing cost of agricultural implements and other supplies for their business. The "Iowa Idea" that the tariff should be lowered on trust-made products gained converts during the spring and summer of 1901. McKinley saw his treaties as a way of modifying the protective system in a gradual and controlled manner without abandoning the tariff altogether. Many Republicans were suspicions of what the president proposed, but his credentials as the "Napoleon of Protection" were so good that he could not receive direct criticism for his ap-parent heresy.

How the history of the Republican Party might have differed had McKinley lived to serve his full second term is conjectural. Much of what happened under Theodore Roosevelt—lawsuits against the trusts, the canal across Central America, and the settlement of the boundary dispute with Canada over Alaska—all these would likely have occurred in a second McKinley term. Although the Senate would not have accepted the reciprocity treaties without a struggle, in the end the lawmakers would probably have given way. Progressive reform would have begun in a more sedate and measured way. Would the GOP have escaped division and discord in 1912? No one can say.

On September 6, 1901, while McKinley was standing in a receiving line at the Temple of Music at the Pan-American Exposition in Buffalo, New York, an assassin, Leon Czolgosz, shot him. (Czolgosz, who became an anarchist after he lost his job, viewed McKinley as a symbol of oppression.) The president died eight days later. McKinley had been a major architect of Republican success in the 1890s and a forceful consolidator of presidential power. Now the nation turned to see how his youthful successor would perform in the White House.

When Theodore Roosevelt came to the presidency, the United States had left behind the hard times of the 1890s. Americans enjoyed the fruits of prosperity that had arrived during the waning years of the nineteenth century. According to the 1900 census, there were almost seventy-six million Americans, the majority of them white, with more than nine million blacks, and 238,000 Native Americans. Most people lived in the Northeast and north central areas, some fifty-six million in all. More citizens lived in rural than urban areas, though the trend of urbanization was accelerating. In the first full year of Roosevelt's administration, almost 649,000 newcomers entered the United States from abroad. The tide of immigration swelled throughout Roosevelt's presidency. Some welcomed the new diversity; others among the older American stock tried to restrict immigration. These crosscurrents shaped politics in the years ahead.

In economic terms, the country was well off. The gross national product had reached almost $20 billion by 1901, and per capita annual income was $569 by Roosevelt's first term. The money that people earned faced no income tax at either the state or national level, and other levies were low, except on luxuries and imports. Yet for all the collective wealth that Americans enjoyed at the beginning of the twentieth century, the nation was confronted with serious social inequities.

Victims of work-related injuries, which included some twenty thousand killed per year and another half million maimed or hurt, had little assurance of medical assistance. Skilled workers received some protection through craft unions such as the American Federation of Labor, but unskilled workers were at the mercy of the marketplace. There were few old-age pensions and no federal unemployment insurance. The welfare state as the twentieth century would know it did not yet exist.

Power in society rested with corporations and banks, which dominated the economy. The antitrust law had been rendered impotent, and there was real doubt about the power of the federal government to supervise business. Theodore Roosevelt believed that it was necessary to alter that balance, saying, "The absolutely vital question was whether the government had the power to control them at all. This question had not yet been decided in favor of the United States Government."³⁰ For the majority of Republicans in 1901, the dominance of business presented no philosophical problems. For Roosevelt and dissident party members in the Middle West who were starting to call themselves progressives, the party needed to engage the issue of bringing corporations to heel.

Two changes in American attitudes shaped the future of the Republicans during the decade that followed. Ever more citizens called for the government to regulate an industrial society at the state and national levels. That pressure challenged the Republicans who believed in a strong government that would promote economic growth but not by interfering with business itself. The other new force was a developing suspicion of the value of political parties. After more than a generation in which parties were regarded as necessary to democracy, Americans asked whether parties contributed to the problems of society and needed to be limited in their influence and power. Because they were the majority party, Republicans became the focus of measures limiting the ability of partisan politics to shape national policy.

Theodore Roosevelt was forty-two years old when he became the twenty-sixth president of the United States. He had been a Republican since his boyhood, but

Addressing a crowd during his presidency, Theodore Roosevelt exuded the energy and passion that made him a favorite among Republicans in the first decade of the twentieth century. Library of Congress, LC-DIG-ppmsca-36630.

his allegiance to the Grand Old Party was not that of a regular partisan. He had little interest in the protective tariff and was not a fan of businessmen or the process by which they made their money. Instead, as a member of the New York aristocracy, he saw his duty as representing the American people in their adjustment to the promises and perils of industrial growth.

For Roosevelt, the Republicans were the party of constructive nationalism. The new president believed that government power could be employed to enable all citizens to share in the bounty of an expanding economy. In time he would come to believe that some government regulation of the economy was also necessary. Democrats were the party of ineptitude and state rights who could be counted upon to thwart the positive work of Roosevelt and the Republicans. While Roosevelt was adroit at the political fighting that allowed him to win the Republican nomination in 1904, over the long haul he was not skilled in persuading his fellow party members to follow his policies.

Where Roosevelt excelled was in the public conduct of his office. He governed with energy and excitement. For the first time the president became a celebrity in his own right, and the newspapers tracked the president's frenetic schedule and the antics of his brood of young children. Roosevelt was the first chief executive to use his family in a conscious way to enhance his own appeal.

He was also the first president to make the most of the celebrity potential of his office. Newspapers covered him as though he were a modern film star. The president conducted public quarrels with a number of Americans, which only added to the fun of his years in the White House. Leaving the presidency, Roosevelt attributed part of his success to the publicity value that the presidency had given him. "I have got such a bully pulpit," he told a reporter in February 1909.[31]

In the initial months of his administration, Roosevelt pledged to carry on McKinley's policies, and in substance if not in style, that is what he did. He soon demonstrated that he had a flair for the dramatic and the timely that his predecessor had not displayed. To build up support among southern Republicans, Roosevelt entertained the African American leader Booker T. Washington at the White House in October 1901. The South reacted with outrage when it became known that an African American had dined with the president and his family. The episode illustrated the continuing power of racism in early twentieth-century America. It did not stop Roosevelt from pursuing Republican delegates for 1904 among the shrinking number of Republicans in the South.

In one key area, however, Roosevelt did abandon a McKinley initiative, and the consequences of that decision proved difficult for the Republicans. The reciprocity treaties that McKinley had championed were still pending before the Senate, and it would take a fight to gain approval for them. For Roosevelt, who found the tariff boring, the prospect of such a struggle was dismaying. As a result, he deferred to the Senate leadership, including Nelson Aldrich of Rhode Island, and gave the pacts only a tepid endorsement. The Senate did not act on them, and they lapsed.

What that meant was that no meaningful action on the tariff could take place in Roosevelt's first term. When he again postponed the issue in his second term, the task of dealing with protection fell to his successor. Meanwhile, the tensions between advocates of tariff revision in the Middle West and defenders of protectionism in the Northeast and Mid-Atlantic states intensified. Democratic assaults on the tariff as a cause of higher prices and the outside power of industry added to Republican vulnerability on the issue. The return of inflation and rising consumer prices during the first decade of the century gave Democratic arguments more bite with middle-class consumers. But Roosevelt left the issue alone to fester and divide the Republicans.

The new president decided to emphasize the control of big business as one of his salient priorities. In February 1902, the Justice Department filed an antitrust suit against the Northern Securities Company, a holding company for railroads in the Northwest. Unpopular in the region that these lines crossed, the company had been under legal attack from the governors in the states affected. Roosevelt was determined to demonstrate that the power of the federal government was more potent that any combination of private capital. Once that supremacy was established, Roosevelt believed that government could then encourage socially useful enterprises ("good trusts") and discourage ones that misbehaved ("bad trusts") through an ongoing regulatory process.

Roosevelt's assault on Northern Securities prompted the financier J. P. Morgan to hurry to Washington to express his personal concern about the treatment of a firm he had helped put together. In a celebrated White House meeting on February 22, 1902, the investment banker told Roosevelt, "If we have done anything wrong, send your man to my man and they can fix it up." Roosevelt and his attorney general, Philander Knox, informed Morgan, "We don't want to fix it up, we want to stop it." Roosevelt assured Morgan that his other interests would not be attacked "unless we find out that in any case they have done something we regard as wrong." Once Morgan had left, Roosevelt told his attorney general, "That is a most illuminating illustration of the Wall Street point of view. Mr. Morgan could not help regarding me as a big rival operator who either intended to ruin his interests or else could be induced to come to an agreement to ruin none."[32]

The episode and Roosevelt's comments showed one part of his attitude toward big business. By prosecuting Northern Securities and obtaining a favorable ruling from the Supreme Court, as he did in 1904, he demonstrated that the government was more powerful than any single corporation. Once he had done so, however, he followed a policy that worked along the lines Morgan had suggested. The White House distinguished between socially useful corporations, such as United States Steel, and the ones that operated in a more predatory fashion, such as Standard Oil or the so-called Beef Trust of meat packers. The "good trusts" received government support for their economic programs; the "bad trusts" risked antitrust prosecution.

Roosevelt enhanced the popularity he had gained from the Northern Securities case when he intervened in the Anthracite Coal Strike in the fall of 1902. He thereby averted a crisis in those areas of the country that depended on coal for their winter heat. Summoning the mine owners and union leaders to the White House, Roosevelt helped broker a settlement with the United Mine Workers of America that ended the threat of a prolonged walkout. The most important aspect of the episode was the implicit recognition that the president gave to labor. It represented a philosophy that Roosevelt called the "Square Deal," one that refuted the popular idea that "the Republican party always legislates to aid the rich and oppress the poor."[33]

The settlement of the strike helped the Republicans in the 1902 congressional elections. The census of 1900 served to increase the size of the House of Representatives, and so each party gained seats. The Democrats added twenty-seven members; the Republicans gained eleven. The GOP still held a majority of thirty in the lower house. The party's prospects for electing Roosevelt on his own in 1904 seemed very good. Within the party he had already obtained more than half of the nearly five hundred delegates needed to assure his nomination. Some of these successes had occurred in the South where the incumbent president usually controlled the predominantly black delegates. But the enthusiasm for Roosevelt extended across the entire rank and file of the GOP.

One important segment of the Republicans remained cool to the new president. Business leaders feared that he might pursue even more government regulation. In the year before an election, though, these qualms were muted and not widely discussed. Some capitalists hoped that an alternative to

Roosevelt might emerge. They looked to Senator Mark Hanna to supply them with that alternative.

By 1904, Hanna had achieved a legendary reputation as both the architect of McKinley's success in 1896 and his political confidant during the ensuing presidency. Opponents of the Ohio senator had characterized him as "Dollar Mark," a business ally who fostered trusts and oppressed the workingman. In fact, Hanna envisioned a society where business and labor worked together toward common ends. He looked with scorn on those employers who refused, as he put it, to meet their men halfway. He was far from the reactionary force that Democrats assailed him as.

But Hanna's reputation outpaced his real power in the Republican Party. Much of his influence rested on his presumed closeness to McKinley. When the president died in September 1901, much of Hanna's clout died with him. The senator was not in good health either. Most of all, he knew that a presidential nomination obtained through the defeat of a popular incumbent would be worth very little. The Republicans were hardly likely to select a politician who symbolized corporate power after rejecting a trustbuster. There was a degree of improbability in Hanna's candidacy from the outset.

Nonetheless, the Ohio senator wanted to be consulted about the nomination. He said in August 1902 that it was "out of place to permit so much discussion about the future selection of the candidate for the Republican party." He wanted to see how well Roosevelt performed and keep his options open to support another candidate in 1904. That was not what Roosevelt wanted to hear. Obsessed with being selected in his own right, the president saw conspiracies against him everywhere. He expected unwavering support for his nomination from Republicans, and he had little patience with Hanna's equivocation.[34]

A political enemy of Hanna's in Ohio, Senator Joseph B. Foraker, saw a chance during the spring of 1903 to embarrass his colleague and help Roosevelt's candidacy. Hanna's allies in Ohio said that the Republican state convention, meeting in May, would not endorse Roosevelt's candidacy so far ahead of the national convention. Foraker at once announced that because Roosevelt was "the best known and most popular man in the United States," the convention should express its support for his candidacy in 1904.[35]

Hanna wired Roosevelt to ask that he not support Foraker and force the issue of an endorsement. Roosevelt responded, "Those who favor my administration and nomination" would favor a resolution of endorsement, and "those who do not will oppose them." When confronted with the issue in those terms, Hanna had little choice but to accept a convention endorsement of the president in what one senator called "a back-action-double-spring feat." The episode settled the issue for all practical purposes.[36]

Nonetheless, Roosevelt still wanted to obtain a formal endorsement from Hanna. That did not occur before Hanna's death in February 1904, much to the unhappiness of the man in the White House. Roosevelt believed that he faced a conspiracy among the anti-Roosevelt, pro-business side of the Republican Party. Though there was uneasiness about his policies from that quarter, much of the problem was Roosevelt's obsession with being nominated on his own. With Hanna gone from the scene, that concern faded away, and the months before the national convention became a kind of triumphal procession for the president.

Roosevelt's election seemed a sure thing during the spring of 1904. In the domestic arena, he had the Northern Securities case (which the Supreme Court had just decided in the government's favor), the coal strike, the beginnings of a campaign to conserve natural resources, and a generally high level of prosperity. As a world leader, he had resolved a boundary dispute with Canada about Alaska and, more important, had secured a zone in in the Isthmus of Panama through which a canal could be built. The Democrats had tried to make an issue of Roosevelt's methods in Panama, but most Americans thought his strong stance toward Colombia, which had opposed a treaty allowing the US to obtain the zone, was justified. They endorsed Roosevelt's succinct summation of his approach to foreign policy. "There is a homely old adage which runs 'Speak softly and carry a big stick; you will go far.'" Few presidents have had more going for them as they approached an election than Theodore Roosevelt in 1904.[37]

The Republican National Convention was not an exciting affair. Everyone among the nearly one thousand delegates knew that the gathering would give Roosevelt a unanimous nomination. As his running mate, the party selected the cautious and careful senator from Indiana, Charles Warren Fairbanks. The only riveting moment came when a State Department telegram was read aloud. A bandit in Morocco, known as Raisuli, had seized a man named Ion Perdicaris, believed to be an American citizen. In the diplomatic negotiations for the release of Perdicaris, the State Department wired Morocco: "We want either Perdicaris alive or Raisuli dead." The convention went wild. The disclosure of the telegram did not affect the ultimate decision to release Perdicaris, but it made for great political theater and reinforced Roosevelt's image as a man of action.[38]

The Democrats recognized their weakness and sought to turn it into a positive asset. Instead of opposing Roosevelt as someone who had not done

THE VALUE OF THE BINDER IN HARVEST-TIME

"The value of the binder in harvest time." This cartoon from 1903 shows President Roosevelt rounding up the delegates he needed for the Republican nomination in 1904 well in advance of the party's convention. From Albert Shaw, *A Cartoon History of Roosevelt's Career* (New York, 1910).

enough to curb corporations, they chose instead to run to the right of the president. Thinking that Roosevelt's forceful presidency had alienated conservative Americans, the Democrats nominated a candidate whose life had been spent in the quiet of the judicial chamber. Alton B. Parker was a New York state judge who had won a sweeping victory in his race for chief judge of the Court of Appeals in 1897. To the Democrats that suggested he could carry New York against Roosevelt. Added to the electoral votes of the Solid South, a win in New York for Parker would put the Democrats very close to victory. So the opposition party turned away from their commitment to William

Jennings Bryan and the South and West. They saw Parker as the safe and sane alternative to Roosevelt and his flamboyant conduct in office.

Parker proved to be a dud candidate who inspired no one. He conducted a front-porch campaign from his home in Esopus, New York, a remote spot that attracted few visitors. Moreover, the public liked Roosevelt's energy and fun. They applauded his policies and endorsed the Square Deal. It soon became apparent that Parker was, as one Midwestern Republican called him, "a blank cartridge." With memories of Grover Cleveland still fresh, the electorate outside of the South was not about to opt for another New York Democrat.[39]

Even though it was clear that Roosevelt was heading for a decisive victory in 1904, the president took an intense interest in the campaign and his fortunes. Though it pained him to do so, he observed the custom by which incumbent presidents did not campaign for their own election. The most he could contribute himself was a speech when he accepted the nomination and the letter of acceptance that became a main campaign document. Roosevelt chafed at the enforced inactivity. "I wish I were where I could fight more offensively," he told his old friend Henry Cabot Lodge in July 1904. "I always like to do my fighting in the adversary's corner."[40]

Roosevelt had to let surrogates do the campaigning for him, and the Republicans rallied behind the winning effort. The campaign manager, the former presidential secretary and head of the Department of Commerce and Labor, George B. Cortelyou, managed an efficient canvass. Republicans reached out to a diverse array of ethnic and religious constituencies. African Americans in the North were told to recall "the silent legions which sleep tonight in Northern churchyards and the forgotten buried trenches on the Southern battlefield." Roosevelt had placated the Catholic hierarchy during his first term by protecting the church's interest in the Philippines and also making presidential appointments on a nonsectarian basis. These steps led an editor of a Catholic newspaper to say that he was "a man without prejudice, sectarian bias or intolerance." Meanwhile, party orators proclaimed that the Republicans rode "in the chariot of American glory; the Democratic party in the hearse of dead and discredited theories."[41]

Until the end, the 1904 election was quiet. The military-style campaigning of the Gilded Age ad largely vanished in favor of pamphlets, newspaper appeals, and advertising. Voters displayed less interest in the issues, and observers noted that enthusiasm was paltry. "This is the most apathetic campaign ever heard of since James Monroe's second election," wrote Albert Shaw of the *American Review of Reviews*. Instead of charismatic speakers, the nation responded to "a half dozen bulging browed youths, a set of encyclopedias and a report of the Bureau of Statistics."[42]

With the Democrats headed for a resounding defeat, Parker decided to take up a new issue as the election neared. The Democratic candidate charged that the Republicans were receiving campaign donations from large corporations in return for protection from government regulation. A Democratic newspaper called the issue "Cortelyou and Corruption"; as secretary of Commerce and Labor, Cortelyou had access to corporate records and knew, the Democrats charged, where to tap business for funds. Parker also received information from Democratic businessmen who had attended a meeting where Roosevelt asked for campaign contributions. A participant at this gathering, Henry Clay Frick, later said of Roosevelt, "He got down on his knees to us. We bought the son of a bitch and then he did not stay bought."[43]

Fearful of defeat despite all the favorable signs, Roosevelt had been meeting with corporate leaders such as railroad magnate E. H. Harriman. Whether Roosevelt asked him for money straight out became a source of controversy later. Cortelyou and other Republican campaign officials were getting donations from Standard Oil and other firms. Roosevelt did not inquire into how the campaign funds were being assembled. He covered himself with pro forma letters directing that money from Standard Oil be returned. When told that the money had already been spent, he commented, "Well, the letter will look well on the record anyhow."[44]

Parker's charges outraged the president. He insisted that the money from Standard Oil be returned, and he flooded Cortelyou with letters refuting the Democratic charges. When Parker stepped up his attacks on November 3 with an assault on Cortelyou's "organized importunity," Roosevelt could not keep silent. He related a statement on November 5 that Parker's charges were "unqualifiedly and atrociously false." Now the burden fell on Parker to prove his claims. Without access to Republican campaign records and with his informants unwilling to break confidentiality, Parker could not connect the dots to show that Roosevelt and the Republicans had accepted corporate funds in exchange for promises of special treatment. Parker's lame response convinced few people as the election neared.[45]

While the episode was not significant for the election itself, it did indicate a mounting popular interest in the influence of business in politics. The question of corporate power and its impact on the Republican Party would become more acute within the next few years. Some reformers even discussed placing legal limits on the amounts of money that corporations could contribute to a candidate or a party. The roots of campaign reform legislation extend back to the early years of the twentieth century.

When the voters went to the polls on November 8, 1904, they produced a landslide victory for Theodore Roosevelt and his party. As the votes came in, Roosevelt met with reporters in his private office in the Executive Office Building. He dictated a statement to the press. He thanked the American people for their verdict and then took himself out of any race for another term in 1908. The time he had already spent in the White House, he said, "constitutes my first term. The wise custom which limits the President to two terms regards the substance and not the form, and under no circumstances will I be a candidate for or accept another nomination."[46]

Roosevelt's statement was no spur-of-the-moment decision, as is often claimed. He had discussed the move with Senator Winthrop Murray Crane of Massachusetts and probably with his wife, as well as several other people. Though it turned out to be a political mistake, the declaration made sense at the time. Roosevelt remembered how the press had approved of McKinley's renunciation of a third term in 1901. More important, the statement would counter Democratic charges that he had ambitions to be president for life. He could pursue his agenda in his second term without being accused of seeking personal gain or partisan motivation.

Even if all of this was true, Roosevelt had still erred. To the extent that politicians believed it, and Roosevelt reaffirmed the pledge over the next several years, the choice confirmed his status as a lame duck. Congress knew that Roosevelt would be gone on March 4, 1909, and lawmakers behaved accordingly in light of that assumption. At the same time, friends and enemies of the president parsed his statements to see if there might be a chance he would change his mind. In the end, Roosevelt had managed to box himself in as far as his future ambitions were concerned.

The election of 1904 represented a decisive success for the president and the Republican Party. Roosevelt won 56.4 percent of the vote to 37.6 percent for Alton B. Parker; the president garnered 7,628,875 votes to 5,084,442 for his Democratic opponent. The Socialist candidate, Eugene V. Debs, and the Prohibition Party candidate trailed the two major-party nominees. Roosevelt had 336 votes in the electoral college to 140 for Parker. That represented the most electoral votes any candidate had received up to that time. By carrying the border state of Missouri, the president made a small dent in the Solid South.

The Republican ticket had earned staggering majorities in such party strongholds as Ohio and Pennsylvania, but Roosevelt had also carried New York, Connecticut, and New Jersey by large margins. The argument against

Roosevelt as a potential dictator had fallen flat. Instead, the president ran well among most ethnic groups.

Two important subthemes affected the election. Turnout fell from 1900, with about four hundred thousand fewer ballots cast than four years before. The estimated turnout in the northern states, which had stood at nearly 72 percent in 1900, was just under 65 percent in 1904. Democratic ballots sagged in dramatic fashion, with 1.3 million fewer votes cast for Parker than for William Jennings Bryan in 1900.

Yet the Democrats also elected governors in five states that Roosevelt won, most notably Massachusetts, Missouri, and Minnesota. The ties of party loyalty were beginning to fray. Split tickets indicated that Republicans dominated in the first ten years of the new century, while Democrats retained residual strength in the states. Beneath the surface of an overwhelming Republican triumph, voter trends suggested that the majority coalition of the 1890s was under some pressure.

The election of 1904 was the culmination of the political changes that had begun during the depression of the 1890s. Republicans had come to power behind a program that embraced the protective tariff, a foreign policy of overseas expansion, ethnic inclusiveness, and the return of prosperity. A charismatic and appealing president had brought all these currents together through his vivid personality. But there were signs that a nationalism that promoted economic growth would not be enough to keep the Republicans in power indefinitely. Americans discussed whether the government should do more to regulate the economy. That issue was much on Theodore Roosevelt's mind in late 1904. He dreaded a nation in which the political landscape was "divided into two parties, one containing the bulk of the property owners and conservative people, the other the bulk of the wage workers and less prosperous people generally."[47] To avoid such a situation, Roosevelt believed, the government must do something to curb corporate power and clean up politics. Whether the majority of Republicans agreed with such a shift in priorities would be an issue that determined the fate of Roosevelt and his party in the eight years that followed.

5

The Taft-Roosevelt Split, 1905–1912

NO ONE WHO ATTENDED the Republican National Convention in Chicago in June 1912 easily forgot the experience. In a week of tumultuous proceedings, the Grand Old Party broke into competing factions for Theodore Roosevelt and William Howard Taft. The delegates hurled insults at each other, accused their opponents of theft or worse, and vowed revenge for every slight. Charles D. Hilles, the president's secretary, told his daughter that Roosevelt's movement was "the most horrible attack on constitutional Government with which we have yet been confronted." On the other hand, George W. Perkins, a key Roosevelt supporter, called the meeting that renominated Taft "thoroughly typical of machine politics with utter and complete disregard of public opinion."[1]

The journalist William Allen White, viewing the goings-on from the reporters' gallery, looked down, he wrote, "into the human cauldron that was boiling all around me." A Democratic observer of the proceedings remembered "a flat, flat lake, sizzling asphalt pavements, bands circling and zigzagging along Michigan Avenue, tooting and booming, 'Everybody's saying it, Roosevelt, Roosevelt.'" With his nomination rebuffed and Taft in control, Roosevelt left the Republicans to form a new party. The choice, he proclaimed, was simple: "We stand at Armageddon and we battle for the Lord."[2]

How had this epochal Republican rupture happened? Taft and Roosevelt had been close friends in Washington. They often told associates how their personal ideas meshed in running the government. Together they represented the reforming energies of the Republicans during the period of change that historians have dubbed the Progressive Era. It seemed unthinkable that the party they led could somehow fall from the electoral heights it had scaled in 1900 and 1904. Yet, because of Roosevelt's efforts, the party had been forced to reckon with an issue that was a source of increasing concern. To what extent should the national government regulate the increasingly complex industrial society that the United States had become? Coming up with a response to that central question tested the resilience and cohesion of the Republican Party as it had not been tried since the days of its birth in the 1850s. In the end, the GOP decided that it would not embrace government regulation of business; it would seek to limit and control such a policy.

In November 1904, the Republican Party stood at the pinnacle of American politics. Theodore Roosevelt's defeat of Alton B. Parker was the first true landslide in the modern sense of the term. The Republican candidate had swamped his rival in both the popular and electoral votes, something that had not happened in more than thirty years. The GOP also held secure majorities in both the House and the Senate. Happy party members asked each other, "What are we going to do with our victory?"[3]

In fact, though they did not recognize it at the time, the Republicans were governing a society with changing priorities by the time Roosevelt was inaugurated on March 4, 1905, after being elected in his own right. The United States was moving away from the agricultural society of the nineteenth century and toward an industrialized, urbanized social order. While the country had not yet fully completed this process, the dominance of big business, the swelling tide of immigration, and the shift from country to city seemed unstoppable in the decades ahead. New demands would confront Republicans and Democrats alike, and older philosophies of government would be tested in ways that shifted the ruling assumptions of both major parties.

There were almost eighty-four million Americans in 1905, augmented by a constant flow of immigration. One million immigrants entered the country that year, and similar numbers followed during the next two years. More than three-quarters of the new residents had come from central, eastern, and southern Europe. They provided labor for a robust and growing economy that had left the depression of the 1890s far behind. How these newcomers would sort themselves out in political terms remained to be determined. Some Republicans of old-stock backgrounds regarded immigrants with dismay and suspicion. Others, including Theodore Roosevelt, wanted to bring them into the party's governing coalition.

Prosperity dominated the economic scene in 1905. The gross national product stood at $24 billion, compared with $13 billion just a decade earlier. Yet the new riches of society rested on a foundation of hard work by millions of laborers who did not share in the growing abundance. American workers toiled almost sixty hours a week on average for about twenty-four cents an hour. The annual income of the average worker was less than $600 per year. The rising rate of inflation cut into the purchasing power of many families. There was no federal income tax, but there were also few pension plans, little in the way of unemployment insurance, and no medical coverage beyond what an individual family could afford to pay. If a breadwinner lost a job, the family made do or slipped into poverty.

Republican orators hailed the good times achieved since the start of the McKinley administration eight years earlier. The Dingley Tariff, in their view, had restored business confidence and protected capital and labor from the damaging effects of foreign competition. It was, said one Republican senator in November 1904, "largely to be credited with our wonderful prosperity and present impregnable business position." The best policy was to "let well enough alone" or, as Senator Mark Hanna had said, using an old poker phrase, to "stand pat." Defenders of that position were soon called "standpatters" within the party.[4]

In Congress, the Republicans of the "stand pat" persuasion held the levers of power in the party as Roosevelt's second term commenced. The Republican leader in the Senate was Nelson Wilmarth Aldrich of Rhode Island. Along with Orville H. Platt of Connecticut, John Coit Spooner of Wisconsin, and William Boyd Allison of Iowa, Aldrich led "the Four" who directed the policies of the upper house. Conservative in their views, and defenders of the business community and the protective tariff, they and the Republicans they led had little sympathy with the idea of regulating the economy. Still, they could read the changing public sentiment. Roosevelt would get some of what he proposed during his second term, but he would have to fight to do so.

Across the capital, the leader of the House was Joseph G. Cannon of Illinois. First elected to Congress in 1872 at the age of thirty-six, the bearded, cigar-smoking Cannon, sporting a smashed felt hat that he wore everywhere, was fondly called "Uncle Joe" by his friends. His enemies, who chafed under his firm control of House procedure and substance, labeled him "Czar Cannon." He had been elected Speaker in 1903 and soon gained fame for his blunt, often profane language. He was so conservative that it was said if he had been present when the universe was created, he would have voted for chaos. Or, as Cannon himself remarked, "I am god-damned tired of listening to all this babble for reform."[5]

Despite Republican reluctance to heed them, there were signs in 1905 of fears in the middle class about their own place in society and the country's well-being. That large corporations controlled the productive means of the nation and greatly influenced politics seemed more and more disturbing to average citizens fearful of losing economic opportunity. Daily newspapers reported on corrupt campaign contributions that were revealed during an investigation of the insurance industry in New York. Across the nation, other disclosures about officials with illicit ties to business and favored treatment from corporate allies became commonplace. Investigative journalists uncovered municipal scandals and revealed shoddy practices in the patent medicine and meatpacking industries.[6]

Americans wondered why the government could not do something on the state and federal level to root out these evils. "Corporations have, and ought to have, many privileges," said Governor Albert B. Cummins of Iowa, "but among them is not the privilege to sit in political conventions or occupy seats in legislative chambers." The answer, according to such "progressive" Republicans, was an expanded role for the government. As Theodore Roosevelt put it in January 1905, "Neither this people nor any free people will permanently tolerate the use of vast power conferred by vast wealth, and especially by wealth in its corporate form, without lodging somewhere in the government the still higher power of seeing that this power, in addition to being used in the interests of the individual or individuals possessing it, is also used for and not against the interests of the people as a whole."[7]

Roosevelt was not talking about the modern welfare state. He proposed to use the government to preserve a balance among competing economic interests, as he had envisioned as part of the Square Deal of his first term. The president's first priority in this regard was the railroad industry, which had become the target of complaints from shippers and consumers about high rates for rail services. In his annual message of 1904, Roosevelt asked whether the regulatory power of the Interstate Commerce Commission (ICC) should be increased to deal with high railroad rates and illegal practices by the major lines. Fundamentally he was asking whether the traditional Republican doctrine of promoting economic growth through government action had to give way to increased regulation from the executive branch.

During the eighteen months that followed, Roosevelt used his presidential powers of persuasion to achieve passage of the Hepburn Act of 1906, which would enhance the authority of the ICC. His repertoire included a series of public speeches, leaks to friendly journalists, the threat of legal actions against major rail lines, and pressure on lawmakers to support his program. Conservatives in the Senate, led by Aldrich, tried to block Roosevelt by giving the federal courts the broad power to oversee ICC decrees. There was a protracted legislative struggle that began when Congress assembled six months later, in December 1905. As a result, Roosevelt did not attain everything he wanted in the form of the Hepburn Act that passed. He did get substantially increased powers for the ICC to regulate rail companies. All in all, Roosevelt believed, the final form of the law was "a fine piece of constructive legislation, and all that has been done tends toward carrying out the principles I have been preaching." Yet many conservative Republicans wondered if Roosevelt's regulatory sermons did not include a healthy dose of heresy from party doctrine.[8]

By 1906, Roosevelt's reform principles included other measures to expand the power of the national government. For several years journalists had been revealing fraud and deadly products that plagued the patent medicine industry as well as dangers to the food supply from unsafe meatpacking. Legislation to ensure pure food and drugs languished in Congress, where the Republican leadership, protecting the interests of the patent medicine and packaged-food trade, had kept it buried in committee. But when the unhealthy practices in the Chicago stockyards were revealed in sickening detail in Upton Sinclair's novel *The Jungle*, the disgusted public clamored for governmental remedies in 1905–1906.[9]

Roosevelt responded first to the meatpacking issue. The White House supported an amendment to the agricultural appropriation law providing for stricter meat inspection rules. Congress gave the president what he sought. The resultant publicity intensified demands to pass the pure food and drugs law as well. With Roosevelt backing a measure that the public wanted, the legislation won passage in late June 1906. Roosevelt had succeeded in moving the Republicans toward greater regulation. He termed the three regulatory measures "a noteworthy advance in the policy of securing Federal supervision and control over corporations." That same spring Roosevelt came out for a federal inheritance tax, "a tax so framed as to put it out of the power of the owner of one of these enormous fortunes to hand on more than a certain amount to any one individual; the tax, of course, to be imposed by the National and not the State Government." In that way, the president believed, extremes of wealth and poverty in the United States could be reduced.[10]

The rationale behind Roosevelt's commitment to greater regulation was simple. If the federal government did not address the major social inequities in American society, then agitation for more drastic reforms would gain converts. After all, Eugene V. Debs and the Socialists had won more than four hundred thousand votes in 1904, and there was evidence of growing support for Socialist candidates in states such as Massachusetts and Wisconsin. As Roosevelt wrote in 1908, "We seek to control law-defying wealth in the first place to prevent its doing dire evil to the Republic, and in the next place to avoid the vindictive and dreadful radicalism which, if left uncontrolled, it is certain in the end to arouse."[11]

The Midwestern Republicans who regarded themselves as the progressive wing of the party applauded Roosevelt's actions, even if they sometimes wished to go further than the president. Among those identified with reform were Governor Cummins of Iowa and Senator Robert M. La Follette of Wisconsin. A mixture of motives underlay their desire for a stronger federal presence. Railroads were a particular grievance, as were the high tariff rates that drove up prices on goods their agrarian constituents purchased. These Republicans also disliked the existing party structure that often shut them out of office and power. Insurgents in California, Kansas, Iowa, Minnesota, Wisconsin, and New Hampshire, for example, endorsed direct primaries to choose candidates and reform of campaign funding and practices. These changes would reduce the clout of older, entrenched Republican leaders who had relied on party caucuses, rigged conventions, and backroom deals to stay in power. Now Republican voters could select primary candidates.

The progressive creed that Republican reformers espoused did not attack capitalism as the foundation of the economy. Instead, they wanted their party to do more to challenge the power of corporations. That would make tariff rates less onerous for consumers and reduce railroad rates. Once the proper balance had been restored, then the role of government could be pared back.

Robert La Follette became the national embodiment of this spirit. A short, feisty man with a pompadour and a strident speaking style, La Follette had been a two-term governor of Wisconsin. He had defied the Republican organization in his state by setting up a direct primary, pursuing railroad reg-ulation, and imposing higher taxes on corporations. He also used the aca-demic resources of the faculty of the University of Wisconsin to shape his reform program in what became known as the "Wisconsin Idea." Elected to the Senate in 1905, he came to Washington a year later with his eye on the White House. He had to defer to Roosevelt, but mutual suspicion soon grew between the two men. Roosevelt deemed the Wisconsin lawmaker an im-practical visionary. La Follette saw the president as too willing to compromise with corporate interests.[12]

The progressive Republicans were vocal and articulate; they attracted a good deal of press attention. Yet outside of their regional base, they remained a minority among Republicans. While the party rank and file admired Roosevelt's vote-getting appeal and tolerated the progressive ideas he champi-oned, there was growing unease among the conservatives, strong in the Northeast and in the older states of the Middle West such as Ohio and Indiana, about the direction of the party. Such standpatters as Joseph G. Cannon, Joseph B. Foraker, and Nelson Aldrich asked about the implications of increasing the power of the government and limiting the economic freedom of corporations. The emergence of regulation as a critical issue forced Republicans to reappraise their party's priorities. Perhaps Democrats should not be the only proponents of states' rights and local power.

Some of these crosscurrents were evident in the 1906 congressional elections. The Democrats joined with the American Federation of Labor (AFL) to mount a determined challenge to the Republican majority in the House and the role of Speaker Cannon, who had become the symbol of Republican conservatism. Some Republican progressives in the House saw the Speaker as the major obstacle to the enactment of reform legislation.

A sore point for many Republicans was the protective tariff, the centerpiece of the party's economic doctrine. Prosperity had brought inflation after 1900, and rising consumer prices gave the Democrats a tempting target. The high tariff rates of the Dingley Law, they charged, hiked the prices of what the average American purchased every day. Middle Western Republicans, for whom the issue cut deeply, contended that a downward revision of rates was needed. The president and the Congress, they felt, should pursue "a rational revision of the tariff along protection lines." But Speaker Cannon disagreed. He believed that the Dingley Tariff was, "all things considered, the most perfect and just customs law ever enacted." The Republicans sent out contradictory messages on their main issue in 1906.[13]

Roosevelt threw himself into the fight to save the House for the Republicans. He dispatched Cabinet officers to the stump, wrote public letters, and tried to stoke enthusiasm among the party's candidates. His efforts, combined with Democratic miscues, held Republican losses in the House to twenty-eight seats. The Republicans retained control, however, and picked up strength in the Senate. While the party had escaped disaster, the internal tensions splitting the Republicans over the tariff and the question of government regulation did not augur well. With Roosevelt out of the 1908 race, a bitter battle for the nomination loomed.

Though Roosevelt had several times reaffirmed his 1904 declaration that he would not be a candidate again, the president did not intend to leave the choice of his successor to the party faithful and the nomination process. He knew that such an approach would result in a candidate who did not share his progressive views. He therefore made it clear that he would not accept a nominee who failed, he said, to "carry out the governmental principles in which I believe with all my heart and soul." With that posture, Roosevelt virtually guaranteed the selection of the candidate he wanted, given his enduring popularity with the voters.[14]

By 1908 a substantial element among the Republicans had decided that Roosevelt was too much of a reformer for their taste. His regulatory policies, his advocacy of conservation in the West, and his endorsement of an inheritance tax drove conservatives into paroxysms of rage. A reporter told a prominent senator in mid-1907 that Republicans disliked "the present fire works administration because it squints too much in the direction of Socialism, that is paternalism from which may easily follow various encroachments on property rights and the rights of individual states." These feelings intensified when a severe financial panic occurred in late 1907. For conservatives the business slump and the resulting bank failures were the direct result of Roosevelt's "ill-considered recommendations and hasty policies."[15]

So both progressives and conservatives in the GOP looked to 1908 as their chance to shape the party's future direction. The Republicans were in the midst of a succession crisis that would affect the next twelve years. With Roosevelt out of the running, a number of conservatives hoped to emerge from a crowded field in 1908. There were other progressive aspirants for the prize as well, but none of these potential nominees had any chance of receiving Roosevelt's endorsement.

Among the conservatives with an eye on the White House were Charles W. Fairbanks of Indiana, Speaker Cannon, and Joseph B. Foraker. Fairbanks was a colorless soul who had once been described as too scared to say boo to a goose. "Uncle Joe" Cannon had developed into a political symbol of a reactionary Congress, and he had little support outside of his home state.[16]

Senator Foraker presented a different problem for the White House. Although the Ohio senator had once been friendly with the president, the two men had split over the Hepburn Act; Foraker was one of the few legislators to oppose the measure on the final vote. Then a more bitter rupture occurred. In August 1906, a shooting took place in Brownsville, Texas, and white residents charged that black soldiers stationed in the town had been responsible for the violence. The soldiers, to a man, denied any involvement, and the historical evidence supports their case. The army and eventually Theodore Roosevelt concluded that some of the troops were responsible and that every member of their unit knew who the culprits were. Therefore, he dismissed all three companies from the service in November 1906, a few days before the congressional elections.[17]

Foraker sprang to the defense of the soldiers and accused Roosevelt of unfairness. The senator saw political advantage in appealing to black Republican voters in the North, but he also believed that a miscarriage of justice had happened. The president and the senator had a nasty public quarrel at the annual dinner of the Gridiron Club of journalists in late January 1907. Theodore Roosevelt did not forgive and forget. Thwarting Foraker's presidential bid would enable Roosevelt to defeat a conservative and also punish a Republican who had impugned his integrity as a chief executive.

The problem of designating an acceptable successor remained. If the choice was made purely on a personal basis, the president would probably have picked his secretary of state, Elihu Root. Political disabilities hurt Root's chances. He was sixty-three and perceived as too old. His background as a corporate lawyer also worked against him. On the more progressive side of the party, Roosevelt might have looked to the newly elected governor of New York, Charles Evans Hughes, who had won in 1906 after revealing scandals in the insurance industry. Roosevelt found Hughes too independent. The other possibility, Robert M. La Follette, seemed too radical and unpalatable on personal grounds.

Looking around his cabinet, Roosevelt's eye fell on his secretary of war, William Howard Taft. The president soon decided that he had found just the man to carry on what he had termed "my policies." This decision grew out of a blend of personal interaction and political calculation that often animated Roosevelt's judgment, but it proved to be a fateful one for the Grand Old Party.

In many respects, Taft was a sensible selection. He had a strong record as governor general of the Philippines from 1900 to 1904 and had been a valuable subordinate as secretary of war. As the two men worked together they formed what appeared to be a strong friendship. Roosevelt believed in 1906 that Taft "would be an ideal president" and "the best man to receive it." The links between the president and secretary were genuine but were based to some extent on a misunderstanding of where each of them stood politically within the Republican ranks.[18]

As an attorney, Taft believed in orderly procedures and the rule of law. His fondest ambition was to be the chief justice of the Supreme Court. He had declined two offers from Roosevelt to go on the court as an associate justice because of his desire for the highest judicial place. Within the administration, Taft felt that Roosevelt's willingness to stretch presidential power to accomplish his regulatory goals sometimes went too far. He also thought that Roosevelt went around the backs of his cabinet officers too often and dealt directly with their subordinates. Pulled along by the force of Roosevelt's personality, Taft became identified with the progressive thrust of the administration even though he had reservations about how far such policies should be pushed. He remained a loyal lieutenant to Roosevelt, and the two friends never really examined their potential differences over issues such as conservation, the tariffs, and the trusts.

By mid-1906, Taft seemed the logical choice from Roosevelt's perspective. He could be counted on to implement regulation, and he was not identified with the conservatives. Roosevelt's enthusiasm for Taft intensified after the Brownsville controversy erupted. Since Taft was from Ohio, his candidacy would have the added benefit of frustrating Foraker's hopes. By early 1907, the president had made it clear to everyone in Republican politics that Taft had his full backing.

One key person in the Taft camp resented the time it had taken Roosevelt to choose his secretary of war. Helen Herron Taft wanted her husband to become president. In fact she had been a major force in persuading him not to accept a Supreme Court nomination. She never trusted the good intentions of Theodore Roosevelt. While Will Taft was loyal to the president during this period, the same could not be said for his wife and other members of his family.

Throughout 1907 the Taft campaign gained momentum as Roosevelt emphasized who his first choice was. Meanwhile, the ideological split in the party deepened. Roosevelt became more emphatic in his denunciation of business after the Panic of 1907. A message to Congress in late January 1908 renewed Roosevelt's earlier call for inheritance taxes and stronger legislation to curb corporations. Conservative Republicans reacted with outrage at this presidential endorsement of greater regulation.

Relations between the White House and Congress only worsened during the spring of 1908. The president pushed for antitrust legislation, which Cannon and his allies then rejected. The progressives urged the party in Congress to do more on social justice, downward revision of the protective tariff, and reform of the banking system in the wake of the 1907 panic. The conservatives balked and the session proved less than productive. Roosevelt complained, "The ruling clique in the Senate, the House, and the National Committee seem to regard every concession to decency as merely a matter of bargain and sale with *me*, which *I* must pay for in some way or fashion."[19]

The Taft campaign, for its part, rolled ahead toward a first-ballot nomination. As the national convention approached, the conservatives (or the "Allies," as they were known) tried to make a stand by questioning the legitimacy of some of the Taft delegates from southern states. By this time the Republican Party in Dixie had become largely a shadow organization that existed solely for the purpose of providing delegates. Patronage favors and outright bribery often determined which national candidate secured the votes of southern delegates. The Taft-Roosevelt forces in 1907–1908 had proven superior in providing inducements to support the secretary of war. With the president and his supporters in control of the convention machinery and the Republican National

Committee, these challenges from the Allies were repulsed and the Taft delegates seated. It did not seem important at the moment of Taft's triumph that his supporters would dominate the national committee for the next four years.

Once the procedural roadblocks had been removed, Taft achieved a decisive first-ballot victory in Chicago. The real story of the convention, however, was that Taft and Roosevelt had to accept a more conservative platform than they had hoped for. The most noteworthy language in the document pledged to revise the tariff but did not specify in what direction the changes in rates would be. Taft also had to agree to a conservative House member, James S. "Sunny Jim" Sherman of New York, as his running mate. Coming out of the convention, the Republicans anticipated a tough contest with the resurgent Democrats, particularly since Theodore Roosevelt would not be on the ballot.

Behind the scenes the friendship between Roosevelt and Taft suffered the first of the misunderstandings that would only grow as the months passed. Upon receiving the news that he was the Republican candidate, Taft said in an offhand manner that he wanted the members of Roosevelt's cabinet "to stay just as they are." Whether Taft meant that all these men would be kept in office if he became president is not clear. Yet, with his usual ebullience, Roosevelt conveyed to all cabinet members that Taft was planning to keep them in office after the election.[20]

On the stump, Taft proved to be an effective candidate. Despite warnings from the campaign managers to avoid speaking tours where he might make a verbal slip, the travel-loving Taft went to the Middle West, parts of the South, and the critical state of New York. In all these places, he attracted sizable and enthusiastic audiences. He endorsed the role of labor unions, pledged downward revision of the tariff, and promised to implement the regulatory legislation on the trusts that Roosevelt had obtained from Congress.

But a restless Roosevelt could not sit still in the White House. While he could not by custom go out and tour for Taft, he could infuse, he said, "a little vim into the campaign by making a publication of my own." The public letters that Roosevelt issued made the president the unofficial campaign manager and cheerleader of Taft's candidacy. By overshadowing the party's candidate, however, Roosevelt added to the popular sense that he remained the GOP leader. This appearance did not sit well with Mrs. Taft and others close to the presidential candidate.[21]

Meanwhile, the Democrats and Bryan could not find a winning theme against Taft. As a result, the Republican nominee won a substantial victory. He received 321 electoral votes to 162 for Bryan. Taft rolled up 7,675,000 popular votes to 6,412,000 for the loser. The turnout was about 65 percent of the eligible electorate, as participation receded from the high levels of the late nineteenth century. Taft garnered almost 50,000 more votes than Roosevelt in 1904, but Bryan gained nearly 1,400,000 more ballots than Alton B. Parker.

Behind the victory were some worrying signs for the Grand Old Party. In five states that Taft carried, Democrats elected governors. Ticket splitting showed that the intense partisanship of the previous generation was breaking down, a trend that worked to the disadvantage of Republicans. The factionalism among the party faithful meant that both progressives and conservatives looked to the president-elect to resolve their growing differences. As one newspaper reporter wrote to Roosevelt, "Are we to hope that Taft will be a bigger man than the party?—and that is the hope in which most progressive men are supporting him."[22]

A keystone of Republican unity was the state of the friendship of Roosevelt and Taft. That concord began to fall apart within days of the election. On November 7, 1908, the president-elect sent Roosevelt a thank-you letter, telling the president, "You and my brother Charlie made that possible which in all probability would not have occurred otherwise." Though he said nothing at the time, Roosevelt resented being lumped together with Taft's half-brother, a wealthy newspaper publisher. He later remarked that it was as if someone said "Abraham Lincoln and the bond seller Jay Cooke saved the Union."[23]

The cabinet selections produced the first tangible rift. Having forgotten his comments in June 1908 or not regarding them as a binding pledge, Taft proceeded to make appointments that did not include some key members of Roosevelt's official family. The secretary of the interior, James R. Garfield, and the secretary of commerce, Oscar S. Straus, were informed that they would not be retained. Straus said to Roosevelt that "through influence or surroundings Taft did not wish to take those who distinguished themselves under" the outgoing president. As Roosevelt put it to another Cabinet officer who was not to be reappointed, "Unfortunately you have been too close to me, I fear."[24]

Tension between the Roosevelt and Taft families contributed to the emerging split. Helen Taft pressed for the right to make changes, even before the inauguration, among the White House ushers and doormen, a move that Edith Roosevelt resented. The Tafts told the president-elect "to be his own king" and resist close identification with Roosevelt. When the outgoing president and Congress feuded in the waning days of his term, Taft kept silent. An uneasy state of affairs persisted through the inauguration. The Roosevelts had the Tafts stay over at the White House on March 3, but it was an awkward evening. Taft once described the occasion as "that funeral."[25]

The next day a severe snowstorm pelted Washington. Roosevelt said, "I knew there would be a blizzard when I went out." The inauguration had to be held in the Senate chamber, where Taft read his speech. Roosevelt and Taft then shook hands, and the former president departed for his home in Oyster Bay, New York. President Taft and Mrs. Taft then rode together to the White House, the first presidential couple to do so.[26]

Because his single term fell between the dramatic presidencies of Theodore Roosevelt and Woodrow Wilson, William Howard Taft has been relegated to mediocrity in the pantheon of chief executives. His embrace of Republican conservatism also hurt his historical reputation. To some extent, Taft was defined as much by his weight (he tipped the scales at over three hundred pounds several times during his presidency) and perceived indolence as by his actual conduct in office. In fact, Taft had a creditable record as president, but the currents of the time and the opposition of Roosevelt meant that his administration failed to secure a second term in the White House for him.

Taft was a more interesting person as president and politician than his critics at the time realized. He brought a philosophy to the presidency that grew out of his training as a lawyer. Where Roosevelt believed that a president could do anything that the Constitution did not prohibit, Taft looked for a clear basis for presidential activity policy in the Constitution and existing law. He was convinced that Roosevelt often had stretched the law unduly in support of what he deemed worthy causes. When Roosevelt and his aides ascribed "an undefined residuum of power to the President," they were advancing, according to Taft, "an unsafe doctrine" that "might lead under emergencies to results of an arbitrary character doing irremediable injustice to private right." Taft saw his role as carrying out Roosevelt's policy goals in what he felt was a more legal and constitutional manner.[27]

Taft's background was in the judiciary and administration, and his sense of how Washington should work during his presidency grew out of that experience. He was fifty-one years old in 1908, a native of Cincinnati, Ohio, and a graduate of Yale. He had little experience with electoral politics before he ran for president. What Taft did have was a perceptive mind and the capacity to work hard when his interest was engaged. He did procrastinate, confident that he could get his job done at the last minute. He lacked Roosevelt's brilliance but made up for it with common sense. On an issue such as antitrust laws, he was more of a dedicated believer in breaking up big corporations than Roosevelt was. To that extent, Taft had more in common with Middle Western progressives than Roosevelt did.

Roosevelt's designated successor, William Howard Taft faced challenges from progressives and conservatives that ultimately led to the party split in 1912. Library of Congress, LC-USZ62-122416.

Where Taft came up particularly short, though, was in the public relations that the presidency now demanded. His interaction with journalists had been good when he was secretary of war, but he did little to court reporters when he moved to the White House. More damaging, Taft paid little attention to his public image. He loved to play golf as a form of exercise to curb his weight problem. As a result, he frequented country clubs with rich friends at a time when golf was perceived as an elitist diversion. The president enjoyed traveling around the country, but the purpose of these speaking junkets did not always come through to the public. As a decision-maker, it took him time to come to a judgment, and yet he could be swayed to another course of action at the last moment. One journalist aptly summed up Taft's abilities as a leader. The president's "bump of politics" was "a deep hole."[28]

Taft had also inherited an abundance of problems from Roosevelt. The first and most divisive was the tariff. The new president intended to carry out the pledge in the 1908 platform to revise customs duties. Since the Republicans had not specified the direction that revision would take, Washington braced for a prolonged tariff battle. To get any tariff bill through Congress required the support of Speaker Cannon, who by early 1909 had become more unpopular in the country than ever. Yet the majority of the conservative Republicans in the House stood behind the Speaker. With Roosevelt's endorsement, Taft declined to help the Republican progressives in the House who were challenging Cannon's leadership. Standing with the House Republican hierarchy made good sense for Taft, but it stirred suspicions about the incoming president within the reform wing of the GOP.

During the weeks that followed the inauguration, Roosevelt departed for Africa and a long-planned hunting safari that would take him out of the country for a year. In his absence, Taft would be out from under the ex-president's shadow. (The joke in Washington was that on Wall Street everyone hoped that a lion would do its duty.) While he was away, Roosevelt did not correspond with Taft, as both men waited for the other to make the first move. In that vacuum, hard feelings and suspicions grew between the two leading Republicans.

Meanwhile, Taft addressed the vexing tariff question. He summoned Congress into special session on March 15, 1909. The House approved a measure in early April that lowered rates on such key items as iron (important for construction), sugar (key to consumer products), and lumber (for home building), and also put coal and cattle hides on the free list. Named after the chair of the House Ways and Means Committee, Sereno E. Payne, the bill went to the Senate, where it faced an uncertain future.

In the upper house, the Republicans had a secure majority of thirty-one seats, or so it seemed. According to the press, Nelson Aldrich was the virtual dictator of that body. Like so many other assumptions about the history of the Republicans, this picture was misleading. By 1909 between seven and ten Republicans from the Middle West, such as Robert La Follette, Jonathan P. Dolliver of Iowa, and Albert J. Beveridge of Indiana, were prepared to oppose Aldrich on the tariff. Their defection reduced Aldrich's real majority down to about ten votes.

Both eastern and western Republicans, eager to protect products of their own states, pushed Aldrich for concessions that favored the economic interests of their constituents in the final Senate version. The bill that came out of the Senate Finance Committee had eight hundred amendments, many of which raised rates upward back to the levels of the Dingley Law. The progressives howled and attributed the result to Aldrich's disdain for public opinion. Their protests eroded Republican unity, but Aldrich had kept his fragile coalition together. His version of the bill passed on July 8, 1909, with ten Republicans voting no.

Nelson Aldrich managed the Senate conservatives who became President Taft's allies in the fight over the Payne-Aldrich Tariff of 1909. Library of Congress, LC-USZ62-9351.

Taft was in a bind. The progressives sought his support, but the president did not want to abandon Aldrich. Taft believed in lower rates, but he did not want to accept an amendment, pushed by progressives, that would have added an income tax. In Taft's mind, because of earlier court decisions voiding an income tax, only a constitutional amendment could authorize such a levy. In the end, Taft negotiated a tax on corporations and language endorsing an income tax amendment. In the conference committee to reconcile the Payne and Aldrich bills, Taft secured enough concessions, particularly on cattle hides, to persuade him to sign what was now known as the Payne-Aldrich Tariff. He rebuffed calls from the progressive Republicans to veto the bill. To maintain as much party unity as possible, Taft believed that he had to accept what Congress had done.

The congressional debate over the Pane-Aldrich Tariff marked another turning point for the Republicans. While there would be other protective measures passed under Republican congresses in 1922 and 1930, the Payne-Aldrich measure represented the last time the tariff issue would be at the heart of party doctrine. When the Democrats enacted an income tax in 1913, they made a permanent change in how government revenues were collected. Customs duties became less important, constituting a diminishing percentage of the funds for government operation. Republican attitudes toward taxation, spending, and trade policy commenced a long and slow evolution away from the tariff and toward the commitment to free trade that would characterize the party by the end of the twentieth century. Such a prospect would have seemed rank political heresy to Nelson Aldrich and the defenders of protectionism in 1909.

Taft's approval of the Payne-Aldrich law in August 1909 produced little anger from a public that could not follow the intricate details of tariff making. To further promote party unity, Taft decided to praise the law and all who voted for it. But by extension he was also condemning those who had opposed Aldrich and the Senate bill. At Winona, Minnesota, on a speaking tour in September 1909, Taft called the Payne-Aldrich measure "the best tariff that the Republican party has ever passed." The regulars were delighted. The progressives seethed and could only conclude that Taft had cast his lot with Aldrich, Cannon, and the party conservatives.[29]

The political picture became more complicated for the Republicans in the rest of 1909. The regular session of Congress that began in December 1909 gave advantages to the resurgent Democrats. The rising cost of living angered consumers. Speaker Cannon became ever more of a liability, and House Republicans accepted limitations on his power in March 1910. Absorbing the impact of these issues, Taft and the lawmakers worked together to pass the Mann-Elkins Act, which increased the regulatory power of the Interstate Commerce Commission. Other pieces of progressive legislation were enacted. By the time the Congress left town, the president observed, "I think things are coming our way a little more than heretofore."[30]

This proved to be misplaced optimism. The Democrats sensed that they had an excellent chance to retake the House for the first time since 1894, and they put aside their differences for the sake of unity. They indicted the Republican tariff policy as a major cause of inflation. With strong candidates for governorships, such as Woodrow Wilson in New Jersey, the Democrats had initiative and internal cohesion for the first time in two decades.

Some Republicans hoped that Theodore Roosevelt would return from Africa and use his popularity to salvage the situation. It was not to be. While Roosevelt had been away, the bonds of his friendship with Taft had frayed. The major element in the erosion of trust between the two men had been a controversy over conservation policy. Roosevelt believed that his work on natural resources, with his key aide, Gifford Pinchot, had been a significant legacy to the nation. Taft did not like Pinchot and was convinced that Roosevelt, acting at Pinchot's behest, had been careless in some of his decisions over public lands, forest reserves, and mining policy. When the new secretary of the interior, Richard A. Ballinger, took over in 1909, he and

Pinchot soon clashed over the proper direction of conservation. Pinchot leaked to the press allegations that Ballinger was corrupt, citing some of his actions over Alaska coal lands. The public attack led Taft to fire Pinchot for insubordination in January 1910. A congressional probe revealed no wrongdoing on Ballinger's part, but the controversy damaged both the secretary and the White House with charges that they had covered up Ballinger's actions.

The important political consequence of the Ballinger case came from Roosevelt's reaction to the ouster of his close friend. During the autumn of 1909, the former president's associates had sent him letter after letter with negative assessments of Taft's performance. When he heard the news of Pinchot's dismissal, he said, "It seems to me absolutely impossible that there can be any truth in this statement." But when the report was confirmed, his disillusionment with his successor and his administration was plain. Roosevelt was compelled to admit that Taft "had gone wrong on certain points," adding, "I also had to admit to myself that deep down underneath I had known all along he was wrong on points as to which I tried to deceive myself, by loudly proclaiming to myself, that he was right."[31]

By this time many of Roosevelt's progressive friends wanted him to run in 1912. They formed "Back from Elba" clubs to spur him on. Still a Republican, he downplayed such overtures but did not repudiate them with a definite statement in support of Taft. The president wanted such an endorsement. Roosevelt balked. The former president agonized about his next move. He had loved being the chief executive, and private life was boring after the excitement of the White House.

For Roosevelt to maintain his standing with progressives and remain in the public eye, he had to keep open the chance that he would run in 1912. The longer that option was on the table, the more likely it became that Roosevelt would exercise it. Meanwhile, he convinced himself that he would be the agent through which party unity would be restored. In that sense, Roosevelt was casting himself as the real leader of the party and relegating Taft to a supporting role. Since Taft was the president, what Roosevelt was envisioning was impossible.

Roosevelt returned from Africa to wide popular acclaim based more on his celebrity status than the idea he should be president once again. Republican progressives hoped he would take a clear stand against the Taft administration. At first Roosevelt said he was out of politics, but pressure from his friends soon had him back in the fray in New York State, where the Republicans were in trouble. Taft still sought Roosevelt's endorsement for reelection in 1912, but the former president hedged on the issue. Suspicion mounted between the two camps. The animosity intensified during the summer of 1910. The deeper significance for the party lay in the policy ideas that Roosevelt advanced during a three-week speaking tour of the west that he launched in late August. His articulation of the New Nationalism further exposed the ideological rifts among Republicans.

Roosevelt's key statement of his brand of Republicanism came at Osawatomie, Kansas, on August 31, 1910, in what became known as the "New Nationalism" speech. He called for a "new nationalism" that would have the federal government be more than the neutral umpire he had advocated during the Square Deal. Roosevelt wanted the government to intervene to achieve a higher degree of social justice. "When I say that I am for the square deal, I mean not merely that I stand for fair play under the present rules of the game, but I stand for having those rules changed so as to work for a more substantial equality of opportunity and of reward for equally good service."[32]

In practical terms, Roosevelt advocated policies that very much looked forward to the modern welfare state. He endorsed such progressive reforms as limits on corporate power in politics, greater regulation of big business through government agencies, and laws to curb child labor, provide minimum wages, and install unemployment compensation for workers. "A graduated inheritance tax on big fortunes" and income taxes on "big fortunes" were large elements of his agenda. "The really big fortune, the swollen fortune, by the mere fact of its size acquires qualities which differentiate it in kind as well as in degree from what is possessed by men of relatively small means."[33]

This was Republicanism that went further in the direction of governmental activism than many in the party were willing to accept. Roosevelt was fusing the nationalism that had always been a hallmark of the party with a faith in regulatory power that conflicted with the business orientation of the Grand Old Party. Roosevelt's ideas, said a New York conservative, "had startled all thoughtful men and impressed them with the frightful danger which lies in his political ascendancy." Roosevelt muted his position in response to criticism from regulars, but there was no doubt that he proposed to take the party in a dramatic new direction.[34]

Roosevelt's efforts to achieve party unity behind his new philosophy backfired. The Republicans went into the 1910 elections more divided than before. The voters watched he spectacle of Republican feuding and heeded the Democratic calls for partisan change. With his customary wisdom, Elihu Root captured the spirit of impending defeat. The country was like "a man in bed. He wants to roll over. He doesn't know why he wants to roll over, but he just does; and he'll do it."[35]

The voters rolled over on the Republicans on November 8, 1910, as the party lost control of the House. The GOP dropped fifty-eight seats to the Democrats and saw another ten senators defeated. Woodrow Wilson won the governorship of New Jersey and was immediately mentioned as a likely nominee in 1912. Progressive Republicans claimed that they had done better at the polls than their conservative counterparts. That was true because the Democrats were weak in the states where Republican reformers were strong. Where the two parties were competitive, the conservative Republicans incurred large losses. Roosevelt was the big loser in the election. The Democrats carried New York, where the former president's hand-picked candidate lost.

Taft made the quickest adjustment to the new political reality. During the first half of 1911, he moved well ahead in the race for the party's nomination a year later. He selected a new personal secretary, Charles D. Hilles, who got the president's campaign for renomination under way during the summer of 1911. Meanwhile, Taft launched a series of initiatives including pursuing freer trade with Canada and arbitration treaties to resolve international disputes, which conveyed an impression of effective leadership. By the fall of 1911, Hilles estimated that Taft was closing in on a majority of Republican convention delegates.

The progressives had trouble pulling together behind a single challenger to the president. Senator La Follette wanted to make the race, and he spent a good deal of time organizing a campaign. But there was little support outside Wisconsin for someone whose radical opinions and French name (evoking echoes of the revolution in that country) stamped him as an extremist. A reporter said that the senator could not count on "one delegate from East of Ohio."[36]

The wild card in Republican calculations was Theodore Roosevelt, who had suffered the effects of humiliation through the first half of 1911. While the former president appeared to be in eclipse, his relations with Taft had warmed somewhat. Roosevelt admitted to worried Republican friends, "As things are now it would be a serious mistake from a public standpoint, and a cruel wrong to me, to nominate me." Roosevelt did not take the irrevocable step of endorsing Taft or promising to refuse any Republican nomination. The possibility that he might change his mind kept Republicans on edge as 1912 neared.[37]

A key episode during the autumn of 1911 revived Roosevelt's doubts about Taft. In late October the news broke that the Department of Justice had filed an antitrust lawsuit against the United States Steel Corporation. The wording of the indictment triggered the final, decisive break between Roosevelt and Taft. In the charges, the Taft administration alleged that business leaders friendly to the steel company had deceived Roosevelt during the Panic of 1907. At the height of the financial crisis, Roosevelt had let the steel giant acquire a competing firm, Tennessee Coal and Iron, without fear of an antitrust prosecution. Roosevelt had maintained in public and private that he had done so to protect the fragile economy and the weak banking system. The management of US Steel, he reiterated, had not duped him. The Justice Department was now stating in public that the former president had been fooled. For Roosevelt it was bad enough when Democrats had made the charge in the summer of 1911, but to have a Republican administration say this was to play "small, mean and foolish politics in this matter."[38]

The crucial element of the US Steel indictment was its effect on Roosevelt's thinking about the 1912 Republican nomination. Up to that point he had turned aside suggestions from progressive Republicans that he declare his candidacy. When he attacked the administration's trust policy and made clear his doubts about Taft, the clamor for him to run intensified. His 1904 pledge not to seek another term posed an immediate problem. Roosevelt contended that the statement did not rule out a former president "who is out of office." He avowed that he should not be a candidate unless, he said, "the bulk of the people wanted a given job done, and for their own sakes and not mine wanted me to do that job." Such language gave his supporters a green light to demonstrate to Roosevelt their enthusiasm for him as a candidate. Soon letters poured in to Oyster Bay urging him to challenge Taft.[39]

Confronted with this evidence of the popular will, Roosevelt became increasingly willing moved toward a willingness to accept the nomination. The question was how to announce his candidacy in a way that made it appear he was responding to the urgings of reform Republicans and not just his own ego. It was decided that a group of progressive governors would send him a letter asking him to become a candidate for the party's nomination and he would agree to do so.

As this scenario developed, the lingering problem of Senator La Follette and his claims to be a progressive eased in dramatic fashion. At a banquet on February 2 before an audience of newspaper publishers in Philadelphia, the senator gave a disastrous speech. He was dead tired, distracted by illness in his family, and aware of Roosevelt's impending candidacy. He spoke too long, indulged in vitriolic attacks on the press, and in general made a public spectacle of himself. Those progressives such as James R. Garfield and Gifford Pinchot, who had been nominally with La Follette, jumped ship and went over to Roosevelt. For a few days it looked as if La Follette might leave the race. That did not happen, but the way seemed clear for Roosevelt to declare.

The letter from the seven governors was received, Roosevelt issued his reply, and on February 21, 1912, the candidate said to the press corps that he would be in the race for the Republican nomination. Indeed, said Roosevelt, he felt like a bull moose. Cartoonists lost no time in depicting a political moose disrupting Republican politics.

Roosevelt's decision to run marked a crucial moment in the history of the party. Personality and policy blended in Roosevelt's thinking. He differed with Taft over antitrust and other issues, and he did hope to implement the New Nationalism. He also believed that Taft's nomination would bring about a Republican defeat at the hands of the confident Democrats. But Roosevelt's reasons had a personal dimension. As a political celebrity, he craved the attention that a presidential race would bring. He had felt most alive when he was in the White House, and nothing else quite rivaled it in terms of interest and excitement.

Roosevelt had not really thought his situation through. If he won the nomination, what would that prize be worth after a debilitating fight with Taft? Assuming that he lost, it was unlikely that he would endorse Taft. Chances were that Roosevelt would then bolt the party and run on his own. Roosevelt could make a good case that the Republican Party had not treated him fairly or given his ideas much respect, but at the same time the former president seemed to think he had become bigger than the party in which he had spent his entire career.

Taft and his supporters responded by putting party success at a lower premium than their personal feelings. In the face of a united Democratic Party, only Roosevelt had a good chance of keeping the White House in Republican hands in 1912. To conservative Republicans that meant accepting all or part of the New Nationalism and its expansion of government power. They were unwilling to do so, and the defeat of Roosevelt transcended any temporary party success as their ultimate goal.

Roosevelt's campaign got off to a rocky start. He made his initial speech to the Ohio Constitutional Convention, calling for the recall (or review) of state judicial decisions through popular elections. The rulings of the courts would be subject to the will of the people as expressed at the ballot box. In the early twentieth century Republican conservatives held the state and federal courts in high esteem as bulwarks against the forces of popular reform and radicalism. To suggest that what judges decided could be overturned in an election was heresy. Many moderate Republicans shrank from endorsing Roosevelt on those grounds alone.

With time slipping by and much organizational work to be done, the Roosevelt forces had to devise a way to offset the impression, fostered by Charles Hilles and the Taft headquarters, that the president was gaining delegates every day and moving toward a first-ballot nomination. The Roosevelt campaign decided to challenge the delegates chosen from southern states where Taft was amassing a big lead. Although the Roosevelt men knew that the president would likely end up with most of those delegates, putting them under challenge disguised Roosevelt's predicament. In the newspapers, where running counts of delegates appeared daily, readers saw Roosevelt and Taft with roughly the same number of delegates and a larger number in the undecided category. The national convention would have to decide the results.

To demonstrate how popular he was with the rank-and-file Republican base, Roosevelt called for presidential preference primaries to determine what party members thought about the nomination contest. These elections allowed Republican voters to designate the delegates for the states rather than going through the system of party conventions. Six states decided to have primaries, and these encounters, to be held in April and May, were Roosevelt's main hope. Meanwhile, the president continued to accumulate delegates.

With the nomination set to slip away unless he stopped Taft's momentum, Roosevelt went out on the campaign trail at the end of March. He won the primary in Illinois and picked up fifty-nine delegates. He added another sixty-seven in Pennsylvania and won victories in Maine, Nebraska, and Oregon in state conventions. Suddenly Roosevelt had the advantage. As the campaign heated up, all vestiges of Taft and Roosevelt's onetime friendship disappeared. Roosevelt charged that Taft had no real support beyond what he could acquire through patronage. Otherwise, as he said in Omaha, Nebraska, on April 17, "Mr. Taft's strength would be trivial and indeed negligible in the present contest." He claimed that Taft followed "a policy of flabby indecision and helpless acquiescence in the wrongdoing of the crooked boss and crooked financier."[40]

Taft responded that Roosevelt had failed to give him a "square deal." In Lowell, Massachusetts, he announced, "I was a man of straw but I have been a man of straw long enough; every man who has blood in his body and who has been misrepresented as I have is forced to fight." Or, as Taft said on another occasion, "Even a rat in a corner will fight." Taft warned that once the two-term tradition was breached, Roosevelt would want to serve "as many terms as his natural life would permit."[41]

After the primary battles, Roosevelt had 278 delegates and had received 1,157,397 votes from Republicans. Taft had polled 716,761 votes and had 78 delegates. La Follette trailed with 351,013 votes and 36 delegates. Other delegates were selected in party caucuses and state conventions. On the eve of the convention, Roosevelt had 411 committed votes, Taft had 201, and La Follette had 36. Of the remaining delegates, there were 166 counted as "uninstructed" (meaning they were not pledged openly to any candidate and could vote as they pleased). Another 254 were contested. Actually, Taft could count on most of the "uninstructed" votes, including the large delegation from New York State, because party leaders there, while pro-Taft, wanted to preserve their bargaining power. How the contests were decided would determine which candidate had the 540 delegates needed for the nomination.

The Republican National Committee met in Chicago during the early days of June to resolve the contest. Taft supporters controlled the panel, and they allocated 235 delegates to the president and 19 to Roosevelt. On the merits, Taft was entitled to at least 200 of the southern delegates that the Roosevelt forces had challenged in early 1912. The president's allies in the South had followed the rules and outworked the Roosevelt backers in the region. For Roosevelt's part, he deserved about 30 more delegates than he received. Had he won those seats, Roosevelt might have impaired Taft's control of the convention, but he would not have had a majority of the convention behind him.

Roosevelt convinced himself that he had won a majority of the delegates. He either did not remember or forgot that the contests in the South had been a pro forma exercise. Nor did he think back to the 1908 GOP convention when the national committee, with his endorsement, had acted in the same way to secure Taft's first nomination. As the national committee in 1912 seated Taft delegates from the key states of Arizona, California, Texas, and Washington, states where Roosevelt had a strong case, the former president concluded that Taft was stealing a nomination that belonged to his challenger.

Faced with what he deemed to be outright theft, Roosevelt decided to go to Chicago in defiance of political convention. He was also making plans for a third-party race if that became necessary. "I have absolutely no affiliation with any party," he wrote the week before the convention started. Roosevelt's loyalty to the Republicans had frayed to such an extent that only a nomination to lead the party would keep him in the fold.[42]

The national convention in 1912 was thus a crucial event in the history of the Republicans. The political humorist Finley Peter Dunne depicted his main character, Mr. Dooley, predicting in a parody of an Irish dialect what would happen when the Republicans assembled. It would be "a combynation iv th' Chicago fire, Saint Bartholomew's massacree, the battle iv th' Boyne, th' life iv Jesse James, an' th' night iv th' big wind." The conclave exceeded such expectations. Roosevelt delegates shouted "Steam roller" and "Liar, liar" at the Taft forces. One Taft supporter recalled that "a tension pervaded the Coliseum breathing the general feeling that a parting of the ways was imminent."[43]

Roosevelt appeared on June 17, the night before the Republicans kicked off the proceedings. He told supporters in the Chicago auditorium that "a great moral issue" faced the party. He was entitled to sixty or eighty more delegates than he had received, and the nomination was being stolen from his hands. To prevent fraud, only the delegates whose seats were not in question should be allowed to vote. That would give the former president a majority of the delegates and control of the convention. Assailing Taft in a bitter manner, he then told his audience, "Fearless of the future, unheeding of our individual fates; with unflinching hearts and undimmed eyes; we stand at Armageddon, and we battle for the Lord."[44]

It made for wonderful political theater, but it did not change the hard reality that the Taft men had control of the machinery of the convention. As a result, the president's forces resolved to beat back all efforts to block his nomination. The Roosevelt bloc first sought to elect a friendly politician, the governor of Wisconsin, as temporary chairman of the convention. Instead, Elihu Root was named to the post by a vote of 558 to 501. The votes of Senator La Follette and his delegates helped to block Roosevelt and secure the victory for Root.

Next came the attempt by the Roosevelt contingent to have seventy-two of their delegates seated in place of those pledged to Taft. That initiative went down by 567 to 507. There was still a possibility that Roosevelt could win the nomination. Taft's position was not secure. Had Roosevelt been able to unite with the La Follette delegates and other potential defectors, he might have prevailed. In any case, there was always a chance for a compromise candidate such as Governor Herbert S. Hadley of Missouri. Roosevelt made it clear, however, that he was not going to back down and allow someone other than himself to be nominated.

Instead, Roosevelt had decided to bolt the party. He and his supporters discussed how to organize a third party and raise enough money to make it work. In the meantime, he issued a statement to the convention that accused it of seating "fraudulent delegates" and said it was "in no proper sense any longer a Republican convention." Thus, he instructed his delegates to sit mute and let the proceedings go forward. That made things easy for Taft, who was nominated on the first ballot with 561 votes to 107 for Roosevelt and another 41 votes for La Follette. The party platform said that the Republicans were "a party of advanced and constructive statesmanship." The document promised social justice and praised courts as the guardians of the rights of the people. The party had been "genuinely and always a party of progress; it has never been either stationary or reactionary."[45]

While Roosevelt went off to organize a third party, the Republicans were left to contemplate their situation. Unless the Democrats slipped badly, chances for a Republican victory in the fall seemed remote. For the Republicans who opposed Roosevelt, his departure from the party was what mattered. The important question was who retained control of the party, and on that point the regulars (as the Taft partisans styled themselves) felt secure that they had prevailed.

There was enough blame to go around for everyone in the 1912 debacle. La Follette had allowed his personal ambitions to stymie progressive chances to nominate the only candidate with a chance to win. President Taft, although likely to lose in the fall, pursued his candidacy against all odds. He, too, prevented any kind of compromise candidate from emerging. Taft was an honest man, but in the heat of the nomination campaign, he made deals with some of the shadiest individuals among the party's conservatives to ensure his own success. The Republican notion that no one was bigger than the party was nowhere to be found in 1912.

Most of the onus for the disaster was on Theodore Roosevelt. He began the race for the Republican nomination with the unspoken assumption that he would follow the rules of the party if he won and reserved the right to bolt if he lost. At no time did Roosevelt think through what he would do in the unlikely (to him) event that he lost. In the most basic sense, Roosevelt never had a majority of the delegates at the convention, so the nomination was never his to lose. What Roosevelt could not admit to himself was that Taft had proven the better politician in the nomination contest.

The Republicans torn apart. In this Udo Keppler cartoon from 1912, Theodore Roosevelt tries to drag the Republican elephant into a pool marked "Teddyism" while Taft and the conservatives seek to hold the elephant back. Library of Congress, LC-DIG-ppmsca-27865.

Roosevelt's loss dealt a serious blow to the Republicans that went beyond the results in 1912. His belief in social progress, his willingness to accept change, and his eagerness to engage national problems imparted an energy to Republican affairs that the party needed. His absence made the GOP less receptive to the issues that came with regulating an industrial nation. Although the party talked of its devotion to progress, its emphasis was more on party unity, political caution, and conservative ideas. A certain degree of stagnation and rigidity had crept into Republican thought and governed how the party dealt with national issues for the three decades that followed.

In the months after the convention, Republicans watched as Roosevelt formed the Progressive Party in August and launched a wide-ranging campaign on behalf of his reform ideas and against Woodrow Wilson and the New Freedom. The Republicans were relegated to the periphery of this exciting contest. Observing the tradition that an incumbent president not campaign for the White House, Taft made only a few nonpartisan appearances. With defeat likely in November, party contributors closed their wallets. The general sentiment among the Republican faithful was: "We can't elect Taft and we must do anything to elect Wilson so as to defeat Roosevelt."[46]

A difficult and painful year for the Republican Party finally ended on November 5, 1912. The voters elected Woodrow Wilson in a Democratic sweep. The winner received 435 electoral votes from forty states. Roosevelt garnered 88 electoral votes from six states, and Taft trailed with 8 electoral votes from Vermont and Utah. The Democrats won control of both houses of Congress.

Yet amid the wreckage, there was Republican hope. Wilson was a minority president with only 41.9 percent of the popular vote. Roosevelt and Taft had 27.4 and 23.2 percent, respectively, and the Socialist, Eugene V. Debs, got almost 3 percent. If they remained united, the Republicans were still the majority party. However, in a two-man race against either Roosevelt or Taft, Wilson would likely have been the winner because of his party's increased strength after 1904 and the Republican division. In the long run, the Republicans were likely to win back some of the progressives who had left with Roosevelt and regain their position as the leading challenger to the Democrats. Meanwhile, most of the Republicans shared the conclusion of a party regular. "If the Republican party is to have a future, it must be on conservative lines; it must be the great conservative party of the nation."[47] The eight years of Wilson's presidency would test the validity of that judgment.

6

Republicans during the Wilson Years,
1913–1921

IN 1912, THE REPUBLICANS nominated William Howard Taft for a second term. After his defeat, Taft went on to become the chief justice of the United States. Four years later, the party selected Charles Evans Hughes to run against Woodrow Wilson. After his loss, Hughes became secretary of state and then the chief justice in 1930. In 1920, the Republicans nominated Senator Warren G. Harding of Ohio, who won a landslide victory in the fall campaign. In his brief administration, Harding would go on to be rated one of the worst presidents in the country's history.

How did the Republican Party that had nominated two such intelligent and distinguished candidates as Taft and Hughes decide to select a genial second-rater such as Harding? The political logic behind Harding's victory in 1920 revealed much about the transformation of the Republicans during the presidential terms of their hated rival, Woodrow Wilson. In those eight years, the Republicans turned away from the moderate progressive reform impulses of Theodore Roosevelt and emerged as the conservative party it would remain for the rest of the twentieth century and beyond.

Their 1912 defeat left the Republicans in a temporary state of confusion and disarray. After sixteen years of national power, they lost control of the presidency and the Congress at the same time. They also faced the bitter legacy of the divisive rupture between Roosevelt and Taft. While they might have some confidence that the Progressive Party would soon collapse, no one could be certain Roosevelt and his allies would fail in their attempt to supplant the Grand Old Party. Republicans could only hope that Wilson would repeat the mistakes of Grover Cleveland and that Democratic failure would provide a Republican opening. As Joseph G. Cannon put it, in his state and elsewhere "the party landed in Purgatory, from which according to orthodox teaching there is an escape. We have to be thankful that we didn't land in that other place from which it is said there is no escape."[1]

The general Republican attitude toward the new president was one of suspicion and more than a little contempt. Wilson's shift from Democratic conservatism to a more progressive stance between 1908 and 1910 struck many Republicans as evidence of inconsistency and expediency. The president's condescension toward those with whom he disagreed also grated on Republican sensibilities. His status as a minority president in terms of popular vote share led some Republicans to wonder about his legitimacy. However, the GOP learned that Wilson was a good politician with a shrewd sense of public moods.

In the aftermath of the Chicago convention, some committed progressives wanted to rewrite party rules to institute presidential preference primaries and reduce the influence of the southern delegates. These initiatives attracted ample newspaper attention during the early months of 1913 but did not lead to any important shifts in party practices. The consensus was to leave things as they were and wait for Wilson to slip up.

Wilson did not oblige his opposition. During his first year, he and the Democrats in Congress passed the Underwood Tariff, which reduced rates on imports and put an income tax in place. The president and lawmakers then established the Federal Reserve System. Finally, the new majority in Washington enacted the Clayton Antitrust Act to regulate large corporations. The president had promised to implement his New Freedom program during the 1912 campaign, and he did so. After the Underwood Tariff passed, a magazine editor wrote that the Democrats had "done much to remove the grounds for the criticism which had been consistently and justly leveled against their party in the past, that it is incapable of positive action."[2]

The enactment of the income tax did not diminish the importance of the tariff for the Republicans in the years before World War I. Their platforms continued to stress the virtues of protection as a doctrine. While the party's commitment to this ideology would endure for another fifty years, the greater reliance on the income tax as a funding source for government shifted the debate about federal revenues away from customs duties. The changes in world trade in the years up to and after World War II also discredited protection as an economic doctrine. What had been the main tenet of Republican orthodoxy began a gradual shift away from the center of political debate.

The spectacle of an effective progressive Democrat in the White House threw Republicans off stride during 1913. Opposition to Wilson rested on several assumptions. Some Republicans viewed him as a transitory, even illegitimate presence whom they could confront with their traditional arguments. From the outset, the Republicans predicted that lowering the tariff and regulating big business would hurt the economy. Off-year elections brought gains for the party and signs of waning support for the Progressives and Roosevelt. As 1914 began, political observers detected omens of a Republican electoral revival in the making.

During the first seven months of the year, the trend seemed to be running in the Republicans' favor. A downturn in the economy, reflecting worldwide economic problems, revived memories of the 1890s, on whose economic troubles the Republicans capitalized. The party attacked Wilson for not doing more to stop unrest and violence against Americans in revolutionary Mexico, criticized him for being heavy-handed in his patronage practices, and accused him of antibusiness attitudes. Of the administration's antitrust legislation, the Republican leader in the House, James R. Mann, said, "There is nothing in the Democratic anti-trust bills that will build a fire that is now out, start a factory, or in any way encourage business."[3] The Republicans were confident of an electoral rebound during the summer of 1914 even as the news from Europe foretold an impending war among the major powers.

Throughout the first fourteen years of the twentieth century, foreign policy issues played a secondary role in American politics. The Republicans had been the exponents of empire under William McKinley. In the Roosevelt and Taft years they favored a greater degree of overseas involvement. The Democrats opposed international adventures, sought independence for the Philippines, and advocated a smaller army and navy. Although the United States had become a world power, isolationist sentiment had a strong base in both parties. Americans believed that European quarrels were far away and best avoided.

The sudden outbreak of World War I in late July and August 1914 changed all this. A century of American separation from European conflicts ended. Both sides in the war sought to placate the United States but found that their interests often demanded a confrontation with the American government. The war added a new dimension to the history of both parties. Republicans felt the effects first in the 1914 congressional elections. The Democrats capitalized on the popular desire to remain aloof from the conflagration then engulfing Europe. The president said he would not campaign for Democratic candidates because of the crisis and confined himself to public statements that labeled the Republican Party "utterly unserviceable as an instrument of reform." Democratic Party managers, meanwhile, proclaimed, "War in the East! Peace in the West! Thank God for Wilson!" The nation was expected to rally around the president, and if the Republicans did not do so, they risked being depicted as unpatriotic. That was a new position for the GOP, and one they resented, especially coming from Wilson and the Democrats they had so often criticized.[4]

The outcome of the voting still favored the Republicans. They gained sixty-six seats in the House and reduced the Democratic margin to forty seats. In the Senate, where popular elections occurred for the first time, the Democrats gained five seats. The Progressives lost ten of their eighteen members and did not do well across the country. Roosevelt's third party was collapsing. Republicans were convinced that these results portended a victory in 1916.

Most of the Republicans who won in 1914, such as Boies Penrose in the Pennsylvania Senate race, were on the conservative side of the party. The future suggested that the Republicans would be the conservatives and the Democrats the progressives in partisan battles. Republicans concluded that they would have won the House but for the outbreak of war. Once again, the wily Wilson had escaped their grasp. They expected to trap him for good in 1916.

The war put unexpected strains on the Republican electoral coalition. President Wilson asked Americans to be neutral between the Allies (Great Britain, France, Russia, and later Italy) and the Central Powers (Germany, Austria-Hungary, and later Turkey). Eastern Republicans identified with the British cause, and some leaders, such as Roosevelt and Elihu Root, even thought that the United States should intervene to ensure an Allied victory. German Americans, strong in the Middle West, supported their fatherland and wanted true neutrality or even an anti-British stance. They regarded Wilson as anti-German and looked to the Republicans to sustain their cause. Most Americans, whatever their point of view, believed that the country should not enter the war. Republicans of a progressive bent contended that only big business and Wall Street would gain from such hostilities.

As Theodore Roosevelt moved away from the Progressive Party in 1915, he did so in large part because of his unhappiness with Wilson's neutrality policy and his hatred for the president. In Roosevelt's mind, these considerations outweighed any effort Wilson might be making to enact elements of the progressive agenda. Wilson was practicing cowardly diplomacy that placed him in a class with other inept Democrats such as Thomas Jefferson and James Buchanan.

When a German submarine sank the British liner *Lusitania* on May 7, 1915, Roosevelt asserted that the United States should have declared war on the Germans for an act of piracy. He ridiculed Wilson's statement that a nation could be "too proud to fight" in such a crisis. Throughout the months that followed, Roosevelt kept up his private and public criticism of the president. His ideas won the backing of Republicans sympathetic to the Allies. Much of the country worried, however, that Roosevelt would take the United States into the European war should he become president once again.[5]

During the first half of 1916, President Wilson moved the Democrats leftward in order to secure the votes of former members of the Progressive Party. His efforts included the nomination of Louis D. Brandeis to the Supreme Court, support for a bill regulating child labor, and endorsement of federal loans for farmers. Wilson had also come out for limited woman suffrage. The Democrats were thus expanding the role of government and identifying themselves with social reform. Franklin K. Lane, Wilson's secretary of the interior, exulted at the change. "The Republican party was for half a century a constructive party and the Democratic party was the party of negation and complaint. We have taken the play from them. The Democratic party has become the party of construction." Republicans would have dissented from this assessment, but Wilson's platform of peace, progressivism, and wartime prosperity would prove to have a powerful appeal at the polls.[6]

In 1916, the Republicans needed to select a presidential candidate who could satisfy both the Roosevelt and Taft partisans, the advocates of neutrality and the proponents of the Allies, and the progressives as well as the conservatives. None of the declared candidates in 1915–1916 displayed much strength along all these lines. There was scant enthusiasm for Senator Albert B. Cummins of Iowa or Robert M. La Follette once again. Elihu Root was strong in the East but was unpopular in the Middle West.

Roosevelt wanted the nomination to defeat the hated Wilson. He knew, however, that he could win the nod from the Republicans only if, in his words, "the country has in its mood something of the heroic." Roosevelt criticized German Americans for disloyalty, and he repeated his belief in the need for intervention in speech after speech. He sought the nomination for himself or at worst the selection of a strong anti-Wilson alternative. The more Roosevelt spoke, the more evident it was that he lacked influence and support from Republican voters outside of the East.[7]

The obvious answer for the Republicans and their electoral dilemma seemed to be Supreme Court Justice Charles Evans Hughes. He had been a progressive governor of New York who got to Albany after he exposed wrongdoing on the part of insurance companies. In 1906, he defeated the notorious publisher William Randolph Hearst to win the governorship, and he had made a speech attacking William Jennings Bryan that politicians remembered as a devastating performance. Taft had named him to the high court in

1910, and his judicial duties kept him out of the fray in 1912, when he turned down overtures to be a compromise candidate.

The wife of a Democratic member of the House remarked in June 1916, "Who knows what opinions lurk beneath Hughes' primly parted hair." The last presidential candidate of a major party to wear a beard, Hughes appeared to be a moderate reformer who had no allegiances to political bosses, an ideal combination for the Republicans. Once he won the nomination, however, he would have to take on questions, especially those relating to the war and neutrality, on which the party was divided. As with the Democratic nomination of Alton B. Parker in 1904, a jurist detached from partisan combat struck many Republicans as the best answer to the political challenge that Woodrow Wilson posed.[8]

The Republicans and Progressives met in Chicago in early June in separate conventions, though they kept in constant touch about their activities. Hughes was nominated on the third ballot, and Charles W. Fairbanks of Indiana, Roosevelt's vice president in the second term, once again served as running mate. Roosevelt's candidacy was rebuffed, and the dejected former president told his sister, "We are passing through a thick streak of yellow in our national life." He promised to support Hughes if the candidate agreed with Roosevelt's attitude toward foreign policy.[9]

The last bearded presidential candidate, Charles Evans Hughes left the Supreme Court and won the GOP nomination only to lose a close contest to Woodrow Wilson in 1916. He addressed a large crowd just before the votes were cast. Library of Congress, LC-DIG-ggbain-23176.

The Republican platform tried to attract progressive voters while also reflecting the conservative temperament of the delegates and the party. It reaffirmed the commitment to the protective tariff, declaring that "the Underwood Tariff is a complete failure in every respect." They came out for woman suffrage and a child labor law. While the party favored "rigid supervision and strict regulation" of railroads and "great corporations," Republicans believed "in encouraging American business as it believes in and will seek to advance all American interests." On foreign affairs and the war, it endorsed a "firm, consistent and courageous foreign policy" as well as "a strict and honest neutrality" without specifying how those contradictory goals were to be realized.[10]

Roosevelt maintained control of the Progressive Convention until Hughes was selected. He then turned down the nomination of the party he had created four years earlier. In so doing, Roosevelt made sure that his former colleagues would not designate a candidate who might cripple Hughes. The Progressive Party expired on June 22 when Roosevelt told them that they should endorse the Republican ticket. Men who had supported Roosevelt in good faith went away bitter and disillusioned. While some Progressives accepted Roosevelt's decision to back Hughes, others did not, and they gravitated toward Wilson.

With Hughes as their candidate, the Republicans again sought to be as progressive as they could to suit voter attitudes in 1916 while not relinquishing their conservative stance on domestic issues. For Hughes that choice meant that he would have to move rightward to please the party's base or move left by accepting reform ideas while criticizing Wilson's methods. Foreign policy posed even more delicate problems for the Republican nominee. Hughes could not support Roosevelt's aggressive program for aiding the Allies without alienating German Americans and letting the Democrats take over the peace issue. If he appealed to the German Americans and other Americans distrustful of the Allies, then the Democrats would assail his patriotism and imply that he was not being truly neutral.

Wilson and his party made the problem more acute for Hughes when they adopted the slogan "He Kept Us Out of War." The Democrats stressed peace, prosperity, and reform as the major issues in their national convention. Under Wilson's leadership in 1915–1916, the Democrats had moved leftward to embrace an activist national government on such issues as farm credits and child labor (but not race relations). The president had dropped much of his earlier suspicion of government as a means of pursuing social justice and identified himself with progressive goals.

As the Republicans struggled with a changing opposition, they realized that Hughes was not the exciting candidate they had hoped he would be.

His acceptance speech did not inspire voters, and he did not do much better in a campaign tour across the country in August. Hughes focused his attacks on Wilson's sometimes mediocre appointments to federal offices and the president's mixed record on the civil service. These sallies did not come across as riveting. When the Republican candidate touched on the tariff, he pleased party regulars but did little to win over the progressives. In contrast, the Democrats stressed the prosperity that had come with orders for war materials from the Allies, and thus defused the traditional Republican association of the Democrats with hard times.

The Republican campaign organization, usually a positive element in the party's winning races, proved weak and ineffective. William Willcox, the man Hughes chose as national chairman, was a dud. A British journalist told his superiors in London, "No American campaign that I have seen has been worse managed than the Republican one," and this result occurred even though "the Republicans have lots of cash, the Democrats not much."[11]

Every move that the Hughes campaign managers made seemed to backfire. When they organized a campaign train tour of women who had supported Hughes because of his endorsement of female suffrage, the wealth of these surrogate speakers became a liability. Since some of the participants were socialites, the Democrats dubbed it the "Billionaires Special." Hughes himself slipped up when he appeared to snub Hiram Johnson, a Senate candidate and popular governor in the key state of California. As one reporter argued, "Hughes is dropping icicles from his beard all over the west and will return to New York clean shaven."[12]

Finding a way to distinguish himself from Wilson on the war issue bedeviled Hughes throughout the campaign. The German Americans, united in their dislike of Wilson, seemed a likely source of Republican votes. To gain their allegiance without providing opportunities to the Democrats was a challenge Hughes could not master. The candidate met with German American leaders, and his speeches emphasized the need for American neutrality. But neither Wilson nor Roosevelt would let the Republican candidate finesse the issue.

Roosevelt took to the stump himself to attack Wilson's foreign policy and Germany. His language was harsh and his readiness for war with Germany evident. In one speech, Roosevelt alluded to Wilson's summer residence at Shadow Lawn, New Jersey. "There should be shadows enough at Shadow Lawn; the shadows of men, women, and children who have risen from the ooze of the ocean bottom and from graves in foreign lands" where Wilson's policies had put them. When Hughes did not criticize Roosevelt's rhetoric, there were defections among German American voters in the Middle West.[13]

Wilson and the Democrats exploited Hughes's vulnerability on the loyalty issue. The president said, "The certain prospect of the success of the Republican party is that we shall be drawn, in one form or another, into the embroilments of the European war." The implication that the Republicans were both bellicose and somehow unpatriotic rankled leaders such as Henry Cabot Lodge and Theodore Roosevelt who had long regarded themselves as the partisan arbiters of American values. Hughes never found a way to counter the impression that Theodore Roosevelt would influence him to take the United States into the conflict.[14]

While foreign policy dominated the campaign, Republicans and Democrats also clashed on domestic questions and the role of the federal government. In September, Wilson pushed through Congress the Adamson Act to avert a national railroad strike. The measure gave the railroad workers the eight-hour workday they had long sought instead of the ten- to twelve-hour workday common in the industry. Tilting toward the labor unions struck Republicans as outrageous. Hughes and party attacked the president for pandering to a special interest group. The Republican candidate said he "would not submit to dictation from any power in the country, no matter what the consequences."[15]

The campaign became bitter and ugly. Republicans charged that Wilson was pro-southern, and the party's orators again waved the bloody shirt among Midwestern voters. Gossip circulated regarding Wilson's second marriage in 1915 to Edith Bolling Galt and the president's earlier relationship with a woman named Mary Hulbert Peck. When these stories got back to the White House, Wilson became even less inclined to cooperate with the Republicans. Since he would have to work with the opposition during World War I, this reluctance proved politically damaging.

By the time the election neared, the odds seemed to favor a Wilson victory, although everyone sensed that the contest would be close. On election night, the initial returns from the Northeast and Middle West disclosed a Republican trend. Hughes carried New York, Pennsylvania, New Jersey, and the rest of the Northeast, with the exception of a narrow loss (fifty-six votes) in New Hampshire. Michigan, Indiana, and Illinois also fell into the Hughes column. From the Middle West region only Ohio stayed with Wilson. It seemed as if Hughes would win. Then the tallies from the West indicated gains for Wilson in usually Republican states such as Kansas and Nebraska. In an age of paper ballots and slower communication, several days went by with the result in doubt. When California's late returns went for Wilson three days after the polling, it was clear that Hughes had been defeated.

The final results attested to a nation very much divided in its partisan allegiance. Wilson had amassed 9.1 million votes to carry thirty states with 277 electoral votes. Hughes won 8.5 million popular votes in eighteen states with 254 electoral votes. Almost 60 percent of eligible voters in the North went to the voting booth, though this was another election in which participation fell below nineteenth-century levels. The Republicans did not recapture the Senate, but only the votes of independents and Socialists kept them from retaking control of the House.

Although Wilson and the Democrats had won two consecutive terms, making him the only Democrat since Andrew Jackson to do so, the Republican electoral dominance established in the 1890s would soon reestablish itself. The president had brought together themes of prosperity, progressivism, and peace in just the right mix to stave off the Grand Old Party and Hughes. If any one of these disparate elements turned in favor of the Republicans, they were likely to regain the White House in 1920. With Roosevelt as their anticipated leader and the strife of 1912 in the past, the Republicans could look forward with optimism. As it happened, Wilson's political skills and the run of good luck he had enjoyed up to 1916 deserted him soon after the election. Within a few months, the fragile Democratic coalition started to collapse.

The campaign left abundant hard feelings between the parties. Wilson believed that the Republicans had smeared him with attacks on his private life. Republican leaders trusted the president even less than they had before the election. Henry Cabot Lodge contended that Wilson had made "a sordid and base appeal" to defecting Republicans who had been influenced by the peace issue.[16] The president and the senator had had a bitter exchange of charges in the waning days of the race that left both convinced of the other's dishonesty. The perception among Republicans that Wilson was president only because of a dishonest campaign and manipulation of demagoguery shaped their strategy during the nasty and partisan warfare in which both parties engaged during the ensuing four years. The Republicans granted Wilson power, not legitimacy.

Within a few months after the 1916 election, the United States was drawn into the world war as the Germans launched unrestricted submarine warfare at the end of January 1917. President Wilson had tried to mediate a resolution of the conflict in December, but his efforts had failed. By April the administration decided to seek a declaration of war against Germany. Republicans supported this step in public. In private, they were scathing about Wilson. Lodge said that the president "lowered the American spirit and confused the popular mind" by coming out for war after he had earlier sought "peace without victory" as the only sensible solution to the conflict. Theodore Roosevelt was more blunt: "Wilson and his crowd should be in the Boche trenches."[17]

Wilson indicated that as far as Republicans were concerned the war would be conducted as a Democratic effort. Wilson thought that he was being bipartisan in his approach to the conflict. After all, he named Elihu Root to a diplomatic assignment to aid the democratic government of Russia during the summer of 1917. William Howard Taft served on the War Labor Board. In fact, Republicans did not regard these subsidiary assignments as credible examples of taking their party into the counsels of government in a serious way. It was not clear just what Wilson was supposed to do to satisfy the opposition, but he fell short, in the minds of the GOP hierarchy, of employing an even-handed policy.

For many Republicans, a decisive case of Wilson's aloof attitude was his reaction to Theodore Roosevelt's efforts in the spring of 1917 to raise a volunteer division to fight in France as he had done with the Rough Riders during the war with Spain. On military grounds, the aging Roosevelt, already blind in one eye, was an unlikely warrior. The former president saw his major role as a booster of Allied morale. He told friends, including Elihu Root, that if went to France, he did not expect to return alive. Root quipped that if Roosevelt could give Wilson that assurance, the president would probably let him go. The administration turned down the offer, and Wilson had the better case on the merits. In addition to his physical limits, Roosevelt would likely have been a difficult subordinate at best. The exclusion of Roosevelt and the failure to assign Leonard Wood, a Republican general, to an overseas command enhanced the impression within the Grand Old Party that the president had no real use for Republican help.

Amid the mobilization, social issues also needed resolution. By 1917, the momentum behind woman suffrage had intensified. Its proponents contended that democracy should include all the population without regard to gender. The Democrats were divided. Many southerners opposed an expansion of the franchise that might one day include African Americans. The Republicans provided more substantial support for suffrage in Congress. The Grand Old Party also included women in its affairs to a greater degree than the Democrats. Women such as Ruth Hanna McCormick, daughter of Mark Hanna, and Mary Garrett Hay of New York sought a more significant role in party affairs.

During 1917, the Republicans gained ground as problems vexed Wilson and his party on the home front. The Democratic coalition frayed, and the

Republicans reaped the political rewards. Congress passed the Lever Act, which contained language allowing the president to fix prices on certain farm products. The goal was to encourage production and stem inflation. In the normally Republican grain states of the Middle West, some of which had gone for Wilson the previous year, farmers looked to receive higher returns for their crops and chafed at the prospect of price controls. Southern Democrats, using their dominance of congressional committees, made sure that no regulations limited cotton prices. When Wilson fixed the price of wheat at $2.20 a bushel, farmers grumbled that they were being denied profits while cotton growers went unregulated.

Republicans also denounced the tax policies of the Democratic Congress. Its leaders believed that Americans in the cities with high incomes should bear the cost of the war while their rural constituents should be less burdened. This sectional disparity struck Republicans as unfair, and their supporters in the prosperous Northeast concurred. The repressive policies toward those who opposed the war rebounded against the administration. While Republicans applauded the hard line on peace advocates and socialists, they resented it when the government criticized Roosevelt and others who wanted more vigorous prosecution of the war.

Although the tide of events ran toward the Grand Old Party in 1918, the Republican organization still reflected the tensions of 1912 and 1916. In February 1918, the Republican National Committee convened to select a new chair who would replace the holdover from the Hughes campaign. The front runner appeared to be John T. Adams of Iowa, but he had the liability of pro-German statements he had made during the period of American neutrality. After a close vote of twenty-four to twenty-one, the party turned to Will H. Hays of Indiana. Not yet forty, the slight Hays styled himself as "100 percent American." After graduation from Wabash College, he had risen through the ranks of the Hoosier Republican Party until he chaired the state's delegation to the 1916 national convention. His efforts enabled Hughes to carry the state, and he had endorsed the return of Theodore Roosevelt and the Progressives to the Republican fold. His selection, wrote Harold Ickes, a former Progressive, "has paved the way for a reconstructed party organization that can win and hold the confidence of all members of the party."[18]

Hays proved to be just what the party needed in a national chairman. His aggressive tactics restored party morale as the November 1918 contests neared. Hays emphasized Republican unity in all his pronouncements. "Our party has no yesterdays," he wrote; "We do not care how a man voted in 1912, 1914, or 1916, nor his reasons for so doing." He contended instead that the

Republicans were doing more to support the Wilson administration in fighting the war than many of the Democrats. As the campaign got under way, Hays proclaimed, "Every Republican vote cast is another nail in the Kaiser's coffin, every Republican Congressman elected is another stone piled on his tomb."[19]

The Republicans bridled when Wilson sought to identify the administration and the Democrats with the war and national patriotism. During a special election in Wisconsin for a Senate seat, Wilson attacked the Republican candidate, Irvine Lenroot, for his "questionable support of the dignity and rights of the country on test occasions." Vice President Thomas Riley Marshall claimed that the Lenroot campaign relied on the "sewage" vote of German sympathizers in the state. This episode unified Republicans, and Lenroot won the race. In another sign of growing Republican cohesion, Taft and Roosevelt staged a well-publicized, if somewhat bogus, reconciliation in late May 1918.[20]

From the spring of 1918 onward, the Republicans went on the offensive. Wilson espoused the lofty position that "politics is adjourned," but both parties continued their partisan sniping with abandon. Theodore Roosevelt attacked Wilson for "inefficiency, incompetence, hesitation and delay." Chairman Hays denounced "the socialistic tendencies of the present administration." The administration's tax policies and reliance on bureaucracies for managing the food supply and overseeing American industry all proved tempting areas for Republican criticism.[21]

As the election neared, Allied fortunes on the battlefield improved, and the Germans asked for peace terms. The Republicans dropped their criticism of Wilson's war tactics and demanded a harsh settlement for the beaten foe. "We stand not for a Democratic peace but an American peace," Roosevelt said in October. With the Republicans maintaining that only they could keep the Democrats and Wilson in check with control of Congress, the president concluded that he should make a personal appeal to Americans to cast their votes for Democratic candidates.[22]

On October 25, 1918, Wilson addressed the nation. Republicans had "unquestionably been pro-war, but they have been anti-administration." To elect Republicans, Wilson said, would be seen "on the other side of the war as a repudiation of my leadership." With its implication that the Republicans had been less than helpful in the war effort, the statement sparked Republican outrage. "The President makes the demand of unconditional surrender upon the voters of the United States. We asked for meat and he gives us a stone," wrote Charles D. Hilles, Taft's former secretary.[23]

The Republicans emerged victorious on November 5, 1918, in one of the most important congressional elections of the first half of the twentieth century. The Democrats suffered the losses to be expected in the sixth year of a two-term presidency, and the delicate majority they had assembled since 1910 disappeared. After the votes were counted, the Republicans had 240 seats in the House to 190 for their rivals. Republicans picked up six seats in the Senate to gain a 49 to 47 majority. Most of the contested Senate races broke for the Republicans in the last weeks of the campaign. The issues of sectionalism and wheat prices cost the Democrats twenty-one House seats in the farm states. The Wilson coalition collapsed into bickering, and the Republican coalition of the 1890s reappeared. For the moment, the voters had had enough of higher taxes, government regulation, labor unrest, and progressive reform.

The 1918 elections were more than just a sweeping Republican success. For the party they represented a triumph of the conservatives after the turmoil that began at the end of Theodore Roosevelt's presidency. The decision that William Howard Taft and his allies made in 1912 to retain control of the machinery of the party had long-term consequences. The conservatives had the power to enforce their agenda as progressive Republicans faded away in the face of Wilson's activist agenda. When the Democrats moved left under Wilson, the Republicans took up a conservative posture on regulation of business, the role of taxation, and the size of government that remained in place for the rest of the century. The Democrats had not yet decided to become the party of liberal reform and government regulation; that would not occur until the ascension of Franklin D. Roosevelt in the early New Deal. The position of the Republicans on the right side of the political spectrum was now one of the defining points of American partisan life.

The armistice brought World War I to an end six days after the 1918 election. The nation turned its attention to the problem of moving from war to peace amid concern over the way in which President Wilson would negotiate a peace treaty to provide for a lasting settlement. While the 1918 election had been hard fought and bitter, it proved only a prelude to a more impassioned struggle over the League of Nations that defined the foreign policy positions of both parties for decades.

One major figure in the history of the Republican Party did not live to see the outcome of the battle between Woodrow Wilson and the Republican Senate over the League. On January 6, 1919, Theodore Roosevelt died in his sleep at his home in Oyster Bay, New York. Roosevelt was a controversial part of Republican history, and his legacy is still debated within the Grand Old Party. For all of his vigorous nationalism and defense of American interests overseas, Roosevelt also believed that Republicans needed to address the nation's domestic problems. Had he lived, Roosevelt would have had to come to terms with the conservative tone of the party after 1918. Perhaps his anti-Wilson sentiments would have kept him loyal as he had not been in 1912. In any case, the Republicans had to look for another presidential candidate in 1920.

The Republicans found the political environment even more favorable to their cause in the eighteen months that followed the 1918 balloting. Control of Congress enabled them to expose the failings of the Democratic administration. Meanwhile, Wilson himself pursued policies that infuriated the Republicans and created rifts in his own coalition.

President Wilson sought to realize his dream of a League of Nations in 1919, but he did so in a high-handed manner that intensified Republican hard feelings. When he traveled to Paris to negotiate the peace treaty, he refused to bring any prominent Republicans in his delegation. Had he decided to include any senators in his diplomatic party, he would have been compelled to ask Senator Henry Cabot Lodge, the new chair of the Foreign Relations Committee, to go with him. Since Lodge and Wilson hated each other with a passion that was rare at any time in American politics, inviting Lodge was not an option. As he had done during the fighting, Wilson decided not to add other prominent Republicans such as Taft or Elihu Root to his team. The president regarded both men as hopeless partisans and his intellectual inferiors. The man he did invite to join his negotiating delegation, Henry White, was a veteran Republican diplomat but not a partisan.

While Wilson was in Europe, the Republicans delayed action on key bills in a lame-duck Congress from December 1918 through March 4, 1919. Since the new Congress was not scheduled to meet again until December 1919, that meant that the president would have to summon a special session where Republicans would be in control. Under the leadership of Lodge, Republican senators also circulated a "round-robin" document that insisted on changes in the proposed League of Nations before they would accept any treaty. Enough senators added their names to deny a two-thirds majority for approval of a pact. An irritated Wilson had to renegotiate some key provisions in Paris to appease his domestic critics.[24]

Wilson returned to the United States in July 1919 with the Treaty of Versailles, the central provision of which was the League of Nations. Article Ten of the treaty bound member nations to come to the assistance of any state in the organization that was the victim of aggression as the League defined it. That meant a diminished role for Congress in deciding whether the nation went to war overseas. Lodge and other Republicans called this clause an infringement of American sovereignty since it would compel possible military action without the consent of lawmakers. Lodge told his colleagues, "We would not have our country's vigor exhausted, or her moral force abated, by everlasting meddling and muddling in every quarrel, great and small, which affects the world." Most Senate Republicans shared Lodge's view to some degree. Those known as "Irreconcilables" wanted no treaty at all. Others labeled "Mild Reservationists" would accept a pact with amendments in the less binding form of reservations.[25]

Whether the Treaty of Versailles succeeded or failed depended on the competition between Wilson and Lodge for the wavering Republicans in the middle. The president tried to appeal over the heads of the senators and made a speaking tour to rouse public opinion in September 1919. By the end of month, as he spoke out for the treaty in the West, Wilson's health collapsed. He returned to Washington, where he suffered a disabling stroke on October 2. When the nation realized the severity of Wilson's condition, sentiment against the Democrats mounted. Beyond the League issue, rising prices, repeated strikes, race riots, and an anti-Communist Red Scare convinced voters that the nation was undergoing a crisis of significant magnitude. There seemed for a time to be no effective government in Washington. Rumors circulated that Wilson had gone mad and his wife was in charge. A change in political leadership seemed inevitable.

While Wilson recuperated, the League of Nations came up for a vote in the Senate. The president insisted that his treaty be approved without change. On November 19, both the treaty without amendments and the version with Lodge's reservations were defeated. The Senate made another try in March 1920 in a vote on the treaty, this time with Lodge's language. Wilson told the Democrats to oppose the deal. With the Democrats doing the president's bidding and the Irreconcilables voting no, the treaty came up seven votes short of approval. The United States stood aloof from the League and ignored its deliberations throughout the 1920s.[26]

This result did not mean that the Republicans opposed American involvement in the world for the next decade. Lodge, Root, and Charles Evans Hughes believed that the United States had to exert its power on the world stage. As secretary of state for Warren G. Harding, Hughes played a constructive and creative part in dealing with issues of European war debts, the Far East, and disarmament. A tradition of strong international power that reached back to William McKinley and Theodore Roosevelt maintained its place in the hearts and minds of eastern Republicans.

In defeating Wilson, however, Lodge also accommodated senators from the Middle West who were suspicious of world power. The arrangement that Lodge had achieved also meant the emergence of a more isolationist foreign policy position among Republicans that was skeptical of military involvement, imperialism, European diplomacy, and overseas commitments. The sense that the United States could and should play a limited role in the world established itself as political dogma in many areas of the nation's heartland where the Republicans were strong after 1920. The increasing influence of this faction in the party would have serious consequences during the rise of the dictators in the 1930s. For now, the United States and many Republicans could think of themselves as safe behind the comforting barrier of two oceans.

After their success in the League of Nations battle, the Republicans could taste victory in the fall of 1920 as they prepared to select their presidential nominee. The process by which Senator Warren G. Harding prevailed as the GOP candidate soon became the stuff of political legend. His selection, so the story went, occurred on June 11, 1920, when a cabal of conservative senatorial kingmakers gathered in a smoke-filled room and anointed a flawed Harding as the Republican choice. There was such a room, and there was a meeting with the candidate, but beyond that the legend yields to a more complex reality.

For the first time since 1888, the Republicans had no clear front runner or incumbent president to place on their ticket. There were a number of hopefuls. General Leonard Wood campaigned as the heir of Theodore Roosevelt but lacked his idol's interest in social justice. He recommended that the nation follow the advice of a clergyman who proposed that suspected Bolsheviks be sent away "in ships of stone, with sails of lead, with the wrath of God for a breeze and with hell for their first port." Frank O. Lowden was the governor of Illinois, an important state, and had ample funds from his wife's links to the Pullman railroad car millions. Neither man did well in the primary season leading up to the convention. Whatever remained of Republican progressivism was embodied by Senator Hiram Johnson of California. With only one hundred delegates, he had an outside chance at best.[27]

The fourth major candidate in the race was Warren G. Harding of Ohio. A newspaper publisher in Marion, Ohio, who was finishing his first senatorial term, Harding would be fifty-five by Election Day. Republicans warmed to the affable politician. William Allen White recalled him as a "handsome young dog, a little better than six feet tall, straight, with well-carved mobile features, a good shock of black hair, dark olive skin fine, even teeth, and an actor's mouth." No one thought of Harding as a brilliant intellect, but

Warren G. Harding, a golfing candidate relaxing under a tree, won a landslide victory over the Democrats in 1920. Library of Congress, LC-USZ62-130972.

the party had seen enough of intelligent candidates in Roosevelt, Taft, and Hughes. As the governor of Kansas put it, "I have a feeling that we have had all the superman business the party is likely to want and what the period really needs in my judgment is the man who is a product of our institutions and not the product of a peculiar period."[28]

Handsome and a pleasing orator, Harding reassured voters that he would not press for more reform in office. In his most famous statement of his placid philosophy, he avowed: "America's present need is not heroics, but healing; not nostrums, normalcy; not revolution, but restoration; not agitation, but adjustment; not surgery, but serenity; not the dramatic, but the dispassionate; not experiment, but equipoise; not submergence in internationality, but sustainment in triumphant nationality."[29]

Known only to a few intimates and his neighbors in Marion were Harding's personal failings. Although his alleged illicit romance with Nan Britton seems to have been only a product of her fertile imagination, the senator had pursued an extramarital relationship with Carrie Phillips, the wife of a friend in Marion. The romance became "a primrose detour from Main Street, which Florence Kling [Harding], the Duchess, had chosen to ignore." In his ardor

Harding had written Carrie letters that could have occasioned blackmail or embarrassment had they become public. Harding's managers, led by Harry M. Daugherty, made sure that word of these indiscretions did not reach the press and public. Harding did not do well in the Republican primaries, but his backers saw him as a logical compromise candidate after the initial balloting of the convention concluded. Daugherty touted Harding as the choice who could unite the party in victory.[30]

The Republicans met in Chicago and made a gesture toward their history of progressivism with a promise in the platform of "an enlightened measure of social and industrial justice." What that entailed was not defined. For the most part, however, conservative themes dominated the document. The Wilson administration was guilty of "complete unpreparedness for war and complete unpreparedness for peace." The platform writers attacked high taxes, promised "honest money and sound finance," and pledged they would "free business from arbitrary and unnecessary control." As for the League of Nations, the delegates endorsed "an international association of nations" as long as it was "based upon international justice." Above all, the Republicans vowed "to end executive autocracy and to restore to the people their constitutional government."[31]

The national convention unfolded according to the script of the Harding strategists. Lowden and Wood stalled in the early balloting with about three hundred delegates each. Harding trailed with only sixty delegates. By the time the convention adjourned for the night on June 11, 1920, the stalemate was evident. Rumors flew that Harding was the choice of influential senators. The candidate had been summoned to the room at the Blackstone Hotel, where he was asked if he knew of any reason why he should not be president. Aware of bogus rumors that he had African American ancestors, his dalliance with Carrie Phillips, and his weak heart, Harding nevertheless responded that he saw no reason why he could not be selected.[32]

These events did not produce a seal of approval for Harding, however, or make his nomination inevitable. For the next three ballots on June 12, the front runners remained deadlocked. After a three-hour recess, the ninth ballot saw Harding surge into the lead with 374½ votes. On the next ballot he became the nominee. Harding himself said it best. "We drew to a pair of deuces and filled." In the context of 1920, Harding made sense as a compromise candidate. He could carry Ohio, he had no serious enemies within the party, and he was a winning figure on the stump. Once again, Ohio had produced another Republican who looked like a president.[33]

Party leaders wanted to balance the selection of Harding with Senator Irvine Lenroot of Wisconsin, but the weary delegates preferred a more popular

choice, one not tainted with any links to the reform ideas of Robert M. La
Follette. During a police strike in Boston the previous year, Governor Calvin
Coolidge had proclaimed, "There is no right to strike against the public safety
by anybody, anywhere, anytime." Although Coolidge had not been instru-
mental in resolving the labor dispute, his ghostwritten words captured the
nation's conservative trend in 1919–1920. In a wave of enthusiasm, his name
was placed in nomination, and he swamped Lenroot.[34]

The Harding-Coolidge ticket faced a demoralized Democratic Party.
President Wilson had some late delusional thoughts of a third nomination,
but his friends advised him that the convention delegates would reject him.
Democrats opted for another Ohioan, the former governor James M. Cox, to

The Republicans and Radicalism, 1919. When Calvin Coolidge denounced the Boston
Police Strike in 1919, cartoonists showed him directing the Republican elephant to stamp
out radicalism. The episode won Coolidge a place on the ticket in 1920. Library of
Congress, LC-USZ62-85471.

lead the ticket. Franklin Delano Roosevelt, a distant cousin of Theodore, became the running mate. The Democrats never had a chance in light of Wilson's pervasive unpopularity. The only real question would be the size of Harding's triumph.

Rather than make an ideological appeal to the voters, the Grand Old Party sought to capitalize on the voter discontent with Wilson and the Democrats. The Harding managers wanted to assemble as many sympathizers as possible without alienating any large interest group in society. Anti-labor elements in the party found their message muted so that Harding could reach out to workingmen. Even former Progressives were given a reason to support the Republican ticket.

In 1920 women voted for the first time in a national election. The suffrage amendment had been adopted in 1919 and then ratified in the late summer of 1920. Republicans had a better claim to the credit for the adoption of the reform, since many southern Democrats had opposed the expansion of government power inherent in expanding the vote to females. The Republicans, however, had not moved as quickly as their Democratic counterparts to integrate women into the party structure. At the Republican convention, twenty-seven women were duly elected delegates; another 277 women served as alternates. Women were on committees and made half a dozen seconding speeches for presidential candidates. The party welcomed women into its ranks, and the platform contained language endorsing a number of issues important to female voters. Yet equality for women in the political operations of the Republican organization was still decades in the future.[35]

In the 1920 campaign, Republicans saw a chance to attract black votes in the North from African Americans whom the segregationist policies of the Wilson administration had alienated. Harding met with black leaders and promised a sympathetic ear for their grievances. The initiative soon encountered problems that would shape Republican efforts in this area for the next ninety years. Migration of blacks to the North during the preceding decade had begun to create large blocs of potential Republican supporters in major cities. At the same time, the movement of whites from the North to warmer southern states meant that Republican chances of making cracks in the Solid South looked more promising than they had been since Reconstruction. The dilemma was that the policies that spoke to one group put off the other. If Republicans such as Harding pledged to support measures in Congress to eradicate lynching, they risked the wrath of southern whites who would move back toward their Democratic home. Yet if they advanced policies that pleased the South, such as "lily white" Republican parties from which

African Americans were excluded, they would risk the displeasure of northern black voters.[36]

So Republicans tried to have the best of both worlds. Harding argued
in July 1920 that "the Federal government should stamp out lynching and
remove that stain from the fair name of America." The Republicans also
made a strong effort to rally black voters in Tennessee, one southern state
they thought might go for their ticket. At the same time, when Harding
appeared in the border state of Oklahoma, on October 9, a local newspaper
carried Harding's answers to questions about segregation and black voting. "You can't give one right to a white man and deny it to a black man. But
I want you to know that I do not mean that white people and black people
should be forced together in accepting their equal rights at the hands of
the nation."[37]

The race issue surfaced toward the end of the campaign when the charge
that Harding had black ancestors appeared in several places. This rumor had
been circulating in Ohio politics for years, and the Republicans responded
with a listing of Harding's family roots that said he came from "a blue-eyed
stock from New England." Afraid of a popular backlash, Democrats refused
to touch the rumor in the press, and the episode did no damage to Harding.[38]

Harding's overall campaign style looked back to McKinley's front-porch
style of 1896, and large crowds came to Marion to view the candidate. As the
election neared, demands for Harding to be seen led to tour of the Middle
West and the East. The candidate equivocated at first on the League of Nations
and then settled on a stance of strong opposition. None of these issues really
did anything to disturb the Republican march to victory, because the public
was ready for a change. The election, said Woodrow Wilson's secretary, Joseph
Tumulty, "wasn't a landslide. It was an earthquake." In one of the most sweeping
Republican victories in the party's history, Harding amassed more than sixteen million popular votes to more than nine million for Cox. Cox carried
only the Democratic South, with 127 electoral votes; Harding piled up 404
electoral votes in the rest of the country. The Republicans carried thirty-seven
states and achieved big majorities in the House and Senate.[39]

The Republicans were once again the majority party of the nation. Women
voters cast their first-time ballots for Harding. Democratic ethnic groups
such as Irish Americans and Italian Americans turned to the Grand Old Party.
Bitterness over the territorial settlements of the League of Nations produced
some of these defections. Woodrow Wilson had revived the Democrats for a
season, but the domestic disasters of his second term had reduced the party to
a minority status.

Two turbulent decades had elapsed since William McKinley stood in the receiving line at Buffalo and shook the murderous hand of his assassin. Theodore Roosevelt's two terms brought an acceptance of some government regulation as part of an enlightened conservatism for an industrial society and its problems. The exercise of national power to regulate business could be justified, as Roosevelt tried to do, as a way of staving off more radical changes. For the majority of Republicans after 1910, the more preferable course was to limit the power of government and oppose regulation. Some restraints on business could be tolerated, but not many. A place for organized labor existed in American society, but its power, it was felt, should be constrained.

As the two parties struggled with the question of how to manage an urbanized, industrial polity, the Democrats edged leftward (except on race) while the Republicans occupied the right side of the spectrum in opposition to more government power and more regulation. This pattern of political discourse proved to be enduring when it came to domestic issues for the nine decades that followed.

The task that lay ahead for Warren G. Harding and the Republicans was an imposing one. The Wilson years had left a legacy of social unrest, government debt, and popular suspicion of the political system. High taxes and an intrusive government seemed to be the legacy of a generation of progressive reforms. Instead, as the 1920s began, the Republicans looked once again to the energies of business enterprise and the individual initiative of the American people to supply what government could not.

The Age of Republican Dominance, 1921–1933

WARREN G. HARDING DIED with dramatic suddenness in the middle of his first term in August 1923, and the nation mourned. The funeral train that took his body across the United States was flanked by the grief-stricken all along the way. When the procession reached the Middle West, great crowds lined the route. In Pittsburgh, industrial workers stood crying as the train passed by. An outpouring of sorrow swept the entire country as people wept for their fallen leader. Yet within a decade the memory of Warren Gamaliel Harding would become a kind of national joke, his presidency shrouded in scandal and ineptitude.

Few periods in the history of the Republican Party have received more scorn than the brief presidential tenure of Harding. One of the most famous scandals in American history, Teapot Dome, symbolized the sordid record of a man whose performance fell well below the high standards of his office. By the time he died, Harding knew he was facing the embarrassment of seeing some of his close associates under investigation for official misdeeds. While these transgressions did not touch Harding himself, they reflected his inadequacy as president. How did Harding, now rated as one of the nation's least successful presidents, evoke such reverence when he was alive and incur such devastating criticism after his death?

A point often forgotten about Harding is the poor reputation of Woodrow Wilson when he left office in March 1921. Even some liberal voices welcomed the change from the repudiated Democratic president. Harding did not have an inaugural ball, and the promised simplicity garnered wide praise even though Wilson had done the same thing in 1913. The new first lady, Florence Kling Harding, opened up the White House after the seclusion of the war period and the president's illness. The mansion became more accessible to visitors. This shift back toward a president who was only the "First Citizen" provided Harding a surge of popularity during his early days in office.[1]

Harding was a kindly man. Eugene V. Debs, the Socialist leader, had been imprisoned during the Wilson years for expressing antiwar sentiments, and the Democratic president had vowed he would remain in jail until the end of his term. After some initial hesitation, Harding pardoned Debs in December 1921. Other radical prisoners were released during the remainder of Harding's tenure.

On racial issues, Harding made some mild overtures toward African Americans and attacked lynching in a message to Congress in April 1921. The administration did not follow up on this initiative with support for an anti-lynching bill then in Congress. Nor did Harding assail the Ku Klux Klan, which was growing in power, or encourage his Department of Justice to investigate the hooded order's violent activities.[2]

The United States over which Harding presided was transformed from the nation that Theodore Roosevelt had governed in September 1901. A generation earlier, agriculture and rural life had shaped the values and experience of most citizens. The 1920 census revealed that a majority of Americans lived in cities or towns of 2,500 or more inhabitants, rendering those who resided in the countryside a minority. Throughout the next decade Americans left the country for the city in growing numbers. They brought with them attitudes and mores bred on the farm, but they embraced as their future the bustle of Chicago, the magic of Manhattan, and the excitement of Hollywood.

After a slow start in the first two years of the Harding presidency, the economy boomed through 1927. The gross national product rose 40 percent from 1922 to 1927, and in the latter year the unemployment rate stood at only 4 percent. Republican dominance rested on the surge of prosperity and economic change. A new consumer culture brought cars, appliances, and the mass media to millions of homes. Movies and radio shaped the common experience of the average citizen. Labor unions lost power and influence as business installed the nonunion "open shop" (in contrast to the all-union "closed shop") and offered more benefits through what was called welfare capitalism. The social conflict of the Progressive Era, while it had not disappeared, seemed to have receded from the minds of most political leaders. Magazines asked what had happened to the prewar reformers.

One sector of the economy, however, was not lifted by the rising economic tide. In the agricultural belt, overproduction of crops marked the decade as wheat and cotton prices slumped from their wartime levels. Farm incomes remained well below what city dwellers were earning. A "farm bloc" of Republican senators pushed for government help for their constituents throughout the 1920s, a drive that both the Harding and Coolidge administrations resisted. The result was often Republican discord in Congress, as these senators also opposed greater involvement overseas and business-oriented trade policies.

For organized labor, the 1920s were a time of retreat and confusion. The antiunion sentiment that followed the world war discredited the American Federation of Labor (AFL) and its leader, Samuel Gompers. Composed of craft and skilled worker unions, the AFL did not reach out to organize the unskilled, lower-paid workers who faced the most economic hazards. Court decisions limited the effectiveness of strikes while the Republican presidents had little tolerance for labor's agenda.

A central element of public policy during the 1920s was the effort to stem the flow of immigration following World War I. In 1921 805,000 people entered the country, a number that aroused the fears of restrictionists in and out of Congress. Lawmakers responded with an emergency bill to limit immigration from Europe to six hundred thousand per year. Three years later, Congress approved the National Origins Quota Act, which restricted annual immigration from Europe to 150,000 entrants, with preference given to those who came from northern Europe. Representative Albert Johnson, a Washington Republican and chair of the House Committee on Immigration, observed in 1927: "The day of unalloyed welcome to all peoples, the day of indiscriminate acceptance of all races, has definitely ended."[3]

Though Harding was far from a great president, his brief administration could claim some tangible accomplishments. Aware of his own limits, the new president sought to enlist "the best minds" in the key Cabinet posts. Charles Evans Hughes became secretary of state, while Herbert Hoover took over the Department of Commerce. Hoover proved to be an energetic and activist administrator who extended his reach into many other departments of the government. Hoover picked Andrew Mellon for the Treasury. His connections to his family's banking interests in Pittsburgh reassured the financial community of the president's conservatism and fiscal soundness.

The rest of Harding's official family was undistinguished. The president named Albert B. Fall, an old friend from the Senate, to head the Department of the Interior. From that place, Fall would set in motion the events that led to the Teapot Dome scandal. Harding's attorney general was Harry Daugherty, his campaign manager and political associate from Ohio, who proceeded to compromise the ethical standards of the Justice Department. Under his lax rule, the criminality of the "Ohio Gang" flourished as favors and pardons were bought and sold through some of Daugherty's cronies. Harding knew little of these developments, but he allowed them to happen.

Yet the administration achieved some creditable results. The Republican Congress passed the Budget Act of 1921, setting up the Bureau of the Budget to give the government a means of managing its expenditures. In the first two years of the presidency, ambitious plans for government reorganization went forward but had not reached fruition when Harding died. The president named conservatives to fill places on regulatory agencies that the progressives had created, demonstrating that political reform could have unexpected consequences.

In foreign affairs, while not recognizing the League of Nations, the administration did summon the Washington Conference on Naval Disarmament in 1922, and Secretary of State Hughes secured important reductions in the naval strength of Great Britain, Japan, and the United States. That same year Congress enacted the Fordney-McCumber Tariff, which undid some of the provisions of the Underwood Tariff of 1913 as far as rates were concerned. Lawmakers also restored much of the protective structure of the Payne-Aldrich Tariff of 1909. Protectionism was among the core beliefs of the GOP.

Ultimately, the first two years of the Harding presidency did not satisfy the voters. The Republicans suffered serious reverses in the 1922 congressional elections. The postwar slump continued, and unemployment hovered at around 11 percent. Meanwhile, the anti-labor sentiment that the war had fostered had weakened the unions. As hard times intensified, strikes became more common and more violent.

Republicans sensed that voter unhappiness would be intense, but little prepared them for the depth of resentment that the Congress and the presidency encountered. In the balloting the Republicans lost nearly eighty seats in the House and eight in the Senate. The GOP retained control of both houses but by much reduced margins. Conservative Republicans were highly vulnerable, and their losses moved the party more toward the center. Harding's reelection chances seemed doubtful.

Warren G. Harding worked hard at being president, but after two years in office he regarded the position as a burden more than as an opportunity to improve the lot of Americans. The duties of the chief executive had expanded as the office became more bureaucratic after World War I and with the increased media focus on the presidency itself. Harding struggled to deal with the flood of letters he received. No longer able to control his own schedule as he had in the Senate, he complained to one Republican, "I am not fit for this office and should never have been here." While most presidents gripe at some point about the rigors of the job, Harding felt the disconnect between his ambitions and his ability more acutely as his presidency developed.[4]

In early 1923, Harding's friends sought to quell doubts about his intention to run in 1924. Harry Daugherty told reporters in March, "President Harding will be a candidate for renomination." The president thought the declaration premature, since he intended to make a speaking tour of the Pacific Northwest not as an announced candidate but as the president during the coming summer. At the same time, his health was deteriorating. A bout with the flu in January 1923 intensified his existing heart problems, and his blood pressure soared. Despite these warning signs, Harding remained a heavy smoker and did not obey his doctor's orders to slow down. Overweight and experiencing chest pains, Harding was a classic candidate for a heart attack.[5]

By this time scandals had begun to dog the White House. The president's appointee to the Veterans Bureau, Charles Forbes, had been forced to resign in February 1923 after disclosures of kickbacks and secret deals in contracts with his agency. At the Justice Department, Daugherty had let a crook named Jess Smith gain access from which pardons, appointments, and contracts were sold. Smith and his cronies traded on their presumed closeness to Harding. The president confronted Smith about his conduct in late May, and the day after the meeting Smith blew his brains out in a Washington apartment. Harding did not know about the looming Teapot Dome scandal in any detail, but by the time he left for the West, he sensed that his administration was under a cloud. According to William Allen White, the president told him, "My God, this is a hell of a job! I have no trouble with my enemies. I can take care of my enemies all right. But my damn friends, my God-damned friends, White, they're the ones that keep me walking the floor nights."[6]

Harding and his party left for the West on June 20, 1923. His speeches seemed to go well, and the president told the press that the American people were "hopeful and confident of the future and manifestly glad to live in this wonderful republic of ours." Harding then left for Alaska, where his speeches pleased his audiences, but his health suffered further reverses. After retreating to the care of his doctors in late July, he succumbed to a fatal heart attack in San Francisco on August 2, 1923. The nation went into mourning.[7]

In the years after Harding's death, macabre stories circulated about the circumstances under which he died, suggesting murder by his wife or presidential intimates. Sensation seekers and confidence men offered lurid stories of how the conspiracy had supposedly been carried out. Since there was no autopsy of the president, theories about his death became more elaborate. The simple reality was that Harding was a middle-aged man with a bad heart who had indulged in all the wrong habits for a person in his condition. That he suffered a fatal heart attack was hardly a surprise.[8]

The most sensational scandal associated with Harding's presidency did not become public knowledge until after his death, and it did not involve the president himself. Teapot Dome was an oil-rich geological formation marked by Teapot Rock, a rock formation in Wyoming that when viewed from the proper angle revealed a vague resemblance to a teapot. Underneath the surface were reserves of oil that the Navy had administered for use in the event of war. In 1922, Secretary of the Interior Albert B. Fall convinced Harding to transfer control of this reserve and another in California to the Interior Department. The oil reserves were then leased to oilmen Harry F. Sinclair and Edward L. Doheny. Subsequent probes revealed that Fall had received more than $400,000 in loans and government bonds from the two oil executives. Congressional inquiries in late 1923 and into 1924 spread the story on the nation's front pages, posing problems for Harding's successor, Calvin Coolidge. At no time were there credible suggestions that Harding was aware of, approved of, or profited from Fall's private transactions.[9]

The revelations of corruption in his administration sent Harding's reputation into a downward slide from which it has never recovered. Historical efforts to rehabilitate his record have shown that Harding did his best and was honest. He sought to implement the conservative policies that his party favored and that the American people wanted after a generation of reform. By no means an above-average president, Harding reflected a return to a kind of pleasant mediocrity that accorded with the temper of his times.

Calvin Coolidge received the news of Harding's death while he was working on his farm in Plymouth Notch, Vermont. By candlelight his father, who was a justice of the peace and notary public, administered the oath of office to the new president. Coolidge has enjoyed something of a resurgence in recent years, especially among Republican conservatives, as a kind of tax-cutting precursor of Ronald Reagan and the supply-side economics of the 1980s. His belief in smaller government and economic self-reliance has added to his reputation in these quarters.

Leaving later parallels aside, Coolidge was an interesting figure for the 1920s. He avoided the scandals of his predecessor and was lucky enough to retire from office before the emergence of the economic problems that would engulf Herbert Hoover. In his handling of the office of the presidency, Coolidge employed image-making techniques that came to be associated with Franklin D. Roosevelt. He was adroit on the radio, relied on his wife's glamour as first lady to increase popular support for his administration, and mastered the political environment of his party. In his frequent press conferences, Coolidge belied his reputation as a man of few words. He could be

The terse, austere figure of Calvin Coolidge won plaudits from Americans in the 1920s for Republican economic policies linked to economic prosperity. Library of Congress, LC-USZ62-93286.

quite voluble with reporters without saying much of substance. He was also adept at deflecting blame onto other officials for the problems within the administration.[10]

Coolidge celebrated his fifty-first birthday on July 4, 1923, a month before he became president. Born in Vermont, he was educated at Amherst College and then read for the law in Northampton. Soon he was active in local Republican politics. In 1905, he married Grace Goodhue, a teacher at a local school for the deaf. Coolidge served in a variety of local posts in Northampton and spent two one-year terms in the Massachusetts House of Representatives. By 1911 he was in the state senate, moving on to lieutenant governor in 1915, and three years later was governor. The Boston Police Strike in 1919 made Coolidge a national figure and put him on track to reach the White House in 1923.

There was always a sense about Coolidge that his achievements had more to do with luck than his own abilities. When he was selected to be Harding's running mate, a Boston newspaperman at the convention "offered to bet all comers that Harding, if elected, would be assassinated before he served half of this term." Warned by his colleagues that "any talk of assassination was unwise and might be misunderstood, for the Armistice was less than two years old and the Mitchell Palmer Red hunt was still in full blast," the reporter refused to stop talking. "I am simply telling you what I know. I know Cal Coolidge inside and out. He is the luckiest _____ _____ in the whole world."[11]

Coolidge was not an activist president in the mold of Theodore Roosevelt or Woodrow Wilson. He believed in his party's conservatism with more conviction than Harding had displayed, and he resisted efforts to expand the role of government. "I favor the American system of individual enterprise, and am opposed to any general extension of government ownership and control," he said in accepting the Republican nomination in 1924. He also believed that the high taxes inherited from World War I were a drag on business enterprise. With the support of Secretary of the Treasury Mellon, he sought to have them lowered or repealed.[12]

Before he could implement any specific programs, Coolidge had to ensure his own nomination for president in 1924. Given his relative obscurity within the Republican Party and the prospect of more scandals, his chances did not seem promising during the summer of 1923. He soon showed an ability to relegate possible rivals to the sidelines. Coolidge named C. Bascom Slemp, a West Virginia Republican, as his secretary. Slemp knew the southern Republican ranks from the inside, and he was indispensable in rounding up delegates for the president. As a result, potential candidates such as Governor Gifford Pinchot of Pennsylvania, Henry Ford of Michigan, and William E. Borah of Idaho found that Coolidge had preempted them and almost locked up the nomination.

The Teapot Dome scandal broke in the months after Coolidge took office. The looming opportunity for the Democrats to wound the new administration never truly presented itself. While the probes on Capitol Hill revealed Fall's involvement with the oilmen Sinclair and Doheny, there was no smoking gun linking Harding to what had happened. Moreover, in his testimony before Congress, Doheny revealed that leading Democrats had accepted payments from him for legal and other services. The most notable example of these relationships involved former secretary of the Treasury William G. McAdoo, who was Wilson's son-in-law. McAdoo was a leading candidate for the Democratic presidential nomination, but Doheny's revelations rendered him damaged political goods. The public soon tired of the hearings on the affair, and the case fizzled rather than helping spark a Democratic victory.

Meanwhile, the new president eased out of office those Harding holdovers who might be an embarrassment in 1924. It took some delicate maneuvering to convince Attorney General Daugherty to depart, but Coolidge secured his resignation in late March. In his place, Coolidge named Harlan Fiske Stone, who went on to become chief justice of the United States. The Bureau of Investigation, tainted by wrongdoing under Harding, gained a new director, J. Edgar Hoover, who installed more honest agents and more modern investigative procedures.

By the spring of 1924, Coolidge had outdistanced all of his potential rivals, and the only issue was his running mate. The president sought to persuade the maverick Republican from Idaho William E. Borah to run with him. The story goes that Coolidge said he wanted Borah on the ticket, to which Borah is said to have replied, "Which place, Mr. President?" With Borah eliminated, Coolidge decided to pick Charles G. Dawes, a former associate of William McKinley and a banker in Chicago. The Republican convention was broadcast on the radio, a sign of the increasing role of the mass media in national politics.[13]

Once nominated, Coolidge faced two rivals in the presidential campaign. After a convention in New York that took 104 ballots to reach a decision, the Democrats selected John W. Davis, a corporate lawyer, to head their ticket. Senator Robert M. La Follette ran as the candidate of the Progressive Party, an alliance of reformers and organized labor. The Republicans painted the Wisconsin senator as a dangerous radical and the choice as "Coolidge or Chaos." Meanwhile, Davis and the Democrats, whom the Republicans did not regard as a legitimate alternative to the GOP, were obscured, "concealed in the crowd, like a bootlegger at a wedding," in the words of H. L. Mencken.[14]

The sudden, tragic death of the president's son Calvin Coolidge, Jr., from an infection during the summer spared the incumbent the need to campaign in person. As Coolidge told reporters, "I don't recall any candidate for President that ever injured himself very much by not talking." He did make effective radio addresses as Election Day neared, but none of this really mattered to the final result. The Republicans had a big war chest and an abundance of speakers for the campaign. Most of all, the return of prosperity lifted the Republican cause. The protest vote that La Follette expected did not materialize, and Davis proved to be a bore. The Republican campaign used Hollywood stars to its advantage. A delegation of cinematic idols came to the White House to pose with the president, and the first lady, Grace Coolidge, led the assemblage in the campaign theme song, "Keep Cool with Coolidge."[15]

In 1924, the voters decided to keep Coolidge. He won a landslide victory over Davis and La Follette. The president drew 15.7 million popular votes to almost 8.4 million for Davis and another 4.8 million for La Follette. Coolidge's 54 percent of the vote gained him 382 electoral votes. Voter turnout, which had been declining since 1900, rose slightly in 1924 to just over 51 percent of the eligible voters casting ballots. The Republicans had substantial majorities in both the House and Senate. With the Democratic Party in disarray and the Republicans united behind Coolidge, there seemed little prospect of a return to power for the opposition party. The increasing Democratic share of the vote in northern cities was not seen as a serious threat to the continuation of Republican rule.

The most famous words that Calvin Coolidge uttered as president came in the waning days of his first term when he spoke to the American Society of Newspaper Editors on January 17, 1925. He said, "A press which maintains an intimate touch with the business currents of the nation is likely to be more reliable than it would be if it were a stranger to these influences. After all, the business of America is business." Taken out of context, Coolidge's words have been seen as a justification for whatever business did during the 1920s. While he was no enemy of business as such, Coolidge thought that material success was only justified as a means to a better society.[16]

One key to that endeavor was, in the president's mind, lowering tax rates and government expenditures, as well as paying down the national debt. In that sense, Coolidge's tax reduction program was not a 1920s version of the supply-side doctrines of the 1980s under Ronald Reagan. Accordingly, in 1926 the president proposed to Congress that tax rates be lowered. The resulting legislation reduced the surtax on individuals who made more than $100,000 each year, lowered the taxes on estates to 20 percent, and eliminated the gift tax. The exemption for married couples was set at $3,500, a figure that few Americans earned. Only about four million taxpayers submitted returns annually during the 1920s. The measure did raise the corporate tax. As a sign of the growing importance of the income tax, the rate of federal income taxes averaged more than 3 percent of the gross national product, up from the rate of 1 percent before World War I.

The continued problems of American agriculture during the 1920 challenged financial policy in another way. Thanks to huge surpluses that they could not sell, farmers found themselves facing falling prices for their crops. They looked to Washington for assistance on behalf of what was known as the McNary-Haugen plan, named after its Republican sponsors, Charles L. McNary of Oregon and Gilbert N. Haugen of Wisconsin. McNary-Haugen proposed to solve the farm problem through government purchase of the farm surpluses at the market price, after which it would dump the goods on the world market. The resulting monetary loss would be covered by an "equalization fee," or processing fee, that would be charged to the farmers whose crops benefitted from the government program. The major criticism of the plan was that it forced the government into the process of fixing prices for an agricultural commodity. Increasing prices would also lift production, of course, and thus only exacerbate the overproduction problem that caused the farm crisis in the first place. The powerful farm bloc passed the McNary-Haugen measure twice, and Coolidge vetoed it twice, in February 1927 and again in May 1928. However, the farm problem would not go away and remained a source of vexation for both Herbert Hoover and Franklin D. Roosevelt.

The 1920s are often portrayed as a decade of American isolationism as the nation stood aloof from the problems that culminated with the onset of the Great Depression and the rise of the dictators. While neither Harding nor Coolidge reversed the Senate's decision to stay out of the League of Nations, neither did they turn their backs on all world issues. Under Harding the Washington Naval Conference pursued disarmament in the Pacific. Coolidge pushed for the United States to join the League of Nations Permanent Court of International Justice (known as the World Court), but the Senate insisted on so many limiting requirements for entry that the campaign for membership collapsed in 1925 and 1926. The Republican administrations sought to expand American business across the globe, relying on business executives to fill ambassadorial positions in key countries. The United States also remained much involved in the turbulent affairs of Mexico, where American oil interests were threatened with expropriation, and in Nicaragua, where civil war often flared.[17]

The United States became involved in the intricate system of international debts and reparations payments that followed the end of World War I. In the Treaty of Versailles, Germany was forced to pay reparations for its role in the war. During the Coolidge years, the administration pushed for a series of agreements to lower the amount of debt that Germany had to pay the Allies. It has often been written that President Coolidge was reluctant to reduce what Great Britain and France owed the United States from the war. The phrase he was said to have used was "They hired the money, didn't they?" While it was something Coolidge might well have said, the evidence suggests that it was one of those presidential tales that gathered around Coolidge. The structure of international loans and debts that the Coolidge administration put in place proved impossible to sustain when the Great Depression hit, but it represented what was possible and feasible at the time.[18]

In the 1926 congressional elections, six years after the election of Warren G. Harding, the Republicans lost ten seats in the House of Representatives and dropped another seven in the Senate, where their control rested on a shaky three-seat margin over the Democrats. The outcome of the congressional contests foreshadowed more legislative trouble for the White House, but no one thought that Coolidge would be in any political trouble should he decide to run again in 1928.

After four years in office, Coolidge could likely have had the Republican nomination if he wanted it. The country was prosperous and at peace, the Democrats were still divided, and the Republicans had united behind the president. In Coolidge's mind, the situation had a different look. The death of his son in 1924 had cast a permanent pall over his presidency. Moreover, his health and the health of the First Lady were more fragile than the public realized. Coolidge had severe chronic allergies, and his heart was also weak.

Whether Coolidge sensed the economic storm over the horizon is impossible to tell, although Mrs. Coolidge told a friend, "Poppa says there's a depression coming." The president was convinced that another term would mean ten years in Washington, and that seemed to him too long. As he wrote in his autobiography, "An examination of the records of those presidents who served eight years will disclose that in almost every instance, the latter parts of their term have shown very little in the way of constructive accomplishments. They have often been clouded with grave disappointments." Sometime in the spring and summer of 1927, Coolidge made his decision not to seek another term.[19]

With typical Coolidge understatement, he picked the fourth anniversary of his accession to the presidency, August 2, 1927, to drop his bombshell, while the Coolidges were vacationing in the Black Hills of South Dakota. That day there was a press conference scheduled at a local high school. As the reporters filed in, they were handed a small piece of paper on which appeared the sentence "I do not choose to run for President in 1928." The decision was Coolidge's alone. He had not even mentioned to his wife when he had the announcement distributed.[20]

The statement set off a flood of speculation about whether Coolidge was orchestrating a draft or in fact intended to leave politics. In the end, that did not matter. Once Coolidge stepped aside, the race for the Republican nomination opened. With his usual political sagacity, Coolidge had decided to leave while he was still admired and wanted, and he let his successor grapple with national issues. As president, Coolidge embodied competence without distinction. He deserved credit for the prosperity that Americans enjoyed during the 1920s, but he did little to dampen the speculative fever that preceded the Stock Market Crash of 1929. He left the government's finances in good shape, the national debt lowered, and the budget in balance. He mastered the Republican Party as it was but did little to expand its base among urban ethnics or to reaffirm the historical allegiance of African Americans to the Grand Old Party. Neither the boob of later Democratic portrayals nor the precursor of supply-side economics as depicted by some Republicans in the 1980s, Coolidge carried out his duties with proficiency but without distinction.

The front runner for the Republican nomination soon became the secretary of commerce, Herbert Hoover. Because of the repudiation he suffered at the hands of Franklin D. Roosevelt four years later during the depths of the Great Depression, Hoover's political abilities have often been underestimated. In 1928, however, he was a strong candidate for a Republican Party still riding the crest of national prosperity. The Democrats had not yet overcome their cultural divisions. When they nominated Governor Alfred E. Smith of New York, a Roman Catholic, they ensured that the election would reveal the prejudices and rifts that filled American politics. Historians have raised the question of whether any Democrat could have beaten Hoover in 1928; the consensus is that in a Republican year he was the strongest candidate the party could have chosen.[21]

In 1928, at the age of fifty-four, Herbert Hoover seemed to be one of the dazzling success stories of American politics. Orphaned at a young age and cared for by relatives in Iowa and Oregon, he attended Stanford University, studied geology, and then pursued a career as a mining engineer. For a decade and a half he amassed a personal fortune before retiring to pursue more fulfilling interests. He and his wife, Lou Henry Hoover, had raised two sons and in their spare time translated and edited a Latin treatise on mining. After the outbreak of World War I, he helped provide food to millions left destitute by the fighting, first in Belgium and later in Russia. When the United States entered the conflict in 1917, Hoover came home to direct the Food Administration for Woodrow Wilson. His efficiency in obtaining the resources the Allied cause needed made him a world figure. In 1920 he made a brief run at the Republican nomination and then accepted the post of secretary of commerce in Harding's cabinet.[22]

In office, Hoover expanded the role of the Commerce Department and involved himself in the business of other departments as well. An efficient public relations staff talked up his accomplishments, and he became the best-known official in the government below the president. Fighting floods, making policy on the expanding radio industry, and promoting the interests of corporate America, Hoover was everywhere in the 1920s. Hoover gained the title of "the busiest man in Washington," and reporters gushed over his ability and the potential of a Hoover presidency if Coolidge stepped aside in 1928.

When the president withdrew in August 1927, Hoover's candidacy prospered. By the time he made an official announcement in February 1928, he was well ahead of all the other challengers. Hoover swept most of the primaries and soon had more than 400 delegates of the 545 needed for the nomination. The convention in Kansas City selected Hoover on the first ballot and named Senator Charles Curtis of Kansas as his running mate.

The party's platform proclaimed that under Coolidge "the country has been lifted from the depths of a great depression to a level of prosperity." The delegates praised the tax reduction policies of the Coolidge years, reaffirmed their belief "in the protective tariff as a fundamental and essential principle of the economic life of this nation," and indicted any Democratic effort to increase the role of the federal government, which "weakens the sense of initiative and creates a feeling of dependence which is unhealthy and unfortunate for the whole body politic." The Republicans also sought a larger role for women in politics and renewed their call for a federal act to eradicate lynching.[23]

Accepting the Republican nomination on August 11, 1928, at Stanford, California, Hoover spoke the words that four years later would come back to haunt him: "We in American today are nearer to the final triumph over poverty than ever before in the history of any land. The poorhouse is vanishing from among us. We have not yet reached the goal, but given a chance to go forward with the policies of the last eight years, we shall soon with the help of God be in sight of the day when poverty shall be banished from this nation."[24]

In the heady days of prosperity in 1928, such a lofty goal seemed attainable. The gross national product stood at $98 billion, with only 4.4 percent of the workforce unemployed, up slightly from the preceding year but far below the levels of the Depression decade to follow. In his campaign speeches, Hoover emphasized the spread of automobiles to American families, the labor-saving benefits of electric power, and the larger homes in which Americans lived. As he later remarked in New York City, "Every man and woman knows that their comfort, their hopes, and their confidence for the future are higher this day than they were seven and one-half years ago."[25]

Because his likely opponent in the election would be Governor Alfred E. Smith of New York, a well-known opponent of Prohibition, Hoover also spoke out on that controversial reform. In his acceptance address he came out against repeal of the Eighteenth Amendment, which had passed in 1919 and had ushered in the Prohibition Era, because the nation had "deliberately undertaken a great social and economic experiment, noble in motive and far-reaching in purpose." In later years the phrase would be compressed, and he would erroneously be credited with calling Prohibition a "noble experiment." For now, his identification with the dry cause sharpened the cultural divisions that separated the two candidates in 1928.[26]

Two weeks after the Republican convention, the Democrats met in Houston to nominate Al Smith. Because Smith was the first Roman Catholic to receive the nomination of a major political party, the 1928 election became a contest in which religious feelings ran high. Protestant fears about a Catholic president fueled bigotry directed against Smith that dominated political discourse. While Al Smith was a very attractive personality in 1928, he had liabilities as well that the Republicans sought to exploit. Within the spectrum of the Democrats, Smith, for all the reforms he endorsed within New York State, was a conservative candidate who proclaimed that "government should interfere as little as possible with business." Rather than focus on issues such as public ownership of electric power companies and Republican tax policy, Smith came across as someone who was very close to Hoover on most issues other than Prohibition. On that divisive problem, the Democratic candidate made clear his commitment to changing the alcohol laws. As a result, Smith did little to ease the feelings of Americans outside the Northeast about whether he understood their lifestyle.[27]

More important, Smith's religion aroused suspicions in large parts of the West and South. The Republicans faced a possible backlash if they made Smith's Catholicism an issue themselves, but they did not have to do so publicly. The press and the Protestant churches did that for them in what became a vituperative attack on the Democratic nominee. The contrast between the eastern cultural provincialism of Smith, who was very much the New Yorker, and the rural cultural provincialism of many Hoover supporters worked to the advantage of the Republican candidate.

Throughout the Republican campaign, Hoover's public stance indicated that he was above the battle and the specifics of attracting votes. He did not make many speaking tours and confined himself to seven public speeches that were spread out at regular intervals. Hoover did not much like the rigors of campaigning, so radio's ability to attract large audiences suited his shyness and dislike of personal contact. In 1928 it did not matter that his delivery was flat and uninspired. Against Smith, it was enough that he sounded like a competent engineer who would manage the country's affairs with efficiency and honesty.[28]

The Republicans exploited radio with surrogates for Hoover, known as the "Hoover minute men," a variation of the "Four Minute Men" of World War I who made brief speeches on behalf of war bonds. A radio division of the campaign supervised the activities of men and women who spoke out for Hoover. The Republicans used some celebrities of the theater such as Walter Huston in their appeal. Most of the effort was directed at the smaller rural communities of the nation where the Grand Old Party was strong.

As the campaign deteriorated into religious name calling against Smith, the Hoover headquarters maintained an air of detachment from the controversy. Behind the scenes, however, Hoover encouraged attacks on Smith and the skillful manipulation of anti-Catholic sentiments. The Republicans gave a discreet push to propaganda against Smith without leaving any fingerprints. State and local Republican campaigns distributed pamphlets that assailed Smith and Catholicism.

Both sides sought to exploit the race issue in the South. Hoover appealed to whites in Dixie when he eliminated language from the platform favoring enforcement of the Fourteenth and Fifteenth Amendments. The pledge against lynching was widely regarded in the black community as empty language, and southern whites ignored it. Republicans also alleged that Smith had encouraged racial intermarriage in New York City, and they circulated photographs showing mixed couples and literature discussing Smith's racial tolerance.

At the same time the Democrats charged that Hoover had abolished segregation in the Department of Commerce, an allegation that the Republican candidate's camp denied. "I can state to you positively that there has been no change whatever in the Department of Commerce since the Wilson administration regarding the treatment of colored people," said Hoover's secretary in late October 1928. While most black voters stayed with the Republican ticket in the Hoover-Smith race, the African American leadership, alienated by the Republican courtship of southern whites, drifted toward the Democrats in a process that accelerated in 1932.[29]

After all the tumult of the 1928 election, the voters selected Hoover on November 6. Hoover amassed 21.4 million popular votes to 15 million for Smith. The electoral total stood at 444 votes for Hoover to 87 for Smith. The Democratic candidate carried only Rhode Island and Massachusetts in the North as well as six states in the South. Hoover broke the Democratic hold on Dixie with victories in Texas, Florida, Tennessee, North Carolina, and Virginia. The Republicans piled up big majorities in both houses of Congress. Hoover told the press, "There has been a vindication of great issues and a determination of the true road of progress. The Republican Party has again been assessed with great responsibility."[30]

Since the Republican triumph proved short-lived and the New Deal coalition emerged within a few years, much attention has been given to the ways, if any, in which Al Smith's showing in 1928 anticipated the success of Roosevelt four years later. In that sense, Hoover's victory was soon eclipsed and forgotten. But Hoover also anticipated what would happen to the Republicans after the trauma of the Great Depression. In the 1950s, as the Democrats became more identified with the cause of civil rights and the votes of African Americans, the strategy that Hoover applied to the South would be reborn under Dwight D. Eisenhower and Richard Nixon.

Herbert Hoover's presidency ended in such disaster for the Republican Party that it is hard to imagine the contented mood of the country during much of the first year of his administration. With prosperity still secure during most of 1929, Hoover focused his activism on the nation's problems. He summoned Congress into special session to address the farm problem, looked into reform of the prison system, and launched initiatives into international disarmament in foreign policy. One magazine review of the president's early performance concluded, "Washington is a center of news these days, not because a corps of hardworking newspaper correspondents is doing its best to pick up tidbits out of a great laissez-faire but because a quick-witted and aggressive Executive is plainly on the job."[31]

By the time that issue of *Literary Digest* appeared, the first signs of trouble at the New York Stock Exchange had appeared. Stocks had peaked on September 3, and then prices decreased throughout September and October. Still, brokers and their customers remained optimistic. The New York Times Index of industrial securities had been at 245 in 1927. In 1928 it had risen to 331. The increase continued until the index stood at 452 in September 1929. A Yale economist, Irvin Fisher, downplayed warnings that the market might be overvalued. Stocks had "reached what looks like a permanently high plateau," he said.[32]

On October 24, 1929, traders discovered that there were no buyers for the stocks that they wished to sell. Prices sagged as thirteen million shares were traded, then a record day. Bankers under the leadership of J. Morgan and Company stepped in to settle the market and succeeded in doing so for several days. The panic resumed on October 29, when more than 16,400 shares were traded. The Times Index slumped forty-three points on what became known as Black Tuesday. Theodore Roosevelt's son Kermit predicted on October 30, "When the smoke is cleared away, there will be a great many Humpty Dumpties."[33]

The stock market crash was a calamitous event, but it was not the sole cause of the Great Depression of the 1930. Economists and historians still debate what destroyed the prosperity of the 1920s and brought about a downturn that would not end until the United States geared up to fight World War II. Various causes have been singled out. The Federal Reserve, the Smoot-Hawley Tariff of 1930, the intricate relationship between war debts and loans following World War I, the Democratic Congress of 1931–1932, and the speculative fevers of the 1920s have all been blamed at one time or another. In terms of the history of the Republican Party, however, the causes of the Depression are less important than how President Hoover responded to the economic crisis.

Hoover's performance following the crash has also been the subject of much controversy. On one level he did much more to fight the Depression than any previous president had done when faced with an economic downturn. Hoover rejected the view of some in his party and his government that the collapse of the economy was a natural event that simply had to be endured before a return to national well-being could take place. The president knew that such a policy, following the precedent of Grover Cleveland in the 1890s, would be political suicide. Naturally an activist himself, Hoover believed that the president could encourage his fellow citizens to work together to lift the country out of the doldrums. His policies sought to instill renewed confidence in the nation that the Depression would soon come to an end—but without expanding the role of government to fight the economic crisis more than was necessary.[34]

In the process, Hoover broadened the government's ability to help the unemployed through a variety of voluntary programs in which the government sponsored and coordinated the activities of private groups. As time passed and the limits of voluntary programs became evident, Hoover endorsed such programs as the Reconstruction Finance Corporation (RFC), which Congress created in 1932 to lend money to banks, railroads, and insurance companies in danger of collapse. The RFC showed that the government had to take action during a depression, and it represented a turning away from private solutions and passivity from Washington during a slowdown.

After the stock market crash, it took a while for the Depression to hit with full force. The market recovered somewhat during 1930, and it seemed as if the economy might straighten itself out. The president sounded an encouraging note in late 1929, saying, "The fundamental business of the country, that is production and distribution, is on a sound and prosperous basis." In 1930, Congress passed the Smoot-Hawley Tariff, thus returning the Republicans to their protectionist roots. Republicans contended that the answer to the business problems of the nation was tariff protection for industry and farmers, and Hoover signed the measure with some reservations. When they became a free-trade party during the 1980s, Republicans often blamed the Smoot-Hawley Tariff for the Depression rather than Hoover's policies. The adverse effects of the bill have probably been exaggerated in comparison with other causes of the downturn, but this last gasp of Republican orthodoxy on the tariff certainly did not help promote world trade and revive American business.[35]

By mid-1930 the effects of the Depression became more evident. Bank failures grew and corporate profits declined. Unemployment moved upward until by 1930 nearly 9 percent of the labor force was looking for work, a problem that worsened during the year that followed. Unemployment stood at 16 percent by 1931. Farm prices fell as production of crops continued to increase. The homeless and unemployed took to the railroads seeking work anywhere they could find it. Gradually, the animus against Hoover rose. The shantytowns outside of big cities became known as "Hoovervilles," and an empty pocket turned inside-out as a sign of poverty was dubbed a "Hoover flag." Jokes about the president proliferated. It was said that if you put a rose in his hand, it would wilt. Another described Hoover as asking the secretary of the Treasury, Andrew Mellon, for a nickel so he could call a friend. "Here's a dime," said Mellon. "Call all your friends."[36]

Although he had been a master of public relations during the 1920s when times were good and his reputation was riding high, Hoover proved to be inept at inspiring national confidence during the Depression. At first, White House reporters anticipated an open administration as they remembered how accessible Hoover had been as secretary of commerce. In the presidency, however, Hoover became more terse and dismissive, and the press corps soured on the administration. To stimulate confidence, Hoover called business leaders to the White House, and they duly issued positive statements about the future of the economy. When the Depression did not lift, such occasions had less effect and even undermined what the president sought to do.

The Hoover administration displayed difficulty in grasping what Americans were going through in the hard times. After a drought hit the Middle West in 1930 and 1931, Congress allocated $60 million to help those in need acquire food and fuel. Hoover agreed that farm animals could be fed, but he disapproved of spending money on farmers and their families. An Arkansas Democrat alleged that the administration believed in feeding "jackasses but...not starving babies." Hoover's administration was more sensitive to the crisis, but the president's dogmatic belief in maintaining the limited role of the federal government proved disastrous for himself and his party.[37]

The 1930 congressional elections occurred before the full effects of the Depression were felt. Nonetheless, the Republicans suffered a fifty-one-seat loss in the House, retained only a one-seat margin, and gave that up by the time Congress convened in December 1931. The GOP also kept control of the Senate by a single vote. The Democrats did not make the Depression itself a major issue, but they were able to tap into resentments over the Smoot-Hawley Tariff, the problems of agriculture, and Republican factionalism. The Democratic National Committee and its publicity director, Charles Michelson, also mounted a very effective, unrelenting assault on the administration that the White House often let go unanswered. Meanwhile, the governor of New York, Franklin D. Roosevelt, won a landslide reelection victory and was viewed as a "formidable contender for the Presidency" in 1932.[38]

By 1931 the Depression hit the nation with full force, and the president's political situation worsened. When the lame-duck Congress met in December 1930, the calls for more presidential action to provide relief for distressed farmers and the unemployed surged. Hoover resisted these efforts on the grounds that direct assistance would sap the self-reliance and healthy spirit of the population. In a speech in mid-July 1931, he asked his audience, "Shall we abandon the philosophy and creed of our people for 150 years by turning to a creed foreign to our people? Shall we establish a dole from the Federal Treasury?" For the moment, Hoover's commitment to a less active government than many Democrats and insurgent Republicans wanted continued to hold sway, but the tide was turning against the president as unemployment worsened throughout 1931. Other indices told the same story, as the gross national product had fallen some 30 percent since 1929.[39]

When the Democrats took control of the House of Representatives in December 1931, the Hoover administration in response proposed the creation of the Reconstruction Finance Corporation. Later in the session, Hoover approved the Emergency Relief and Construction Act, albeit with severe limitations, to provide some relief funds for states to start projects to put people to work. Further than that the president would not go.[40]

As the government's finances worsened, Hoover believed that balancing the federal budget was imperative. The Democratic Party leadership in Congress concurred, despite the opposition of some Democrats and progressive Republicans who sought more spending on public works. The end result was a tax that raised rates on income as well as on luxuries and gifts. Maintaining the confidence of the business community and the banking industry was the rationale for this step. At a time when a balanced budget still represented economic orthodoxy, the idea that the government should spend money to stimulate economic growth was anathema to conservatives in both parties. The economic effect, of course, was to worsen the impact of the Depression by taking money out of the economy at a time when it was most needed.[41]

As the 1932 election loomed, with the potential for a disastrous Republican defeat, party members looked around for a possible alternative to Hoover, but none had much credibility. With the memories of 1912 still fresh, the choice of a protest candidate that might split the party seemed unlikely. Few names presented themselves, in any case. Former president Coolidge, already ailing with the heart condition that would kill him in early 1933, had no interest in taking on Hoover. Charles G. Dawes was an improbable choice, and a boomlet for Pennsylvania governor Gifford Pinchot encountered a frosty response. While most Republicans expected the president to lose, they stuck with him.

Hoover and his vice president, Charles Curtis, were chosen to run again at the party convention in June. The platform praised Hoover as a "wise, courageous, patient, understanding, resourceful" leader who had acted to meet the economic distress of the nation. The party pledged to maintain a balanced budget, to keep the currency sound, and to eliminate waste. Meanwhile, the gathering attacked Democrats in Congress for offering "proof of the existing incapacity of that party for leadership in a national crisis." Questioning the legitimacy of the opposition to govern remained a proven posture for the Grand Old Party.[42]

Another sensational incident tested Hoover's leadership in the weeks after the Republican convention. Following World War I, Congress had authorized the payment of a bonus to members of the American Expeditionary Force (the US World War I military in Europe) to be made in 1945. Veterans of the war asked in the Depression why the bonus could not be paid to them when they needed it so badly. Congress was reluctant to appropriate money for the bonus, and legislation failed to pass. To put pressure on lawmakers, the veterans marched to Washington, where they encamped on Anacostia Flats while Congress deliberated. The presence of the so-called Bonus Army in the nation's capital stirred fears of social unrest and perhaps violent revolution. After Congress adjourned in mid-July, pressure mounted on the District of Columbia police force to disperse the marchers from their encampment.

Late in the month the police were ordered to remove the marchers from government buildings they had occupied. In the melee that ensued, two Bonus Marchers were killed. Hoover ordered in federal troops commanded by General Douglas MacArthur to restore order. The resulting panic when the Army attacked was recorded on newsreels. The Hoover administration labeled the marchers as Communists, and many newspapers applauded the president's action. The incident did not, however, assist Hoover's flagging popularity, and for those opposed to him it seemed further confirmation of his insensitivity to the plight of struggling citizens caught in the Depression.[43]

Within another month the campaign for the presidency had begun. As the Democratic candidate, Franklin D. Roosevelt exuded optimism and a sense of confidence about the future. Roosevelt was a distant relation of Theodore Roosevelt, and his wife, Eleanor, was the former president's niece. The New York governor had followed the Democratic tradition of his father and had gained an appreciation for an active government during his eight years as assistant secretary of the Navy under Woodrow Wilson. He had carried on that commitment during his four years in Albany.

Roosevelt's specific plans for fighting the Depression were vague. He criticized Hoover as a big spender and for doing too little to address the economic crisis. This inconsistency irritated Republicans in 1932, and they regarded Roosevelt as an opportunist. For his part, the president made more formal

Herbert Hoover preferred to share his views with Americans through radio broadcasts, but even that modern technique failed him when the Great Depression hit. Library of Congress, LC-USZ62-92155.

speeches than he had in 1928, most of them written in longhand and delivered in a dry, impassive manner. Some of his campaign stops attracted only apathetic or hostile crowds. Elsewhere the audiences were enthusiastic. All informed Republicans expected Hoover to lose. He was glum; Roosevelt was confident. Hoover endorsed Prohibition; Roosevelt promised repeal. Few listened when Hoover said that the Democrats were out "to change our form of government and our social and economic system." Such dire warnings failed to sway by an electorate ready for a new team in Washington.[44]

The election results bore out the gloomy predictions Republicans had been making throughout 1932. Roosevelt swamped Hoover by more than seven million votes and rolled up 472 electoral votes to 59 for the president. Hoover carried Pennsylvania, Delaware, Connecticut, Rhode Island, New Hampshire, Vermont, and Maine. Roosevelt won everywhere else. In Congress the Democrats gained big majorities in both houses. The Republican coalition that had dominated American politics during the 1920s had collapsed along with the economy.

Protest against the Depression was the major element in the Republican debacle in 1932, but other reliable sources of GOP support faltered in the Hoover-Roosevelt race. For the campaign, Republican fundraising, impacted by the economy, was well down from 1928. Only $2.54 million came in, compared with nearly $7 million four years earlier. Prominent business figures split their donations between the two parties instead of tilting Republican. In the western states, factionalism between progressives and conservatives gave the Democrats an edge in a region that had been solid for the GOP. While black voters remained loyal Republicans by and large, there were signs in such cities as New York that unhappiness with the party was mounting among African Americans. The early years of the New Deal would accelerate that process.

Amid the ruins of the Hoover campaign and the stinging defeat in 1932, Republicans could find little consolation. They had been blamed for the Depression and all of its attendant ills. The Democrats had capitalized on popular unhappiness and Roosevelt's skills as a candidate to capitalize on the mood of protest. In all probability, given the severity of the Depression, Hoover never had a chance of reelection, and the Republicans were bound to suffer for his political sins.

Despite all of these obstacles, the Republican Party retained the allegiance of more than fifteen million Americans, who represented 40 percent of the electorate in 1932. If a candidate with such grave liabilities as Hoover could rely on such a base of support, then a more effective challenger to the Democrat might revive the party's fortunes four years later. For all the loose talk about the decline in Republican effectiveness, the party was still a potential force on the national political scene. Much would depend on how Franklin D. Roosevelt implemented his promise of a "New Deal" for the American people.

In American political history, the election of 1932 would become a major turning point between the welfare state that emerged from the New Deal era and the business-dominated politics that had preceded it. For twenty-four out of the first thirty-two years of the century, the Republicans had accomplished some notable legislative and policy achievements. These included the Hepburn Act and the Pure Food and Drugs Act under Theodore Roosevelt, the Budget Act under Harding, and tax reduction under Coolidge.

Among conservative Republicans in the 1930s and for decades thereafter, however, even these accomplishments would be seen as a fatal compromise with party principles. They knew that articulating such an austere vision of American society would be unpopular, and so the goal of rolling back even the modest expansion of government between 1900 and 1932 remained unstated. Soon the enactment of Franklin D. Roosevelt's New Deal gave Republicans even more to resent and oppose. During the next eighty years, the Republicans would present a pleasing face to the public in congressional and presidential campaigns. In their innermost thoughts, however, they embraced a social vision of a nation that rewarded the affluent and the productive and rejected those who depended on the government for their survival.

Thus the Republicans felt little remorse that in 1932 the United States was a nation that did not provide old-age pensions for retired workers, did not regulate its banking and securities system in a meaningful way, did not limit the impact of child labor on its youngest citizens, and did not have the national means to ameliorate the effects of mass unemployment. There were ideological and political reasons that the Republicans had not moved to enact any of these measures during its years of power; each reform would have threatened a major constituency of the Republican coalition. At bottom, however, the party did not implement such changes because it did not believe in the society where these programs would be a reality.

These conditions meant that the United States confronted the worst economic depression in its history with an unmet agenda of pressing social reforms to make society more equitable and just for all its citizens. The Republican Party had possessed the power to address these problems during its long tenure of power but had chosen not to do so. In the 1930s it felt the effects of its historic failure at the ballot box.

8

The Republicans and the New Deal,
1933–1945

IT WAS HOT IN PHILADELPHIA in June 1940. Delegates to the Republican National Convention crowded into Convention Hall, a structure built with just such gatherings in mind. The seating capacity was fifteen thousand. Everyone who was there remembered the galleries packed with supporters of Wendell Willkie, chanting "We want Willkie." The Republicans were on the verge of nominating a defector from the Democratic Party to run against Franklin D. Roosevelt. Representative Charles Halleck, a Willkie supporter from his home state of Indiana, asked the crowd as he placed Willkie's name in nomination, "Is the Republican party a closed corporation? Do you have to be born into it?" The galleries rocked with the response: "No, no."[1]

Some Republicans were less thrilled with Willkie. When he told former senator James E. Watson of Indiana that he had once been a Democrat, Watson replied, "Well, Wendell, you know that back home in Indiana it's all right if the town whore joins the church, but they don't let her lead the choir the first night." The specter of World War II hung over the nation. Democracy seemed to be under assault. Republicans concerned about the place of the United States in the world wanted a candidate who would defend the country against the danger of Nazi Germany and Imperial Japan. They also looked for someone who could beat Franklin D. Roosevelt. If a former Democrat could do that, these Republicans were prepared to nominate him. The shouts from the gallery continued: "We want Willkie!" After six tumultuous ballots, the Willkie supporters got their wish. The new candidate told them he would wage "an aggressive fighting campaign." As he left the podium, the organist played "God Bless America," and the delegates sang in unison as the convention ended. It was a moving moment in an era of defeat and discord for the Republicans as they watched Franklin D. Roosevelt dominate American politics during the New Deal.[2]

Elected in 1938, Robert A. Taft arrived in Washington determined to cut the federal budget in half. He posed for photographers with a copy of that document in 1939. Such attacks on the New Deal soon won him the title of Mr. Republican. Library of Congress, LC-DIG-hec-27889.

The nomination of Willkie began a twenty-five year struggle between the eastern wing of the party, more conservative than the Democrats but willing to accept some aspects of the New Deal, and the Republicans of the nation's heartland, who believed that the party must oppose Roosevelt and all of his programs. The battle was always between differing visions of a conservative ideology, but the Republicans who wanted to endorse the more popular programs of the New Deal and expand the nation's role in the world became known as "liberals" within the party. While their strength in Congress was always marginal, their ability to install their candidates as the GOP's presidential nominees between 1940 and 1960 continued to irritate their more conservative brethren. In the end, however, the conservative vision of Republicanism prevailed.

The 1932 presidential election represented a huge political repudiation for the Republican Party. Then things got even worse. Herbert Hoover and Franklin D. Roosevelt wrangled during the four month transition over what, if anything, could be done for the economy in the face of failing banks and mounting unemployment. Hoover's efforts to tie his successor to his own policy answers collapsed by March 4, 1933. A friend of Hoover's said that it would be "hard on H. to go out of office to the sound of crashing banks." By the time Roosevelt was inaugurated, the banking system stood on the edge of disaster.[3]

In his inaugural address and decisive actions during the "First Hundred Days" that followed, Roosevelt injected a dose of political energy into the government that was in striking contrast to Hoover's dour approach to his job in 1931–1932. The New Deal, as Roosevelt called his program, began with a flourish of activity that galvanized Congress and the American people. So responsive was Capitol Hill to what Roosevelt requested that some of the early New Deal measures were enacted without dissent.

The New Deal has taxed the ability of historians to explain its impact because it did so much in so many areas. For Republicans key points of disagreement were Roosevelt's willingness to use the power of government to establish permanent programs such as Social Security, his sympathy for organized labor, and his reliance (albeit reluctantly in some cases) on deficit spending to pay for his initiatives. New groups—blacks, union members, ethnics—rallied to the Democratic banner. The previous Republican dominance of the electorate faded away. Roosevelt and his party seemed to be everywhere. There were projects to put people to work, to encourage theater and the arts, to develop the resources of the Tennessee Valley. A man who came from a wealthy background, Roosevelt, so the Republicans contended, was betraying his own heritage, igniting class warfare, and making the opposition swallow everything. Opposition turned to bitterness and in some instances even hatred for "that man in the White House."

As many historians have noted, much of what Roosevelt did worked at cross-purposes to the goal of economic recovery. His initial measure to cut government spending, to restore the banks, and to abandon prohibition did not embody long-term solutions to the crisis of an economy working at less than full capacity. Yet even these limited steps were more than the Republicans offered during the spring of 1933 and the months that followed.[4]

While the small cadre of Republicans in Congress could do little to counter the wishes of the Democratic majority in 1933–1934, some opposition members managed to shape aspects of key legislation. Senator Arthur Vandenberg of Michigan pushed for federal insurance of bank deposits as a means of shoring up banks that were not part of large urban banking companies. Vandenberg's initiative led to the incorporation of the idea in the Glass-Steagall Act of 1933, and the provision became one of the most important parts of the early New Deal because it introduced stability into the financial system.[5]

Throughout Roosevelt's first two years in office, the Republicans groped for a way to deal with the popular Democratic president. Heavily in debt after the 1932 campaign, the Republican National Committee assailed Roosevelt's policies at a time when the man in the White House was riding high. As a result, more moderate Republicans endeavored to couch their efforts in more attractive terms by creating new committees among House and Senate Republicans to help candidates in the 1934 congressional elections. These panels would try to adopt a more constructive tone than what the national committee employed.[6]

The Republicans faced a dilemma that dominated their internal debates for the next dozen years and beyond. Conservatives argued that the best and most intellectually honest course was to oppose the New Deal and all its works from the start. As an Ohio senator told Herbert Hoover, "I would rather be defeated in antagonizing this program of economic absurdities than to have been elected either by advocating them or sneaking in as noncommital." On the other hand, Republicans in the Northeast, where Roosevelt's policies had much resonance with the voters, contended that simple naysaying would be suicide. A New Yorker observed, "It is no longer good political strategy to abuse and denounce everyone and everything without regard to the facts or the temper of the times."[7]

In 1934, neither ideological purity nor political expedience did much to help Republican congressional candidates fight against the New Deal tide. The usual pattern of the opposition party gaining seats two years after a presidential election did not hold up. Going into the voting, the Grand Old Party held 117 seats in the House. They saw their numbers drop by thirteen in that chamber. Another ten senators went down to defeat as well, leaving the party with only twenty-five senators to oppose Roosevelt.

The bulk of the losses that the Republicans suffered were in the Northeast and Middle Atlantic states. In the Middle West more moderate Republicans were defeated, so the conservative bloc of Republicans in the House was actually strengthened in terms of its influence with the party. Disgruntled conservatives blamed their losses on timely relief payments that the Roosevelt administration had made in key states. Moderates in the party contended that the results showed the party had to move to the center.

Following the 1934 elections, the New Deal moved further leftward during the spring of 1935 as Congress passed Social Security, the Wagner Act to provide bargaining rights for organized labor, the Public Utility Holding

Companies Act, and the Banking Act of 1935, and approved some $4.8 billion for relief. The Roosevelt administration also introduced major legislation to raise income tax rates on the wealthiest Americans. These measures intensified the existing Republican opposition to Roosevelt and his programs. The business community, some of whose members had been sympathetic to early New Deal programs such as the National Recovery Act in 1933, moved back toward the GOP and lent their financial support to the beleaguered Republican treasury.[8]

In Congress, Republicans fought a rearguard action against what has been called the "Second Hundred Days" during the spring and summer of 1935. Their dissents anticipated the critiques that the party would make of Roosevelt and the New Deal for decades. On Social Security, Republicans saw "no compelling reason" for dealing with this reform prior to recovery. Taking money out of the economy to pay for old-age pensions was not a step that would put people back to work. The White House claimed, on the other hand, that some kind of provision for people's welfare in their old age was necessary. Republicans expressed their disapproval of this move away from individual self-reliance. Representative James Wadsworth of New York argued, "Once we pay pensions and supervise annuities, we cannot withdraw from the undertaking no matter how demoralizing and subversive it may become." Charles Eaton of New Jersey charged that "the ultimate aim of the New Deal is to place all American industry, business, and individual liberties under the control of Government here in Washington." After failing in an effort to have Social Security sent back to committee, most Republicans then went on record as endorsing the popular bill on final passage. That tactic enabled later generations of Republicans to disguise their party's visceral and abiding dislike of Social Security.[9]

As for the Wagner Act, Republicans stood against the "closed shop" that mandated union membership when organized labor won an election in a factory or business. They also condemned Roosevelt's 1935 tax measure increasing levies on inheritance, gifts, and high individual incomes. Senator Vandenberg called it "a tin foil measure which snipes inconclusively at wealth, but will neither produce revenue commensurate with our spending nor achieve any useful social purpose." The Republican reaction to the second hundred days was not monolithic. Western Republicans such as George W. Norris of Nebraska gave a greater degree of support to the Democratic administration than their eastern counterparts. Yet overall, congressional Republicans were becoming more conservative and more cohesive as the New Deal progressed.[10]

By 1935, discontent with Roosevelt among conservative Democrats led to the emergence of the American Liberty League, designed to counteract Roosevelt's dominance within his own party. Such dissent from the president's policies encouraged Republicans to believe that the political tide might be turning. One newspaperman on the right observed in August 1934 that "the chance of a Republican comeback has been strengthened." A year later, after the Second Hundred Days, increased contributions from business helped the Republicans pay off the debt from 1932. The Republicans devoted themselves to restoring party unity and, more important, finding a presidential candidate who could win in 1936. If the conservative elements in both parties worked together, defeat of Roosevelt and the Democrats actually seemed possible.[11]

The key to success against Roosevelt, Republican strategists believed, was to bring the normally Republican states of the Northeast and Middle Atlantic regions back into harmony with the Plains and Middle Western states. In short, the Republicans needed to recreate the coalitions that had elected William McKinley, Theodore Roosevelt, and Warren G. Harding. In light of that theory, it made sense to look for a presidential candidate from west of the Mississippi River who could appeal to both sections. But after the 1934 disaster, there were not many attractive candidates who fit that set of requirements.

Only one incumbent Republican governor had been returned in 1934, Alfred M. Landon of Kansas. The other GOP presidential possibilities did not evoke much enthusiasm. Herbert Hoover hoped for another nomination even though most realistic Republicans knew his selection would spell disaster. Under pressure from party regulars, he withdrew from consideration in September 1935. Senator William E. Borah of Idaho, a progressive on domestic issues and an isolationist in foreign policy, was seventy years old and had little strength outside the Rocky Mountain region. Other contenders such as Frank Knox and Arthur Vandenberg were not credible alternatives.

Landon seemed in 1935 to have real potential as a rival to Roosevelt. He had supported Theodore Roosevelt in 1912, but since then had backed Republican candidates. Some styled Landon a "Kansas Coolidge." His ally, William Allen White, called him "a bigger man than Coolidge was the day he went to the White House" and a candidate who "outsizes most of the Republican aspirants." Landon was forty-nine in 1936, a successful oil operator in Oklahoma, and a liberal on social matters. Otherwise his opinions tracked Republican orthodoxy. He supported a balanced budget, opposed attempts to inflate the currency, and believed Roosevelt and the New Deal had shifted too much power from the states to Washington.[12]

In the absence of a serious challenge, Landon glided toward the Republican nomination during the first five months of 1936. He united his western support with the big states of the East and locked up the nomination on the first ballot. At first the convention leaders wanted to name Senator Styles Bridges of New Hampshire as the running mate until someone pointed out the dangers of "Landon Bridges falling down." Frank Knox became the vice presidential nominee.

The Republican platform endorsed in principle a number of New Deal programs, including Social Security, the right of labor to organize, and the desirability of regulating business. The delegates promised to balance the budget by cutting expenditures "drastically and immediately" rather than by raising taxes. In foreign affairs they pledged not to join the League of Nations or the World Court, and to seek resolution of disputes among nations through international arbitration. The foreign policy section was very brief—the last time it would be in the twentieth century. The Democrats did not receive much explicit criticism, though the Republicans wavered between their conservative impulses and the need to craft language that supported popular New Deal programs in principle.[13]

The course of the Landon campaign contradicted all the optimistic forecasts of his electoral appeal and the possibility of real voter discontent with Roosevelt's leadership. Landon proved to be a lackluster candidate who was no match for Roosevelt at the height of his popularity. As his chances receded, Landon attacked Roosevelt increasingly from the right, and thus ceded to the president the middle ground, which is where the voters were in 1936. The Republicans made the sunflower their symbol in 1936 and "Oh! Susanna" their campaign song. Nostalgia did not work, nor did predictions of impending national doom from the right. The electorate did not see tyranny but rather better times coming from the president and the Democrats.

The Republicans did carry Maine, which in those days voted in September. If the familiar slogan, "As Maine goes, so goes the nation," were true, then Roosevelt might have been in trouble. The *Literary Digest* magazine offered polls showing Landon competing well with the president. Unfortunately, the *Digest* surveyed only those voters with telephones, missing the massive surge for Roosevelt among those who were less well off. When Landon carried only Maine and Vermont in November, the chairman of the Democratic National Committee retorted, "As Maine goes, so goes Vermont."[14]

The Landon-Roosevelt race intensified a sharp ideological division between the two parties. Landon said that only his election would preserve "the Constitution and the American form of government." Though it was harder now to argue that the Democrats lacked the capacity to govern, casting doubts on their legitimacy within the American system reappeared as a consistent GOP theme. The New Deal, the Republican candidate charged, believed "in an all powerful chief executive" as well as "the destruction of state's rights and home rule." In short, the Roosevelt administration had "betrayed" American principles.[15]

Roosevelt reciprocated with tough rhetoric of his own. In his final speech at Madison Square Garden in late October, he linked the Republicans with "organized money" that was "unanimous in their hatred for me—and I welcome their hatred." He promised that in his second term "the forces of selfishness and lust for power" would meet "their master." This strident language intensified the already powerful Republican dislike for the president.[16]

The 1936 campaign also saw the business community rally behind the Republican ticket and supply the bulk of the party's funds for the national campaign. Some segments of corporate America, such as the Du Ponts, who had large chemical holdings, had contributed to the Democrats in 1932, and they moved back into the ranks of the GOP. Most major business leaders had endorsed Hoover with their checks in 1932 and did the same for Landon four years later. The Republicans spent $14 million in 1936; the Democrats and their allied groups expended more than $9 million. The Republicans believed, however, that the president and his supporters used ample government funds, especially relief payments, to bolster the incumbent's chances for victory. Democratic victories were, in the minds of Republicans, not legitimate expressions of the will of the people, but rather the result of tricky and often illegal political manipulations.

However it was achieved—and the evidence indicates that it embodied the popular will—Roosevelt amassed a landslide of seismic proportions in 1936. He won nearly twenty-eight million popular votes to slightly under seventeen million votes for Landon. The Republican candidate increased the party's total over Hoover's in 1932, but Roosevelt gained almost eight million votes over his 1932 total as well. The electoral vote tally was 523 for Roosevelt and only 8 for Landon. The Democrats controlled the Senate eighty to sixteen. There were only eighty-nine Republicans in the House. The Republicans had reached such a low ebb that there was talk of their imminent demise as a party.

President Roosevelt soon took care of reviving Republican fortunes, but on the national level he had assembled an electoral coalition that would win five of the next seven presidential elections. The New Deal coalition became a dominant feature of American political life for a generation, and its ultimate breakdown in the 1960s was what enabled the Republican ascendancy in the last third of the twentieth century. The component parts of Roosevelt's electoral team included contradictory and unstable elements, but when they worked together, as they did in 1936, the Republicans were at a disadvantage.

The oldest building block was the still solid Democratic white South. The Depression restored Dixie to its traditional allegiance as New Deal programs poured money and jobs into the region. Democratic lawmakers supported social welfare initiatives as long as their white constituents received the bulk of the funding. Should the White House display any regard for blacks in the South on a sustained basis, then cracks would appear in the white commitment to the New Deal.

The newest component of the New Deal coalition was the vote of African Americans in the North; they had moved there during the "Great Migration" of blacks from the South during and after World War I. Beginning slowly in 1928 and with increasing speed in the four years that followed, blacks had left the Grand Old Party and identified themselves as Roosevelt Democrats. The Roosevelt administration was cautious in assisting African Americans because of the power of southern Democrats in Congress, but even the modest steps that the White House took to distribute relief payments and provide government jobs for blacks brought its reward at the polls. Eleanor Roosevelt's evident sympathy for the aspirations of African Americans helped as well. For the moment, Republicans competed for black voters, but the conviction was forming within the GOP that the New Deal had bought black ballots. That assumption would in time result in Republican efforts to suppress black voting.

Urban voters and organized labor provided other key components of FDR's new coalition. The various measures that assisted the American Federation of Labor and the Congress of Industrial Organizations moved union members into the Democratic ranks. As Alf Landon put it, "The labor leaders are all tied up with this administration." As long as these disparate forces remained in the Democratic column, the Republicans faced an uphill battle in a presidential contest.[17]

Even amid this electoral disaster, there were some reassuring signs for the Republicans. With a weak candidate and facing a popular president, some 40 percent of the voters remained loyal to the Grand Old Party. Once the natural balance of American politics reasserted itself and the economic crisis ebbed, the Republicans would again be competitive with their rivals. That historical trend was confirmed during the two years that followed the 1936 election. Because of fissures within the Republican Party and the skill of Roosevelt as a president and campaigner, the return of the Republicans to power on the presidential level took longer.

The other significant aspect of the 1936 presidential contest was the way it underscored the lineup of ideologies that had been in the process of development since the Wilson-Hughes race in 1916. Following the era of Theodore Roosevelt, a progressive, reformist group resided within the Republican Party, albeit with diminishing influence during the 1920s. By the mid-1930s, conservatism prevailed as the dominant party stance on domestic issues. "Liberal" Republicans were willing to accept some aspects of the New Deal for electoral reasons. Moderates were less enthusiastic about this strategy, but would go along when a winning campaign seemed a likely prospect. Conservatives, who made up the majority of the party, believed that the New Deal represented a revolutionary shift in values that should be rolled back when the party regained political power. The faith in national power that had been at the heart of Republican thinking in the mid-nineteenth century was replaced by an increasing commitment to state's rights, smaller government, and a limited executive, all of which became hallmarks of twentieth-century Republicanism.

From the heights of his electoral triumph in 1936, Franklin D. Roosevelt committed a significant blunder that enabled the Republicans to move out of the wilderness for the first time in the 1930s. In February 1937, Roosevelt launched his plan to transform the Supreme Court by adding new justices, up to as many as six, to the existing nine members. The "court-packing plan," designed to make the high court more liberal and responsive to public opinion, flopped. Even some liberals who disliked the court's anti–New Deal decisions did not approve of Roosevelt's initiative. At a time when the court was still held in awe, Roosevelt created a controversy that united some liberal and many conservative Democrats in opposition to the scheme. A wave of protest erupted.

The small minority of Republicans in Congress opposed what Roosevelt wanted to do, but they recognized that their public opposition might drive Democrats back into Roosevelt's camp. With Democrats in the Senate attacking the court plan, the Republicans let members of the party in power fight among themselves. The result was a stinging defeat for Roosevelt. He achieved from Congress only a greatly watered-down version of his original proposal that left the Supreme Court intact. The controversy prompted conservative Democrats in Congress to explore ways in which they might cooperate with their Republican colleagues to stymie additional New Deal measures.[18]

Other forces aided Republican fortunes in 1937–1938. Labor militance, expressed in sit-down strikes in the automobile and steel industries, brought outbreaks of violence that frightened middle-class citizens who were otherwise sympathetic to the administration. The Congress of Industrial Organizations (CIO), which tried to organize unskilled workers into unions, became the symbol of labor's new aggressiveness. An advertisement in a Boston newspaper sought to capitalize on the apprehensions that the sit-down strikes evoked: "Come on down to Cape Cod for a real vacation where the CIO is unknown and over 90 percent are Republicans who respect the Supreme Court."[19]

The final lift for the Republicans came from the deep recession that started in the spring of 1937 and belied the promises of the president that the Depression was on the run. Industrial production sagged some 30 percent during the sixteen months after April 1937. Unemployment surged from about five million in August 1937 to 9.6 million the following spring. Roosevelt's efforts to balance the budget, the reduced purchasing power brought on by Social Security taxes, and the loss of business confidence all contributed to the abrupt downturn. Blame fell on the president and his policies. Republicans talked of the "Roosevelt recession," and even the "Roosevelt Depression."[20]

The Republicans saw their fortunes revive further during 1937 when Thomas E. Dewey won election as district attorney in New York City and sometime Republican Fiorello La Guardia also gained reelection as mayor. As 1938 opened, polls showed Republican gains in the Middle West. Meanwhile, the Democrats divided into warring factions when the president sought to "purge" conservatives within his own party. After six years Roosevelt's popularity sagged during what everyone assumed would be the last term of his presidency.

For the first time in a decade the Republicans were on the offensive, and their newspapers proclaimed "American Voters Return to Sanity." When the results of the 1938 elections were tabulated, the GOP had reestablished itself as a real alternative to the Democrats. The party picked up seven senators, elected twelve governors, and added seventy-five seats in the House. Some new faces emerged on the national scene. Robert A. Taft, son of the former president, won a Senate seat in Ohio. Harold Stassen was elected governor of Minnesota, and even Thomas E. Dewey's close but unsuccessful race for governor of New York made him a rising figure within the party.[21]

Wendell Willkie stormed to the Republican nomination in 1940 as he aroused the party's grass roots with his charisma and energy. Library of Congress, LC-USZ62-38331.

The surge of Republican strength in Congress, combined with southern Democratic unhappiness with Roosevelt over both his economic policies and the race issue, facilitated the rise of the conservative coalition that dominated the legislative stage for the next twenty-five years. As a result the New Deal had to face lawmakers in 1939–1940 who were intent on cutting back social programs such as the Federal Theater Project. An ambitious White House effort to reorganize the executive branch produced a bitter struggle on Capitol Hill during 1938, and the president had to compromise to get even some of what he sought in 1939.

The political events of 1938 took place while the international scene darkened for both the European democracies and the United States. The Munich Agreement dismembered Czechoslovakia at the behest of Adolf Hitler, while the tide of anti-Semitism rose in Germany. Japan seemed an aggressive challenger to the American position in the Pacific. Foreign policy surged to the forefront of the national debate. As it did so, serious internal divisions among Republicans plagued the party.

In the nation's heartland, far from Europe and its troubles, sentiment to stay out of the quarrels of the Old World had wide support among Republicans. Disillusion with the outcome of World War I, antipathy toward Great Britain, and some degree of anti-Semitism moved together in varying degrees to feed the argument on behalf of continued isolation. Senators such as William E. Borah of Idaho and Gerald P. Nye of North Dakota led the bloc of Republicans in the upper house who wanted to avoid European disputes. The *Chicago Tribune* under "Colonel" Robert McCormick provided a powerful editorial voice for this brand of Republican thought.

In the East, other Republicans looked with apprehension at the string of German triumphs in 1938 and worried about the foreign policy dangers to the country if Hitler prevailed. After World War II began in Europe with the German invasion of Poland on September 1, 1939, these interventionists wanted the United States to aid Great Britain and France. Such newspapers as the *New York Herald Tribune* trumpeted the cause in their editorials. Less conservative on domestic issues than their Middle Western counterparts, these Republicans believed in a strong national defense and aggressive opposition to German designs. With money from the business and banking communities and good connections to the mass media, through such magazines as Henry Luce's *Time*, the interventionist side had greater capacity to influence Republican conventions on behalf of the candidate they favored.

As 1940 neared, the choice of the Republican presidential candidate was not at all clear. The party's victory in 1938 had made the nomination worth having, especially if Roosevelt decided to step down at the end of his second term. None of the Democrats mentioned as the president's possible successor seemed of heavyweight caliber. In that setting the Republican nomination seemed a very attractive prize, and a number of aspirants entered the race.

Senator Robert A. Taft had already followed the course that would earn him the title "Mr. Republican." Party conservatives admired Taft's intellectual rigor and commitment to pre-1932 doctrines of small government that favored business enterprise. Later, Taft endorsed government intervention in the form of public housing, which raised eyebrows on the right. Before the war, however, he was a staunch exponent of anti–New Deal thinking and strong isolationist sentiments. He was also dull. Alice Roosevelt Longworth said that having Taft follow Roosevelt "would be like taking a glass of warm milk after taking a slug of benzedrine." From the beginning of the race, Taft's cold and stern personality hampered his appeal to the voters. Balding, with steel-rimmed glasses and a dry speaking style, Taft seemed austere and aloof. The best one of his friends could do to humanize him was to tell the 1940 convention that the candidate was "as common as an old shoe."[22]

The ostensible front runner in early 1940 was Thomas E. Dewey, the district attorney of New York City. Just thirty-seven years old in 1939, the diminutive, mustachioed Dewey had built a reputation as a racket-busting prosecutor who had taken out "Murder Incorporated," as the New York tabloids dubbed organized crime. He had lost the governor's race to Herbert H. Lehman in 1938 but had come so close to the popular incumbent that it was in essence a moral triumph. Dewey had a very pleasant speaking voice on the radio, and he told his audiences, "There is no limit to America. There is a force in America that has been held in check which, once released, can give us the employment we need."[23]

For all Dewey's charm, he impressed some who met him as icy and arrogant. An aide later called him "cold—as cold as a February icicle." The Democrats mocked his youth. Secretary of the Interior Harold Ickes quipped that when Dewey announced for president, he threw his diaper into the ring. Despite these difficulties, Dewey established a lead over Taft and Senator Arthur Vandenberg when he won primaries in Wisconsin and Nebraska in April and May.[24]

Then the international scene further deteriorated. On May 11, 1940, the Germans invaded Holland and Belgium, and soon went deep into France with their Panzer divisions. As the cause of democracy wavered and Germany seemed ascendant, previous calculations of Republican politicians went out the window. Neither Dewey nor Taft seemed up to the task of managing the country's defense in a time of crisis. Talk began in Democratic circles that the president might seek an unprecedented third term. As the Republicans assembled for their convention in steamy Philadelphia in June 1940, they faced a situation as confused and uncertain as any in their party's history. Many Republicans argued that the best course was to select a man who only a few short years earlier had been a utility company executive and a Democrat, Wendell Willkie of Indiana.[25]

Few events in the history of the Republicans were more improbable than Wendell Willkie's capture of the presidential nomination in 1940. In May, Willkie was the choice of only 3 percent of Americans in a presidential poll, but that result was hardly surprising. Forty-eight-year-old Willkie was not known to most Americans that tumultuous spring. He grew up in Elwood, Indiana, graduated from Indiana University with a law degree, and went to work for the Commonwealth and Southern Corporation, a public utility. In 1935, he became the company's president. In that position he came into conflict with the Roosevelt administration over its Tennessee Valley Authority project to provide inexpensive electric power to that region. Willkie was an effective and articulate defender of the interests of private power companies, and his views soon attracted the attention of other corporate executives and opinion makers in the East. As a conservative Democrat, Willkie had few realistic options other than to move toward the Grand Old Party.[26]

The burly Willkie was only an average orator with a prepared text, but when he spoke ad lib he had the ability to excite a crowd. He was especially appealing to women, who found that he had "the well-organized bulkiness of a healthy bear, and singularly brilliant eyes." His marriage had long been in name only, but his wife kept up the pretense that they were a happy couple. To the public, Willkie seemed a breath of fresh air: a critic of the New Deal and its excesses who also maintained some objectivity about what was valuable within Roosevelt's record. As war engulfed Europe, Willkie's belief in aiding the Allies struck internationalist Republicans as what the leaders of their party should be promoting. To the conservatives of an isolationist bent, the candidacy of this lapsed Democrat was dismaying and dangerous.[27]

Willkie registered as a Republican before local elections in November 1939. Then in the April 1940 issue of *Fortune* magazine, Willkie proclaimed, "It makes a great deal of difference to us—politically, economically, and emotionally—what kind of world exists beyond our shores." With words like that, Willkie set himself apart from the isolationist attitudes of Taft and Vandenberg as well as the equivocations that Dewey had expressed in the many speeches he made that spring.[28]

While the Republican convention was in progress, President Roosevelt surprised the delegates and the nation with the selection of two prominent Republicans for his cabinet. He named Henry L. Stimson as his secretary of war and Frank Knox as secretary of the Navy. Stimson had held the same post under William Howard Taft a generation earlier and then had been secretary of state under Hoover. Knox had run with Landon four years earlier. Angry Republicans said that the two men were no longer party members in good standing, but the episode illustrated Roosevelt's skill in co-opting his political enemies and defusing the appeal of the opposition.[29]

In 1940 it was still possible for a candidate such as Willkie to come from nowhere and seize the Republican nomination. Although primaries were held, they did not lock up the prize in advance for any single candidate, and the party structure was fluid enough to enable an insurgent to outwit the established Republican leadership. Many elements contributed to Willkie's striking victory. The course of the war in Europe made all the other candidates seem wrong for the presidency. With no clear front runner to beat, Willkie divided and conquered. He had intense popular enthusiasm on his side. Younger Republicans, led by an attorney named Oren Root, Jr., created Draft Willkie for President clubs that sprang up across the nation among young professionals who identified with the moderate wing of the party. The candidate also had the support of such publishing giants as Henry Luce, the Cowles family of *Look* magazine, and other print moguls.

At bottom, however, the rumpled, heavyset, plainspoken Willkie caught the imagination of those Republicans in the summer of 1940 who did not want their party to stand aside from the dangers of impending war. The leaders of the Willkie bandwagon provided fuel for the vehicle, but popular enthusiasm and the sense that Willkie could beat Roosevelt impelled the Hoosier newcomer toward the nomination. The packed gallery, the chanting crowd, the telegrams that deluged the delegates, all attested to the charisma of this new Republican hero. Willkie still might have been stopped had the Taft and Dewey delegates combined, but that alliance did not occur because neither candidate would defer to the other. Once Willkie had won, the convention chose Senator Charles L. McNary of Oregon as his running mate.

The platform that the delegates adopted in Philadelphia reflected the crosscurrents among Republicans as World War II intensified. "The Republican Party is firmly opposed to involving this Nation in a foreign war" was the first line in the plank on national defense. Elsewhere in the platform was a promise to "revise the tax system and remove those practices which impede recovery" in favor of policies "which stimulate enterprise." The delegates urged Congress to submit the Equal Rights Amendment to the states. They also condemned "the New Deal encouragement of various groups that seek to change the American government by means outside the Constitution" and pledged "the Republican Party to get rid of such borers from within." The platform writers did not specify whether such threats came from Nazis or Communists, but the underlying suspicion of the patriotism and legitimacy of the Democrats persisted.[30]

Had Willkie gone on to capture the presidency, his nomination would not have had the traumatic effect on the party that it did. Since he lost to Franklin D. Roosevelt, the choice of Willkie came to be seen as the first of several cases in which eastern Republicans forced a liberal nominee perceived as electable upon middle western and western conservatives, only to have him go down to defeat anyway. The argument that more conservative choices would have done worse against Roosevelt in 1940 and 1944 and Harry Truman in 1948 is plausible but impossible to prove. The right wing believed that it had been betrayed for expediency's sake and had nothing to show for the degrading experience.

Willkie's campaign peaked the day he was nominated. In his acceptance speech he referred to "you Republicans." From the outset of his race against Roosevelt he demonstrated an insensitivity to party regulars when he installed a new chair of the Republican National Committee after promising to retain the incumbent. The new nominee was not well organized, nor did he have a consistent strategy to beat President Roosevelt. So chaotic did the Willkie campaign become that one of the speechwriters said, "This place is like a whorehouse on a Saturday night when the madam is out and all the girls are running around dropping nickels in juke boxes."[31]

Willkie started out looking for the middle ground. He agreed not to attack Roosevelt's deal with the British exchanging obsolete American destroyers for British bases in North America. The arrangement strengthened American defenses against Nazi submarines. However, Willkie moved rightward as the campaign progressed. By October, when the polls showed him trailing Roosevelt, Willkie played the isolationist card with increasing vehemence. "We can have peace but we must know how to preserve it," he told the nation over the radio. "To begin with, we shall not undertake to fight anybody else's war. Our boys shall stay out of Europe." Willkie's energy and the appeal of his dynamic personality helped the challenger close the gap as the election neared a climax.[32]

The 1940 election was hard-fought and bitter, and its residual impact on the Republicans was profound. The issue of Roosevelt's unprecedented third term received much attention. GOP buttons proclaimed, "Two times is enough for any man." Others said, "We don't want Eleanor either," a reference to Mrs. Roosevelt's growing status as a controversial advocate of African American rights. Democrats countered with a button that said, "Better a third-termer than a third-rater." Secretary of the Interior Harold Ickes called Willkie "a simple barefoot Wall Street lawyer." The campaign strengthened Republican resolve that no president in the future be allowed to duplicate Roosevelt's multiple term tenure.[33]

Outside of the public view, the Republicans gained access to letters that the Democratic vice presidential candidate, Henry Wallace, had written to a personal adviser who happened to be an Eastern mystic. The missives painted Wallace in a naive and foolish light. Roosevelt also played hardball. A White House conversation was taped on a crude device in the president's office that Roosevelt had installed. In the recording, Roosevelt planned to counter any anti-Wallace effort with a whispering campaign of his own against Willkie. It would reveal the Republican candidate's longtime extramarital relationship with Irita Van Doren of the *New York Herald Tribune*. In the end neither side used their clandestine information.[34]

As the presidential race tightened, Roosevelt went out on the stump. In two statements FDR seized the initiative from his rival. During a speech at Boston Garden on October 30, Roosevelt reminded his audience: "I have said this before but I shall say it again and again and again. Your boys are not going to be sent into any foreign war." The speech outraged Willkie when he heard it on the radio. "That hypocritical son of a bitch! This is going to beat me." In a final speech at Madison Square Garden in New York City, Roosevelt assailed three isolationist Republicans in the House by name: Joseph W. Martin of Massachusetts and New Yorkers Bruce Barton and Hamilton Fish. He gained roars from the crowd when he denounced "Martin, Barton, and Fish." As the president pressed the crowd to identify Republican culprits on issues of defense and preparedness, the throng shouted back "Martin, Barton, and Fish." The isolationist wing of the GOP proved Willkie's heaviest burden in 1940.[35]

Willkie made the 1940 election close, but he fell short of victory. The Republican candidate came within five million votes of the president but lost in the electoral college 449 to 82. The Republican ticket did well in the Middle West and made gains among Irish Americans who resented the emerging alliance with Great Britain and Italian Americans who bridled at the president's criticism of Benito Mussolini. Roosevelt ran strongest in the cities and piled up large margins in precincts where lower-income Americans lived. Dominance in that area as well as the impact of the war effort offset Willkie's robust showing in the suburbs, the Great Plains, and the Pacific Coast. The continuing Democratic stranglehold on the South gave Roosevelt a strong base that Willkie's impassioned campaign could not overcome.[36]

The 1940 election created a permanent sense of grievance within the conservative base of the Republicans. Reliance on the moderate Willkie and the eastern Republicans who supported him had not brought victory and ousted Roosevelt. Instead, in their view, the party had compromised its core principles without winning national power. Some Republicans believed that eastern media interests had engineered Willkie's nomination for the express purpose of denying the nation an honest choice between Roosevelt's prowar policy and genuine isolationism. Had Willkie taken a clear position against war and Roosevelt's pro-British stance, this argument ran, the Republican candidate would have made a better showing in the Middle West. The sense that the Republicans needed to be true to their fundamental beliefs would animate conservatives for the next four decades.

In the aftermath of the 1940 election, the Republicans remained at odds with one another. Roosevelt's initiative to help Great Britain through the Lend-Lease program, announced in early 1941, sharpened the divisions. Willkie and his friends saw the United States as tied to the fortunes of the global conflict. Senator Taft and the isolationist wing believed that the country must not be drawn into Europe's battles. The idea of making war supplies available to Great Britain during the fighting and receiving payment only after the war was won seemed fiscally unsound and, worse yet, a blatant violation of neutrality. As Taft told a friend in January 1941, "I feel very strongly that Hitler's defeat is not vital to us, and that even the collapse of England is to be preferred to participation for the rest of our lives in European wars."[37]

The political battle that ensued over Lend-Lease in 1941 led some Republicans to support the Roosevelt administration's stance on national defense, aid to Great Britain, and, after Hitler's invasion of the Soviet Union in June 1941, assistance to the Soviets. William Allen White, the Kansas editor, for example, formed the interventionist Committee to Defend America by Aiding the Allies. Willkie testified on behalf of Lend-Lease. In the midst of his appearance, Senator Gerald P. Nye of North Dakota asked him if he still believed, as he said during the presidential campaign, that Roosevelt would have the nation in the war by April 1941. Willkie responded that what he had said "was a bit of campaign oratory." The candid remark outraged Republican conservatives who believed that it revealed Willkie's true colors on foreign policy. Their 1940 candidate had never been truly committed to the Republican cause, or so they thought.[38]

These conservative Republicans comprised the other side of the foreign policy divide in their opposition to Roosevelt, the British, and American involvement in the war. The America First committee attracted their support, especially in the Middle West. Organized in September 1940, the committee achieved its greatest prominence during the Lend-Lease debate. Republicans used the committee and other such foreign policy interest groups to make the case against the president and his proposal. Among them were Alice Roosevelt Longworth, Herbert Hoover, and Arthur Vandenberg. The Michigan senator noted in his diary when Lend-Lease passed the Senate that he "was witnessing the suicide of the Republic." Led by Senator Taft, seventeen Republicans voted against Lend-Lease on final passage. Ten GOP senators voted with the administration.[39]

Republican isolationists in 1941 proved in the end to have chosen the wrong side of the historical debate. They voted overwhelmingly against the extension of the selective service law as a means of drafting young Americans into the armed forces when it came up for a vote in the House in August. Their strong opposition accounted for the tough fight that Speaker Sam Rayburn and the House leadership faced in passing the measure, ultimately by a single vote. In the months that followed, Republicans in the Senate also opposed more money for Lend-Lease and the arming of merchant ships.

Later revelations about the Holocaust and the enormity of the crimes of the Nazis and Adolf Hitler have complicated the debate about the prewar period. Why the United States did not do more to defeat Germany and Japan has seemed a salient historical issue. While the position of the isolationists was misguided, it was honestly held and reflected deep currents of American thinking about the world. That Franklin D. Roosevelt was not always candid in his diplomatic and military efforts to aid the British and their allies in 1940–1941 is also clear. Some of the tactical criticism he incurred about his undeclared naval war with Germany in late 1941 had validity. Republican warnings about the dangers of unchecked presidential power would also seem prescient a generation later during the Vietnam War. Nonetheless, the way in which war came to the United States and the consequences that followed undermined the doctrine of Republican isolationism within the Grand Old Party of the 1940s. Still, the impulses that isolationism embodied did not easily die.

The Japanese attack on Pearl Harbor on December 7, 1941, ended the debate over the active participation of the United States in World War II. Republicans rallied behind the administration in the immediate aftermath of the assault. Willkie's running mate, Senator McNary, said, "Our first duty now is to knock down the ears of those little yellow rats of the Orient." Senator

Taft told the press, "Undivided and unlimited prosecution of the war must show the world that no one can safely attack the American people."[40]

While pledging their support for the war in principle, Republicans did not believe that there was any reason to abate their political criticism of the Roosevelt administration. As Taft put it: "I believe there can be no doubt that criticism in time of war is essential to the maintenance of any kind of democratic government." Republicans in Congress contended that war was no time to continue costly New Deal programs, especially since the return of prosperity had ended any need for them in the first place. Republicans insisted that such initiatives as the National Youth Administration, the Civilian Conservation Corps, and the Works Progress Administration be stopped within six months in the interest of the war effort. Faced with a Congress where conservatives dominated, the Roosevelt administration acquiesced in terminating the New Deal.[41]

The war did not end the internal debate among Republicans over foreign policy and the nation's future role in the world. To some degree the aftermath of Pearl Harbor intensified the disagreement between isolationists and interventionists. Both Democrats and Republicans remembered World War I and the experience of Woodrow Wilson with the League of Nations. Roosevelt looked for ways to avoid the mistakes of his Democratic predecessor, while the Republicans endeavored to prevent a commitment to a modern variant of the League. The result was a contentious foreign policy dialogue that continued throughout the war and beyond it.

While the war evoked a surge of patriotic fervor in early 1942, the Democrats did not gain a political advantage from the fighting. For most of the year the war news was bad. The Japanese advanced in the Pacific with stunning speed, taking the Philippines, a US territory. The enemy's naval power in the Pacific was checked at the Battle of Midway in June, but the turn of the tide on the ground did not come until the struggle for Guadalcanal ended in early 1943. In Europe the Germans once again seemed to be on the march in Russia until their advance was checked at Stalingrad late in the year. American forces did not go on the attack until the invasion of North Africa five days after the congressional elections in November 1942.

World War II produced new political circumstances to which both parties had to adapt. Government spending on the conflict fueled an economic boom that ended the Depression once and for all. It has become an article of Republican faith that New Deal spending failed to relieve the hard times until the war lifted the economy. Of course, the war instigated government spending at a rate that would have been unthinkable a few years earlier.

While World War II would become enshrined by the 1990s as the heyday of the "Greatest Generation," the home front witnessed its share of social turmoil, wrenching change, and self-interested behavior. The Japanese relocation program, race riots in major cities, wartime profiteering, and the ever-present casualty lists were also part of the American experience between 1942 and 1945. The nation was more prosperous than ever before, even if citizens had little on which to spend their increased paychecks. As war workers moved to follow the relocation of many industries to the Sunbelt and other Americans began to trek to the suburbs, a shift toward conservatism and traditional social values vied with the painful memories of the Great Depression in shaping political attitudes toward the Republicans and their presidential candidates.

The war and its aftermath were the probable causes of the Grand Old Party's inability to regain national power for two additional presidential contests, in 1944 and 1948. The Republicans did enjoy greater success at the congressional level in the 1940s, yet their internal differences over foreign policy limited their effectiveness in shaping alternatives to the overseas initiatives of the Democrats.

In 1942, the Republicans gained another victory in the congressional races. The slow pace of the war, along with recurrent Allied defeats, stirred unhappiness with the Roosevelt administration. Isolationist views were still strong in the Middle West, where voters also disliked the price controls that had been imposed on food crops to stem inflation. Turnout in the election was depressed, especially among the low-income groups that formed the Democratic base. With soldiers away, only twenty-five million voters went to the polls, a sharp drop from the 1940 total.[42] The Republicans added forty-four seats in the House to raise their total to 208. They were now within sight of a majority for the first time in twelve years. The GOP added nine Senate seats, which increased their delegation to thirty-seven. The working arrangements with southern Democrats that started a few years earlier meant that the Senate was not a reliable asset for the Roosevelt administration.

The big winner in 1942 was Thomas E. Dewey. He achieved a decisive victory over divided Democrats in New York State in his bid to become governor. Elsewhere, Earl Warren became governor of California, Harold Stassen won the Minnesota statehouse, and John W. Bricker, a Taft conservative, triumphed in Ohio in his bid for a third term. Bricker's victory made him a potential presidential contender, too, as leader of the conservatives and isolationists. In 1943, both Taft and Vandenberg took themselves out of the 1944 contest, and the battle for the prize shaped up as a contest among Willkie, Dewey, and Bricker.

Despite his continuing national popularity, Willkie saw his standing among Republicans erode in 1942 and 1943. His defense of the Roosevelt administration on foreign policy did not help him, nor did his decision to make a round-the-world tour rather than campaign for GOP candidates in 1942. Above all, Willkie's internationalist views made him anathema to the party's rank and file. Neither Taft nor Dewey liked or trusted Willkie, whom Dewey called "my fat friend" in private. As Willkie became yet more internationalist and more critical of his party's leaders, his Republican base shrank.[43]

Dewey saw his fortunes improve at Willkie's expense. As governor of New York, he did well on issues such as housing, agriculture, and taxes. He also staked out a moderate position on foreign policy between Taft and Willkie. A private poll of 1940 convention delegates showed Dewey ahead of Bricker 36 percent to 21 percent. Willkie trailed badly, as did General Douglas MacArthur. When prominent Republicans assembled at Mackinac Island in Michigan in 1943 to discuss postwar foreign policy, Dewey grabbed the headlines when he proposed an alliance between the United States and Great Britain after the fighting ended. The move irritated isolationists. The *Chicago Tribune*, ever ready to rebuke signs of internationalism, responded with a banner headline: "Tom Dewey Goes Anti-America." The episode further bolstered Dewey's standing as a Republican moderate.[44]

The Mackinac Conference, designed to smooth over Republican tensions, achieved its desired result by scripting language on foreign policy that all factions could endorse. The resulting document spoke of "responsible participation by the United States in postwar cooperative organization among sovereign nations to prevent military aggression and to attain permanent peace with organized justice in a free world." That inclusive rhetoric enabled Republicans, whether isolationist or internationalist, to coexist without fratricidal debates over foreign affairs as they headed into the 1944 presidential race.[45]

During the first half of 1944, Willkie's star dimmed among Republicans. When Dewey trounced him in the Wisconsin primary in April, Willkie withdrew from the presidential race. By the fall of 1944, he was dead of pneumonia and a heart attack. His role in the Republican Party receded from memory as the party moved further to the right during the rest of the decade. Yet Willkie had been an important Republican during his all-too-brief season in the party's leadership. He provided a voice for the internationalist wing and the more moderate policies associated with eastern Republicans. Had the GOP sought to rely only on its isolationist base during the 1940 and 1944 presidential contests, Roosevelt would likely have won more decisive victories. By keeping the Republicans closer to the middle in both domestic and foreign affairs, Willkie maintained their competitive posture. In that sense Willkie was an important transitional figure for the presidency of Dwight D. Eisenhower.

After Dewey ousted Willkie, the nomination was his to win. The determined New Yorker believed that he could beat Roosevelt on themes of economic conservatism and moderate social policies, a combination that had worked for him as governor. As he told newspaper publishers in late April, he rejected the view implicit in the New Deal that the economy "can continue to function only by constantly taking ever more expensive patent medicine." Instead, Dewey affirmed that "America is still young, still vigorous, still capable of growth." Privately, he insisted, "If [the electorate] can give their full attention to domestic problems, they will vote Roosevelt out unanimously."[46]

As Dewey neared clinching the nomination, latent conservative restiveness about the candidate and his political style simmered. Someone, perhaps actress Ethel Barrymore, but not Alice Roosevelt Longworth, had said that the diminutive New Yorker looked like "the little man on the wedding cake." Imperious and disinclined to suffer fools, Dewey did not ingratiate himself with his GOP colleagues. With his lead in the delegate race and with John Bricker fading as the conservative alternative, the right wing of the party saw Dewey as their only hope to unseat Roosevelt.[47]

The convention met in Chicago summer heat that hovered around one hundred degrees, and the proceedings went forward in a kind of stupor. Dewey wanted Earl Warren to be his running mate, but the Californian declined. That left Bricker, whom Alice Roosevelt Longworth had dubbed "an honest Harding." A man noted for his dynamic oratory but not for his brains or political flexibility, Bricker was the darling of the right. As a newspaper columnist noted after Bricker joined the ticket: "Mr. Average Delegate's mind and judgment is all for Dewey, but his heart belongs to Bricker."[48]

Senator Taft framed most of the platform in Chicago. It incorporated the language of the Mackinac Conference into the plank headed "War and Peace." On other subjects, the convention again endorsed the Equal Rights Amendment, favored a two-term limit on the presidency, and attacked lynching and the poll tax. "Four more years of the New Deal policy," said the Republicans, "would centralize all power in the President, and would daily subject every act of every citizen to regulation by his henchmen; the country would remain a Republic only in name."

Yet after twelve years of the New Deal, the Republicans also endorsed many Democratic programs, albeit with a heavy emphasis on the role of the states. They favored extension of Social Security "to all employees not already covered." Calling their party "the historical champions of free labor," the delegates accepted "the purposes of the Wagner Act, Social Security and the Wages and Hours Act," as well as other "Federal statutes designed to promote and protect the welfare of American working men and women." They did "reject the theory of restoring prosperity through government spending and deficit financing." Nonetheless, the rhetoric of the GOP's official statement of party policy went further in the direction of the welfare state than would have seemed possible a few years earlier.[49]

The 1944 campaign proceeded in the context of war news that had brightened for the Allies. Nazi Germany faced armies pounding it from east and west. The Americans were driving the Japanese back across the Pacific and invaded the Philippines in the autumn. The Roosevelt administration received credit for the good war performance, though the White House knew that hard fighting remained. By 1944, people close to Roosevelt recognized that his health was failing and he was unlikely to serve another four-year term. The Democrats selected Harry S. Truman as his running mate, and many people expected him to occupy the Oval Office soon if Roosevelt was reelected. Yet the Republicans faced risks if they invoked the issue of the president's health. They had to rely on public perceptions about Roosevelt's physical condition, and there Roosevelt proved adept at defusing the problem.[50]

Dewey and Bricker raised a number of domestic issues in their effort to throw the president off stride. One topic that received much attention turned on the role of the Congress of Industrial Organizations and its political action committee (CIO-PAC), headed by the labor leader Sidney Hillman, which raised money for Democratic candidates. Hillman became notorious when the president issued instructions during the Democratic convention that aides should "clear" the vice presidential choice with Hillman. The tag "clear it with Sidney" passed into political folklore as evidence of the power of left-wing labor leaders in the Democratic Party.[51]

The turning point in the campaign came in late September. A Republican member of the House named Harold Knutson charged that Roosevelt had wasted taxpayer money on his pet Scottish terrier, Fala. During a trip to the Aleutians, Fala had supposedly been left behind, and allegedly a destroyer had been dispatched to retrieve the presidential pooch. Roosevelt pounced. During a speech to the Teamsters on September 25 he ridiculed the charge as an example of chronic Republican exaggeration of his failings. As for Fala, he said, "When he learned that the Republican fiction writers had concocted a story that I left him behind on the Aleutian island and had sent a destroyer back to find him—at a cost to the taxpayer of two or three or twenty million dollars—his Scotch soul was furious. He has not been the same dog since." The sarcastic attack on the Republicans energized the Democrats while enraging Dewey and his aides.[52]

During the later stages of the campaign, Dewey and his running mate turned to an issue that would loom large for Republicans in the years that followed. Addressing alleged ties between the Roosevelt administration and the American Communist Party, Bricker told a Texas audience that "to all intents and purposes the great Democratic party has become the Hillman-Browder Communist party with Franklin Roosevelt as its front." Dewey echoed the theme. Through Hillman, he said, "the Communists are seizing control of the New Deal through which they aim to control the government of the United States." With the Russians fighting the Germans and driving toward the enemy's capital, the invocation of domestic Communism as an issue did not have the resonance it would gain just a few years later. But since Republicans believed that the Democrats were treasonous by nature and the New Deal was anti-American in its essence, a link with subversive elements was a natural connection to make.[53]

Another incident in the campaign illustrated the mutual suspicion and rancor that marked the Dewey-Roosevelt confrontation. Many Republicans believed that the president had been negligent, if not an outright liar, in the case of the Japanese surprise attack on Pearl Harbor. Rumors that the government had broken the Japanese diplomatic code circulated in Washington during 1944. Republicans concluded from these leaks that Roosevelt had been aware of the impending Japanese strike. While the diplomatic codebreaking gave clues to Tokyo's intentions in 1941, it did not supply the time or place of the attack. That information was contained in the naval codes, which were not being read in late 1941 in sufficient amounts to provide clues to what the Japanese Navy planned.

More important, the United States was still reading the Japanese cable traffic between Tokyo's ambassador in Berlin and his superiors, and the decoding of this communication was a source of valuable information. If Dewey made an issue of the matter and the codebreaking success was revealed to the Japanese, this window into Nazi strategy would be closed. General George C. Marshall, acting on his own, prevailed on the Republican candidate to keep the matter out of politics. Dewey did so, and the secret was preserved. However, the belief that Roosevelt had been at fault remained an article of Republican faith.[54]

The last month of the 1944 race became quite bitter as Dewey pressed the attack while Roosevelt campaigned in person to dispel rumors about his health. His eight-hour ride in pouring rain through New York City did much to silence the whispering about his imminent demise. The two candidates felt an abiding dislike for each other. Roosevelt said of Dewey on election night, "I still think he is a son of a bitch."[55]

In a heavy turnout of forty-eight million voters, Roosevelt beat Dewey and won his fourth term with 53 percent of the vote and a 432–99 result in the electoral college. The margin in the popular vote was about 3.5 million ballots. Dewey carried nine states, including Bricker's Ohio, but not his own state of New York. Meanwhile, Senator Taft won reelection and emerged as a likely presidential candidate for 1948. The Republicans foresaw that, with the war presumably over by 1948 and Roosevelt not a candidate, they would have a better than even chance in four years.

In January 1945, an ailing Roosevelt left for a final wartime conference with Joseph Stalin and Winston Churchill at Yalta in Crimea. The resulting deliberations produced one of the long-running political controversies of the Cold War era. The Allies agreed to divide Germany into occupied zones, designated four-power status on Berlin among the Soviet Union, the United States, Great Britain, and France. The best Roosevelt could get out of Stalin was a pledge to have free elections in Poland at some time in the future. Roosevelt's bargaining power was limited since Russian armies occupied Poland and other Eastern European countries.

When the details of the Yalta agreements became known, Republicans believed that the president had made concessions to the Soviets that put Eastern Europe in Communist hands. A Democratic administration had watched as millions fell captive under Soviet sway. Republicans wondered what other secret agreements might exist of a dastardly nature. That Communists had swayed Roosevelt's decisions became a working Republican assumption. The Democrats were not just inept and deceitful; they had forfeited their legitimacy by their flirtation with treason.[56]

On April 12, 1945, Franklin D. Roosevelt died in Warm Springs, Georgia, and Harry S. Truman succeeded to the presidency. After twelve years of the New Deal, its architect was no more. During his tenure, Roosevelt had reshaped American politics by creating the welfare state and broadening the nation's role in the word. The Republican Party had been divided on both achievements, and that fracture persisted after Roosevelt was gone. On the right of the GOP, sentiment was strong to repeal as much of the New Deal as the voters would allow. More moderate elements among the Republicans, while critical of the premises of Democratic programs, wished to retain the popular and workable results of the Roosevelt era while trimming away excessive bureaucracy and holding down spending.

On questions of foreign policy, Republicans diverged over whether the United States should revert to an isolationist past or continue in its role on the international stage. During the early months of the Truman administration, as first the war in Europe ended and then the Japanese surrendered, Republicans watched the new president and looked ahead to the 1946 congressional elections. These contests loomed as their first opportunity to return to national power. The onset of peace also brought disturbing signs that victory over Germany and Japan had not ended the challenges facing the nation. Tensions with the Soviet Union mounted as 1945 unfolded. The era of Roosevelt was over. The Cold War was beginning.

From "Had Enough" to Modern Republicanism, 1945–1961

THE REPUBLICANS WERE once again meeting in Chicago in July 1952 amid intense passions as Robert A. Taft and Dwight D. Eisenhower struggled for the nomination. After twenty years out of power, victory against the Democrats in the fall seemed probable. First the party had to decide between "Mr. Republican" and the American military hero of World War II. The contest was close, hinging on a cluster of disputed delegates from the South. The Eisenhower forces charged that Taft's allies were trying to steal delegates, and they sought "fair play." The Taft camp believed that their candidate was being cheated out of a nomination that belonged to him. Once again, they felt, eastern Republicans were thwarting the will of the party. A decade and a half of strife between the factions swelled to a climax.

The symbol of frustration for the Taft delegates was the New York governor, Thomas E. Dewey, the losing presidential candidate in 1944 and 1948. Now Dewey was the brains behind the effort to put Eisenhower in the White House and the spirit behind the claim that Taft "can't win." At a key moment in the struggle over the delegates, the Taft leaders decided to make Dewey the issue. They selected Senator Everett M. Dirksen to speak on Taft's behalf during the debate over the issue of the contested delegates. The Senator's real task was to take on Dewey and his controversial role in the party. With his wavy hair and stentorian voice, the grandiloquent Dirksen assailed the New Yorker. Spotting Dewey in the audience, he said, "We followed you before and you took us down the road to defeat."[1]

Dirksen's words set off a spontaneous outpouring of Dewey denunciation. Boos rang out through the hall, some of them intended for Dirksen, but most directed at Dewey. From the galleries, jeers rained down on the imperturbable New Yorker. A national television audience (or as national as it was in those days) watched as the pent-up animosities of the New Deal and Fair

Deal were unleashed on the convention floor. The next day the Taft leaders styled Dewey as "the greatest menace that the Republican party has."[2]

In the end, Dewey's cause triumphed and Eisenhower was nominated, but the long-term victory would rest with the conservatism that Taft and Dirksen represented. During the 1940s and 1950s, the Republicans sought and then won national power. Nonetheless, their own sense of themselves as a party remained in flux during the years between the end of World War II and the presidential candidacy of Richard Nixon in 1960.

That television viewers saw for themselves Dirksen's attack on Dewey was one major indicator of how politics had changed for both parties after the end of World War II. In 1948, under 1 percent of American homes had a television set. By 1952 the number had risen to more than 34 percent. Televised hearings of Senator Estes Kefauver's investigation of organized crime attracted big audiences in 1951. A new age of politics was dawning as the old alignments that had dominated public life since the turn of the century gave way to a new culture of celebrity and mass media that tested the resilience of both parties.

Although many Americans feared that the depression of the 1930s might return once the fighting stopped, the exact opposite occurred. The nation had become so prosperous during wartime that consumers had built up large amounts of savings as their weekly wages rose by almost 100 percent. Government spending on veterans also increased in the late 1940s. With money at their disposal and marriage rates soaring, couples poured savings into suburban homes for their baby boom offspring by the end of the decade. Mothers stayed home to raise their families, and the couples acquired cars, appliances, and all the trappings of the good life.

With prosperity came moves to warmer climates as veterans who had been stationed in the Sunbelt returned there to make a new start. Fresh from the Navy and then Yale, George Herbert Walker Bush ventured into the oil business in West Texas, and soon his growing family found other Republican-minded friends in Midland and later in Houston. Barry M. Goldwater welcomed newcomers to Phoenix after the war. Still a liberal Democrat, Ronald Reagan witnessed Los Angeles explode with new arrivals after 1945. Richard Nixon accepted the invitation of local Republicans to seek the congressional nomination in his southern California district that same year.

Many Roosevelt Democrats found their allegiance to that party eroding as they acquired a home and achieved prosperity in their businesses. The militance of labor unions now seemed a threat to social stability, and attacks on management had less resonance. Other forces also undermined the New Deal. As Communism loomed, Democrats of Eastern European extraction saw their party as less concerned about the Russian threat and the plight of the satellite nations. The influx of blacks in the North strengthened the Democrats, but the resulting racial tensions also strained white ties to the party of Roosevelt and Truman. These pressures emerged slowly but by the 1950s were tilting voters toward the Republicans.

In the South, Democrats chafed at the evident sympathy of their northern colleagues for the aspirations of African Americans following World War II. They began to consider either a third party to represent southern interests or the even more profound heresy of making common cause with the Republicans. White migrants to Atlanta, Houston, Birmingham, and other southern cities found only a shell of a Republican Party in most instances. For decades the Grand Old Party had existed there only to distribute patronage when Republicans held the White House or to furnish delegates to the party's national conventions. These entrenched leaders did not seek out new converts during the late 1940s even as some of their electorate expanded for the first time since the Civil War. New Republicans would make a powerful statement when Dwight D. Eisenhower ran for president.[3]

The style of national politics also shifted during the postwar era. Radio in the 1920s and 1930s had provided an aural window into a culture that had not changed much since the late nineteenth century. Newspapers had reported conventions and rallies in some detail, and the full text of key speeches often appeared in major urban dailies. The media had only covered what politicians did and had little effect on how politicians conducted themselves. Television proved a devastating blow to "business as usual" for politicians. Lengthy speeches were boring when cameras looked on. Contested conventions proved embarrassing to winner and loser alike when the proceedings ran into the night and disrupted programming schedules. Photogenic qualities trumped sober substance.

Television also created new ways for the parties to market their appeal through commercials. Access to a mass audience came with the costs associated with a national medium. Soon the expenses of campaigns grew in an inflationary cycle that made fundraising a key skill for a politician. Dependence on large donors, whether personal or corporate, became an integral part of political life. Republicans in the 1950s and 1960s combined cultivation of small supporters among their rank and file with the largesse of corporate America.

The century-long trend of declining interest in politics accelerated. Despite periodic surges in voter participation, such as the 1952 and 1960 elections, citizens took a smaller role in partisan affairs during the second half of the twentieth century. Other diversions—ample leisure time, professional sports—wooed people away from politics year after year. The number of self-styled independents rose to one-third of eligible voters. Parties became an arena where activists dominated. Ideological differences between Republicans and Democrats become more intense.

The issue of Communism and internal subversion was perhaps the most striking factor in the postwar political equation. The emergence of the Cold War and the rivalry with the Soviet Union and, later, Communist China had turned victory in World War II into a dangerous worldwide struggle with a totalitarian creed. That the USSR took advantage of its military triumph over Germany to dominate Eastern Europe was not sufficient explanation in the eyes of Republicans. Nor did the ability of the Chinese Communists to capitalize on the weakness and corruption of their Nationalist rivals appear to explain the "fall" of China. Franklin D. Roosevelt and his administration must have been sympathetic to Communism or been taken in by the Soviet agents working in the government. Since the Republicans believed that the Democratic Party was illegitimate in the first place and the New Deal an alien creed on its own terms, a connection between Roosevelt and the Communist threat was easy to make.[4]

Subsequent revelations taken from Soviet archives and American code-breaking have disclosed the presence of an active Soviet espionage network in the United States. Its membership and impact is a matter of intense dispute. To assert, for example, that Alger Hiss was a spy is to ignite a clamorous controversy. While the weight of the evidence does indicate that Hiss was a Soviet agent, the work of Hiss, Harry Dexter White, and others did not change in a fundamental manner the direction of American foreign policy between 1941 and 1947. Cooperation with the Soviets made sense during World War II, since the Red Army was the main force confronting the Wehrmacht until 1943 or 1944. Historians on the left now believe, moreover, that Harry Truman was too much the belligerent anti-Communist in 1946–1947 rather than the dupe of left-wing advisers.[5]

Republican attacks on Democrats for their alleged softness on Communism offered tempting rewards beyond asserting a position that many Republicans accepted as an article of faith. It provided the prospect of recapturing the allegiance of voters of Eastern European ancestry who disliked the Soviets. Roman Catholic voters also found the Republicans more palatable because of their stance on Moscow. Anti-Communism put the Democrats on the defensive about their patriotism, while serving to emphasize the differences within the majority party over how to handle the Communist challenge. There seemed to be no political risks in the campaign, since being too patriotic in the fight against Communism could never be perceived as a liability among Republicans.

The practical effect was another matter. Rooting out the real Soviet spies was a laborious process for law enforcement and not something done well in the glow of publicity. Labeling as security risks all those in government who had once sympathized with Communism ignored the changes that had occurred in people's thinking during the 1940s after such events as the Nazi-Soviet Pact of 1939. Moreover, the effort to instill conformity on anti-Communism wasted much valuable energy without producing real results in the struggle with Moscow. For more than a decade, however, allegations of disloyalty became a staple element in Republican attacks on the Democrats.

Though Harry S. Truman is now regarded as a great president, his administration got off to a clumsy start in 1945–1946. The dropping of the atomic bombs in August 1945 ended the war with Japan, and the economy lurched into peacetime in the months that followed. Organized labor sought to realize wage gains that had been deferred during the fighting, and strikes became a chronic part of American life. Price controls added to the continuing pressure that consumers experienced. Truman stumbled from one crisis to another without the united support of his own party. Liberal and conservative Democrats battled for influence within the new administration over civil rights, foreign policy, and the economy. Martha Taft quipped, "To err is Truman," and much of the middle class took up the refrain. As the Republicans put it to the voters, "Had Enough?"[6]

The Republicans also fielded new faces among their candidates. In California a young Navy veteran named Richard Nixon ran against the liberal House member Jerry Voorhis with an indictment of the incumbent's record "as more Socialistic and Communistic than Democratic." Joseph R. McCarthy in Wisconsin portrayed himself as "Tail-Gunner Joe" (an exaggeration of his military record with the Marines in the South Pacific) in his race against Senator Robert M. La Follette, Jr., to win the state's Republican primary. John Bricker of Ohio ran for the Senate and won, as did John Sherman Cooper in Kentucky. Henry Cabot Lodge, Jr., won reelection in Massachusetts.[7]

The issue of Communism loomed large in the Republican surge. The chair of the Republican National Committee, B. Carroll Reece, told voters, "The choice which confronts America this year is between Communism and Republicanism." Senator Taft was at the forefront of this effort. He argued that the Democrats were "so divided between Communism and Americanism" that the party's "foreign policy can only be futile and contradictory and make the United States the laughing stock of the world." A single phrase summed up this aspect of the Republican campaign. The Democrats were guilty of the "Three Cs," which were "Confusion, Corruption, and Communism."[8]

In fact, the election results produced a Republican sweep. The party gained 13 seats in the Senate to establish control with 51 senators to 45 for the Democrats. In the House, their net gain was 55, and they had a strong working majority with 245 members. The Republicans also elected twenty-five governors in what the *Chicago Tribune* called "the greatest victory for the Republicans since Appomattox." For the first time since 1930, the Republicans had control of Congress, and prospects for 1948 seemed bright.[9]

Congressional Republicans, flush with success, thought they knew what the election meant. As Taft put it, the party should "restore those principles of freedom which had been the foundation stone of America's historical development." Most of the Republicans agreed that they had a popular mandate to repeal as much of the Roosevelt program as President Truman would allow. This postelection enthusiasm was misguided. The Republicans had not campaigned on the issue of overturning the New Deal and repudiating the policies of the past fourteen years. The party had won because of discontent with the excesses of organized labor and the early ineptitude of the Truman administration. By going too far in their zeal to reject the New Deal, the Republicans in Congress played into Harry Truman's hands in 1948.[10]

In the Eightieth Congress, which convened in January 1947, Robert Taft was the major Republican leader. He did not take the post of majority leader, but he dominated the upper house on domestic issues. Although conservative on most subjects, he advocated government support of housing and federal aid for education. For the most part, however, Taft pursued the agenda of the right wing of his party.

The main Republican voice on foreign policy was Arthur Vandenberg, who had renounced his earlier isolationism in favor of the internationalism of Roosevelt and Truman. He and Taft were sometimes at odds because the Ohioan was suspicious of the administration's attempts to involve the United States overseas. As a result, the Republicans did not have a coherent voice as the White House developed its containment policy toward the Soviet Union in 1946–1947.

The House, under the leadership of Joseph Martin of Massachusetts, was more determined than the Senate to roll back the New Deal. Legislation came out of the lower chamber that often put the Republican senators in the awkward position of disagreeing with their House colleagues or accepting proposals that would hurt the party's chances in 1948. The reluctance of the

House to compromise provided the president with ample evidence to use against the Republicans when 1948 rolled around.

Divisions among the Republicans frustrated the hopes of Taft and his associates to build a platform on which the party could run. In foreign affairs, the Grand Old Party fell in behind the administration on the main components of containment. Congress did pass the Taft-Hartley law aimed at organized labor in 1947 over Truman's veto. Despite charges that it was unfair to unions, and even a "slave labor" measure, the Taft-Hartley Act became a lasting part of labor law. The unions resented most the measure's abolition of the closed, all-union shop where every worker had to be a union member. In the short run, therefore, organized labor's unhappiness with Taft-Hartley helped Truman's election chances.[11]

On the issue of Communism, Truman took much of the sting out of the Republican attacks. Aid to Greece and Turkey in 1947, along with the Marshall Plan to rebuild the war-torn economies of Western Europe, showed that the White House was as anti-Communist as the GOP. Truman also launched a large-scale government program to root out alleged subversives, a tactic that preempted that issue. As left-wing elements in the Democratic Party moved away from Truman and toward the presidential candidacy of Henry Wallace, Truman came to seem even more of a battler against Communist influence in the United States.[12]

Meanwhile, the congressional Republicans made substantial cuts in farm programs, declined to increase the minimum wage, and rejected housing legislation that Senator Taft had introduced and supported. The assumption that the American people wanted to have the New Deal overturned proved to be out of step with the popular mood in 1947–48. Yet the congressional Republicans declined to modify their conservative positions even to help their party's chances in the 1948 presidential race.

That contest proved to be the last of the New Deal confrontations between Democrats and Republicans. When the year began the fundamentals seemed to be on the side of Truman. The nation was prosperous and once again at peace within the context of the Cold War. In political terms, dark clouds threatened the incumbent's chances. On the left, the candidacy of Henry Wallace attracted many Democrats who were not convinced that a hard-line policy toward the Soviet Union was needed. In the South, resistance to Truman's ambitious civil rights program stirred talk of a revolt among Dixie Democrats (Dixiecrats) against party loyalty because of the race question. The Democratic coalition, so long an amalgam of contradictory elements, seemed to be coming apart.

The Republicans appeared to have a good chance of winning against Truman, whose popularity remained vulnerable to political downdrafts. Their available candidates had weaknesses that made the possibility of an outside alternative more attractive. So in late 1947, much talk went around within both parties about the potential of Dwight D. Eisenhower as a presidential candidate. The general had not yet revealed his strong Republican leanings. His Republican supporters entered him in the New Hampshire primary, and Eisenhower was forced to respond. Serving as president of Columbia University and not wishing to enter politics at that time, he wrote a public letter to the publisher of a New Hampshire newspaper that conveyed his decision, in his words, "to remove myself completely from the political scene."[13]

That left the Republicans with their main hopefuls, Thomas E. Dewey, Robert A. Taft, and Harold Stassen of Minnesota. Though he would later turn into a political joke, Stassen had real appeal in 1948 as a young (he was forty), dynamic, liberal Republican who had been governor of his state at the age of thirty. Behind a campaign that aimed to rally grass-roots Republicans and the attractive personal facade was a shallow, self-absorbed individual so sure of his own destiny that he could not recognize his own vulnerabilities. Stassen won a number of primaries in the spring but stumbled when he debated Dewey during the Oregon primary. The Minnesotan advocated outlawing the Communist Party, Dewey demolished his argument, and Stassen faded as a candidate.[14]

Senator Taft still had to overcome the belief that he could not win because of his dour personality. A public relations campaign to humanize the Ohio senator only ended up emphasizing his sterner qualities. Taft may have been "Mr. Republican," but there persisted in the ranks of the faithful the nagging sense that he would be a poor choice in a presidential race against Truman. Neither he nor his supporters really liked Dewey and his icy efficiency, but Taft's lack of charisma was his main drawback in 1948.

Despite his loss in 1944, Thomas E. Dewey appeared to be the strongest Republican choice. The defeat by Roosevelt was blamed on wartime conditions, and in an election against the less commanding Truman, Dewey's victory seemed probable. He could carry his home state against the president and would do well on the eastern seaboard. With Republican strength in the farm belt and the West, a winning electoral coalition seemed to be within reach. Dewey had been a popular governor of New York, where he blended fiscal conservatism with moderation on social issues. During the primary season, Dewey put special emphasis on the struggle with Communism and urged the American people to "insist that government stop listening to the left-wingers, the communist propaganda and its own fears and doubts and start believing in our system and telling all the world about it."[15]

While Dewey stood in the mainstream of Republican thought, he did not believe that his party would win simply by denouncing the New Deal and all its works. Yet by offering more conservative policy alternatives that still resonated with the goals of the Democrats, he came across to many of his fellow Republicans as a "me-too" candidate. As a result, conservatives thought that Dewey did not attack the opposition with sufficient gusto. A street fighter by instinct, as he had proven in his war with organized crime in the 1930s, Dewey concluded that his slashing attacks on Roosevelt in 1944 had not worked, and he resolved to take a higher road against Truman toward what seemed an inevitable victory.

Many Republicans fretted that Dewey had an unattractive personality. The wife of a Republican leader in New York once said, "You have to know Mr. Dewey very well in order to dislike him." The working press regarded him as secretive and arrogant. Dewey's mustache put voters off, but his wife liked it, and he refused to change his appearance. With a poll-driven organization that pretested his views on disputed issues, Dewey often came across as soulless and calculating. As long as he seemed like a winner, the GOP would tolerate him, but he never won the party's heart in his two presidential campaigns.[16]

With Truman beset on all sides during the first half of 1948, Dewey disposed of Harold Stassen in the primaries and won the nomination on the third ballot over Taft and the other candidates at the Philadelphia convention. Both parties met in the same city that year because network television coverage over AT&T's coaxial cable from Richmond to Boston enabled them to reach the small number of set owners in the Northeast. For his running mate, Dewey selected Earl Warren, the popular governor of California. The two men did not get along, and Dewey criticized Warren's intelligence in private.

In his acceptance speech on June 24, 1948, Dewey sought to rise above the partisan fray and strike a note of unity and national resolve. "Our people are turning away from the meaner things that divide us," he told the delegates. The Republicans "must be the instrument of that inspiration." In its lofty tone it read and sounded more like an inaugural address than a call to arms. From the outset of the campaign, the Republican assumption that victory was theirs informed the strategy that Dewey followed. The platform was moderate in its language and centrist in its substance. It called for the Equal Rights Amendment, stood for broader civil rights including abolition of the poll tax, and proposed a "reduction in the enormous burden of taxation." While there

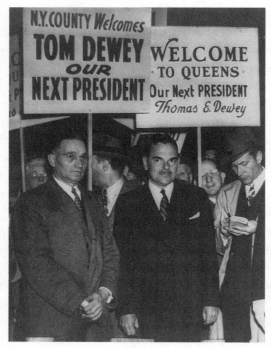

Everyone expected Governor Thomas E. Dewey to win
the presidency in 1948 and return the Republicans to
power. Supporters reflected that confidence in New
York when he returned from a campaign tour. Library
of Congress, LC-USZ62-94135.

was a pledge "to expose the treasonable activities of Communists," the wording did not link the Democrats with subversion. There was a plank supporting
the United Nations and the concept of "collective security."[17]

The Republicans left Philadelphia confident of their success in November.
The postconvention polls showed a "bounce" for Dewey, and he was reported
to be eight to ten points ahead of Truman, whose troubles persisted. Southern
Democrats, angry about the administration's civil rights program, split off to form
the States' Rights Party, with Strom Thurmond of South Carolina as its presidential nominee. The Progressive Party behind Henry Wallace was certain to
draw off voters from Truman's left. How then could the Democrats ever expect
to win? As Dewey's campaign manager, Herbert Brownell, wrote, "Our optimism
for a Republican victory was based in large part on Truman's political woes."[18]

Republican confidence in victory bred a sense of impending entitlement within the party. With polls showing Dewey well ahead, Republicans
made plans for a move to Washington in January 1949. Partisans readied their

résumés and thought about how new policies would be developed. All that remained was the formality of the election itself before the Republicans would retake control of the government and once again play their natural role as the majority party.

Nothing went as the Republicans had planned. Truman made a hard-hitting acceptance speech at the Democratic convention that assailed the Eightieth Congress as the worst in the nation's history. He promised to summon the lawmakers back into a special session in late July (on "Turnip Day," as the president put it) to address the nation's unmet needs on housing, education, civil rights, and economic issues such as rising prices. The strategy was risky, since the Republicans could enact some substantial laws and leave the president looking foolish.[19]

The Republicans chose principle over tactics during the special session. The lawmakers deadlocked on most issues, even proving unsympathetic to Dewey's needs. The candidate wanted modifications in the restrictive law governing the admission of refugees from Europe that had alienated urban Catholic and Jewish voters. The Republicans on Capitol Hill took no action on the measure. This episode and other roadblocks solidified the stereotype about a "Do-Nothing" Congress that Truman was now using as a whipping boy in his reinvigorated campaign.[20]

Both Truman and Dewey campaigned in the fall in the last of the railroad-based presidential contests. The Republican and his team rode the "Victory Special," with polls showing him some thirteen points ahead in mid-September. Dewey let Taft, Stassen, and other Republicans do the heavy lifting in attacking Truman and his policies. Dewey himself stumped like an incumbent facing a defeated opponent. His propensity for sonorous banalities soon became a trademark. In Arizona on September 23, he told his audience: "You know that your future is still ahead of you." The next day at the Hollywood Bowl he proclaimed, "We will go forward to develop our resources." Several weeks later in Kansas City, Dewey intoned, "As never before we need a rudder to our ship of state and a firm hand on the tiller."[21]

Dewey's speeches did have substance, but they often resembled position papers more than exhortations to the faithful to turn out and vote. Truman and the Democrats were not often mentioned, and the record of the Republican Congress received little attention. Like a football team with a secure lead in the fourth quarter, the Dewey camp planned to run out the clock. The problem was that President Truman did not intend to perform the political equivalent of taking a knee. As Dewey's momentum slowed, the president kept hammering away at his "Give 'em Hell" campaign to large and enthusiastic crowds. In his battle, Truman sometimes tinged his remarks with dema-goguery: in late October he likened Dewey to a "front man" for fascism on the model of Hitler's Germany and Mussolini's Italy. Dewey wanted to strike back hard but backed off on the advice of his strategists. He chided Truman for a "new low in mud-slinging" but went no further.[22]

These events would become part of Republican lore. Dewey's defeat convinced many conservatives that only an all-out attack would work in the future. If Truman could raise the specter of fascism, then Republicans could invoke the more damaging image of Communism at home and abroad. In the mutual exchange of invective that marks American politics, both parties enjoyed playing hardball when they were pitching. The Truman-Dewey campaign left lasting scars on the GOP, and the party would not soon again be outdone in vitriol on the trail.

A key element in Dewey's loss had little to do with ideology but emerged from a sector of the economy where the party had done well in the past. A revolt in the farm community, unanticipated by the Republicans, cost Dewey crucial votes and the presidency. With crop surpluses at high levels, farmers needed storage capacity for their products or they would have to sell their goods for whatever the market would bear. The Eightieth Congress had not funded the expansion of such facilities when it reauthorized the Commodity Credit Corporation. When farm prices fell in the autumn of 1948, Middle Western farmers blamed the Republicans for their plight. As a gentleman farmer from New York, Dewey seemed less interested in the problem than did Truman, who had been a Missouri farmer. The issue collapsed Dewey's support in key farm states as the election neared.[23]

On Election Day, November 2, 1948, everyone expected a Dewey victory. Some pollsters had even stopped taking surveys in late September because Dewey was perceived as so far ahead. The conventional wisdom was that voters made up their minds by Labor Day and rarely changed them after that date. In fact, Dewey lost supporters and Truman picked up votes as the campaign wrapped up. Still, as the returns started to come in and Truman moved into the lead, commentators expected Dewey to bounce back and pull the contest out based on the rural vote in the West.

It never happened. Truman won more than twenty-four million votes; Dewey received just under twenty-two million. The president garnered 303 electoral votes to 189 for Dewey, while the States' Rights Party carried four southern states with 39 electoral votes. Henry Wallace and the Progressive Party came in a badly beaten fourth. The Democrats also regained control of the House and Senate. Truman carried much of the old Democratic South and border states, did well in the Middle West, and scored west of the Rockies. Dewey ran well in the East, picked up Michigan and Indiana, but carried only four states west of the Mississippi. Despite the excitement of the election, fewer voters went to the polls than expected. Republican turnout was not robust, probably because Dewey's success seemed so certain. The campaign that had begun with so much confidence for the Republicans ended in one of the great electoral surprises in the nation's history.

The Republican Party spent the postelection season eating political crow. The *Chicago Tribune*, convinced that the Republicans had won on election night despite all the negative indicators came out the next morning with the banner headline "Dewey Defeats Truman." Alice Roosevelt quipped as the returns came in: "You can't make a soufflé rise twice." The defeated candidate well summed up Republican feelings in private: "What do you know? The son of a bitch won."[24]

The outcome of the 1948 election hinged on Dewey's lapses as a candidate. Had he campaigned with half of Truman's vigor and invective, he would have spurred Republicans who stayed home in their confidence of success. Had Dewey been more approachable and trusting of the voters, he could have blended his skill as an administrator with just a touch of humanity. As it was, the American people realized that Dewey was not really one of them.

The results of the 1948 election produced important results for both parties. The Democrats were a tired organization by 1948 after sixteen years in power. While Truman was an effective foreign policy president and pioneer in civil rights, his administration lacked the energy and talent of the New Deal. It was probably time for a change. Had Dewey triumphed, the Korean War would have been fought under Republican auspices, and the issue of domestic Communism might not have taken the virulent form that it did. The country was not as liberal as Truman's victory made it appear, and Dewey's administration would probably have reflected the country's real mood.

As it was, the Republicans were convinced that the combination of Truman's demagogic campaigning and Dewey's ineptitude had cost them an election that belonged to them. If Truman could toss charges of fascism against them, then why should the GOP not hurl charges of Communist subversion against their political rivals? After all, most Republicans knew in their heart of hearts that these allegations were true. If pursuing the Communist issue attracted new voters to the Republicans, that was a pleasant dividend from their honest patriotism.

After Dewey's loss, the conservative and moderate wings of the party argued about the cause of the 1948 debacle in a debate that raged for another decade. One influential conservative, Clarence Budington Kelland, complained in February 1949 that the party "had appeased groups and blocs." He continued, "We have fished for racial voters or sectional votes with evasions. We have not realized our duty, to our party, to our country and posterity." Faced with a tide of Democratic efforts to take away freedom in the name of liberalism, Kelland added, the Republican Party, "if it deserves to survive, must erect itself as a restraining dam to contain and hurl back this flood."[25]

Dewey himself contended in a speech that same month that the Republicans could not win if they joined those "who honestly oppose farm price supports, unemployment insurance, old age benefits, slum clearance, and other social programs." Should the Republicans come out against these measures, he said, "You can bury the Republican party as the deadest pigeon in the country." The Republicans sympathetic to Dewey's point of view made speeches while the conservatives and their supporters worked at the grass roots to reaffirm their dominance within the party. Liberal Republicanism in its twentieth-century form always had an air of electoral expediency rather than real conviction about it. As a result, that faction's hold on the GOP was more tenuous than it seemed.[26]

The Democratic victory in 1948 soon turned sour as the Republicans reasserted themselves in and out of Congress. The coalition of Republicans and southern Democrats on Capitol Hill stalled most of the initiatives, including a civil rights program that Truman proposed in 1949. At the same time a series of foreign policy shocks raised questions about the Truman administration's competence and revived the controversy about Communism in government. In the first half of 1949, the position of the Nationalist Chinese forces deteriorated, paving the way for a Communist takeover in December. The trial of Alger Hiss on charges that he had lied under oath about spying for the Soviets was in the headlines. Most ominous was the news in September 1949 that the Russians had detonated the atomic bomb. The American nuclear monopoly no longer existed.

Republican criticism of the Truman administration's performance intensified throughout the year. Bipartisan foreign policy continued, since Republican votes helped approve the pact creating the North Atlantic Treaty Organization in the spring. On other issues, however, Republican ire mounted, particularly against Secretary of State Dean Acheson, who seemed to embody the administration's failure to take a harder line toward the Soviets. Haughty and aristocratic, Acheson drove his political enemies to distraction, especially when he did not rush to condemn the accused spy Alger Hiss.

With the White House under siege, the Republicans looked to win back some of the ground they had lost in the House and Senate in 1948.

Though few recognized it at the time, the political landscape in the United States shifted in February 1950. In a speech to the Ohio County Women's Republican Club in Wheeling, West Virginia, Joseph R. McCarthy, an otherwise obscure Republican senator from Wisconsin, told his audience, "I have in my hand fifty-seven cases of individuals who would appear to be either card-carrying members or certainly loyal to the Communist party" in the State Department. McCarthy went on to say, "The reason we find ourselves in a position of impotency is not because the enemy has sent men to invade our shores, but because of the traitorous actions of those...who have had all the benefits that the wealthiest nation on earth has had to offer—the finest homes, the finest college education, and the finest jobs in the Government we can give."[27]

This speech launched McCarthy's rise to national influence as the embodiment of the anti-Communist spirit that dominated in the early 1950s. "McCarthyism" soon became a label. Decades after his death in 1957, McCarthy's place in history still stirs acrimony and debate. The man himself was forty-one on February 9, 1950, when he spoke in Wheeling. He had been elected as a circuit judge in 1939 at the age of twenty-nine and then served with the Marines as an intelligence officer in the Pacific. While his actual war record was respectable, McCarthy inflated the performance to include dangerous missions and phony war wounds. In 1946, he defeated the Republican incumbent in the primary and then went on to win a Senate seat during the Republican sweep in November.

Once McCarthy earned national fame, legends about the impetus behind the speech proliferated. Facing a difficult reelection campaign in 1952, he needed a winning theme, but he had not yet fixed on subversion in government when he appeared in Wheeling. The intense public response to his remarks made McCarthy realized what a rich vein he had tapped, and his campaign took shape from there. As numerous students of McCarthy have noted, he proved to be a master of publicity who used the press to make sensational charges he could never sustain in fact. But for Republicans in 1950, McCarthy was a political asset, and the party establishment in the Senate approved his efforts. "If one case doesn't work, bring up another," Taft told McCarthy. From the outset of McCarthy's rise, there were Republicans such as Margaret Chase Smith of Maine who disapproved of his methods and questioned his effectiveness. For the most part, however, Republicans fell in line behind McCarthy through the 1952 election.[28]

The Wisconsin senator's profile increased as the troubles of the Truman administration mounted during the second half of 1950. The outbreak of the Korean War in late June produced a brief moment of bipartisan support for the president, but soon Republicans resumed their criticism of the administration. Popular unhappiness about the Korean conflict, where Truman had introduced American troops to counter the North Korean advance into the South, helped the GOP. Republicans argued that a lack of readiness and a soft policy toward Communism accounted for the initial military setbacks that the country experienced in Korea.

The elections produced Republican gains but fell well short of a landslide on the scale of 1946. In the Senate, the GOP picked up five seats. Richard Nixon defeated Helen Gahagan Douglas in California in a bitter campaign where the issue of Communism dominated. Everett Dirksen beat the Democratic majority leader, Scott Lucas, in Illinois. Taft won a smashing reelection victory in Ohio despite the stiff opposition of organized labor. The Democrats kept control of both houses of Congress, but the Truman administration was now on the defensive with no political mandate.

Joseph McCarthy was the big winner in 1950. He made many speeches around the country as the best drawing card for the GOP. His efforts were credited with bringing down Democrat Millard Tydings in Delaware and in assisting Republican candidates in general. The accepted judgment in Washington was that defying McCarthy on Communism was political suicide. For the next two years, fears of his wrath shaped the nation's discourse about Communism.

When the president relieved General Douglas MacArthur of his command in the Far East in April 1951, Republican outrage boiled over. Tension between the general and the president had been building for months, and the Republicans took MacArthur's side in the dispute over military strategy in Korea. MacArthur believed that with the Communist Chinese involved in combat in Korea, the war should be extended into China and total victory pursued even at the risk of nuclear war. The administration countered that such moves would risk an even wider war with the Chinese and the Soviet Union with no guarantee of victory in the end.

The general's ouster occurred after MacArthur praised a speech by Republican House leader Joseph W. Martin that proposed using the forces of Nationalist China to open a second front against Communist China. In the letter that he wrote Martin after he read the speech, MacArthur renewed his own call for success in Korea by attacks on the Communist Chinese inside their own nation. "As you pointed out," MacArthur said. "There is no substitute for victory." Truman had decided to fire MacArthur before his letter to Martin became public, but the general's response encapsulated what MacArthur was proposing to Republicans and the nation.[29]

MacArthur returned home later in April 1951, addressed Congress in a sensational speech, and was met with a wave of popular adulation. Republicans sang his praises and decried Truman, Secretary of State Acheson, and the British government for his dismissal. The GOP in Congress called for hearings on the war and its aims, which the Democrats had no choice but to hold. Yet the discussion of foreign policy did not produce the political bonanza that the Republicans expected. As the Joint Chiefs of Staff rebutted MacArthur's arguments for a wider war in Korea and China, some of the steam went out of his presidential bid as the public realized the dangerous implications of his aggressive approach. The Republicans maintained, however, that a negotiated settlement of the war that left Korea divided between North and South was unacceptable. As Senator Taft put it in July 1951, "There is no satisfactory protection against socialism at home and war and ignominy abroad except an overwhelming Republican victory in 1952."[30]

The urgent question among Republicans in 1952 was the identity of their presidential candidate. With no major moderate-conservative hopeful left on the scene after the defeat of Dewey, it looked at long last to be Senator Taft's turn. On October 16, 1951, he summoned reporters to a news conference where he said he would enter the race for the GOP nomination. In the weeks that followed, Taft forged ahead among the Republican regulars, and by the end of the year he estimated that he had as many as six hundred delegates who were "clearly favorable" to him. That total would put him within a few votes of a convention victory. By the start of 1952, Taft was the front runner by all conventional measures of Republican sentiment.[31]

Lurking behind Taft's apparent strength were two nagging issues that caused some Republicans to look for an alternative. The first was the well-known fear that the Ohioan could not be elected. Beyond his lackluster personality on the campaign trail, Taft's record of opposition to so many of the domestic programs of the Democrats led even those favorably disposed to him to wonder whether, in the words of one of them "he can revise his thinking and be positively for something." More damaging was the perception that Taft was a dedicated isolationist who would pull the nation back from its recent commitments to the defense of Europe. Eisenhower later revealed that he had offered to stay out of the 1952 race if Taft would agree to a larger role for the United States abroad, but Taft refused.[32]

The logical choice for internationalist-minded Republicans was the military hero of World War II, General Dwight D. Eisenhower. Ever since his withdrawal from electoral politics in 1948, Eisenhower had received appeals from Republicans of all stripes to run in 1952. These party members were convinced that only someone of his popular stature could produce a GOP victory and win the White House. In addition, Eisenhower would see to it that internationalist ideas prevailed in the party, a key point with eastern Republicans. On domestic issues Eisenhower's thinking was as conservative as Taft's, perhaps even a little more to the right than the senator on questions such as government support for housing. Yet Eisenhower came across as a moderate, balanced politician who would not approach public issues in a radical way.

Eisenhower is one of several major figures in the Republican past who have been airbrushed out of party history since the ascendance of the conservatives. Underrated as a politician while he was alive and downgraded by historians in the 1960s and 1970s, Eisenhower is now recognized as a forceful chief executive and very canny national leader. While he was suspicious of many aspects of the New Deal, he recognized the wide public support for measures such as Social Security and believed that attacking such programs was suicidal. For many Republicans on the right at the time and in the decades since his death in 1969, that made Eisenhower an apologist for what Franklin D. Roosevelt had done. He has faded as a Republican and now seems less significant than Barry Goldwater.[33]

Eisenhower was no liberal, and he became more conservative as his presidency advanced. He had little regard for Democrats and liberals, but he was equally scathing about the right wing of his own party, which he believed was impractical and often reckless. His disdain was reciprocated. While Eisenhower believed in a strong national defense, he thought that the Pentagon often asked for more than it needed. In the president's mind, a balanced budget and fiscal prudence were as important an index of the nation's health as the number of its weapon systems. His emphasis on arms control was another of his departures from Republican orthodoxy.

Eisenhower's first task in 1952 was to win the Republican nomination. Although Taft was far ahead in the delegate race, Eisenhower had an asset in the form of his broad popularity with the American people, which his rival could not match. As Eisenhower got into the race in the spring of 1952, his allure as a military hero above political strife crossed partisan barriers. He had some learning to do about campaigning and national politics, but he proved a very quick study. With the support of Dewey and his organization, several prominent media outlets, including *Time* and the *New York Herald Tribune*, and rank and file Republicans across the country, Eisenhower had nearly drawn even with Taft in delegate strength by the time the national convention arrived in Chicago in June 1952.

The Eisenhower forces were close to nabbing the nomination, but Taft likely would still prevail unless some of his pledged delegates could be jostled loose. Eisenhower's candidacy had prompted a surge of enthusiasm in the South, where conservative white Democrats in states such as Texas had flooded into Republican caucuses. Old-line Republicans who had dominated the party's deliberations for years fought with these newcomers (in some cases to the point of fist fights) and then used their control of the party machinery to send pro-Taft delegations to Chicago. The Eisenhower Republicans, in turn, contested these results and dispatched competing slates on the grounds that Taft leaders had acted outside the rules. The question turned on whether, as the Eisenhower camp charged, the Taft campaign was trying to steal the nomination.

The Eisenhower leadership knew that if Taft had his disputed delegates from Texas, Georgia, and Louisiana seated, then the general's candidacy was doomed. Their strategy became to adopt a "fair play" amendment to the convention rules that would preclude the Taft delegations from these states from voting on their own right to be seated (as had been done in past conventions). Equally important was the need to cast this battle as a struggle between virtue (Eisenhower) and old-style machinations (Taft). When the credentials committee tried to meet in secret, Eisenhower's managers clamored for television coverage of the panel's proceedings. The Taft men had to give in on that point, and the televised deliberations of the committee built support for Eisenhower outside the convention hall. As a result, the convention adopted the fair play amendment, which meant that Taft's total vote was reduced. Then debate began on the Georgia, Louisiana, and Texas slates.[34]

When Senator Dirksen launched his attack on Thomas E. Dewey, he illustrated the fissures that remained in the party from the defeats of Willkie and Dewey. The spectacle again worked in Eisenhower's favor, since the Taft delegates seemed relics of an older tradition of backroom deals. Eisenhower succeeded in all the key votes about seating contested delegates, and the number of votes committed to him rose. On the first ballot, Eisenhower was within nine votes of victory. After the convention nominated the general, Taft was gracious in defeat, and Republicans hoped that Eisenhower could bring them victory.

The convention's final task was the selection of Eisenhower's running mate. The choice of Senator Richard M. Nixon of California was a decisive step for the party's future. Well before Eisenhower even got into the race, political insiders had seen the young California senator as the logical choice.

Eisenhower was sixty-two and needed youth to balance the ticket. California was a crucial state in a close election, and Nixon had proven he could win statewide. Nixon's reputation as a foe of Communism made him an ideal foil for Eisenhower's foreign policy skills.

Following his nomination, Eisenhower prepared to face the Democratic nominee, Governor Adlai E. Stevenson of Illinois. The bitter Republican convention left some hard feelings, and so Eisenhower met with Taft in New York City on September 12. The candidate was already under attack for the lack of energy in the Republican campaign. The influential Scripps-Howard newspapers, which spoke for the Republican middle, said that Eisenhower was "running like a dry creek." In the meeting, Taft received most of what he wanted from Eisenhower. The national budget would be kept at $60 billion, taxes would be reduced, and the Taft-Hartley law would remain. The episode underscored the unified Republican commitment to ousting the Democrats in 1952.[35]

The Republicans took the fight to their opponents in what Eisenhower styled a "crusade" to redeem the nation. Nixon and Joseph McCarthy pounded the Democrats on the issue of Communism, while other Republican orators indicted the president for the ethical lapses of his aides (including the receipt of freezers and mink coats). The upshot of twenty years of Democratic rule was a "mess in Washington" that only Eisenhower and the Grand Old Party could clean up.

In this setting, the news that Richard Nixon was the beneficiary of a secret fund of $18,000, collected from his supporters in California, that paid for his office expenses disrupted the Republican momentum. Disgruntled California Republicans, angry at how Nixon had treated Earl Warren at the convention, leaked the news to the press. To some extent, Nixon was the recipient of a bum rap. He did not spend the money for personal needs but only for his political activities and projects.

There was, however, evidence of tangible benefits for some donors. The seeming contradiction between Eisenhower's ethical standards and Nixon's apparent transgressions launched a wave of criticism. Calls arose for Nixon to leave the ticket. Thomas E. Dewey urged the vice presidential candidate to give a full accounting on national television. The episode became legendary in American politics for Nixon's refusal during his half-hour address to return one gift, a cocker spaniel named Checkers that his daughters had received. The public applauded Nixon's earnest, open demeanor. The candidate urged listeners to send telegrams to the Republican National Committee (not the Eisenhower campaign), and his retention on the ticket was assured.[36]

With the Nixon campaign fund fracas behind him, Eisenhower put the election away when, late in the race, he said that he would go to Korea as president-elect to inspect the military situation. Since the general would not make such a trip to intensify the war, the implications were clear that he meant to end the conflict. Stevenson and the Democrats were outmatched as the voters clamored for a change in leadership. The result was a landslide for Eisenhower. The Republican candidate received 442 electoral votes to 89 for Stevenson. In the popular vote, Eisenhower led by 6.6 million ballots. The Republicans gained control of both houses of Congress. Eisenhower won four states in the South, including Texas, and initiated the

Dwight D. Eisenhower ended the twenty-year Democratic hold on the White House in 1952. Library of Congress, LC-USZ62-104961.

long-term buildup of Republican strength in that region. After two decades, Democratic dominance of American politics had ended.

In historical perspective, the presidency of Dwight D. Eisenhower would come to seem a period of peace and prosperity before the tumult of the 1960s. For Republicans, however, Eisenhower is now a forgotten and indeed somewhat embarrassing figure. His acceptance of the New Deal's main programs made him anathema to conservatives in the 1950s and afterward. A campaign to achieve what he called "modern Republicanism" by making his party more popular with the broader electorate failed to make any lasting impression on the GOP.

Eisenhower was a strong conservative, becoming more so as his presidency progressed. He was not, however, an intense partisan in his Republicanism, and he regarded many on the right as impractical and often obstructive to his administration. In terms of foreign policy, he did not believe in military power as an end in itself and was convinced that simply accumulating nuclear weapons did not enhance the nation's security. He was thus willing to negotiate with the Soviet Union over arms control in ways that dismayed the Republican right. Given Eisenhower's military credentials, it was almost impossible to make a credible case that he was too soft on the Soviets, even though many Republicans chafed at the president's efforts on arms control. Eisenhower resisted GOP efforts to limit presidential power in foreign affairs. The Bricker Amendment to curb the impact of treaties on the Constitution, which Senate Republicans endorsed, was defeated in large part because of Eisenhower's unrelenting opposition.

Once in power in 1953, the Republicans expected that they could turn from Truman's policy of containing Soviet expansion to an approach that sought to undo the Communist domination of Eastern Europe. It turned out that the containment policy was easier to denounce than abandon. The concept of liberating the captive nations faded away in the face of Soviet power in that region. On defense policy, even though it was called the "New Look," the Eisenhower White House relied on nuclear weapons to deter Moscow, much as Truman had done. Promising "massive retaliation" in the event of Soviet aggression did not answer the question of when such action was justified.

Eisenhower negotiated a truce in Korea based on the current military balance and an acceptance of a peninsula divided between North and South Korea. He also resisted efforts by the French to involve the United States in a direct military intervention in Vietnam in 1954. When the Hungarians revolted against their Soviet masters in 1956, Washington accepted the incursion of Russian tanks to crush the uprising. Republican critics of Eisenhower noted with dismay the continuity with the Truman years and expressed their disappointment that the government had not been more willing to have a showdown with Moscow.

While Eisenhower worked hard to hold down government spending and achieve a balanced budget, he did not share the suspicion of Social Security that some conservative Republicans felt. As he told his brother Edgar, "Should any political party attempt to abolish social security and eliminate labor laws and farm programs, you would not hear of that party again in our political history." He was convinced that Social Security helped maintain national stability and economic health. For conservative Republicans who wanted to overturn the New Deal, Eisenhower seemed to offer a strategy of expediency rather than principle.[37]

Eisenhower had never liked the tactics of Senator Joseph McCarthy but had tolerated them in 1952 in the interest of party harmony and his own election. When the Wisconsin senator continued his course of exposing alleged Communists after January 1953, Eisenhower bristled at tactics that embarrassed a Republican administration. Avoiding a public confrontation, Eisenhower allowed the senator to hang himself. McCarthy obliged in 1954 through the celebrated Army-McCarthy hearings over alleged subversion in the military. Viewers who saw McCarthy's badgering of witnesses and arguing with fellow senators found the senator a less attractive figure. When McCarthy attacked fellow Republicans, he went too far. The Senate rebuked McCarthy and ended his influence. A broken, alcoholic McCarthy died three years later. The episode damaged the right, which believed that McCarthy had not gone far enough in rooting out subversives. Some even suggested that Eisenhower had served the Communist cause.

Had Eisenhower's approach to the Republicans proven successful at the polls for candidates other than himself, he might have persuaded Republican critics of the merits of his view of the electorate. Unfortunately for the president, the GOP suffered losses in the three congressional elections that followed Eisenhower's elevation to the presidency. In 1954, the Republicans lost eighteen seats in the House and one in the Senate as the Democrats reestablished control of Congress. Two years later, even though Eisenhower was reelected, the Republicans dropped another House seat and one in the Senate. The big loss for the GOP came in 1958 when their party went through a fifty-eight seat loss in the House and saw twelve seats go into the opposition column in the Senate. The Republicans would not regain control of the Senate for more than two decades and thirty-six years for the House.

During the 1950s, the Republicans confronted both opportunities and challenges stemming from the emerging issue of civil rights. The Supreme Court's decision in the case of *Brown v. Board of Education* (1954), ruling school segregation unconstitutional, won praise from blacks who credited the Eisenhower administration for the result. Eisenhower shared the prevailing southern view on race, however, and did little to push desegregation during his first term. The president did well with blacks in the 1956 election, securing as much as 30 percent of their vote. At the same time, the increasing Democratic identification with civil rights was opening the door for Republican gains in the South a decade later.

To capitalize on Eisenhower's strength with southern white voters, the Republican National Committee created a southern arm of its organization and launched "Operation Dixie" in 1957 to expand the Republican base below the Mason-Dixon Line. The initiative appealed to the expanding postwar white electorate of former Democrats defecting in the wake of their party's rising commitment to civil rights. Operation Dixie provided the foundation for the emergence of the southern Republican Party during the presidency of John F. Kennedy.

Any Republican ideological restiveness about Eisenhower as a party leader was well submerged in the 1956 presidential election. The president had suffered a heart attack in September 1955, but his recovery and his party's need for a strong candidate justified his decision to seek a second term in early 1956. Eisenhower toyed with the idea of replacing Richard Nixon on the ticket until it became clear that there was no acceptable alternative. Coolness between Nixon and Eisenhower lingered. As Nixon himself later wrote of the president, "Beneath his captivating personal appearance was a lot of finely tempered cold steel."[38]

At the national convention, the platform sang Eisenhower's praises while reflecting some elements of his desire to move the GOP away from reflexive conservatism. The delegates promised "to seek extension and perfection of a sound social security system" as well as a balanced budget and a "gradual reduction of the national debt." As they had done since 1940, the Republicans endorsed "the submission of a constitutional amendment providing equal rights for men and women." On the time-honored issue of the tariff, the party now said that "barriers which impede international trade and the flow of capital should be reduced on a gradual, selective and reciprocal basis, with full recognition of the necessity to safeguard domestic enterprises, agriculture, and labor against unfair import competition." Protectionism was yielding to the new world of free trade. The delegates praised Eisenhower's record in the world, which allowed, the platform stated, "our people to enjoy the blessings of liberty and peace."[39]

The 1956 presidential race was never a real contest. Adlai Stevenson was again the Democratic nominee, but his campaign lacked focus and energy. When he called for a ban on nuclear testing, Nixon and others denounced Stevenson's idea as impractical. Republicans said that the proposal demonstrated that Eisenhower was a trusted world leader and Stevenson was not. Outside events, including the Hungarian Revolution and the Suez Canal crisis, convinced most voters that Eisenhower should remain at his post. The reluctance of the United States to get involved on the side of the rebellious Hungarians demonstrated that Republican talk of "rolling back" Communism had been political rhetoric and nothing more. Eisenhower secured a landslide victory with 457 electoral votes and a margin of 9.5 million popular ballots. However, the GOP failed to regain control of Congress. The Democrats benefitted from ticket splitting for their candidates, and made small gains in the House and Senate. Eisenhower proclaimed: "Modern Republicanism has now proved itself. And America has approved modern Republicanism."[40]

Eisenhower misread the direction of his party. Instead of accepting the president's vision of where the Republicans should go, conservatism stirred and then gained momentum during the 1950s. Because of their rules allowing representation at all levels of the party's conduct, a determined Republican faction could gain control of the grass-roots machinery. Conservative voices such as William F. Buckley's *National Review* and the growing number of Young Republicans on college campuses combined to help move the party rightward during the 1950s. Their presence did not yet threaten Richard

Nixon's control of the 1960 presidential nomination, but the tension between Eisenhower's brand of conservatism and the more ideological variety on the right foreshadowed the struggles of the 1960s.

The new champion of the resurgent right in the GOP was a first-term Arizona senator named Barry M. Goldwater. Elected in 1952, Goldwater was handsome, photogenic, and a compelling speaker before a friendly audience. In 1957, he looked over Eisenhower's budget, which called for $71.8 billion in spending, up some $2.8 billion over the previous year. After reviewing the budget that reflected the assumptions of "Modern Republicanism," Goldwater denounced the excessive spending, which confirmed how Eisenhower had been enchanted by "the siren song of socialism." More money was needed for national defense, but funds for what Goldwater called "squanderbust government" were out. Republicans fought among themselves over the size and direction of the government.[41]

In addition to their internal disputes, the Republicans faced problems in civil rights and foreign policy as they headed toward the 1958 congressional elections. African Americans had given Eisenhower a healthy share of their support in 1956, and the enactment of the mild civil rights law of 1957 provided more credit for the GOP. The crisis over integration later that year set back Republican hopes in the South when Eisenhower used National Guard troops to enforce court decisions that allowed black students to attend Little Rock High School. Southern Democrats drifted back to their traditional allegiance. The future direction of the GOP on race was still in flux. Such young conservatives as William F. Buckley and his *National Review* were skeptical of a pro-civil-rights stand. As Buckley's father told Strom Thurmond, his son was "for segregation and backs it in every issue."[42]

The Soviet launch of the Sputnik satellite in the fall allowed Democrats to raise more questions about the state of the nation's defenses. Eisenhower knew but could not say for security reasons that the United States was well ahead of the USSR in retaliatory power. There was a sense of the president and the administration as listless and unfocused as the second term got underway.

A major target for the Republicans in 1957–1958 was organized labor and its political clout, most notably in the case of Walter Reuther and the United Auto Workers. In the 1958 elections, the Republicans pushed the virtues of "right-to-work" laws that prevented closed, union shops. The tactic backfired when labor in key states organized effective voting drives. Adding to the Republican problems were allegations of corruption against White House Chief of Staff Sherman Adams. He had taken gifts from a favor-seeking friend. The embattled aide stepped down a month before the voters went to the polls.[43]

When the effects of a sharp recession were added to the political mix, Republican defeats in the sixth year of a two-term presidency were to be expected. Their scope staggered the party, as the Democrats added fifty seats in the House and sixteen in the Senate. The loss of such conservative stalwarts as William F. Knowland of California and John Bricker underlined the sweeping nature of the setback. Goldwater won reelection to a second term, confirming his status as the darling of the conservatives. On the other side of the country, Nelson Rockefeller secured the governorship of New York and was recognized as a contender for 1960. Yet the likely nominee remained Richard Nixon, who had piled up credits from Republicans while campaigning for party candidates in 1958.

Nelson Rockefeller soon emerged as a wild card in the Republican contest, but in the process he alienated himself from the mainstream of the party. The distaste for the New York governor was not so much because of his views, which tended to be conservative except on civil rights. Rockefeller seemed to think that his money and celebrity appeal entitled him to leadership. He made little secret of his disdain for the opinions of rank-and-file Republicans. Dominant in New York, where his money and a divided Democratic Party helped him, Rockefeller was not a very good national politician. Along with indecision went a tin ear for Republican attitudes, and his casual approach to his marriage vows compounded the problem. Through his array of publicists and sympathetic journalists, he could make noise about Republican issues whenever he chose.[44]

After testing the waters and finding that Nixon had a lock on the nomination, Rockefeller announced in December 1959 that he would not be seeking the Republican nomination in 1960. His withdrawal cleared the way for Nixon, or so it seemed. Then the first half of 1960 produced a series of crises that appeared to threaten the standing of the United States in the world. The shooting down of the U-2 spy plane, the failure of Eisenhower's summit with the Soviets, and Democratic complaints that the country was falling behind in defense because of a "missile gap" with the USSR put the Republicans on the defensive in an area that was usually their strength. The Democratic front runner, John F. Kennedy, was already sounding the theme of getting the nation "moving again."[45]

Into this volatile environment stepped Nelson Rockefeller in early June with the announcement that he was back in the race for the GOP nomination. He urged the party to "save the nation by saving itself." Selecting him, so the argument went, would put in the White House someone committed to rebuilding defense and pushing civil rights. Rockefeller's strategy was Willkie-like. By making an issue of the convention's platform on foreign policy, he hoped to unsettle the race and sway the delegates to his cause. The approach made little sense. In the unlikely event of Nixon being stopped, the delegates would be much more inclined to switch to Goldwater, who already had a good deal of support as a vice presidential candidate.[46]

Faced with a Rockefeller insurgency whose power he overestimated, Nixon decided to make concessions to his putative rival. The two men met at Rockefeller's lavish apartment in New York on July 22, 1960, and produced a joint declaration that became known as the "Compact of Fifth Avenue." In it, Nixon came out for an increase in defense spending to meet the Soviet challenge. He had in effect endorsed the criticisms of President Eisenhower's stewardship in foreign affairs. Nixon backed other social causes, among them a plan seeking vigorous support for civil rights and black protestors who had begun "sit-ins" in the South.[47]

The outreach to Rockefeller backfired. It irritated Eisenhower, who did not appreciate having his defense policy repudiated. More important, it infuriated Barry Goldwater and his conservative base. Goldwater declared that what Rockefeller had agreed to, if it became part of the platform, "will live in history as the Munich of the Republican Party." A rebellion brewed among southern delegates over civil rights. Nixon decided that retaining Eisenhower's support was more important than southern electoral votes. The nominee dropped the criticism of Eisenhower and agreed to make the civil rights plank more assertive.[48]

A compromise was worked out that allowed everyone involved to rally behind the semblance of unity on the platform. Rockefeller dropped out, Nixon received the nomination, and a divisive floor fight was avoided. A cohesive Republican Party presented a positive face to the voters. There was one unscripted, spontaneous moment that cast a spotlight on the Republican future. On Wednesday night of the convention, when nominations were made, Barry Goldwater's name was placed before the delegates. The Arizona senator then made a speech of withdrawal; that became the first move in the 1964 presidential race and a pivotal event in the history of the GOP.

Before a responsive, cheering crowd, Goldwater proclaimed to his fellow conservatives, "This great Republican party is our historic house. This is our home." Denouncing the Democrats as a "party which has lost its belief in the dignity of man," he urged that Nixon be elected. In his closing, Goldwater told the throng: "Let's grow up, conservatives. If we want to take this Party back, and I think we can some day, let's get to work." Goldwater did not say from whom the Republican Party should be reclaimed, but he meant

Rockefeller and by extension Richard Nixon. For Goldwater the task was to render a conservative party even more conservative.[49]

The presidential race of 1960 was the most exciting and nail-biting race of the second half of the twentieth century. Nixon's narrow defeat at the hands of John F. Kennedy has produced a number of plausible explanations for the Republican setback. An array of negative circumstances helped cost Nixon the White House. Eisenhower delivered the opening rebuff to Nixon in August. Asked at a press conference several times how Nixon had contributed to the decisions of the administration, the president evaded his questioners. Finally, a reporter at the end of the session sought, in his words, "an example of a major idea of his that you had adopted," Eisenhower replied, "If you give me a week, I might think of one. I don't remember." The comment dogged Nixon throughout the campaign.[50]

Nixon also faced problems of his own creation. Overconfident about his debating abilities, he agreed to four televised encounters with his Democratic opponent. The first debate, in which Nixon was both recovering from an infection and poorly prepared in terms of makeup and overall readiness, elevated Kennedy to an equal status with his Republican rival. The two men did equally well in the remaining debates, but the political damage to Nixon had been done. As the British prime minister, Harold Macmillan, told Eisenhower after watching the first debate, Nixon "looked like a convicted criminal," while Kennedy appeared to be "a rather engaging young undergraduate."[51]

Promising to campaign in all fifty states, Nixon spread his energies too thin and never developed a clear electoral strategy for winning. The choice of Henry Cabot Lodge as his running mate was also whimsical. Lodge was not going to help Nixon in his home state of Massachusetts, which Kennedy was sure to carry, and Lodge's patrician style of campaigning was lazy and self-indulgent.

Still, despite all the advantages that Kennedy had, including more favorable press coverage, Nixon very nearly won. Last-minute campaigning from Eisenhower, a strong late surge by the candidate himself, and doubts about Kennedy's youth and Catholicism tightened the race at the end. Nixon came within one percentage point and 118,000 popular votes of besting Kennedy. The Democrat captured 303 electoral votes to 219 for Nixon.

In his memoirs a generation later, Nixon blamed the press, especially television, for his unfavorable coverage. The Kennedys themselves also stirred his wrath. The Republicans, he wrote, were "faced by an organization that had equal dedication and unlimited money, that was led by the most ruthless group of political operators ever mobilized for a presidential campaign." He resented the way that, in his mind, the Democrats had capitalized on the issue of Kennedy's religion. Any criticism of Kennedy's relationship to the Catholic Church was denounced as bigotry, but the Democratic candidate also stressed his faith in appealing to his coreligionists.[52]

These elements were important, but they did not account for Nixon's failure to focus his campaign on a winning strategy, make the case for extending the Eisenhower record, and present his message in a clear and forceful manner. Conservative Republicans also thought that Nixon had not given the party's base a reason to turn out and vote for him. Nixon believed that Kennedy had stolen the election from him, but decided not to contest the result. The 1960 election became another in a list of Republican losses that would be attributed to Democratic chicanery rather than a lack of GOP appeal to the voters.[53]

The defeat in 1960, while frustrating to the Republicans, did not represent a decisive setback. So tenuous were Kennedy's coattails that the Democrats lost a few seats in the House and Senate. Nixon's loss and the eclipse of Rockefeller left a vacuum in the party that the conservative troops devoted to Barry Goldwater intended to fill in 1964. The process of taking back the Republican Party was already ongoing days after Nixon conceded defeat. A new and turbulent era in the history of the GOP had opened.

IO

From Goldwater to Watergate,
1961–1974

MANY REPUBLICANS, GATHERED for their national convention in San Francisco's Cow Palace on that memorable July evening in 1964, had been waiting for this moment for four years and more. Through precinct conventions and county caucuses, they had pledged themselves to the faith of conservatism and its champion, Senator Barry Goldwater of Arizona. The eastern press had called them extremists, and Governor Nelson Rockefeller of New York had denounced them just a few days earlier. They knew their cause was just and that Barry Goldwater would carry them to victory in November against the socialistic policies of the hated Lyndon Johnson and the Democrats. The delegates on the floor and the passionate throng in the galleries had seen Goldwater nominated. Now it was time for the acceptance speech that would be a prelude to the White House.

In other years at other Republican conventions, unity had been the theme after the nominee was chosen. Conservatives had been made to swallow Wendell Willkie, Thomas E. Dewey twice, Dwight D. Eisenhower twice, and then Richard Nixon. Even when Eisenhower led them to victory, winning seemed to come at the expense of principle. Eisenhower had promised a crusade to take back America for conservative ideals and instead delivered the "modern Republicanism" that Goldwater and his followers detested. Richard Nixon had rebuffed Goldwater and then lost to John F. Kennedy in another "me-too" campaign that failed to be conservative enough. Conservatives believed their time had come at last.

The business of the night was soon finished. Goldwater's personal pick for vice president, Representative William E. Miller of New York, was nominated with virtual unanimity. Richard Nixon then introduced Goldwater, and the Republican nominee strode to the podium. Handsome, bespectacled, and determined, Goldwater had not come to mollify his party's defeated moderates or to reach out to undecided voters in the biggest audience he would ever command. He had stepped forward to sound a call to arms to the conservative faithful in the hall and the armies of like-minded Republicans across the country.

And so he did. Like an Old Testament prophet, Goldwater urged the nation to return to the tried and true America that he believed had disappeared since the New Deal. The United States must not "stagnate in the swampland of collectivism" or "cringe before the bully of Communism." Democrats had let the nation's defenses weaken and allowed a billion people to be "cast into Communist captivity." The key element in Goldwater's appeal came near the end in two sentences that summed up his appeal and foreshadowed his electoral fate several months later. "I would remind you that extremism in the defense of liberty is no vice," he said, as the audience responded. Then, after a pause, he added, "And let me remind you that moderation in the pursuit of justice is no virtue."[1]

The audience cheered as Goldwater began his campaign to oust Lyndon Johnson from the White House. Though the Republican candidate went down to defeat in November 1964, the Republican Party of the second half of the twentieth century had been born. The course of its development would not be smooth nor would its progress be without setbacks. Nonetheless, the Goldwater speech marked a pivotal juncture after which the Grand Old Party moved ever rightward as Republicans followed the legacy of Barry Goldwater and his loyal legions.

The Republican Party looked the same in the aftermath of Richard Nixon's defeat in 1960, but beneath the surface the nature of the GOP was shifting. The party's establishment, rooted in the East, saw its power and influence ebb as the Republican center of gravity moved to the South and West. To some extent the core of the rightward trend lay in the Sunbelt states. Whites who had migrated to California, Arizona, and the old Confederacy after World War II hated Communism, distrusted the federal government, wanted to protect their stake in society, and feared for the moral future of the nation. An intense desire to block the civil rights efforts of Latinos and African Americans underlay a sizable proportion of the conservative endorsement of states' rights and limited government as well. Belief in the values of Christianity and a virtuous lifestyle also impelled the new adherents of conservatism in the early 1960s.[2]

Barry Goldwater's ghostwritten book, *The Conscience of a Conservative* (1960), embodied conservative Republicanism in these years. It sold millions of copies and inspired a generation of young people to take up the causes the senator had espoused. Before the demands of the campaign trail in 1963–1964 tempered his rhetoric, Goldwater offered a heady appeal of drastic change. "I have little interest in streamlining government or making it more efficient for I mean to reduce its size. I do not undertake to promote welfare for I propose to extend freedom. My aim is not to pass laws but to repeal them." The Arizona senator called federal matching funds for the states the equivalent of bribery, asked that farm subsidies be ended, and sought the dismantling of the income tax and annual reductions of 10 percent in the federal budget. He also contended that Social Security was also a questionable idea that at best should be voluntary.[3]

Goldwater declared that the Communists were winning because timid liberals were fearful of standing up to the USSR. As a result, the Soviet Union was on the march as liberals made concession after concession. Goldwater was skeptical of the United Nations, arms control, and the idea that nuclear weapons had established a balance of terror in the world. Winning a war, even by using nuclear arms, was the main point for the United States, and the American people should be willing to take risks for peace. In the end the Soviet Union would back down before the threat of a resolute United States.[4]

Barry Goldwater's nomination for the presidency in 1964 occurred because of the grass-roots efforts of thousands of conservative activists. They were inspired when he appeared on national television, as in this 1962 photograph. Library of Congress, LC-DIG-ppmsca-19601.

A central element of Goldwater's creed was his stance on civil rights. Since he had without fanfare supported the rights of African Americans in Arizona, including making contributions to the National Association for the Advancement of Colored People, he was confident that he was not guilty of racism—a conviction he shared with many whites in the 1960s.

If the senator endorsed, as he did, states' rights and the power of the people of the South and Southwest to make segregation the law in their states, then Goldwater believed that the freedom of whites to do so was of higher value than black equality. In his mind, none should dare call that bigotry. His stance had a powerful appeal for white voters in the South who increasingly identified the national Democratic Party with the interests of African Americans. Goldwater had once said that in seeking votes the Republicans should go hunting "where the ducks are." Southern whites, particularly males, committed to white supremacy, would be a key element in the new Republican electoral coalition.[5]

In the first three years of the 1960s, Goldwater had become the charismatic figure the Republican right had long sought. The candidate's firm beliefs precluded the possibility of compromise, and Goldwater himself did not examine the premises of his own convictions. Political campaigns in Arizona in 1952 and 1958 had not tested his skills on the stump, and friendly reporters had never pressed him to define his policy positions. As a result, Goldwater was a novice as a national candidate when he began his race for the White House. While he could dish out the hot rhetoric that pleased his audiences, it was not clear how he would do when the Democrats attacked him.

Pushing Goldwater in the early 1960s was a broad alliance of conservative activists that ranged from William F. Buckley, through the young party members, to fringe groups such as the John Birch Society. This society was named after a Baptist missionary in China and sometime American agent whose death at the hands of Communists in 1945 was, at least to the organization's founder, Robert Welch, proof of the extent of the State Department's culpability in the ultimate loss of China. When Welch charged that Eisenhower was not just a dupe of the Soviets but an active Communist agent, he alienated the *National Review* and other usually sympathetic allies. Yet the Republicans could not disavow the Birchers completely without losing supporters and contributors.

For conservatives in the early 1960s, John F. Kennedy was far from the cautious, moderate chief executive of his later reputation. Instead they saw the New Frontier as a continuation of the Democratic charge toward collectivism and further evidence of their illegitimacy in the American system. In foreign policy, Republicans assailed Kennedy for the failure at the Bay of Pigs to oust Fidel Castro from Cuba in 1961, and they saw the Cuban Missile Crisis a year and a half later as another missed opportunity to confront the USSR. In the mounting American involvement in Vietnam, Republicans saw victory over North Vietnam as the only rational goal.

The first chance for the GOP to test the popularity of the Kennedy administration came in the 1962 congressional elections. The results were disappointing at the national level. The Democrats held down their losses in the House to two seats, and they added four new senators. Conservative Republicans took heart from the results in key individual contests. Richard Nixon lost the race for governor of California, which removed him from the 1964 presidential derby. Nelson Rockefeller won reelection but with a smaller margin than in his first race in 1958. The Republicans gained five seats in the South, came close to winning a Senate seat in Alabama, and did well in an unsuccessful battle for governor of Texas. With anger mounting among white voters at Kennedy's civil rights policies, the prospects for Goldwater to turn racism into votes for Republicans seemed limitless, especially if Goldwater faced off against Kennedy.[6]

While Goldwater gained strength, Rockefeller wounded his own candidacy. In the spring of 1963, he divorced his wife of more than three decades and a month later wed Margaretta "Happy" Murphy, herself a recent divorcee with four young children. For mainline Republicans mindful of what a later generation called family values, Rockefeller's actions exemplified eastern liberalism at its worst. With typical obtuseness, he stayed in the race, but his candidacy was effectively over. Other potential moderate candidates, such as Governors George Romney of Michigan and William Scranton of Pennsylvania, were much talked about in the press but lagged well behind Goldwater among the party's base.[7]

Goldwater benefitted from one of the most efficient and well-organized grass-roots efforts in modern American politics. A New Yorker named F. Clifton White orchestrated the campaign to gather delegates out of Suite 3505 of the Chanin Building in New York City. Short of cash but long on dedication, the Draft Goldwater Committee organized enthusiastic rallies and courted potential delegates. When Goldwater, doubtful about his chances, hesitated over deciding to run for president in January 1963, one supporter told the core group around White: "There's only one thing we *can* do. Let's draft the son of a bitch."[8]

The Republican Party in 1963–1964 was ready to respond to the Draft Goldwater effort. Representative William E. Miller of upstate New York chaired the Republican National Committee and supported Goldwater's cause. Throughout the rest of the party, from the Young Republicans to the National Federation of Republican Women, conservative activists had come to the meetings, elected their members to key committees, and drafted pro-Goldwater resolutions. Moderate Republicanism, which looked so imposing both in terms of governors in the East and Middle West and in opinion polls, was a hollowed out shell. The days when money men from New York and the dictates of eastern newspapers would prevail in choosing Republican candidates were about to end.

So confident were the Goldwater leaders and their followers that they boasted that President Kennedy could be defeated in 1964 if their champion won the Republican nomination. Had Kennedy lived, a race with Goldwater would have been much closer than the Lyndon Johnson–Goldwater matchup. Goldwater would have polled stronger in the South and would probably have carried Texas, for example. Yet his problems as a national campaigner would still have made him vulnerable to Kennedy's superior skills as a candidate.

In any case, Kennedy's murder on November 22, 1963, changed the political equation for the Republicans and impaired Goldwater's chances for victory. In the long run, Lyndon Johnson would prove to be an inept leader of his party, but from late 1963 through November 1964, sympathy arising from Kennedy's death, the new president's mastery of Congress, and his command of the foreign policy apparatus appeared to make Johnson the proponent of prosperity at home; the heir of Roosevelt, Truman, and Kennedy; and the preserver of peace abroad.

After some initial hesitation about whether he still wanted to run in 1964, Goldwater made his formal declaration from his home in Phoenix on January 3, 1964. He promised "a choice, not an echo" against Lyndon Johnson and Democratic liberalism. The American people should not become "just cogs in a vast government machine." Upon his announcement, Goldwater trailed Johnson by wide margins in the major public opinion polls. The president had already put the GOP on the defensive with his legislative activism and ambitious program for a civil rights bill and a tax cut, with a war on poverty soon to come. Goldwater, however, regarded Johnson as an unworthy opponent and a politician "who never cleaned the crap off his boots."[9]

The opening months of the campaign produced mixed results for Goldwater's candidacy. In the contest for convention delegates, his bandwagon rolled on, picking up votes in the South, Middle West, and West with striking efficiency. As he went out to meet the voters in person and came under intense press scrutiny for the first time, his defects as a candidate emerged. While Goldwater could work hard when he wished, he lacked the discipline to stay on message in this early phase. These inconsistencies tended to confirm the senator's self-evaluation to a newspaperman in August 1963: "You know, I haven't got a really first-class brain." He could have avoided the New Hampshire primary, but he decided to make a test of his strength there. Goldwater campaigned hard but committed some damaging gaffes that haunted him for the rest of the year.[10]

Goldwater liked to speak off the cuff and answer questions informally. That had worked for him in Arizona, where the obliging press had tidied up his awkward phrasings and fixed his mistakes. Now the reporters printed most of what he said. In answer to a question in New Hampshire, he argued that Social Security ought to become a voluntary program. "If a person can provide better for himself, let him do it. But if he prefers the government to do it, let him." Conservatives at the time and since contended that it was a mistake to assume, as opposing newspapers did, that Goldwater wanted to end Social Security. Leaving aside Goldwater's imprecise language, there remained the point that if Social Security was made voluntary, its character as an old-age insurance program would end. Goldwater was articulating what most Republicans then and since believed about Social Security, but to offer the idea as a casual response to an inquiry illustrated how much of a political amateur Goldwater was.[11]

A similar slip occurred regarding the candidate's stand on nuclear weapons. While Goldwater's ideas about the North Atlantic Treaty Organization's commanders having the authority to use nuclear weapons in the case of a Soviet attack reflected government policy, the senator discussed the issue in a way that suggested a rather cavalier attitude toward the matter. By raising the question in the context that he did, Goldwater enabled first Rockefeller and later Lyndon Johnson to depict him as unreliable and intemperate on the topic of nuclear weapons. The later complaints by Goldwater defenders that these charges were untrue obscured the harder political axiom that allowing opponents to define a candidacy is no way to win an election.

Goldwater lost the New Hampshire primary to Henry Cabot Lodge, the American ambassador to South Vietnam, who gained from a write-in campaign that two young supporters organized. That slip in Goldwater's fortunes did not interrupt the senator's progress toward the nomination. The climactic encounter with the flagging campaign of Nelson Rockefeller came in early June in the California primary. Rockefeller had won the Oregon primary, in which Goldwater did not participate. If the New York governor could defeat his conservative rival in that large state, he might disrupt Goldwater's momentum enough to deadlock the convention. Given the passion with which the delegates favored Goldwater, if his candidacy had been stopped, the convention would never have endorsed Rockefeller. The New Yorker had become little more than a potential spoiler.

In a hard-fought primary, Goldwater and Rockefeller waged an ugly contest. Both sides hurled charges at the other. Rockefeller had a slight edge in the polls as the voting neared, but then the picture changed days before the election. His new wife gave birth to their first child, recalling the Rockefeller divorce, especially when the New Yorker left California to be with Happy and the new baby. Goldwater partisans asked, "Do you want a leader or a lover in the White House?" Goldwater's victory was narrow, with only sixty-eight thousand votes separating the two men. Nonetheless, he had beaten Rockefeller and was on a clear path to the nomination.[12]

Faced with the prospect of Goldwater's nomination, moderate Republicans had no credible alternative to challenge him with. Professionals regarded the candidacy of Senator Margaret Chase Smith of Maine, the first woman to seek the GOP nomination, as only an amusing sideshow. The men running to block Goldwater were hardly more believable contenders. Between the California primary and the national convention in mid-July, the abortive "Stop Goldwater" efforts from Pennsylvania governor William Scranton proved futile. The Goldwater delegates were not to be shaken loose from their man, especially not at the eleventh hour by an eastern moderate. Despite qualms about Goldwater's electoral chances in the fall, the effective opposition dwindled as the convention at San Francisco's Cow Palace neared.[13]

While Goldwater was locking up the nomination, events in Congress posed a test for his leadership and for his party in response to the rising tide of the civil rights movement. The Kennedy administration had proposed a bill in the summer of 1963 that provided access to public accommodations for all Americans regardless of race. After Kennedy's death, Lyndon Johnson made civil rights a keystone of his legislative program. Passage in the House came with the crucial support of 138 Republicans. Then Johnson insisted that the Senate act on the measure in 1964. The White House pushed hard to break the filibuster of southern Democratic senators opposed to the measure. Everett Dirksen assembled a majority of Republican senators, whose votes were indispensable to ultimate passage. By the summer of 1964 it was evident that the bill was going to become law.[14]

Goldwater had supported the civil rights laws of 1957 and 1960, but he stopped short on the 1964 proposal. The Arizonan believed, based on the anti–civil rights views of such legal advisers as William Rehnquist and Robert Bork, that the measure was unconstitutional. As a result, Goldwater decided that he would vote against the law in the Senate. "The problem of discrimination cannot be cured by laws alone," he told his colleagues. States' rights prevented the government from interfering with local issues such as race relations.[15]

Goldwater's position mixed conviction and expediency. His hopes of winning the presidency hinged on a strong showing in the South, where he hoped to get the largest share of the votes he needed to prevail in the electoral college. This judgment represented an important shift in the party's strategy for presidential contests and thus anticipated subsequent Republican campaigns. A vote for the civil rights law would doom his chances and leave the South in Johnson's hands. With Governor George C. Wallace, an avowed segregationist, embarrassing the Democrats with his presidential campaign in the primaries, talk of a "white backlash" against civil rights suggested that opposition to racial justice might be good politics in the North. Moreover, a dislike of an intrusive federal government brought conservative Republicans into an alliance with defecting southern Democrats and restive ethnic Democrats in the North fearful of desegregation in their all-white neighborhoods. Playing the race card offered rich rewards for the GOP in 1964.

Citing Goldwater's support for the National Association for the Advancement of Colored People in Phoenix and his role in desegregating the Air National Guard in Arizona, as well as the senator's declared lack of racial prejudice, Goldwater's biographers attribute his opposition to the 1964 law to constitutional principle. Fear of an oppressive federal government telling the states what to do in private matters was Goldwater's worry. In time the South would see the error of discrimination. Until then, patience and noninterference were the proper approaches.

Black Americans and Democrats found Goldwater's logic flawed. He placed greater emphasis on the rights and opinions of white southerners than the fair treatment of African Americans in public places and employment. Goldwater and his allies had made an electoral calculus. There were more white votes to be gained by opposing civil rights than black votes to be lost. Since Goldwater and like-minded Republicans knew in their hearts that they were not bigots, they believed that they could court the South without adopting the prejudices of white southerners. The question was whether Republicans would in time find the South's racial views transformed or in fact become converted to the region's pro-white ideology.

Lyndon Johnson told Bill Moyers after the civil rights law was enacted, "I think we have just delivered the South to the Republican party for a long time to come." The election did not go the Republicans' way in 1964, but in the years that followed the GOP gathered in a rich harvest of ballots in the South and elsewhere from white Americans who prized social order. Like the Democrats in the nineteenth century, the Republicans found that states' rights, calls for limited government, and lower taxes had an enduring appeal. To what extent that meant making the GOP the party of white Americans remained to be seen. The percentage of black Americans who identified themselves as Republicans skidded from 23 percent four years earlier to 12 percent on Election Day 1964.[16]

The Republican National Convention proved two points beyond question. Goldwater and his conservative supporters had gained control of the Republican Party. More important, they intended to win or lose the presidency on their own terms. Goldwater's managers controlled the proceedings through an elaborate system of telephones and walkie-talkies. Despite this conservative discipline, the delegates and the galleries let a national television audience know about their passion for their cause. They cheered when Dwight D. Eisenhower attacked the news media in passing, and they booed Nelson Rockefeller when he spoke on behalf of a platform plank denouncing extremism. The plank was defeated, but the way Rockefeller was treated backfired against the Goldwaterites.[17]

The Republican platform, as adopted by the delegates, backed away from the 1960 document on civil rights by promising "full implementation and faithful execution" of the new civil rights law while at the same time asserting that the elimination "of any such discrimination is a matter of heart, conscience, and education, as well as of equal rights under law." The delegates supported an amendment to allow prayer in public schools, endorsed Social Security "with improved benefits to our people," and sought a reduction in government spending of at least $5 billion. In foreign policy, the GOP opposed the admission of Communist China to the United Nations, promised victory in South Vietnam, and pledged to "never unilaterally disarm America." While couched in conservative language, the Goldwater platform was less confrontational than some of the delegates might have wished in that it did not seek abolition of Social Security, denounce civil rights, or seek repudiation of other New Deal measures.[18]

Conciliation or even electoral success was not Goldwater's priority, as evidenced by his choice of a running mate and his acceptance speech. The selection of Representative William E. Miller, the chair of the Republican National Committee, brought a hard-working moderate to the ticket. This choice was premised not on emphasizing Miller's positive qualifications but rather on the grounds that Miller's partisan attacks would, in Goldwater's phrase, drive Lyndon Johnson "nuts." The nominee would have been better advised to have selected a figure from a border state or the Middle West, but Goldwater made his choice without consulting any major party leaders.[19]

The acceptance speech provided Goldwater with a last chance to woo Republican moderates back to his camp and to convince independent voters that he was not the demon that had appeared in the media since January. Goldwater felt understandable anger about the treatment he had received from the press and other Republicans. Some commentators had questioned his mental health, and others had attacked his intelligence. As a result, Goldwater saw the speech not as a time to heal wounds but as a moment to chart "a new course in GOP national politics." So the rhetoric of the speech was intensified. Unlike the inclusive Ronald Reagan sixteen years later, Goldwater's approach did not increase his chances of winning the White House. He and his speech-writers, particularly Professor Harry Jaffa of Claremont McKenna College, wanted to send a message to the American political world. Thus, the famous statement about "extremism in the pursuit of liberty" became what Goldwater's acceptance speech will always be remembered for.[20]

Seasoned politicians such as Richard Nixon understood that the Republican nominee, often unfairly attacked for his alleged ties to the radical right, had handed his enemies a rhetorical gift. Not only did Goldwater fail to close the rifts in the party and heal its wounds, Nixon recalled, "He opened new wounds and then rubbed salt in them." The Goldwater campaign deflated as soon as the words were delivered. One reporter in the crowd said, "My God, he's going to run as Barry Goldwater." The Republican candidate had provided the opposition with evidence to support their charges that Goldwater himself held extreme views. That the Democrats and moderate Republicans used Goldwater's words against him was hardly surprising.[21]

While some Republicans remained loyal to the national ticket, others made it clear that they were either not voting for Goldwater or providing only token support for his candidacy. The Johnson administration found it easy to recruit Republicans for financial support and as members of Republicans for Johnson committees. While the moderates defected, Goldwater moved his friends into key positions within the GOP and the Republican National Committee. Arizonans whom the presidential candidate had known for years ran the campaign and excluded outsiders. Even among conservatives the Goldwater forces proved less inclusive than was prudent. Goldwater was never comfortable with those outside of his inner circle. The resulting campaign was very insular and ineffective.[22]

As a contest, the 1964 race for the presidency was one-sided in its results and ugly in its tone. Little in the campaign itself affected the final outcome. Lyndon Johnson enjoyed a big lead in the polls over Goldwater in August 1964, and that advantage expanded into a landslide Johnson victory in November. Everything seemed to go Johnson's way. The Tonkin Gulf episode in August, involving naval encounters between North Vietnamese and American ships in the waters off North Vietnam, allowed Johnson to appear strong in defending American interests and moderate in his response to what was portrayed as a Communist challenge to the United States. For a public that did not want war in Southeast Asia but sought a defense of American rights, Johnson's actions appeared at the time to be appropriate.

The historical importance of the 1964 election lay in its enduring effects on American politics for the next thirty years. The defection of moderate

Republicans from the Goldwater-Miller ticket assured continuing conservative dominance of the party once the election results were counted. Whatever moderate Republicanism was, that faction of the party shrank and moved rightward at the same time to remain within the party.

Although Goldwater lost in a national rout, he established a more permanent base for the GOP in the South. The Republican candidate carried Alabama, Georgia, Louisiana, Mississippi, and South Carolina, and ran well in the rest of the Deep South even in states that he lost. In South Carolina, Senator Strom Thurmond made a public conversion to the GOP that proved significant for the party in the future. The process by which the South became a Republican bastion took time to unfold, but Lyndon Johnson accurately predicted the impact of Democratic adherence to civil rights and the Goldwater candidacy on the political allegiance of the states of the old Confederacy.

The Goldwater-Johnson race featured a degree of negative campaigning, especially on television, that anticipated the techniques common by the end of the twentieth century. The Republicans believed that the Johnson White House had gone well beyond the boundaries of political fair play in its advertising against Goldwater. The major exhibit in this argument was the so-called Daisy Field commercial, which showed a little girl with daisy petals that dissolved into a nuclear explosion. Johnson's voice intoned under these images: "These are the stakes—to make a world in which all of God's children can live, or to go into the dark." Aired only once but repeated often on news broadcasts, the Daisy Field commercial became a symbol of the willingness of Johnson and his aides to stop at nothing to defeat Goldwater. Moreover, those close to Goldwater were sure that the president used the Federal Bureau of Investigation to tap phones and place listening devices on Goldwater's campaign plane.[23]

The 1964 campaign was not one of virtue against vice when it came to the tactics of the two parties. Goldwater's canvass gained from widely circulated anti-Johnson literature such as J. Evetts Haley's *A Texan Looks at Lyndon* and Phyllis Schlafly's *A Choice Not an Echo*. The Republicans prepared a tough film about Johnson and the Democrats but withdrew it on Goldwater's orders. Spots that were aired emphasized crime in the streets and Johnson's shady past. Since they were constantly on the defensive, the Republicans were not able to "go negative" against Johnson as they would with other Democratic candidates in future contests. Nonetheless, the 1964 race would linger as a touchstone for Republicans that the Democrats had been the first to use attack ads on national television.

The most significant moment of the Goldwater campaign did not involve the candidate himself. A former Democrat turned Republican, Ronald Reagan, delivered a nationally televised speech on October 27 called "A Time for Choosing." In it, Reagan invoked many of the policy themes and much of the appealing rhetoric that would mark his political career. "We'll preserve for our children this, the last best hope of man on earth, or we'll sentence them to take the last step into a thousand years of darkness." The speech, delivered with Reagan's oratorical skill, sparked a flood of contributions, made Reagan a national political personality, and encouraged talk of a race for governor of California in 1966. Though Barry Goldwater did not yet realize it, his moment as a leader of conservatism within the Republican Party ended even before his presidential campaign did.[24]

When the votes came in on election night in 1964, Goldwater's candidacy went down to a crushing defeat. The Republican candidate carried six states, five in the South, along with Arizona. He trailed Johnson in the popular vote by more than fifteen million votes, and his twenty-seven million popular votes were nearly seven million fewer than Nixon had received four years earlier. The Goldwater-Johnson race brought a smaller percentage of Americans to the polls than the exciting Kennedy-Nixon encounter.

The Democrats controlled both houses of Congress by wide margins, and the president had the legislative muscle he needed to enact his Great Society program embracing a war on poverty, Medicare, and sweeping environmental measures, among other initiatives. The pundits likened the contest to a rerun of the 1936 debacle for the GOP. Forecasts of the demise of the Republicans proved premature. Within two years the Republicans bounced back, and four years later Nixon was in the White House. Lyndon Johnson's victory proved temporary as the combination of racial tensions, domestic unrest, and the costs of the Vietnam War unhinged the Democratic presidency. Barry Goldwater brought conservatives to dominance within the Republican Party but other men such as Ronald Reagan and Richard Nixon inherited his mantle and returned the GOP to national competitiveness in the mid-1960s.

In fact, the aftermath of the 1964 election demonstrated that the Democratic grip on American politics was not permanent. Although he had assured voters that he sought no wider war in Vietnam, Johnson escalated the conflict with bombing in North Vietnam and the introduction of American ground troops in the summer. Republicans endorsed these moves, eager to end Communism in Southeast Asia. Many Republicans criticized Johnson for not using enough military force, for his willingness to negotiate with the North, and for his reluctance to pursue total victory. The nature of this total victory was not usually defined with precision, but the idea that some other course, whether more escalation or the threat of nuclear weapons, could bring an end to the conflict became embedded in conservative thinking.

From these presumptions another idea emerged once the Vietnam conflict was lost in the mid-1970s. The concept gained currency among Republicans that the Democrats under Johnson had not pushed hard enough to achieve victory. The answer in the next American war was to amass overwhelming force and allow the military, not civilian politicians, to make the key strategic decisions. In that way the Democratic errors of slow escalation and an unwillingness to employ the full weight of military power in Vietnam would not be repeated. The rise on the left of Democratic protest against the war provided Republicans with abundant confirmation of what they always knew—the Democratic Party was unpatriotic and prone to treason. Future Republican administrations would end the "Vietnam syndrome."

In the mid-1960s, it was not the war in Vietnam that destroyed the Democratic coalition of Lyndon Johnson. The issue of race, submerged in the election, reappeared to bedevil the Democrats. During the summer of 1965, twenty-three of thirty-two Republicans in the Senate provided crucial support for the enactment of the Voting Rights Act of 1965. Though it was not apparent at the time, the tide of the civil rights movement had crested, as had Republican support for the goals of African Americans.[25]

Within a week of the signing of this law the Watts Riots erupted in Los Angeles and continued for five days. The National Guard had to restore order after thirty-four people were killed and much property was destroyed. In the three years that followed, "long hot summers" brought racial uprisings to major cities. Advocates of "black power" represented the more militant opinions of African Americans. Democratic liberalism became identified with the resentments and demands of the black underclass. Whites who had supported the party since Franklin D. Roosevelt began to defect. Two British politicians who toured the country after the elections of 1966 "found an undercurrent of resentment concerning civil order and gains made by the Negro population."[26]

The Republicans came into the 1966 elections well positioned to capitalize on the sudden Democratic disarray. On the organizational side, a new chairman of the Republican National Committee, Ray Bliss of Ohio, brought efficient fundraising and ideological tolerance to his duties. While Bliss emphasized the problem of inflation as a gut issue in the fall elections, the question of race was just beneath the surface. A poll taken in September 1966 found that 52 percent of Americans believed that the Johnson administration was moving too fast on civil rights.[27]

A particular target for Republican complaints was the Supreme Court under Chief Justice Earl Warren. The decision of *Miranda v. Arizona* affirming the right of criminal suspects to remain silent during police questioning was denounced as procriminal and antipolice. Richard Nixon would promise in 1968 to appoint judges who would favor law and order. These Republican themes resonated with an electorate worried about social stability and the prospect of becoming victi of crime. The Johnson administration found itself on the defensive and never identified a persuasive theme to offset the GOP attacks.

The election results revived Republican spirits after the 1964 debacle. The GOP gained forty-seven seats in the House, elected three new senators, and won eight gubernatorial races. The party suddenly had fresh faces to present to the American people. Spiro T. Agnew won the Maryland statehouse. On the other side of the country, Ronald Reagan defeated the incumbent California governor, Edmund G. "Pat" Brown. Charles Percy won a senate seat in Illinois by ousting longtime liberal Paul H. Douglas. In Massachusetts, Edward Brooke gained a Senate seat and became the first African American to sit in that body since Reconstruction. "We've beaten the hell out of them," said Richard Nixon of the Democrats, "and we're going to kill them in '68."[28]

In the long-range perspective, the most significant result in 1966 was Ronald Reagan's victory in California. Building on his television appearance for Goldwater in 1964, the personable, attractive Reagan won the party's nomination and easily defeated the overconfident Brown. While his views were as hard-edged as Goldwater's, Reagan presented them with charm, plausibility, and a winning smile. Not for the last time did the Democrats underestimate Reagan's skill as a campaigner and communicator of conservatism. His opposition to the Civil Rights Act of 1964 no longer seemed unreasonable in the wake of Watts. The student upheavals at the University of California at Berkeley gave Reagan even greater appeal to middle-class voters who wanted calm as well as patriotism on their nightly news programs. Some of Reagan's supporters began thinking of a presidential race in 1968 based on their candidate's sweeping victory in California.

The big winner in 1966 was Richard Nixon, who now saw his path to the nomination in 1968 open up. Written off as a political has-been after his loss to Pat Brown in 1962, Nixon had supported Goldwater two years later when so many Republicans stayed home or supported Johnson. When the Democrats ran into trouble, Nixon went out on the hustings on behalf of Republican candidates. The political credits he gained in 1966 would turn into delegate votes two years later.

President Johnson had given Nixon a lift as the congressional elections neared. After the Republicans assailed the president's policy on Vietnam, Johnson fired back that Nixon was "a chronic campaigner." Nixon responded that the remark represented "one of the most savage personal assaults ever leveled by the President of the United States against one of his political opponents." Johnson had treated him as a major Republican leader, and this allowed Nixon to depict GOP gains as a triumph for himself personally.[29]

Nixon's fortunes brightened during the rest of 1967. He built a well-financed organization and went on a series of foreign tours that provided even more visibility for his candidacy. The key for Nixon was to erase the "loser" image that he had acquired in 1960 and 1962. As the Vietnam War stalemated and urban rioting plagued the home front, Nixon seemed like a moderate, credible alternative to Johnson and his failing policies.

The main Republican rival to Nixon in 1967 was Governor George Romney of Michigan. Handsome and impressive-looking before television cameras, Romney had served three terms and blended public service with executive experience in the automobile industry. His Mormon faith never had the chance to become a salient issue in his presidential run. The governor was not a gifted speaker or a fast thinker, and his campaign was always vulnerable to a verbal slip. After a trip to Vietnam, a reporter asked him why his position on the war had changed to one of opposition to American involvement. Romney responded, "When I came back from Vietnam, I just had the greatest brainwashing that anybody can get when you go over to Vietnam, not only by the generals but also by the diplomatic corps over there." Ignoring the substance of Romney's comments, the press treated the brainwashing remark as evidence that the candidate lacked the smarts to be president. Private polls showed him well behind Nixon. As a result, the Michigan governor took himself out of the race in late February 1968.[30]

The other potential challengers for Nixon were Nelson Rockefeller and Ronald Reagan. Rockefeller was never a serious threat because of the hatred he aroused among conservatives. Reagan, however, was already beginning to create the buzz among Republicans that would continue for the next two decades. He represented a real threat to Nixon's quest for the nomination if he could dispel the impression that the former vice president had a lock on the prize. A quiet struggle between Reagan and Nixon for supremacy among Republicans ensued during the first half of 1968.

The nation experienced a chaotic first three months of 1968. The Democratic Party shook itself to pieces as first Senator Eugene McCarthy of Minnesota and then Senator Robert F. Kennedy of New York sought the nomination against Lyndon Johnson. The Tet Offensive of North Vietnam undermined popular confidence in the progress of the war. Then Johnson's surprise with-drawal from the race on March 31, 1968, as his political base collapsed further scrambled the political scene. All these events worked in favor of Nixon and the Republicans. In the New Hampshire primary, Nixon trounced Rockefeller, who was not a formal candidate, by an eight-to-one margin. Only the potential threat of a Reagan candidacy stood in Nixon's way.

In later years, the allegation that Nixon had claimed to have a "secret plan" during the campaign to end the Vietnam War produced much debate. Publicly, he asserted his intention to provide "new leadership" that would "end the war and win the peace in the Pacific." That goal would be achieved, he said, "if we mobilize our economic and political and diplomatic leader-ship." Though he did not say so, Nixon intended to play the Soviet Union and China against each other to pressure North Vietnam into a negotiated settlement of the conflict. At the same time, American troops would be pulled out and the war put in the hands of South Vietnam. Nixon said that he could not reveal the specific details of his approach lest he interfere with Johnson's leadership or commit himself about his own presidential agenda. So calculated artful and ambiguous was Nixon's stance that oppo-nents of the war and those who wanted victory could both take comfort in Nixon's words.[31]

The Nixon campaign's priority at this point was to change the way the press viewed the candidate himself. Though he disliked and dis-trusted journalists after his 1960 campaign, Nixon knew that careful management of the media was essential to a successful run. The candidate gave few press conferences and emphasized events, such as scripted meetings with voters, that were staged for television. Nixon and his campaign portrayed him as a "new Nixon," a man of more mature judgment and less volatile temper than earlier in the decade. One of his aides put it well: "It's not the man we have to change, but rather the *received impression*."[32]

Richard Nixon brought the Republicans to power in the late 1960s. The Watergate scandal, however, ended his presidency and set back the GOP. Library of Congress, LC-USZ62-13037.

Johnson's departure from the race further aided Nixon's candidacy. Reporters had been clamoring for the details of Nixon's Vietnam ideas, but the surprise an-nouncement of Johnson's withdrawal allowed the Republican front runner to remain silent while the president opened the negotiations with North Vietnam that Johnson had coupled with his departure from politics. Meanwhile, Nelson Rockefeller had concluded that Nixon could not be beaten. He declared on March 21 that he would not run. The statement outraged and embarrassed Spiro Agnew, who had started a Draft Rockefeller Committee. Agnew and Nixon began quiet conversations about the future.

Then a month later, urged on by President Johnson (who at the time feared the race might be between Nixon and Senator Robert F. Kennedy on the Democratic side), Nelson Rockefeller reappeared as a candidate. The strategy of the New Yorker was bizarre. He argued that he was electable and Nixon was not, based on public opinion polls. The polls he commissioned did not show the support Rockefeller anticipated. Rank-and-file Republicans, most of whom hated Rockefeller, were not buying. Should Nixon falter, they would turn to Reagan, but the front runner did not collapse under the Rockefeller barrage. By the early part of June 1968, the inept Rockefeller campaign was moribund.

The spring of 1968 brought dramatic events for an already lurching nation. Martin Luther King was murdered in early April, and Senator Robert F. Kennedy was assassinated two months later after he won the Democratic primary in California. While the Democrats descended into bitter infighting, Nixon campaigned on themes that resonated with voters for decades to come. He stressed the needs of "the silent center, the millions of people in the middle of the political spectrum who do not demonstrate, who do not picket or protest loudly." Moreover, there was, he said, "a rebellion against taxes, and against the ever-higher piling of Federal tax on state tax on local tax."[33]

Nixon's election chances seemed more and more promising as the summer of 1968 unfolded. On the Vietnam issue, Nixon worked to hew as closely to Johnson's negotiating stance as he could. He feared that the president might announce something approaching peace before the election, boost the Democrats, and undercut Republican hopes. Vice President Hubert Humphrey, the likely Democratic nominee after Robert F. Kennedy's death, was trying and failing to escape from the embrace of Johnson's Vietnam policy, which was so unpopular among Democrats. Meanwhile, Nixon was opening up backchannels to the South Vietnamese government that could be used to send private messages to the politicians in Saigon in the event Johnson launched a peace offensive.

As the Republican convention neared in early August, Nixon's victory seemed assured, barring the emergence of a Rockefeller-Reagan coalition to block the front runner on the first ballot. The former vice president had long feared the charismatic appeal of the California governor to Republican conservatives. Although his administration in Sacramento had gotten off to a shaky start, Reagan displayed an ability to rouse the party faithful to even greater heights of enthusiasm than Goldwater had achieved. Inevitably, the Californian's campaign had to be something of a stealth enterprise. He dared not oppose Nixon in public, but he could watch for an opening should Nixon falter. With his usual wariness, Nixon recognized the threat that Reagan posed.

At the last minute before the convention, Reagan got into the race. A media event with the California delegation provided the platform and hinted at the "Great Communicator" to come. The Reagan slate adopted a resolution requesting that the governor be "a leading and bona fide candidate for President." Reagan then strode into the room and told the group, "Gosh, I was surprised. It all came out of a clear blue sky." If Reagan was to win, he would have to dislodge Nixon's grip on Republicans from below the Mason-Dixon Line. Should Nixon waver on the race issue or, worse yet, choose a northern, liberal Republican for his running mate, then a break for Reagan might take place.[34]

Nixon moved to forestall Reagan on two fronts. He and his surrogates assured southerners that, while he believed in desegregation of schools, he was opposed to busing children to schools outside their neighborhoods in pursuit of racial balance. Moreover, he thought that the South should be allowed to comply voluntarily with judicial decrees before being compelled to do so. Second, in these private sessions with southern delegations, Nixon made clear his opposition to federal judges who interfered with the working of local schools. "I think it is the job of the courts to interpret the law and not make law," Nixon commented.[35]

The assistance of Strom Thurmond of South Carolina was crucial in demonstrating Nixon's devotion to the South and its racial arrangements. As a result, Nixon subdued any potential Reagan rebellion among southerners and held on to the crucial delegate votes there. The actual voting for the nominee went as the Nixon camp anticipated. Their candidate went over the top on the first ballot with twenty-five more votes than he needed. Although Reagan, Rockefeller, and several minor candidates trailed, their combined total revealed how narrow Nixon's victory had been. Nixon now turned to the choice of his running mate.

Weeks earlier, Nixon had concluded that Governor Spiro Agnew of Maryland was the best choice. On the surface, Agnew had much to recommend him in terms of Nixon's emerging strategy toward the white South. In 1966,

Agnew defeated a racist Democrat to claim the Maryland statehouse. After the embarrassment of supporting Rockefeller before his withdrawal, Agnew moved toward Nixon, especially about civil rights. He also reacted to the rioting that followed the murder of Martin Luther King, Jr., with stern denunciations of black leaders and attacks on urban unrest. Here was the man Nixon required to help him win the South and border states by appealing to white voters. With Governor George C. Wallace running as a third-party candidate, Agnew seemed an ideal choice to counter Wallace's allure without getting into the racial gutter with the Alabama leader.

One thing Nixon had not done was launch an investigation into Agnew's background and financial affairs. Nor had Nixon and his men questioned Agnew about potential problems that might affect his fitness to serve as vice president. Nixon had made a mistake. Agnew was involved in several conspiracies in Maryland that included bribery, tax fraud, and extortion. He had been taking bribes from state contractors. These arrangements continued once he became vice president; Nixon had chosen an active participant in criminal enterprises as his pick for the nation's second highest office.[36]

At the convention, Nixon made symbolic offers of the vice presidency to two other Republicans, both of whom declined. Nixon then chose Agnew and made the announcement to the surprised press corps. It became apparent that Agnew was not a strong choice, but he suited Nixon's purposes in August 1968. The criticisms of the media were only nagging distractions as he prepared for his moment of vindication and triumph.

In his acceptance address, Nixon cast himself as the champion of "the great majority of Americans, the forgotten Americans, the non-shouters, the non-demonstrators." He contended, "America is in trouble today not because her people have failed but because her leaders have failed." The problems of Vietnam, racial unrest, and crime were compelling reasons that it was "time for new leadership for the United States of America."[37]

Nixon began the campaign with obvious advantages over his main opponent, Vice President Humphrey, and his third-party challenger, George C. Wallace. He was well ahead in the public opinion polls with a 45–29 spread over Humphrey, and Wallace trailing with 18 percent. The electoral map also looked promising for the GOP. There were many states where Nixon was certain of victory. Humphrey had no such cushion. The Republicans had built up a big lead in campaign funding and had more than $30 million in the presidential-campaign war chest. For all of his assets, however, Nixon relied on voter discontent with the Democrats, not on an ideological appeal. Unlike Goldwater four years earlier, the Nixon effort was empty of programmatic content. If the Democrats reunited and Humphrey closed the gap, then Nixon and his party might be in difficulty, As Nixon aide William Safire later wrote, "Nixon was playing not to lose."[38]

At first it seemed that Nixon had very little to fear in his cautious approach to the campaign. The turbulent Democratic Convention, blighted by riots and the heavy-handed tactics of the Chicago police, pushed Humphrey even further behind. With his lead, Nixon could devote his resources to those states where his candidacy seemed strong. Had Wallace not been in the race, a Republican landslide would likely have occurred, since the majority of voters for the Alabama governor would have gone Republican. By the end of September, the prospect of a decisive Republican triumph seemed possible, especially because the underfunded Humphrey campaign was doing so badly.

Yet problems lingered. Nixon seemed stuck at around 40–45 percent. Wallace faltered in early October because organized labor attacked him in the North with effective advertising. Like many third-party candidates, Wallace lost ground when voters realized he could not be elected. Meanwhile, Nixon ran to protect his lead rather than seeking to expand it. Nor did he run in a way that energized the campaigns of other Republican candidates for the Senate and the House. Safely tucked behind his campaign apparatus, which was out of sight of the media, Nixon sought to run out the clock as the election neared.

Humphrey revived his candidacy by breaking away from Johnson on Vietnam in late September. A few weeks later prospects for negotiations with North Vietnam improved and hopes or peace rose. By October 24, Humphrey was eight points down in the polls and closing the gap as traditional Democrats returned to their party. In the last two weeks of the election, the margin between Nixon and Humphrey tightened almost daily.

The final days of the 1968 contest saw an intricate interplay between President Johnson and Nixon over a halt to bombing in Vietnam. Both sides played hardball. Nixon used his backchannel in Saigon to prevent South Vietnam from backing Johnson's initiative. The president brought in the FBI and used wiretaps to keep track of what the Nixon camp was doing. In the end, the bombing halt did not lead to peace talks because of Saigon's reluctance to sit down with the North. Although the public knew little of these events, the process had major consequences. Having endured political surveillance from the Democrats, Nixon and his men came to believe that they could take similar actions when they were in power.

Despite the last-minute Democratic surge, Nixon and the Republicans held on to win in 1968. The victor secured 31,770,237 popular votes to 31,270,533 for

Humphrey. Wallace trailed with 9,906,141. Nixon garnered 43.4 percent of the vote to 42.7 percent for Humphrey and 13.5 percent for Wallace. In the electoral college, Nixon had the votes of thirty-two states for 301 electoral votes to Humphrey's 191 from thirteen states and the District of Columbia. Wallace captured five states and 46 electoral votes.

While the election represented a significant repudiation of the Democrats, it was not a major endorsement of the Grand Old Party. In four years the Democrats had dropped twelve million votes from Johnson's 1964 total, and Nixon had run four million votes better than Barry Goldwater. The big element in the shift was race. The Republicans gained from the movement of white voters away from the Democrats. The Republicans now had the prospect of majority status if the party could solidify the gains that the 1968 presidential contest had produced.

The Republicans came out of 1968 with several enduring advantages over their opponents. The Republicans had learned how to frame issues so that key elements of the Democratic coalition defected from that party. Nixon drove a wedge into the South with his "southern strategy," and Republicans duplicated that feat in subsequent presidential contests. Indeed, in the 1970s, the South moved toward its ultimate role as Republican bastion, despite the temporary victory of Jimmy Carter in 1976.[39]

The success of Nixon's fundraising also reflected what would be a lasting GOP strength. While Nixon had not helped Republican congressional and senatorial candidates much, the base of small and large donors meant that the party would always be competitive across the country. Finally, the organization that Nixon put together in 1968 helped create a cadre of seasoned political operatives in the Republican presidential races that followed for the next twenty years. Whoever the Republican candidate was in that period, he could count on practiced strategists and advocates to sign on for another campaign. In that area, until the arrival of Bill Clinton in 1992, the Democrats were outmatched.

For all these positive strides, the Nixon presidency and the Watergate scandal that ensued proved a dramatic setback for Republican hopes of building a national majority. Even though Nixon won a huge reelection victory in 1972, the Democrats retained control of both houses of Congress throughout his presidency. Nixon's resignation in 1974 and the brief presidency of Gerald Ford laid the basis for the election victory of Jimmy Carter in 1976.

Of all the Republican presidents in the twentieth century, Richard Nixon is the most complex and controversial. He had great ability as a practitioner of foreign policy, and his administration was innovative in its handling of many domestic concerns. So activist was his presidency on environmental matters, welfare reform, and Native American rights that Nixon has been called, with a touch of irony, the last liberal president. In many respects, Nixon was a Republican moderate, to the left of his mentor Dwight D. Eisenhower on a number of social and economic questions. In his rhetorical animus against big government and his dislike of bureaucracy, of course, Nixon articulated more conventional Republican thinking.[40]

For all of Nixon's abilities as a politician and diplomat, he had corresponding flaws that led him into disaster by 1974. The new president trusted almost no one, and he viewed the world with deep suspicion. Convinced that he had been cheated out of the presidency by the press, liberal Democrats, and the Kennedys in 1960, he regarded himself as surrounded by enemies while he sat in the White House. So he sought to use the power of the presidency to strike back in an often bitter, ruthless fashion. As he told his aide H. R. Haldeman in September 1971, "Bob, *please* get me the names of the Jews, you know, the big Jewish contributors of the Democrats.... All right. Could we please investigate some of the cocksuckers? That's all." Out of this sense of persecution and potential betrayal came a need to control all aspects of the political environment, even by illegal means if necessary. Politics for Richard Nixon was not like war; it was war.[41]

This deep-rooted conviction led Nixon to view the apparatus of the Republican Party as inept and lacking in the ruthlessness his needs demanded. He wanted to advance the interests of the party but was not willing to use the GOP organization to do so. As a result, the Republican National Committee became a figurehead with no real power or authority. Nixon and his aides ran the 1972 election as a separate operation apart from the Republican parties in the states. As the chairman of the RNC, Senator Robert Dole, put it with his usual brand of sarcastic realism: "The Republican party was not only not involved with Watergate, but it wasn't involved in the nomination, the convention, the campaign, the election or the inauguration."[42]

Despite his reputation as a fierce Republican partisan, Nixon often was not in step with his fellow party members. He once remarked to former Texas governor John Connally that, compared with the Democrats, "The Republicans are more restrained, more proper. The Democrats let it all out and love to shout and laugh and have fun. The Republicans have fun but they don't want people to see it. The Democrats, even when they are not having fun, like to appear to be having fun." Nixon even contemplated before and after the 1972 election creating a new party to replace the Republicans. The new organization would be on the right side of the spectrum but would be moderate on social policy and conservative in foreign affairs and on the economy. In that sense, Nixon shared sentiments that Dwight Eisenhower had expressed a decade and a half earlier.[43]

For their part, conservative Republicans eyed Nixon with suspicion as well. They had to tolerate a president who sponsored such initiatives as a guaranteed annual income, the Environmental Protection Agency, greater spending on social programs at a rate higher than under Lyndon Johnson, and affirmative action on racial problems. In foreign policy, while Nixon sought to achieve "peace with honor" in Vietnam, he also pursued detente with the Soviet Union and opened up relations with the Communist leadership of China.

Nixon wanted the Republicans, as he conceived them, to become the majority party during his presidency. He dreamed of redefining American politics as Franklin D. Roosevelt had done during the 1930s. To reach that goal, Nixon exploited the changes in political demography that the 1960s had produced. The future of the Grand Old Party lay in the South and West where explosive population growth and conservative values offered ripe pickings for the Republicans. With a conservative agenda that appealed to Middle Americans, Republicans could outgain the Democrats with key voting groups. These Americans became known in the Nixon White House as the Silent Majority.

The Nixon Administration moved with skill and determination to attract these voters. Division and discord among the Democrats after 1968 made these White House initiatives successful among many Americans. Outside the South, Nixon targeted blue-collar Democrats in the Middle West, especially those who belonged to the unions of the AFL-CIO and Jimmy Hoffa's Teamsters. A timely commutation of Hoffa's prison sentence in December 1971 helped win Teamster support for Nixon in the 1972 presidential race. The White House also reached out to Catholics with public statements of Nixon's opposition to abortion and his belief that the federal government should assist parochial schools.

A key factor in Nixon's political equation was the South, but the president had to tread with care because of the sensitivity of the civil rights issue. The Republican administration was generally popular with southerners because of Nixon's opposition to student busing and his efforts to appoint a southerner to the Supreme Court. At the same time, the Nixon administration brought public school segregation in the South to an end and advanced affirmative action programs in the North. Although these activities produced grumbling from the unions and scattered unhappiness in parts of the South,

Nixon and the Republicans did not suffer at the polls. The blame for civil rights advances always fell on the Democrats. The Republicans were recognized in the North and South as the party of states' rights and for their willingness to restrain the aspirations of black Americans.[44]

The congressional elections of 1970 offered the first test of the success of Nixon's political approach. He had begun to withdraw American troops from South Vietnam and to pursue "Vietnamization," which gave Saigon more responsibility for their own defense. The president had thus defused some of the antiwar sentiment. It flared again in the spring of 1970 with the invasion of Cambodia, the deaths of students at Kent State University in Ohio and Jackson State University in Mississippi, and a resulting wave of student protest. With the economy lagging, the best tactic for the White House and the Republicans in the fall seemed to be to concentrate on law and order issues.

The campaign did not go as the White House had hoped. The Democrats co-opted many of the social issues and thus blunted the Republican offensive. Vice President Agnew was supposed to be point man for the party, but he proved ineffective. To save the situation, Nixon himself campaigned during the last two weeks. In San Jose, California, an angry crowd taunted the president, who stood on the hood of his car and waved his fingers in the "V" sign at the protestors. The White House released a film of another campaign address on election eve that backfired because of the poor quality of the images and the president's frenzied appearance. A response by Democratic senator Edmund Muskie countered Nixon with a calm, well-produced statement of the issues.

The results of the 1970 elections left Nixon and his party very disappointed. The Republicans picked up two Senate seats but fell short of gaining control of the upper house. The Democrats added nine House seats and eleven governorships. Nixon declared the results a success because the Republicans had not suffered greater defeats two years after their presidential victory. Yet the prospects for Nixon's reelection two years later were in question.

The Democratic victory, which turned mostly on a weaker economy and Republican miscues, was transient. When it came to nominating a candidate to run against Nixon, the fault lines in the opposition, which were first opened up in 1968, were still evident and raw. The Democratic Party's new rules for electing delegates, which made their process more open to determined minorities, created problems for a moderate centrist seeking support from activist liberals. In short, Nixon and the Republicans faced a wounded, demoralized Democratic party in the run-up to 1972.

The conclusion that Nixon and his aides drew from the 1970 outcome, however, was that the president's reelection effort had to be directed from the White House. Although he spoke to the men around him about "introducing dynamic campaign management into the Republican National Committee," the president wanted little to do with Republican professionals on the committee or in the various states. The obvious choice in Nixon's mind was to have at hand "the formidable political muscle that goes with being the party in the White House." Democrats had done it since Franklin D. Roosevelt, Nixon wrote later, and, he said, "I planned to take no less advantage of it myself."[45]

Convinced from the outset of his presidency that he faced a coordinated and ruthless opposition from Democrats and a liberal media, Nixon had already taken steps to employ "formidable political muscle" in clandestine ways. Wiretaps of White House aides and reporters, on Nixon's orders, had begun as early as 1969. The Internal Revenue Service, building on what Kennedy and Johnson had done in probing right-wing enemies, had audited the tax returns and launched investigations of radical groups, journalists, and Democratic critics of the president. In 1971, after Daniel Ellsberg leaked the Pentagon Papers to the *New York Times* and the *Washington Post*, the administration created the "Plumbers," a secret group of illicit operatives, to forestall further leaks by illegal means. Other White House insiders coordinated efforts to disrupt Democratic political campaigns. Meanwhile, in 1971, the White House installed an audio taping system that was recording Nixon's conversations in the Oval Office. All the elements for a major scandal were in place, but few Republicans outside of Nixon's immediate circle had any hint of what was happening.[46]

For conservative Republicans who remained loyal to Nixon in public, the president's policies were troubling. Nixon's endorsement of Keynesian economics as well as his commitment to wage and price controls flouted right-wing economic orthodoxy. More problematic still was the dramatic opening to China, which outraged many conservative pundits. The resulting hard feelings led Representative John Ashbrook of Ohio to mount an ineffective challenge to Nixon's renomination, although it drew only minimal support in the two primaries that the maverick lawmaker entered. On the left, Representative Pete McCloskey of California launched an antiwar insurgency against Nixon that drew few Republican voters. Discontent with Nixon faded as the 1972 campaign loomed and the traditional unity among Republicans reasserted itself.[47]

The 1972 presidential race was no contest. The Democrats selected their most vulnerable candidate, Senator George S. McGovern, whose liberal campaign encountered endless troubles, produced defections to Nixon among key voting groups, and never found a winning theme on major issues. The Republicans depicted McGovern as out of touch with mainstream opinion because he favored a negotiated settlement in Vietnam. The Democrats were painted as advocates of drug use and abortion. McGovern's campaign collapsed and the president hardly needed to campaign. The Nixon camp did not intend, however, to rely on the mistakes of their opponents. "We have to develop a sense of mission," Nixon told a key aide, "and not back into victory by default."[48]

Nixon and Spiro Agnew achieved the landslide victory that they sought. The president won every state but Massachusetts and the District of Columbia, received more than an eighteen-million-vote margin over his rival, and gained 60.7 percent of the vote. He made inroads into such former bastions of Democratic strength as union members and Roman Catholics. Only African Americans and traditional Democrats stayed with their party. On a personal level, Nixon had built the New Majority he had been proclaiming during his first term.

It was not yet a Republican majority. Down the ballot, the Democrats held their own. The Republicans picked up a dozen House seats, not enough to threaten Democratic control. The Republicans dropped one Senate seat. In Maine the lone woman in the upper house, Margaret Chase Smith, was defeated after four terms in Washington. A sometime irritant to the White House, Smith had not been able to persuade Nixon to campaign for her. During the 1972 campaign, Nixon did not risk his own political capital to advance the hopes of his party in Congress.

In the aftermath of his electoral triumph, Nixon intended to move back toward conservatism by restructuring the government to make it smaller and less intrusive. To that end he sought the resignations of most of the senior government officials in the White House and the government, a move that damaged morale within the administration. Having achieved an end to US involvement in Vietnam by early 1973, Nixon turned to domestic change as his main agenda. He would seek to implement his New Majority. Having allowed the government to grow larger as he pursued reelection, Nixon proposed to do in his second term what he had not shown the will to do in his first administration.

Of course, Nixon's mandate of 1972, such as it was, never was exploited in the ambitious form that the president envisaged. By early 1973 the Watergate scandal was already corroding the administration and, to a significant extent, the Republican Party as well. The break-in at the Democratic Party headquarters in the Watergate complex in June 1972 had been part of the effort of the Nixon White House to manage what the president and his men regarded as a hostile political environment. Along the same lines, Nixon had authorized criminal acts against Democrats, dissenters, and journalists. By late 1972 a variety of "White House horrors," in the words of Attorney General John Mitchell, were being covered up lest the public, Democrats, and law enforcement learn about them. The reporting of Bob Woodward and Carl Bernstein in the *Washington Post* was laying out much of the scandal, but their revelations attracted little interest during the second half of 1972.[49]

The Watergate scandal began to unfold early in 1973 and continued to worsen until Nixon's resignation in early August 1974. For Republicans the disintegration of Nixon's administration was protracted and painful. Although many prominent leaders within the party had long harbored private doubts about Nixon's character, Democratic attacks on the White House in 1973 elicited staunch defenses of the president from Republicans on Capitol Hill. Barry Goldwater had once labeled Nixon "a two-fisted, four-square liar," but he stood behind him until the spring of 1973, when he likened Watergate to the Teapot Dome scandal of Warren G. Harding a half century earlier. "I mean, there's a smell to it. Let's get rid of the smell."[50]

Other Republicans had different reactions. George H. W. Bush, the new chair of the Republican National Committee after the 1972 election, noted that Nixon had "said repeatedly he wasn't involved in the sordid Watergate affairs," and added, "I believe him." Ronald Reagan defended Nixon against the attacks of what the California governor privately called a "lynch mob" until just a few days before the president's resignation.[51]

As evidence of Nixon's wrongdoing accumulated, Republicans were important actors in revealing the extent of the scandals in the White House. Senator Howard Baker became a key figure on the Senate committee to investigate Watergate during the spring of 1973. Baker's famous question about what the president knew and when he knew it zeroed in on the main issue of the Watergate affair. A year later Republican senator James Buckley of New York called for Nixon's resignation, because he had lost "credibility and moral authority." When Nixon made a damaging partial release of White House tape recordings, Republicans such as Hugh Scott of Pennsylvania called the disclosures, which revealed Nixon's coarse language and machinations, "shabby, disgusting and immoral." On the House Judiciary Committee, four Republican members provided key votes against Nixon and joined with conservative Democrats in a coalition that sealed the president's fate when impeachment votes were taken.[52]

As the Watergate scandal ran its course, the leadership of the Republicans changed in ways that scrambled the party's future. Vice President Spiro Agnew proved to be a criminal who had continued to take bribes after 1968. His resignation in a plea bargain with federal prosecutors removed a potential conservative rival to Ronald Reagan in 1976. Agnew's departure posed a more immediate challenge for the embattled Nixon, who had to select a successor that Congress would confirm as vice president.

Nixon opted for Representative Gerald Ford of Michigan, the Republican leader in the House, to replace Agnew. Ford had several political assets. He would have no difficulty in winning approval from his fellow lawmakers. Ford also offered Nixon insurance against impeachment, because legislators, so the president believed, would not want to replace the incumbent with such an untrained man. In fact, as Watergate pressed on in 1974, Ford's personal honesty appeared as a refreshing contrast with Nixon's criminality.

The Watergate mess hit the Republican Party at the ballot box in 1974. The Republicans lost several special elections in the spring arising from the death or resignation of incumbents, including one for Gerald Ford's seat in Michigan. An electoral disaster loomed in the November contests as the GOP faced the voters in the sixth year of a two-term presidency. With a presidential impeachment becoming likely, the Republicans had little joy in the summer of 1974.

By that time, however, Nixon's political position was collapsing. The Republicans in Congress contended that Nixon had to be proved guilty of an illegal act for impeachment to occur. When a tape of a Nixon conversation of June 23, 1972, was released in July 1974, it showed the president was involved in the cover-up of the Watergate break-in. This "smoking gun" made Nixon's departure from the presidency inescapable. Congressional Republicans informed the president that he had only a handful of supporters remaining on Capitol Hill. On August 8, 1974, Nixon resigned, and Gerald Ford became president. In his first address to the nation, Ford proclaimed, "Our long national nightmare is over."[53]

Richard Nixon's public relationship with the Republican Party, which stretched over nearly three decades, from 1946 to 1974, has yet to be understood in all its complexity. Because of his participation in Watergate, he remains an embattled figure and a reminder to Republicans of one of their shabbier hours. As historians and political scientists have chronicled the increased government spending and expanded social programs that marked Nixon's tenure, conservatives have discovered even less to admire. The foreign policy accomplishments—detente with the Soviet Union, the opening to

China, the end of the Vietnam War—are regarded by many on the right as negative features of Nixon's record. Whether he was the last liberal president or not, he was never a conservative true believer in the mold of Ronald Reagan.

Yet Nixon left important legacies to the GOP in both substantive and tactical ways. His conviction that he faced ruthless enemies bent on his destruction harmonized with the sentiment among conservatives that liberals and Democrats were not just political adversaries but active opponents of American values. Unrelenting efforts to achieve complete electoral dominance were thus more than justified, since Democratic victories lacked basic legitimacy. The training that Republican politicians received in Nixon's hard school carried into campaigns for the next four decades.

While Congress under the Democrats sought to reform fundraising practices in 1974, the ties that Nixon had established with the business community in 1968 and 1972 translated into continuing access to big money for the GOP. As electioneering became a year-round endeavor, the Republicans outstripped their opponents in both resources and expertise without serious challenge until the arrival of Bill Clinton on the national scene in the early 1990s.

Although he lived until the mid-1990s, Richard Nixon seems like a throwback to an earlier era—the age of anti-Communism, a divisive war, and a protracted political scandal. The ousted president spent the rest of his life trying to rebuild his reputation and had succeeded in large part by the time of his death. Yet it seems unlikely that Nixon will ever enter into the pantheon of Republican heroes. As happened with the presidencies of Ulysses S. Grant and Warren G. Harding, a stain of scandal and disgrace will always color Nixon's career, in contrast to the esteem that Republicans feel for Ronald Reagan, whose moment in the sun dawned with Nixon's ruin.

II

Republicans in the Reagan Era, 1974–1988

THE 1980 PRESIDENTIAL ELECTION was still close as the Democratic president, James Earl "Jimmy" Carter, and his Republican challenger, Ronald Reagan, prepared for their only debate. The two candidates had been jockeying for position on the debate issue since the campaign began. While the Carter campaign at first thought Reagan would be a pushover in the contest for the president, they had come to respect the Republican candidate's skill in public settings. The Reagan camp, on the other hand, needed to have their man on the same stage with Carter to reassure Americans that, contrary to the claims of some Democrats, the Republican candidate was not a menacing figure who was likely to imperil the nation. After much deliberation, the aides to the two presidential hopefuls agreed to hold a single debate late in the campaign on October 28, 1980.

Two moments defined the encounter. The first came as Carter was discussing the issue of arms control and nuclear weapons. Perhaps to underline his empathy with the younger generation, perhaps to show his sensitivity on the matter generally, the president said, "I had a discussion with my daughter, Amy, the other day, before I came here, to ask her what the most important issue was. She said she thought nuclear weaponry and the control of nuclear arms." Carter's invocation of his daughter as an element in his thinking fell flat.[1]

The more crucial moment came when Carter went after Reagan for his opposition to Social Security and Medicare in the 1960s when he was a conservative spokesman and later a candidate for governor of California. The president's hard-edged, accurate criticism gave Reagan his chance to display his skill as a platform debater. When Carter contended that Reagan had begun "his career campaigning around the nation against Medicare," Reagan looked at his adversary and said, "There you go again." In a phrase Reagan summed up how many Americans felt about the president's preachy tone and his strident attacks on his rival. Reagan had articulated the doubts about Carter's personality and political leadership. At that moment the tide that had been running in Reagan's favor turned into a tsunami, and a landslide victory ensued when the voters went to the polls a week later.[2]

The Watergate scandal and the political fate of President Richard M. Nixon defined the Republican Party in the early 1970s. While their national leader was resigning in disgrace in August 1974, within the Grand Old Party itself new issues and new forces were arising that would shift its direction during the remainder of the decade. Conservatism was becoming more ideological and confrontational, underscoring the existing Republican opposition to Democratic liberalism on economic matters. The Republican stance on the economy would soon grow even more strongly predicated on the idea of lower taxes in almost all circumstances.

In retrospect, the second half of the 1970s came to be identified with Ronald Reagan's emergence as the party's face. Yet Reagan's rise to power was derived from a fresh generation of activist Republicans who transformed the energy of Barry Goldwater and his supporters in the 1960s into a new brand of social conservatism that spoke to the fears and hopes of middle- and lower-class Americans during a turbulent period for the nation.

Neither of the two parties had been especially hospitable to women before the 1970s, but the Republicans were marginally more inclusive than the Democrats. The GOP had specified in the convention rules in 1940 that women should have equal representation on committees of the Republican National Committee and mandated a similar balance on the platform committee of the national convention four years later. From 1940 through 1960 the Republican platform had endorsed the Equal Rights Amendment (ERA). By 1964 the statement disappeared when the Goldwater delegates wrote the document. It reappeared in 1968 with Nixon. Four years later, when Richard Nixon was renominated, the convention delegates in the platform "continued [their] support of the Equal Rights Amendment to the Constitution" and promised to work toward its ratification.[3]

But the mood within the party was shifting. Phyllis Schlafly, who had written the best-selling *A Choice Not an Echo*, in support of Barry Goldwater in 1964, came to the forefront among opponents of the Equal Rights Amendment after Congress sent it to the states for ratification in March 1972. Although thirty states had endorsed the amendment within a year, Schlafly rallied opponents of the ERA to block the ratification process. She charged that the document would infringe on the rights of mothers and housewives while at the same time promoting gay rights, unisex toilets, and taxpayer-funded abortions. Schlafy's STOP ERA campaign drew conservative women into Republican politics at all levels. The ERA was not ratified, and Republicans moved into opposition of much of the feminist agenda of the 1970s. In the process, the Republicans enjoyed the allegiance of conservative women in the South and West who found what feminists were calling for to be anathema.[4]

The United States Supreme Court decision in the case of *Roe v. Wade* in 1973 further persuaded conservatives to move toward the Republicans. The high court's ruling made abortion legal in the United States, thereby triggering protests from opponents of abortion who presented themselves as defenders of the unborn. Roman Catholics were at the forefront of what became the pro-life movement, with evangelical Protestants going in the same direction during the mid-1970s. The goal of these groups was to amend the Constitution to outlaw abortion. Their power at the ballot box, along with the similar convictions of many Republican lawmakers, impelled GOP leaders to identify the party as antiabortion. The inroads that Republicans made among previously Democratic Catholic voters, especially men, provided a crucial difference for the party in the elections of the late 1970s and early 1980s.

The Republicans also gained from the appearance of "neoconservatives" within the party's ranks. Drawn from former Democrats put off by their party's views on domestic and especially foreign policy issues, these intellectuals and polemicists found the Republicans more congenial as the 1970s wound down. These individuals included Irving Kristol, Jeane Kirkpatrick, Ben Wattenberg, and Michael Novak, and they moved into well-funded conservative think tanks in Washington, most notably the American Enterprise Institute. There they preached their doctrines of a strong national defense, militant anti-Communism, and economic policies of deregulation and a smaller national government.

One intellectual drag on the Republicans was the perception that the party's dislike of unbalanced budgets and deficit spending meant only a willingness to retrench and pare back government programs, which came to be known as "root canal" economics on the right. A more appealing alternative emerged in the late 1970s. Opponents of federal and state taxation contended that substantial tax cuts would in time generate so much economic growth that government revenues would actually increase. This approach became known as "supply-side economics," and it soon captured the allegiance of many Republicans. Ronald Reagan, who paid high taxes as a movie star, embraced the doctrine. Representative Jack Kemp of New York and Senator William Roth of Delaware advocated trimming income tax rates by 30 percent. Other Republicans contended that the capital gains tax rate should be reduced.

The tax reduction ethos had long been part of Republican thinking, but now it could be presented as a fresh and innovative way to overcome the economic stagnation that plagued the United States during the mid-1970s. Conservatives no longer had to stand in the way of liberalism by rejecting social progress. They could be the proponents of progress while they painted Democrats and especially liberals as reactionary defenders of the big-government policies that failed to serve the needs of the American people. In the process, Republicans denounced unpopular manifestations of big government such as welfare and avoided discussion of the popular programs such as Medicare and Social Security that would also have to be cut back if the size of government were to be reduced.[5]

New political fundraising rules favored the GOP. In the wake of the excesses of the Watergate scandal, Congress had updated the laws on raising money for political candidates. A key provision of the measure, passed in 1974, limited individual contributions to $1,000, and $5,000 for political action committees (PACs). With their superior base of small contributors and their ties to corporations that sponsored PACs, the Republicans soon surpassed the Democrats in the money raised for campaigns in presidential and congressional elections.

In 1976, the Federal Elections Commission decided, and Congress wrote the ruling into law in 1979, that parties could raise unlimited amounts of money for general activities of a party-building nature: yard signs, leaflets, and voter registration. These functions were not regulated, and the funds that sustained them came to be known as "soft money," as opposed to supervised "hard money" that went to a candidate. While soft money did not explode into American politics until the late 1980s, the use of it would serve the interests of Republicans because of their greater access to corporate resources.

Republicans also benefitted from the rise of direct-mail political fundraising developed by Richard Viguerie and other conservative activists in the 1970s. Using mailing lists from the campaigns of Barry Goldwater and Alabama governor George Wallace, Viguerie framed messages of stark simplicity that spoke of imminent disaster if liberal initiatives were not fought with a timely donation. The usual response was a gratifying amount of money. The power of such groups as the National Conservative Political Action Committee (NCPAC) grew as they mobilized conservative Protestant evangelical voters for Republican causes. These voters would find their champion in Ronald Reagan in 1980.

The Republican assault on liberals in the mid-1970s coincided with a serious recession following the boom years of the 1960s. A number of worrying developments came together in the last years of the Nixon presidency to shake confidence in the future. After years of postwar prosperity, the prospects for the nation seemed less bright. American workers were no longer as productive as they had been a decade earlier. The goods they made, especially automobiles, did not compete well in world markets. The manufacturing sector was falling behind the rest of the world. In the early 1970s, inflation and unemployment rose at the same time in what was called "stagflation." By 1974, the jobless rate stood at 7.2 percent, the highest in almost a decade and a half.[6]

A major shock to the economy was the Arab oil embargo of late 1973. A brief war between the Israelis and the Arabs in October, known as the Yom Kippur War, raised international tensions and caused the Middle East oil producers to withhold oil shipments for several months. The cartel that controlled world oil supplies, the Organization of Petroleum Exporting Companies (OPEC), raised oil prices shortly thereafter. In the United States this produced temporary oil shortages, long lines at gas stations, and chronic inflation. The United States no longer seemed to be in charge of its own economic destiny.

The economic shocks of the mid-1970s came when the cultural wars of the 1960s were still playing out in the public arena. The women's movement, beyond the Equal Rights Amendment and the abortion issue, pressed forward to achieve greater economic and social equality. The protests of gay Americans, which began in the late 1960s, challenged traditional values as well. On the left, sympathy with gay rights grew in this period after the American Psychiatric Association decided in 1973 that homosexuality was not a mental disorder. Conservatives saw permissiveness and lower moral standards encroaching on the established order in disturbing ways. The Republican Party seemed the best option for countering these unwelcome trends.[7]

Overseas, the dominance that the United States had enjoyed since World War II seemed in doubt. The Nixon administration had terminated US involvement in Vietnam in 1973, but the collapse of South Vietnam two years later ended the longest war and the most painful military defeat in the nation's history. Meanwhile, the Soviet Union appeared disinclined to follow the policy of detente on which Nixon and Secretary of State Henry Kissinger had based much of their international diplomacy. Moscow had aided Egypt against Israel in 1973; the Soviets were abusing human rights and jailing dissidents; and, worst of all, they were building missiles in what many conservatives argued was a clear effort to gain nuclear superiority over the West. The future of the country looked to be at greater risk despite all the sacrifices and social turmoil Americans had endured since Kennedy's death.

The weight of these problems fell first on Nixon's successor, Gerald R. Ford, whose brief presidency began in abrupt fashion on August 8, 1974. A long-time House member from Grand Rapids, Michigan, Ford had risen to lead the Republican minority in the House in the mid-1960s. He was a decent man whose conservatism lacked a hard exterior. His many friends on both sides of the aisle applauded his elevation to the vice presidency after Spiro Agnew's departure in October 1973. Ford was not a glib man, and in Washington, where being able to speak quickly was taken for a bright mind, he gained a reputation as someone whose intelligence was average at best. Lyndon Johnson summed up the Washington consensus in a cruel quip about Ford: "He can't fart and chew gum at the same time."[8]

These judgments were unfair. While Gerald Ford was no intellectual, his record at Yale Law School demonstrated his aptitude. He was not an inspiring speaker, but his character and sincerity showed through in his public appearances. Ford was not a good administrator, and it took him some time to pull together a functioning team in the White House. His reliance on Henry Kissinger on foreign policy generated qualms among many on the right who regarded the Secretary of State as too willing to negotiate with Moscow. Nevertheless, Ford proved to be more than a competent president.

Gerald R. Ford, shown accepting the Republican nomination in 1976 with his wife, Betty; his running mate, Robert Dole; and Nelson Rockefeller, provided a creditable presidency but could not carry the Republicans to victory on his own. Library of Congress, LC-DIG-ppmsca-08488.

Ford enjoyed a brief honeymoon. After the tensions of the Nixon years, the Ford family seemed refreshing and open. Betty Ford's problems with drugs and alcohol were not yet fully known even to her own family. Pictures of the new president making breakfast, his family gathered around, added to Ford's favorable image.

The euphoria lasted one month. On the morning of Sunday, September 8, 1974, Ford told a national television audience that he had pardoned Richard Nixon for any and all crimes connected with Watergate. A storm of protest followed. Ford's press secretary quit in disgust. The new chief executive came across as no more than a Washington insider ready to cut a deal with one of his cronies. His standing in the polls dropped from 71 percent to 50 percent in the week after his announcement. Ford's presidency and the chances for the Republicans in the 1974 and 1976 elections never really recovered from the episode.

By and large pardoning Richard Nixon was a defensible step. A prolonged trial for the former president would have been a major political distraction for the White House. Even if convicted, Nixon would not have received jail time, so the whole exercise would have been largely symbolic. Where Ford and his men failed in the first month of his presidency was in making the case that a pardon was necessary. Instead, the action came out of the blue and seemed like another example of the insider deals that the voters so disliked about Washington in the mid-1970s. There was no bargain between Ford and Nixon, but the look of the arrangement aroused suspicions that the president then had to spend the time putting to rest.

With only two months to go before the congressional elections, the Republicans faced dire prospects in the wake of Watergate and Nixon's departure from the White House. The poor economy worked against the GOP candidates, who were already demoralized by the scandal. Adding to the Republican woes was Ford's nomination of Nelson Rockefeller as vice president to fill that vacancy. Seeing their old adversary elevated to the second highest office outraged the right wing. Ford did his best to campaign for Republican candidates, but nothing worked to help the beleaguered party. The Republican National Committee ran advertisements asking, "When has it been easy to be a Republican?"⁹

When the votes came in, the GOP dropped forty-three seats in the House and another four seats in the Senate. Ford now faced a Democratic majority in the House that could override vetoes and a Democratic Senate where filibusters were less of a threat with only thirty GOP members. The new Congress was more liberal and more reformist. As a result, legislative confrontations loomed as the 1976 presidential election approached.

The president's major political problem among Republicans was the impending challenge from Ronald Reagan. The California governor came to the end of his second term in Sacramento in the autumn of 1974. Already sixty-three, Reagan had to make decisions about his future soon or the window of opportunity to seek the White House might be closed to him. If Ford won the presidency in 1976, he could run again in 1980. That would leave Reagan well past the age of seventy and too old to seek the White House. For him 1976 was an up or out year as far as politics was concerned. In addition, Reagan had little respect for Ford, a sentiment that the president reciprocated.

But going up against an incumbent Republican was a problematic course in a party that placed such a premium on unity, continuity, and loyalty. Reagan himself had often invoked what he called the "Eleventh Commandment": "Thou shalt not speak ill of another Republican." The imperative of winning the White House and implementing his program persuaded Reagan that this self-created limitation could be breached. As Ronald Reagan would demonstrate over the next decade and a half, he was a Republican to whom the customary rules of the party did not apply, both in his appeal to a broad spectrum of the GOP and his mastery of the arts of national politics.

Bringing Ronald Wilson Reagan into clear focus is not a simple proposition. Republican devotion to his legacy became so pronounced that Reagan evolved into a totemic, almost deified figure. In the minds of his admirers, there should be a Reagan memorial in every state, a fifth face on Mount Rushmore, and his image on a dime like (or instead of) Franklin D. Roosevelt. The mania for Reagan has slipped a bit in recent years as his party has moved even further rightward. His willingness to raise taxes during his presidency, his interest in arms control, and his pragmatism in general has caused some to inquire whether he could be nominated by today's Republican Party. There is a skepticism about some aspects of Reagan's career among Republicans now that would have seemed improbable at the time of his death in 2004.

Reagan was sixty-five years old when he began his race against Gerald Ford in 1976. He had been a Republican for fourteen years, switching his registration from independent in 1962. For much of his life Reagan had been a Democrat with an admiration for Franklin D. Roosevelt. In the 1950s he began to move away from that earlier allegiance as he faced high taxes as a movie actor and became disillusioned with liberalism. He opposed Medicare in the early 1960s and warned of the dangers of Communism.

One powerful element in Reagan's thinking was a belief in states' rights and local government. He had opposed the Civil Rights Act of 1964 and the

Voting Rights Act of 1965 as unconstitutional because of their enhancement of national power. He believed that the states had existed before the federal government, a notion with which Abraham Lincoln and several generations of Gilded Age Republicans would have disagreed. As a means of limiting federal regulation over natural resources in the West and business activities in the area of race relations, states' rights became an essential part of Reagan's conservatism.[10]

Reagan brought a well-developed set of ideas to national affairs. The federal government was too big, too costly, and too ready to tax Americans. Running Washington on the domestic side was both crucial and, in the end, Reagan asserted, not too difficult. What was required was a leader with the will to cut spending and abolish unnecessary programs. Since the federal government, he believed, was rife with fraud and abuse, reducing expenditures was simply a matter of determination and persistence.

In foreign policy, Reagan saw the United States as engaged in a death struggle with the Soviet Union that by the mid-1970s his nation was losing. "The evidence mounts that we are Number Two in a world where it's dangerous, if not fatal, to be second best," he said in 1976. As a result, an immediate buildup of American strength was imperative. More important yet was to follow a diplomatic course that identified the Soviet Union as the major source of evil in the world and threatened the remaining bastion of freedom with oblivion. Reagan rejected detente as the Nixon and Ford administrations practiced it. The Republican candidate did not like the idea of containment in principle and saw the eventual end of the USSR as a key goal of the United States.[11]

Other Republicans, most notably Barry Goldwater, had offered views similar to Reagan's, but accompanied by a biting anger and tough demeanor. Goldwater in 1964 had seemed perpetually angry at America's plight. Reagan shared Goldwater's dismay, but his sunnier disposition, affirming optimism, and nonthreatening manner conveyed his ideas to the nation in a more positive way. Not since Theodore Roosevelt had the Republicans had a politician who combined ideology and celebrity. Dwight D. Eisenhower had rarely used his popularity in the cause of party doctrine even when he advanced "Modern Republicanism" in the 1950s.

Reagan came to politics from show business, where he had been a successful film star and a very competent actor. To say that Reagan was not a performer of the top rank in Hollywood is true but misses the point. If a group of excellent screen actors surpassed Reagan, he still stood near the top of his profession. That made him so much better a speaker and advocate of political ideas than his contemporaries, Republicans and Democrats, that he had no equals in the period from 1970 to 1990. Reagan had spent a lifetime mastering the artifices of entertainment. He held his body in just the right position and recounted anecdotes with genial charm. He conveyed conviction and sincerity on the campaign trail. So effortless did his calculated performances appear that the Ford White House and later the Democrats underestimated the extent of Reagan's connection with the American people.

Engaging the substance of public policy was not one of Reagan's strengths. A complex issue can be difficult to explain in compelling phrases. But Reagan was not interested in the nuances of policy. He knew what he knew about the major questions in which he was interested, and he only refilled his store of anecdotes on occasion, without probing his own assumptions. Reagan's power as a communicator lay in his simplicity of expression. For him the truth of an

Ronald Reagan led the Republicans to victory in 1980 and opened an era of conservative electoral dominance that lasted through his two terms and the election of his successor. Library of Congress, LC-DIG-highsm-18335.

episode or illustration mattered less than its capacity to sway an audience. Much as a screenwriter adapts a nonfiction story to be more compelling on the screen, Reagan used tales about welfare queens or racial integration in place of policy analysis. While critics might point out a resulting inaccuracy, an unscathed untouched Reagan had moved on to another speech and another story.

Reagan entered the race on November 19, 1975. He went after Ford on foreign policy and pledged to transform Washington to make the nation more secure. Few Washington insiders thought that Reagan had a chance to win the contest against Ford. Indeed, the Ford campaign was already making plans to quash the Reagan candidacy. They thought they had found a vulnerability in a speech Reagan had delivered in September 1975. In the address Reagan had asserted that transferring federal government programs to the states would reduce federal spending by $90 billion. Doing that, Reagan asserted, would make a balanced budget a realistic possibility.[12]

The statement at first received little press coverage because of the troubles the Ford White House itself was experiencing during the summer of 1975. As Reagan's candidacy loomed, the presence of Nelson Rockefeller as a potential running mate continued to irritate the right wing of the party. Ford asked Rockefeller not to be a candidate for vice president in 1976. Rockefeller obliged with a public statement on November 3, 1975. A day earlier, Ford had sought the resignations of his secretary of defense and director of central intelligence in a shake-up of his foreign policy team. The resulting perception of disarray caused Ford to slump in the polls. By the time Reagan announced, the president was twelve points behind him.

The guiding spirit of the president's campaign was the White House chief of staff Richard B. "Dick" Cheney, along with Stuart Spencer, a former adviser to Reagan in the 1960s. Their strategy was to emphasize Ford as an effective president while going after Reagan for his proposal of $90 billion in spending reductions. The key was the New Hampshire primary, where they charged that Reagan's proposed cuts in federal taxes would necessitate corresponding increases at the state level. This was not an appealing position for Reagan to defend in a state with no income or sales tax. Although Reagan had a long lead over Ford and campaigned well in the state, Ford's effort closed the gap.

The president eked out a close victory on February 24, 1976, by a little more than 1,300 ballots out of a vote of 109,000. Since Ford had exceeded expectations and Reagan had fallen short of them, the win revived the president's chances for the nomination. Two weeks later, Ford won the Florida primary, a race that turned when Reagan came under attack for saying that the government should invest Social Security funds in the stock market.

With Reagan's campaign seemingly on the ropes, the challenger assailed the administration's foreign policy, especially the volatile question of the fate of the Panama Canal. The government had been attempting to negotiate a resolution to Panamanian grievances over the Hay-Bunau-Varilla Treaty of 1903, which had given the United States perpetual control of the ten-mile-wide Panama Canal Zone as if the United States were the sovereign. Diplomatic talks had stalled. On the right deep suspicions existed over the Panamanian ruler General Omar Torrijos, a friend of Cuban dictator Fidel Castro. Reagan asserted that the Canal Zone and the canal itself were part of the United States and should not be ceded to Panama. As he put it to cheering audiences, "When it comes to the Canal, we paid for it, it's ours, and we should tell Torrijos and company that we are going to keep it." The Ford administration reacted too slowly to this Reagan offensive, having assumed that his campaign was failing.[13]

Reagan's turnaround happened on March 23 in the North Carolina primary. Helped by the efficient organization of Senator Jesse Helms, Reagan beat Ford with 52 percent of the vote. Suddenly it was the president who seemed to be in trouble. Reagan swept Texas with its big bloc of delegates and won three other states in the week that followed. Reagan was ahead in pledged delegates and appeared to have momentum. Ford's advantage was in states that chose delegates at state conventions rather than primaries. Exploiting all the benefits of incumbency, Ford wooed the uncommitted delegates. As the Republican convention in Kansas City neared, both Ford and Reagan were close to victory, but neither candidate had yet received a majority.

Then the Reagan campaign gambled. To shake up the race and win voters for his candidate in the East, John Sears, Reagan's campaign manager, proposed that the vice presidential nomination be offered to Richard Schweiker of Pennsylvania, the most liberal Republican in the Senate. When Reagan did so, the conservatives erupted in anger, and the challenger lost delegates. Moreover, Schweiker did not deliver any votes from Pennsylvania, and the tactic made Reagan look like a reckless opportunist. Ford now had a tenuous lead as the convention began.

The Kansas City convention did not become a repeat of earlier battles such as the Taft-Roosevelt showdown of 1912 or the bitter Eisenhower-Taft confrontation of 1952. To avoid any bruising floor fights that might sway delegates to Reagan, the Ford side compromised on major platform issues such as foreign policy. Secretary of State Kissinger was kept out of sight until the final night lest he stir the juices of the right. The platform reflected Reagan's thinking about Eastern Europe and relations with the Soviet Union. On abortion, the convention supported "the efforts of those who seek enactment of a constitutional amendment to restore protection of the right to life for unborn children." In a bow toward Betty Ford, who championed the Equal Rights Amendment, the platform endorsed the "swift ratification" of the ERA. The delegates also supported lower taxes if spending cuts were made, but then added, "Without such spending restraint, we cannot responsibly cut back taxes."[14]

Ford won the nomination by a vote of 1,187 to 1,070. For his running mate, Ford selected Senator Robert Dole of Kansas, at the behest of Reagan, who did not want the second spot on the ticket himself. Dole added little to the Republican chances, since Kansas was in the GOP column, and the senator's abrasive campaigning style later proved a drawback. Ford gave as good an acceptance speech as he was capable of delivering, but the most dramatic moment of the convention came when the nominee, in a gesture of harmony, invited Reagan to join him on the podium to "say a few words at this time."[15]

Reagan endorsed the platform and the party but never mentioned Ford's name. Instead, he spoke of the future and whether Americans a hundred years from 1976 would enjoy the same freedoms and live in a world that had avoided the threat of nuclear war. It was vintage Reagan—broad, thematic, uplifting, and evocative of Republican themes. If it did not do much to help Gerald Ford, it signaled that if the president failed to win in the fall, the hearts of most Republicans were already pledged to Reagan and his vision of the future.

Gerald Ford did not beat Jimmy Carter in November 1976. The Democratic nominee started the campaign with a big lead over the president, based on Carter's appeal as a fresh face who was not a Washington insider. A very effective Republican campaign, however, coupled with Carter's mistakes as a novice in national politics, soon brought the Democratic hopeful down in the polls. The Republican ticket did not do well in the presidential and vice presidential debates. In his encounter with the Democratic running mate, Walter Mondale, Senator Dole said, "If we added up the killed and wounded in Democrat wars in this century, it would be about 1.6 million Americans, enough to fill the city of Detroit." The implied attack on the foreign policy record of the opposition in the twentieth century did not enhance Dole's reputation.[16]

Ford and Carter debated three times. In the second debate, Ford, responding to a question about American attitudes toward the Soviet Union and Eastern Europe, misstated a line from his pre-debate briefing book. "There is no Soviet domination of Eastern Europe, and there never will be under a Ford administration." When the reporter who posed the question gave Ford a chance to clarify his answer, the president stepped into trouble again. "I don't believe the Poles consider themselves dominated by the Soviet Union," he said, and added, "The United States does not concede that these countries are under the domination of the Soviet Union." The episode renewed doubts about Ford's grasp of the issues, and he slipped in the polls. Ford did not repudiate his comments for a week, and the Republicans never quite overcame the Democratic advantage that Carter had taken into the election.[17]

The result was still very close. Carter won 297 electoral votes with 49.9 percent of the vote to 241 electoral votes and 47.9 percent for Ford. The congressional results were a draw. On the surface, the Democrats held the major components of national power. Yet the Democratic success was illusory. Carter had run well in the South because of his religious appeal as a Baptist and born-again Christian. Combined with the reliable African American vote, the return of some conservative Democrats to the party meant that Carter had a strong base in Dixie. The long-term success of the GOP in the South stalled for a moment. The Democrats would now have to run the government, an assignment that would prove to be their undoing.

Most crucial of the factors working against the Carter administration was the poor economy. In 1976, the Democrats had made much of the "misery index" that the country endured under Ford, a combination of the inflation rate of 6 percent and an unemployment rate of 8 percent. Under Carter, however, while unemployment went down to six percent in his first two years, inflation mounted. In 1978, inflation stood at 10 percent annually, producing a "misery index" for the Democrats of sixteen, which then kept climbing.

The administration proposed and Congress passed energy legislation that Republicans attacked for its emphasis on conservation and government regulation. In foreign policy, Carter negotiated a Panama Canal Treaty that relinquished control of the waterway to Panama by the end of the century. Although the Senate approved the pact, with the support of such key Republican senators as Howard Baker of Tennessee, the issue proved a popular theme for Ronald Reagan in his stump speeches in 1978–1979. Panama also galvanized the base of the GOP by eliciting a flood of contributions for the National Committee and political action committees.

Taxes became the major focus of the 1978 congressional elections, especially when California approved a major tax-cutting proposal, Proposition 13. Other states followed suit. The debate over the proper level of taxation developed as the potential key to Republican economic policy and victory in the impending congressional races. One of the effects of rising inflation in the 1970s was that it pushed more taxpayers with lower and middle income into higher tax brackets. What had once been a progressive federal income tax that affected the upper end of the income scale now hit the middle class with effective tax

rates above 20 percent. Combined with rising state and local taxes and property taxes, the impact of federal income taxes caused additional popular
unhappiness and greater receptivity to Republican calls for reductions in tax
rates and curbs on government spending.[18]

The Republicans took advantage of this political windfall by developing the tax-cutting policy that has been the hallmark of the party's domestic
ideology ever since. Their strategy, identified with the term "supply-side economics," has become one of the most controversial courses of action in GOP
history and within the historical legacy of Ronald Reagan. The consensus
among mainstream economists, even some of Republican orientation, is that
tax cutting did not produce the promised revenue increases and caused the
large deficits that characterized the 1980s. That judgment has not lessened the
fervor for further tax cuts among Republicans.

The proposals for cuts in income tax rates welled up from a number of
Republican sources in the mid- to late 1970s. The economist Arthur Laffer
advanced the argument that rate cuts would stimulate economic activity, as
did Jack Kemp, a former pro football quarterback and House member from
upstate New York. The supporters of these reductions in income tax rates did
not say that the improvement in the economy that resulted would restore
all the lost government revenue, but they did assert that there would be some
compensating gains in revenue. To throw the Democrats off stride, the sup-
ply-siders identified themselves with John F. Kennedy's tax cuts of the early
1960s (which some congressional Republicans had then opposed). The move
allowed them to depict the GOP as the party of change and energy. The
Democrats thus became the defenders of the status quo and the repository of
tired, big-government ideas.[19]

The prospect of tax-rate cutting caught on in American politics but did
not appear quite soon enough to translate into large Republican gains in the
congressional elections of that year. The party added twelve seats in the House
and another three in the Senate. Democratic control of Congress persisted.
Yet the ongoing trends favored the Republicans.

Among the new faces that voters sent to Congress were Newton "Newt"
Gingrich from Georgia and Dick Cheney from Wyoming. Gingrich, in particular, soon laid out ambitious plans to recapture the House for the GOP. In the
South the Republicans scored a notable victory when William L. Clements won
the governorship of Texas, the first Republican to do so since Reconstruction.
The support for President Carter was waning in his home region as he moved too
far leftward for the tastes of southern conservatives. The elections also produced
the ouster of several liberal senators by Republican challengers.

On Election Day, the government of the Shah of Iran collapsed, and an anti-American regime led by Muslim fundamentalists took power. The foreign policy position of the United States in the Middle East seemed to be under siege. Meanwhile, the Soviet Union appeared to be gaining power at American expense. Soon the Carter administration was under attack from both the Democratic left and the resurgent Republicans, who saw a return to power in 1980 as a tantalizing prospect. The seizure of the American embassy and its personnel by Iranian militants in November 1979 underscored the persistent problems that the Carter White House faced as the presidential election approached.

The larger national mood was becoming more Republican as the Carter presidency faltered. One of the keys to the president's victory in 1976 had been the support of evangelical Christians in the South who had been attracted by the president's public piety. Disillusioned with Carter's performance, they found more to admire in a new organization created by Jerry Falwell of Lynchburg, Virginia. The Moral Majority, which Falwell established in 1979, used modern fundraising techniques, including direct mailing, and proved an effective means for evangelicals to identify with the Republican Party and its issues.

By 1978, the amount of funds that Republicans raised far exceeded what their rivals collected. In 1980, for example, the Republican National Committee brought in $77 million, compared to $16 million collected by the Democrats. The base of small donors that grew out of the Goldwater Campaign and the efforts of Ray Bliss continued to pay dividends for the GOP. In addition, the Republican organization built the party at the state and local levels with more success than the Democrats. While the Democratic apparatus shrank under Lyndon Johnson and Jimmy Carter, the Republicans were constructing a modern organization that gave it a decided edge in the two-party competition throughout the 1980s.

With the Republican presidential nomination in 1980 a necessary steppingstone to the White House, a number of hopefuls put their names forward. Senator Howard Baker of Tennessee; John Connally, a former Democrat from Texas; George H. W. Bush; and several others all sought to position themselves as the alternative to Ronald Reagan. Each one thought there was either enough potential opposition to Reagan or that the front runner might stumble and give them a legitimate chance at the nomination. As events were to prove, these optimistic scenarios bore little relation to the reality of Reagan's overwhelming popularity within the party. George Bush scared the Reagan campaign with a victory in the Iowa caucuses, but Reagan rebounded to win the New Hampshire primary and then went on to a first-ballot nomination.

At the 1980 convention, Reagan explored for a moment the idea of putting Gerald Ford on the ticket, but the two men and their aides could not work out an acceptable division of presidential responsibility. Reagan then turned to George H. W. Bush for the second spot. There were reservations about Bush in the Reagan camp because he had been critical of the tax-cut proposals the front runner had advanced. At one point Bush had called the idea "voodoo economics." Bush was also believed to favor some abortion rights. His advocacy of population control while in Congress during the 1960s had earned Bush the nickname "Rubbers." Reagan insisted that Bush "support [him] on the issue of abortion," and the Texan agreed. The new vice presidential candidate dropped his backing for the Equal Rights Amendment as well.[20]

The Republican platform in 1980 reflected Reagan's beliefs and the thinking of Republican conservatives who were able at last to tailor the document to their liking. On economic policy the delegates called for lower tax rates and a balanced budget. In a decisive move away from the party's past, they contended that "protectionist tariffs and quotas are detrimental to our economic well being." The platform called for a constitutional amendment "to restore protection of the right to life for unborn children." On the Equal Rights Amendment both sides of the argument were recognized as engaged in "legitimate efforts." As for civil rights and African Americans, "Republicans will not make idle promises to black Americans and other minorities. We are beyond the day when any American can live off rhetoric or political platitudes."[21]

Jimmy Carter's foreign policy received a tongue-lashing from the Republican platform. "For three and one-half years the Carter administration has given us a foreign policy not of constancy and credibility, but of chaos, confusion, and failure." Not since 1941 on the eve of Pearl Harbor had the nation faced such peril, the platform writers argued. Accordingly, they would "build toward a sustained defense expenditure sufficient to close the gap with the Soviets and ultimately reach the position of military superiority that the American people demand." The various proposals included rebuilding nuclear forces and defense systems against a Soviet surprise attack.[22]

Given the disarray of the Carter presidency, Reagan had a clear advantage going into the 1980 election. The American hostages were still being held in Iran, the Soviet Union had invaded Afghanistan, and the United States seemed powerless. The White House failed in a military mission to rescue the hostages in the spring, and in the ensuing months negotiations to free the captives had produced no results. At home the weak economy dragged down

Democratic hopes. In the summer of 1979, Carter had shaken up his administration after a nationally televised address that had warned the American people of a crisis of confidence in their country. Though Carter never used the word "malaise" in his speech, the term became associated with the president's troubles. Carter had to stave off a challenge to his nomination from Senator Edward M. Kennedy of Massachusetts, a battle that left scars on the Democrats. To further bedevil Carter's chances, the candidacy of an independent, John Anderson, a former Republican, gave moderates who did not like Reagan an alternative.

Reagan did show a propensity for verbal gaffes in the early phase of the campaign, but he hit his stride as the election neared. Carter sought to paint the Republican candidate as an extremist using harsh terms, but this tactic backfired when the president came across as strident and Reagan appeared optimistic and confident. The polls indicated that the election was still close, with the voters undecided about the merits of the two major rivals for the presidency.

The election finally turned on October 28, 1980, when Reagan used his "There you go again" line with such effectiveness. Moreover, he posed to voters the devastating question "Are you better off than you were four years ago? Is it easier for you to go and buy things in the stores than it was four years ago?" When the issue was framed in that way, the undecideds broke for Reagan in the waning days of the campaign, and an electoral landslide resulted. Reagan piled up 51 percent of the vote to Carter's 41 percent and achieved an even more decisive sweep in the electoral college. Reagan won 489 electoral votes to 49 for Carter. The independent candidacy of John Anderson drew seven million popular votes.[23]

The triumph for the Republicans was across the board. The GOP turned twelve Democratic senators out of office and regained control of the upper house for the first time since 1955. Republican candidates picked up thirty-two seats in the House. While the Democrats retained control under Speaker Thomas P. "Tip" O'Neill, the Republicans had a good chance of forging a working majority with the assistance of conservative southern Democrats fearful of defeat in 1982 if they did not cooperate with a popular incumbent president. The prospect of a realignment of American politics in a rightward direction and the establishment of a reliable Republican majority was much discussed in the wake of Reagan's success.

The 1980 presidential election illustrated how much the Republican Party had changed since the 1950s. One new area of electoral strength was the South, where white voters held Reagan in high esteem. In Mississippi, for example,

Reagan carried 62 percent of the white vote, and he recorded similar margins across the region. Reagan opened his national campaign after the Republican convention at the Neshoba County Fair in Philadelphia, Mississippi. Sixteen years earlier four civil rights workers had been murdered in that county in one of the most notorious examples of white violence against those seeking to integrate the South. Reagan's speech defended states' rights and private property before a friendly, almost all-white audience of ten thousand listeners. "I believe in people doing as much as they can at the private level," Reagan maintained.

With memories of his opposition to the Civil Rights Act of 1964 and the Voting Rights Act of 1965 still fresh, Reagan couched his conservative message in language that pleased white voters in the South. Like Nixon's southern strategy, Reagan's speech could be defended as racially neutral, but a southerner unhappy with black progress could also interpret it as an affirmation of his opinion. Black southerners in the 1980s disliked Reagan, but his popularity among whites more than neutralized the impact of African American animosity in the South. During the decade that followed, white Democrats moved in huge numbers over to the Republicans to make the southern GOP the bastion of white racial attitudes that had for so long been the property of Democrats in the region.[24]

Appealing to the white vote paid large electoral dividends for the Republicans and Ronald Reagan during the 1980s. Southern white voters, especially males, made up a key element in the party's winning coalitions. With the South, Plains states, and Rocky Mountain region in the GOP column in most presidential elections, the party had what one commentator called "a lock" on the presidency in the electoral college. With immediate advantages came long term problems as well. As southerners moved into positions of power and influence within the GOP, their racial views, cultural conservatism, and religious moralism grated on other sections of the nation. There was a harking back to the older Democratic assumption that the South was at heart a white man's country as the Republicans came to champion what they had been created to oppose.

Another characteristic of the changed Republican Party was the new president's attraction among religious conservatives. Despite his own lack of churchgoing and strong public piety, Reagan knew what the religious right wanted to hear. He stood against abortion, supported voluntary prayer in the public schools, and questioned whether evolution was a valid scientific theory. Careful not to push the agenda of the Moral Majority into substantive legislation, Reagan gave these groups and their leaders enough rhetorical endorsement to keep them reasonably contented throughout his administration.[25]

As president, Reagan continued to identify the federal government as the major source of the nation's woes. "In the present crisis, government is not the solution to our problems; government is the problem," he said in his inaugural address.[26] He intended to reduce taxes, balance the budget by 1984, and boost national defenses to offset the threat from the Soviet Union. Congress enacted an even more generous version of his tax proposals during the summer of 1981. Meanwhile, lawmakers approved the sizable buildup of the nation's defenses that the new administration proposed. The failed assassination attempt on Reagan on March 31, 1981, and his bravery in the aftermath raised the president's popularity. So, too, his firm stance against striking air traffic controllers a few months later confirmed his strength as a chief executive. By the end of 1981, despite worsening economic conditions, Reagan dominated the political scene.

The Republican Party did not benefit immediately from Reagan's stature. Turning the economy around took longer than the White House had anticipated, and the nation experienced a sharp recession in 1981–1982. Democrats complained about "Reaganomics," which included some nine to eleven million people out of work and a substantial number of business failures. Reagan's personal approval rating dropped to 41 percent by the end of 1982. The prospect of achieving a balanced budget by the end of 1984, as Reagan had promised during the campaign, faded away.

The Democrats were the short-term beneficiaries of these developments. In the 1982 elections, they added twenty-six seats in the House while the Republicans retained control of the Senate. Reagan urged his fellow Republicans to "stay the course" and predicted that his economic policies would produce a turnaround before the 1984 presidential race. Reagan's prediction proved correct, but not for the reasons he offered. The administration backed away from his tax-cutting policy with a law passed in August 1982 that lifted taxes to close the budget deficit. In addition, the Federal Reserve loosened up on the money supply. The stock market rose in August and the economy began a sustained expansion in late 1982 that continued during the rest of Reagan's presidency.

As the economy improved and memories of the 1970s faded, Reagan and the GOP received credit for the nation's good health. The president seemed impervious to adverse criticism, and critics said Teflon caused negative comments to bounce off the affable Reagan. The president was a likable, engaging leader whose image was calculated to present his policies in their most appealing form. The White House staged his daily activities with an eye to their impact on nightly television news. The upshot was that Reagan remained popular even when his policies were less so.

In foreign policy, Reagan's staunch defense of traditional values and stringent criticism of the Soviet Union also resonated with the voters. His comment in March 1983 that the USSR was an "evil empire" impressed Americans. Two weeks later the president advanced the Strategic Defense Initiative (SDI) to protect the United States against a Soviet missile launch. The US attack on Grenada in October 1983 to oust a left-wing government also contributed to a significant upturn in Reagan's standing as the 1984 election approached.

Under Ronald Reagan's leadership, the ideas of the Republicans set the agenda for American politics in the 1980s. The dominant themes of the GOP were the dangers of big government and the failures of liberalism since the New Deal. At the 1984 national convention, George H. W. Bush declared, "For over half a century the Liberal Democrats have pursued the philosophy of tax and spend, tax and spend," while the Republicans were telling "the tax raisers, the free spenders, the excess regulators, the government-knows-best hand wringers, those who would promise every special group everything... your time has passed." The answer to America's economic problems, Bush said, was a "dynamic private sector that provides jobs, jobs with dignity. The answer lies in limited government and unlimited confidence in the American people."[27]

Restricting government above all meant a reduction in the size of the federal establishment and a lowering of the tax burden. If a choice had to be made between those two options, a reduction in taxes should have priority. A suspicion of the efficiency and value of the national government as a force in regulating the economy underlay much of the Republican ideology. One of the administration's proudest achievements, accomplished in conjunction with Democrats and Republicans in Congress, was the deregulation of the savings and loan industry in the early 1980s. Reagan and other Republicans believed that the government should promote economic growth through favorable tax policies, enterprise zones in economically disadvantaged areas, and subsidies for research and development. On the other hand, programs to supply welfare to the poor had to be reduced because they were unnecessary, inefficient, and wasteful.

The Reagan years saw a turn away from government action on behalf of the environment. Though the Environmental Protection Agency (EPA) had been created during the Nixon years, GOP leaders regarded it as a leading example of overregulation. Reagan's policies reflected the influence of westerners, embodied in the "Sagebrush Rebellion" against government interference, who sought prodevelopment policies in the West. Secretary of the Interior James Watt led this effort until he was forced out of office in 1983 after a series of indiscreet comments. Meanwhile the EPA and Interior were run by individuals with close ties to the business interests they were to oversee.

For all the distrust of government in the economic sphere, Republicans in the Reagan era saw areas in which an expanded federal presence was necessary and desirable. The War on Drugs, begun under Nixon, expanded under Reagan, especially because of Nancy Reagan's "Just Say No" program to change teenage behavior. Other examples of Republican activism included a vigorous assault on obscenity and pornography. Most important, Republicans pursued an antiabortion program on a variety of state and federal levels to curb the availability of abortion.

Republicans grappled as well with the role of government regarding civil rights. Efforts to increase the party's share of African American voters did not bear much fruit. Rhetorical deference to the Civil Rights Act of 1964 did not conceal an opposition to initiatives to implement affirmative action programs. Meanwhile, the need to attract Hispanic and black votes often ran up against the party's growing reliance on white support, especially in the South and West. Long-range campaigns to undermine the legal basis for the Voting Rights Act of 1965 indicated where the major priorities of the party lay.

Ronald Reagan proclaimed his lack of bigotry even as his Justice Department sought to grant tax-exempt status to Bob Jones University, which maintained exclusionary racial policies toward minorities. The White House opposed the extension of the Voting Rights Act of 1965 and only accepted a national holiday for Martin Luther King, Jr., in 1983 when it was clear that congressional passage was inevitable. The president was a master of presenting racial demagoguery with a smiling face. By the end of Reagan's terms in office, the Republicans owed more to the philosophy of the Confederate States of America than they did to the legacy of Abraham Lincoln.

While defining themselves by what they were for, the Republicans in the 1980s also stressed how different they were from the existing Democratic Party. Their opposition, Republicans asserted, was soft on the issue of Communism, permissive on cultural issues, and prone to "class warfare" on economic matters. Making such a case involved finding virtues in past Democratic presidents that few Republicans had acknowledged when these men were in office. Ronald Reagan began this process in his 1980 acceptance speech. He quoted Franklin D. Roosevelt's speeches from 1932 on the balanced budget to show how far the Democratic Party had strayed from these onetime principles. By the 1984 Republican convention, party orators were praising Harry S.

Truman, John F. Kennedy, and Hubert Humphrey as "mainstream" Democrats in contrast to the leaders of the party in the 1980s. With these leaders safely dead, the Republicans could accord them retrospective legitimacy.

The GOP by the 1980s had detached itself from most of its history. There were occasional references at party gatherings to Abraham Lincoln, a quotation or two from Dwight D. Eisenhower, and respectful comments about Gerald Ford. Theodore Roosevelt had vanished from the Republican record, as had the executives of the 1920s and Richard Nixon. The ideological turmoil that had marked the 1940s with Wendell Willkie and Thomas E. Dewey had not left even faint traces. Moderate Republicans had disappeared as if they had never been a force in party affairs. For the moment, conservatism among Republicans dominated all that came before it.

The 1984 campaign was a cakewalk for the Republicans, but an important missed opportunity as well. There was never any real doubt that Ronald Reagan and George H. W. Bush would be reelected. The Democratic ticket of Walter Mondale and Geraldine Ferraro brought together a colorless presidential candidate and an obscure House member from New York whose standing as a vice presidential hopeful owed most to her gender. Mondale's statement at the Democratic convention that he would raise taxes if elected gave Republicans all the ammunition they needed. Mondale enjoyed one bright moment when Reagan faltered in the first of two debates, but even that temporary triumph never altered the political balance.

The 1984 election was made to order for the creation of a sustained GOP majority united behind a set of ideological goals. There were two problems with such an approach. Reagan himself was more popular than his domestic policies. Pushing the envelope by coming out for private control of Social Security, more stringent controls on abortion, and abolishing the Departments of Energy and Education, for example, might disturb the voters and alienate potential support. These limits raised the question of whether a conservative transformation of American society was feasible. The Reagan Revolution was a timid affair once taxes had been cut and defense spending increased. If a president with so much political capital in the summer of 1984 could not advance the harder edge of the Republican agenda, it was difficult to see when such an array of initiatives could be launched.

The second problem arose from the need for the president to explain and rationalize these controversial items if they were made part of his campaign. While opinions differ on how much of a toll Reagan's age had taken on him by 1984, when he was seventy-three, there was a strong sense within the Reagan political operation that the burdens of the campaign should not rest on his shoulders. While Reagan had his good days, he had uncertain ones too, and a slip in a public appearance, while not likely to hinder his reelection, could arouse doubts about his ability to govern. Thus, the decision was reached to run an issueless campaign that affirmed the faith that most Americans had in Reagan but tried to do little else. Skillfully produced commercials proclaimed that it was "Morning in America" to make voters feel good about the choice of their president. The GOP used the national pride generated by the Los Angeles Olympics to reinforce their upbeat message.

Unlike other previous incumbents such as Lyndon Johnson and Richard Nixon who had not debated their challengers as they rode to landslide victories, Reagan agreed to confront Mondale twice. The first appearance went badly for Reagan. The president was listless, appeared confused at times, and rambled in answer to some questions. So poor was Reagan's showing that the age issue, which had not arisen up to that time, became the center of concern. The Republicans attributed Reagan's indifferent performance to overpreparation and promised a better result two weeks later. In fact, Reagan improved only to a marginal degree over the first debate, but he did deliver a devastating one-liner that made the difference. Faced with a question about his age, Reagan said, "I will not make age an issue in this campaign. I am not going to exploit, for political purposes, my opponent's youth and inexperience." For a nation that wanted Reagan to prevail over the fifty-six-year-old Mondale, that statement was comforting enough.[28]

On Election Day, Reagan achieved a personal landslide. He carried forty-nine states for 525 electoral votes. Mondale won his home state of Minnesota and the District of Columbia. With 59 percent of the popular vote, Reagan confirmed his status as a champion vote-getter among all the men who had ever run for president as Republicans. Yet the president proved to have short coattails. The GOP lost two seats in the Senate and gained just a handful of House members. With Reagan's political future settled, political speculation within the party turned to the succession issue in 1988 and the hopes of Vice President Bush.

The second Reagan term brought more problems than political revolutions for the Republicans. The White House team that had worked well for the president split up. Tired by the exertions of the first term, the successful managers of Reagan's presidency wanted new challenges. White House Chief of Staff James Baker moved over to the Treasury Department. In turn, Treasury Secretary Donald Regan took over the White House post. The change, which was developed by the two men and then presented to Reagan, was not an improvement. Regan proved to be heavy-handed and devoid of political skill. The White House lost most of its mastery in showcasing the president.

The events of the latter half of the 1980s tested Reagan's ability to lead. Mounting budget deficits impelled Congress to devise a method of keeping federal spending under control. Republican senators Phil Gramm of Texas and Warren Rudman of New Hampshire, along with Democrat Ernest F. Hollings of South Carolina, confronted Congress with either mandated spending cuts or the prospect of across-the-board reductions in key programs. Their initiative on spending cuts pleased most lawmakers and the White House even though it put off most of the hard choices until after the 1986 elections.

The major legislative achievement of Reagan's second term was sweeping tax reform in 1986. Although the White House pushed for the concept in general, much of the credit for the enactment of the measure belonged to Senator Robert Packwood. The Oregon Republican, chair of the Senate Finance Committee, took up the bill following House passage in late 1985. By April 1986 the prospects for tax reform seemed dim, since most senators were bent on loading up the bill with special deals. Packwood drafted a new bill that provided much lower rates and ended a host of long-standing deductions. The bill went through the legislative process and Reagan signed it into law in September 1986. The new tax act simplified and reduced taxes in a way that helped the economy.

During Reagan's second term, the economic boom continued and the nation experienced a wave of money making and mergers. For Republicans, the rise of corporate acquisitions, the high salaries for executives, and the emergence of young, urban professionals (or "yuppies") were evidence that the policies of the Reagan years were achieving sustained growth as the GOP had always promised. "Contrary to all the doomsayers," said Jack Kemp, "we have witnessed an entrepreneurial renaissance. It's electrified the world. It's raised our standard of living."[29]

Unfortunately for the Republicans in the 1986 elections, the prosperity of the decade did not result in the continuation of their electoral success. In the sixth year of a two-term presidency, when losses usually take place for the party in the White House, the Republicans dropped six Senate seats. The Reagan tide in 1980 had swept in some marginal figures in the upper house. These weaker candidates, without Reagan on the ballot, succumbed to Democratic challengers. The opposition regained control of the Senate. With the 1988 presidential election just over the horizon and Reagan's presidency winding down, the Democrats thought that recapturing the White House was more possible than anyone could have believed after the Reagan triumph of 1984.

On Election Day in 1986, the Iran-Contra Scandal broke in what became the most serious crisis of Reagan's presidency. The revelation of the arms-for-hostages deal with Iran and the diversion of funds to the Nicaraguan Contras, who were waging a guerrilla campaign against that country's left-wing government, staggered the administration. Disclosures that White House staff members, including Colonel Oliver North of the National Security Council, had negotiated with the Iranians and sent money to Nicaragua suggested that a separate foreign policy apparatus had been established outside the restraints of Congress. Republican officials had regarded the Constitution not as a check on their power in conducting foreign policy but rather as a troublesome obstacle to be circumvented by any means necessary to achieve their ends. In that sense, Reagan's conservative administration displayed quite radical tendencies toward the traditional procedures of the American government.

The episode took some of the luster off Reagan's relations with the American people in 1987–1988, but he rebounded with the foreign policy successes he forged in negotiations with the Soviet Union in the same period. Contrary to what the Democrats believed when the scandal erupted, the political fallout did not hurt the GOP. The Iran-Contra episode figured as less of an issue in the 1988 elections than observers might have expected when the news broke in late 1986.

From a long-range perspective, the most significant episode at the end of Reagan's presidency was Robert Bork's nomination to the United States Supreme Court. President Reagan had already made history when he selected Sandra Day O'Connor as the first woman nominated to the high court in 1981. Five years later Reagan elevated Justice William Rehnquist to the position of chief justice of the United States after Warren Burger stepped down. To fill Rehnquist's place, the president named Antonin Scalia, a legal conservative and appeals court judge. Described as "brilliant" by most commentators, Scalia had substantial reservations about the legality of civil rights laws as unduly favoring blacks and Hispanics. The conservative cause did not yet have a secure majority on the Court. When Justice Lewis Powell resigned on June 26, 1987, Reagan turned to Robert Bork, a judge on the US Court of Appeals. A political firestorm then ensued.

A prolific legal writer and professor at the Yale Law School, the scraggly bearded Bork specialized in antitrust law but had provocative views on a number of hot-button issues. He had opposed the Civil Rights Act for intruding on the rights of citizens. Bork disagreed with the court's ruling on privacy in such matters as birth control and was believed to harbor doubts about abortion rights and the decision in *Roe v. Wade*. As a member of the Justice

Department, Bork had fired the special prosecutor Archibald Cox during the "Saturday Night Massacre" of the Watergate period. There were no personal or financial skeletons in Bork's past. His opponents found his views distasteful and disliked him on ideological grounds.[30]

Liberal groups and Democratic senators attacked Bork's opinions in the manner of a political campaign with hard-edged advertising and strong rhetoric. Senator Edward M. Kennedy of Massachusetts said, in remarks that especially angered Republicans, "Robert Bork's America is a land in which women would be forced into back-alley abortions, blacks would sit at segregated lunch counters, [and] rogue police could break down citizens' doors in midnight raids." Kennedy highlighted Bork's beliefs but did not invent them. Still, the use of movie star Gregory Peck in anti-Bork ads, before celebrity political spots had become common, also seemed out of bounds to Republican supporters of the nominee.[31]

Republicans charged at the time and later that this kind of examination of Bork's opinions represented an intrusion of politics and ideology into a Supreme Court appointment. While a Supreme Court nominee's views had not generally been scrutinized, there were exceptions. In 1916 the Republicans had opposed Woodrow Wilson's selection of Louis D. Brandeis because he was a liberal and a Jew. Fourteen years later, labor and civil rights groups had defeated the nomination of John J. Parker under Herbert Hoover. In 1968, Republicans such as Strom Thurmond had opposed Abe Fortas for Chief Justice based on the court's decisions about crime and pornography as well as Fortas's finances.

In 1987, the White House was unprepared to make the case for Bork and let the initiative slide to his well-organized opposition. Bork himself was not an effective witness on his own behalf when he testified before the Senate Judiciary Committee. In fact, he confirmed his beliefs in ways that bolstered the case for the opposition. In the end the nomination went down fifty-eight to forty-two, with a few Republicans deserting Bork on the final vote. After another abortive pick, the White House turned to Anthony Kennedy, an appeals court judge, and he was unanimously confirmed in early 1988. By the time Bork died in December 2012 his views, so debatable in 1986, had become mainstream Republican principles.

By the time the aftershocks of the Bork nomination had subsided in early 1988, the Republicans were well on their way to selecting their nominee to succeed Ronald Reagan as the party's leader. Already efforts had begun to measure the impact of Reagan's presidency, and they have continued ever since. By the time of his death in 2004, his place as an icon of Republican history seemed secure. He towered above Abraham Lincoln, Theodore Roosevelt, Dwight D. Eisenhower, and of course, Richard Nixon. Republicans argued that Reagan should be memorialized through named sites across the United States, and his visage should be added to Mount Rushmore.

History can be ironic, however, and a decade after his passing Reagan's legacy seems more muddled than might have been imagined when the nation mourned his death. By 2012 there were discussions in the press about whether Reagan could have been nominated in the changed environment that saw Willard Mitt Romney selected to be the Republican presidential nominee. After all, Reagan had raised taxes while in the White House, had signed abortion legislation as governor of California, and had struck deals with Democrats in Congress.

Yet in the history of the party his pivotal role in the 1980s seems secure. Reagan transformed the Republican Party into a conservative unit with a diminishing band of moderates on its fringes. His advocacy of smaller government, deregulation, and private enterprise met with general assent while he was in office. In foreign affairs, the debate over whether he helped the nation win the Cold War as president attests to the power of his ideas and personality in the international arena. As a media communicator and presence on the campaign trail, Reagan trailed only Franklin D. Roosevelt among modern presidents. In 1989, Reagan seemed a tough act to follow, as George H. W. Bush would find, to the political detriment of his ill-fated presidency.

12

Bush to Gingrich to Bush, 1988–2000

IT WAS A CLEAR, crisp day in Washington as three hundred Republican members of the House of Representatives and GOP congressional candidates assembled on the steps of the Capitol on September 27, 1994. Behind them was a large blue sign that read "Contract with America." In front of the Republican crowd an array of television cameras and microphones stood ready to relay the party's message to the American people. The architect of the event, Newt Gingrich of Georgia, the minority whip and the presumed next Speaker of the House, came forward to present the message that he had been perfecting for fifteen years.

Ever since he came to Washington in 1979, Gingrich had worked for and thought about a Republican majority. He was convinced that the Democrats had become a corrupt, power-hungry force, committed to a vision of American that no longer worked. He sought, a Gingrich friend said, "to smash 'tax and spend liberalism' which has dominated our politics for sixty years." The whole concept of an activist federal government, so beloved by the Democrats, was misguided, Gingrich believed. As such, the Democrats represented a set of ideas that history had rendered obsolete.[1]

In the fall of 1994, with Republican fortunes on the rise, Gingrich and like-minded Republicans had the wind at their backs. Demoralized Democrats tried to distance themselves from the unpopular administration of Bill Clinton, while resurgent Republicans, energized by conservative radio talk show hosts, longed for Election Day to make their anger known. Suddenly, what had once seemed impossible, a Republican takeover of the House of Representatives after forty years of Democratic rule, appeared to have a chance of coming to pass.

Once in power, Gingrich and his allies had an even larger vision. With their Contract with America enacted, they would move forward to recapture the presidency, implement the Conservative Opportunity Society of Gingrich's dreams, and make the nation Republican for a generation or more. As countless Republicans could have attested, it was much easier to want to change American public life than to accomplish that goal. Gingrich got what he sought—victory in the election and the speakership of the House—only to find that history had other plans for his vision and party.

The relentless rhythms of American politics meant that Republicans were already looking to the future of their party even as they paid tribute to the legacy of Ronald Reagan. At the end of Reagan's eight years there was a moment when the party's future was more open and less settled. Whoever emerged as the party's nominee, if he then won the White House, would determine the direction of the GOP well into the future.

On the other hand, the Republican Party tended to have a clear line of succession already established even in moments of flux. Reagan had made it clear that he believed his vice president, George H. W. Bush, should be the next nominee. That fact, as well as Bush's loyalty to the administration and the party over the years, gave him a presumptive claim to the nomination. Of course, Bush might falter in the run-up to the primaries, but the money, organization, and traditions of the party all favored Bush's chances in 1988.

Still a crowded field of candidates vied for position as the process of choosing a candidate began in 1987. By this time rituals of narrowing down the candidates involved a series of straw votes, public debates, and party caucuses around the country. These "cattle shows" allowed Republican activists a chance to see their prospective leaders perform under pressure and measure their conservative credentials. Changes in state elections during the 1980s had grouped major state primaries on a single date, especially in the South. There, a number of elections would occur on the same day, Super Tuesday, in March 1988. The candidate who won those contests would most likely be the nominee.

The two serious rivals in 1988 were Vice President Bush and Senator Robert Dole of Kansas. Dole had become the GOP leader in the Senate after Howard Baker left politics in 1985. An effective lawmaker best known for his tart tongue and refreshing candor, Dole had flopped as Gerald Ford's running mate in 1976, but he saw his chance twelve years later. A decorated veteran who had been gravely wounded in World War II, Dole knew that Bush would be his most dangerous foe. The Kansan hoped to beat Bush in the Iowa caucuses and the New Hampshire primary. If the race went on too long, Dole lacked the organization and the money to fight the vice president in the southern primaries on Super Tuesday.

Bush, on the other hand, had surface weaknesses and residual strength. A World War II veteran like Dole, Bush had graduated from Yale after the conflict and found success in the oil business in west Texas. He had then moved to Houston and entered Republican politics. He first ran for the Senate and lost in 1964 amid the Democratic wave of that year. Bush spent two terms in the House of Representatives, from 1967 to 1971, and voted for the 1968 Civil Rights Act. In 1970, Bush made another Senate race but lost to Lloyd M. Bentsen, Jr.[2]

For the next decade, Bush held appointive positions in the Nixon and Ford presidencies: chair of the Republican National Committee, ambassador to the United Nations, US representative to China, and director of Central Intelligence. These posts added to Bush's exposure and reputation as a Republican team player. Nevertheless, doubts about his abilities and commitment to conservative values persisted in GOP circles. When his name came up as a possible running mate for Reagan in 1980, the presidential candidate said of the potential choice: "I have strong reservations about George Bush. I'm concerned about turning the country over to him."[3]

Reagan came to like and respect Bush as vice president, but the president's political trouble also posed difficulties for him as a potential candidate. The Iran-Contra affair raised questions about Bush's knowledge of those events. The vice president asserted that he had not been "in the loop" of decision-making about the arms-for-hostages deal with Iran. For the most part Bush succeeded in keeping the issue at a distance during the early phase of the 1988 campaign.

George H. W. Bush, shown here signing an arms control treaty with Mikhail Gorbachev, did well in foreign policy, but domestic troubles cost him a second term. Library of Congress.

As events were to prove, it was easy to underestimate George H. W. Bush as a candidate. Behind his Ivy League demeanor and patrician habits was a man who wanted the presidency and was ready to do whatever he deemed necessary to achieve it. First, he had to secure the Republican nomination, and his campaign encountered problems during the early stages. Since Bush had won the Iowa caucuses in 1980, it was assumed that he would have the advantage eight years later. Reagan's farm policies were unpopular and Iowa was beginning to trend Democratic. As a result, Bush's campaign was in trouble in the state in January 1988.

The vice president's immediate problem was the Iran-Contra scandal and his own role in the affair. To defuse the issue and demonstrate Bush's toughness, his campaign turned to the mass media. He had a live interview with Dan Rather of CBS News on January 25. A symbol of the liberal media, Rather was an excellent target for Bush's wrath. The vice president stood up well to Rather's aggressive questioning and gave as good as he got. The encounter helped Bush with the still-suspicious base. "It was stronger than grits in the South," said campaign aide Lee Atwater. "Rather is a guy people love to hate down there." The staged confrontation eased the perception that Bush lacked courage.[4]

The Rather interview did not turn the tide for Bush in the Iowa caucuses, however. The vice president came in third behind the winner, Dole, and Pat Robertson, a religious talk show host who had made a well-organized effort to rouse evangelicals. Suddenly, Bush's campaign was in trouble again, and some in the press even pronounced his obituary. That judgment was premature. Bush was the only Republican with true national support and a viable organization. His status as the designated heir of Ronald Reagan meant that the conservative base of the party was his if could beat Dole in the New Hampshire primary.

Bush went into the primary behind Dole in the polls by a narrow margin but with all the advantages of money and organization rolling his way. Dole was not a good administrator, and his campaign lacked a defining theme beyond his Senate record. Bush had the backing of Governor John Sununu and a hard-hitting advertising campaign that attacked Dole's votes for tax increases in the Senate. Bush campaigned as a regular fellow in the retail politics of New Hampshire. As a result, Dole was simply overwhelmed as Bush achieved a nine-point win over his main challenger. The campaign then turned south with Bush holding a clear lead.

The importance of Super Tuesday in the Republican nominating process underscored how central the South was becoming in GOP affairs by the end of the 1980s. Originally designed to give Dixie extra clout in the Democratic nomination race, the cluster of presidential contests now had the same impact for the Republicans. If a candidate scored big in the South, an insurmountable lead in delegates could be established. That was what the Bush forces sought in March 1988.

Though he was far from the only southern Republican involved in the Bush campaign, Lee Atwater of South Carolina emerged as the defining presence in Bush's 1988 race both in the primaries and the general election. Atwater, who had turned thirty-seven in March 1988, had come up through the rough school of his state's politics as a protégé of Senator Strom Thurmond and a contemporary of Governor Carroll Campbell. Atwater understood how important southern Republicans were to Bush's chances for the nomination in 1988. The blend of cultural and economic conservatism that played well in the region tapped into feelings about race and religion that had once been the province of the Democrats. Now white voters in the South found these same qualities in the GOP. On Super Tuesday, Bush recorded victories in all the southern state and put Dole's candidacy on the ropes. Further successes in the spring left the vice president the likely Republican nominee.

How much that prize might be worth was still in question during the spring of 1988. The Democrats were on the verge of nominating Governor Michael Dukakis of Massachusetts as their candidate, and public opinion polls gave him a lead of as much as sixteen points over Bush. Running as a moderate, centrist Democrat, Dukakis seemed a fresh face who might be able to tap into a public desire for gradual change after eight years of Ronald Reagan and the Republicans. Accordingly, Bush and his campaign team explored ways to turn the temporary assets of Dukakis into permanent weaknesses.

An additional task for Bush was the selection of a running mate, to be unveiled at the Republican National Convention in New Orleans in mid-August. By the time the Republican delegates assembled, Bush had already cut into the polling lead that Dukakis once held. The Democratic candidate had started to show the vulnerabilities on issues that plagued him during the fall campaign. So Bush knew that if present trends continued he was likely to win. The question was what a running mate could contribute to what now seemed inside the Bush campaign to be a likely presidency.

Some candidates could be ruled out at once. Bush and Senator Dole did not like each other. Jack Kemp had many strong supporters but was perceived as a loose cannon who could not be relied on to stick to campaign themes without adding comments of his own. Most intriguing for Bush and his advisors was a young second-term senator from Indiana, J. Danforth "Dan" Quayle. Much of the appeal of Quayle, a staunch conservative, was cosmetic, since

Bush was certain to carry Indiana anyway. Bush had trouble connecting with women voters. The joke was that he reminded every woman of her first husband. The handsome, energetic Quayle seemed a solid contrast. The problem was that in the haste of the preconvention countdown, a thorough vetting of Quayle's strengths and weaknesses did not occur.

When the choice was announced, Quayle made a lackluster impression. He gushed with enthusiasm to Bush in their joint press conference, but could not handle questions from journalists about his enlistment in the Indiana National Guard in the late 1960s. Since Guard units were unlikely to be called to active duty during the Vietnam War, they had become a favorable option for well-connected young men who wanted to serve but not to fight. Quayle came across as not fast on his feet mentally, and his repeated verbal gaffes did little to refute that impression. One Republican later called the selection "a perfect example of computer dating gone wrong." Bush had erred, as he noted in his diary, but there was no choice but to press forward with Quayle once the selection had occurred.[5]

The high point of the convention came with Bush's acceptance speech to the delegates. He had been the subject of ridicule from the Democrats at their convention. With the polls showing him pulling ahead of Dukakis, a strong speech would give Bush momentum going into the general election. Republican speechwriters, among them Peggy Noonan of the White House, crafted an oration with key applause lines. One of these remarks would propel Bush to victory in 1988 but also foreshadowed the ultimate problems of his presidency.

Before a cheering crowd, Bush assailed Dukakis's record on cultural issues. As governor of Massachusetts, the Democrat had vetoed a bill requiring schoolchildren to recite the Pledge of Allegiance. Bush attacked his rival for failing to get right on this issue. He ended his speech by leading the delegates in the pledge himself. The other phrase that resonated was Noonan's description of America's private charities as "a brilliant diversity spread like stars, like a thousand points of light in a broad and peaceful sky."[6]

What made Bush's oration memorable, however, was his statement on taxes. He contrasted his unwillingness to raise income taxes and other levies with the reluctance of Dukakis to "rule out raising taxes." The Republican nominee predicted, "Congress will push me to raise taxes, and I'll say 'no,' and they'll push, and I'll say 'no'; and they'll push again, and I'll say to them, 'Read my lips. No new taxes.'" The last line, borrowed from Hollywood star Clint Eastwood's films, produced exuberant applause from the delegates and defined Bush's revamped persona. The short-term political gain was large, but Bush had also painted himself into a corner when he became president.[7]

The 1988 campaign shifted toward the Republicans after the national convention. Dukakis did not respond in a timely manner to the attacks on his
character and record, and he performed poorly in the debates with Bush. The
GOP pounded away on the issue of the Pledge of Allegiance and Dukakis's
"liberalism" to create the impression that the Democratic candidate lacked
the stature to be president. When Dukakis, in a photo op on a campaign visit
to a defense manufacturer, rode in a tank with a helmet on, he looked like a
parody of a military leader, a point the Republicans emphasized with relish.
In all of this jockeying, however, Bush was never really compelled to put forward his own vision of where the nation should be going. From an ideological
point of view, it was another empty campaign for the GOP.

One aspect of the campaign became fixed in the public memory. As part
of their effort to indict the Dukakis record, Republicans criticized one of the
policy decisions of the Massachusetts governor, the granting of furloughs to
convicted felons in the state's prisons. The furlough program began under the
Republican predecessor to Dukakis, but it was continued under Dukakis.
Under the policy, an African American convict named William J. Horton, Jr.,
who was serving a life sentence for murder, was released on a weekend furlough.
Horton fled to Maryland, where he assaulted a couple, raping the woman.
A Massachusetts newspaper brought the case to light. One of Dukakis's
Democratic rivals, Senator Albert Gore, Jr., attacked the furlough policy (but
did not mention Horton) in a Democratic debate in 1987.[8]

Looking for issues with which to dent Dukakis's poll standing, Republicans
found the Horton case an inviting target. William Horton became "Willie
Horton" in commercials featuring his mug shot that pro-Bush groups made.
These entities were not affiliated in a direct way with the Bush campaign.
While the Bush campaign distanced itself from the Horton ads, they nevertheless enjoyed the political benefit of the extensive media coverage. "The
great thing about the issue was that any way you spin it, Dukakis loses," said
one campaign aide.[9]

The Republicans had a legitimate issue in the furlough policy. Rarely did
they acknowledge that Ronald Reagan had pursued a similar arrangement as
governor of California. While denying racial motivation in the Horton controversy, the strategists in the Bush campaign made only pro forma gestures to
still the furor over the advertisement and its implications. The episode attested
to the extent that race-baiting attitudes more common to the South had permeated the Republican Party.

When the votes were counted, Bush recorded a seven percentage point
win over his rival, 53 percent to 46 percent. The result in the electoral race was

426 to 112. The Republicans still had their lock on presidential contests, but there were small signs of erosion. The Democrats carried ten states and came close to winning several others. Dukakis did well among skilled workers, a growing segment of the electorate. A more effective Democratic campaigner could build on the centrist argument that Dukakis made to give Bush and the Republicans a real challenger four years later.

During his first two years, George H. W. Bush seemed an activist and very effective chief executive. More involved in governing than Ronald Reagan had been, he moved away from some of the hallmarks of his predecessor. On the surface, everything was amicable within the party. Behind that facade, however, Reagan loyalists believed that their presence was not wanted on the new White House team. A close friend of Reagan's later griped that there had been "a very systematic purge" that included "anyone with any association with the Reagan-Nixon-Goldwater wing of the party."[10]

The new administration was, by most standards of American politics, very conservative. Bush named his old friend and campaign manager James Baker as secretary of state. After a misstep with the selection of former senator John Tower as secretary of defense, whom the Senate rejected, Bush named Richard Cheney to the post. The rest of the cabinet, which combined conservatives and moderates, was well within the GOP mainstream. To run the White House, Bush picked the former governor of New Hampshire, John Sununu, the man whose help had been so critical in the New Hampshire primary against Bob Dole.

Bush distinguished between politics, which he disliked, and governing, which engaged his hyperactive energies. His record in the White House proved creditable. In foreign policy, he and his team managed the fallout from the collapse of the Soviet Union with skill. He sent troops into Panama to capture strongman and drug trafficker Manuel Noriega. The Bush White House had its greatest triumph with the Gulf War and the expulsion of Iraqi forces from Kuwait. On the domestic side, the Americans with Disabilities Act and the resolution of the savings and loan scandal inherited from Ronald Reagan were both to Bush's credit.

By 1990, however, the political quandary that Bush confronted was taxes. The pledge that he had uttered at the 1988 convention was one that he meant at the time and intended to keep as long as he could as president. But if flexibility was required, Bush had the example of Reagan before him. Dedicated tax cutter that he was, Reagan had still agreed to a number of what were in fact tax hikes during the 1980s. What Bush and his advisers did not grasp was that Republican conservatives allowed Reagan these temporary heresies because of their confidence that in his heart he favored lower tax rates.

With Bush there was no such faith in his motives. After all, Bush had once been for birth control and had criticized Reagan's supply-side policies in the 1980 campaign. To staunch conservatives, Bush always had the feel of someone with well-concealed moderate leanings. Many in the GOP feared that Bush, like Robert Dole, did not mind big government in some areas and the taxes that funded it. As the party moved to a stance that regarded all tax increases for any reason as a betrayal of the core values of the Republican Party, any wavering on Bush's part was bound to evoke strident criticism from conservatives.

The Bush shift took place in two stages during the spring and summer of 1990. On May 8, 1990, the White House announced that in dealing with congressional Democrats over the budget, there would be "no preconditions for negotiation," which in itself implied that revenues might rise. The Republican base was angered. A month and a half later, the president issued a statement in which he said that dealing with the deficit might require "tax revenue increases." The 1988 pledge had been breached.[11]

Republicans in and out of Congress were infuriated. The chair of the Republican Congressional Campaign Committee, Ed Rollins, warned that the broken pledge might cost the party as many as ten seats in the fall. Newt Gingrich of Georgia, a rising star in the party and minority whip in the House, made it clear to allies that he would oppose whatever came out of the budget negotiations with the Democrats if it included increased taxes.

The Bush negotiators, John Sununu and Budget Director Richard Darman, did produce a deal with the Democrats in October 1990. The deficit reduction package proposed to raise the highest marginal tax rate, but it would be offset by lowering projected increases in the gasoline tax. Because of Democratic support, the measure passed, even though almost three-quarters of the Republicans in the House and Senate voted against the administration. Gingrich's position, not that of President Bush, represented the party's true attitude. The belief that tax cuts were good in every circumstance and under all conditions was, more than ever before, a fundamental principle of the party. Conversely, tax increases were to be resisted with the most intense fervor possible. Economic policy and governance gave way among Republicans to an almost theological aversion to higher taxes.

At first it did not seem that Bush would suffer any lasting consequences from his political apostasy over taxes. The Iraqi invasion of Kuwait in the summer of 1990 and the events that led to the Gulf War in February 1991 lifted President Bush's popularity to record heights, making the furor among Republicans over the budget seem secondary. The congressional elections cost the GOP eight seats in the House and one in the Senate, but with Bush riding high after the Gulf War triumph a reelection in November 1992 seemed a certainty. Leading Democrats decided to duck the opportunity to face the incumbent. Bush's own burgeoning popularity gave him little incentive to take steps toward building up his Republican base. In the president's mind, when 1992 came around there would be ample time for the Republican partisanship that he regarded as a necessary evil.

Partisanship flared when Supreme Court Justice Thurgood Marshall retired in 1991 and Bush selected Clarence Thomas, an African American appeals court justice, to succeed him. When a black law professor named Anita Hill accused Thomas of sexual harassment, a controversial Senate hearing ensued. Republicans on the Judiciary Committee defended Thomas and attacked Hill's credibility. Republicans believed that a talented, qualified nominee had been the victim of a smear campaign, much like the one Robert Bork had faced five years earlier. Thomas was confirmed by a narrow vote, but the passion his case had aroused spilled over into the political arena and beyond.

Although on the surface President Bush's reelection still seemed likely during the second half of 1991, the ground was shifting under the feet of the Republicans. A brief, sharp recession, the first in eight years, aroused fears among voters about the future. With deficits weighing on the government, Americans asked whether the benefits of Social Security and Medicare would be available to them when they reached retirement age. Citizens told pollsters that the nation was on the wrong track and that national leaders were out of touch with ordinary people. An antipolitical mood, fed by the economic troubles and the sense of failing national leadership, coursed through the electorate. Both parties seemed detached from pressing concerns and the possibilities for a third party or political insurgency grew.

The high ratings that Bush had achieved after the Gulf victory slipped away in 1991 as the White House seemed to become immobilized by the economy. Yet through these months the president seemed oblivious to what was happening to his electoral chances. Even a skid in his job approval rating of almost twenty points in the early fall of 1991 did not seem to jolt Bush out of his self-imposed lethargy.

By December 1991, however, Bush had jettisoned the unpopular and maladroit White House chief of staff, John Sununu, whose nastiness had become legendary in Washington. No one of stature came in to manage the Bush reelection effort, and the leaders of the president's campaign never found a theme or purpose to persuade voters that Bush should receive another term. The president particularly missed the advice of Lee Atwater, the head of the Republican National Committee, who died of a brain tumor in 1991.

While Bush was looking for the proper moment to revive his candidacy, he faced a challenge to his own renomination. Former Nixon and Reagan aide Patrick "Pat" Buchanan left his cable news television show to run against Bush in a symbolic protest against the president's "moderate" policies. His goal was to defeat Bush in the New Hampshire primary and take his conservative insurgence into the South. In the primary itself, Bush defeated his challenger by a vote of 53 to 37 percent. Bush then locked up the nomination in the southern primaries. Buchanan had become enough of a nuisance that he would require delicate handling at the national convention in August. The need to repel Buchanan showed that about a quarter of the Republican electorate opposed the president. He was thus compelled to tack to the right, not something that helped his chances in the general election.

By the spring of 1992, Arkansas governor William Jefferson Clinton had become the Democratic front runner. Because Clinton seemed compromised by personal problems, including marital infidelity, the Bush camp did not see him as a major threat in the fall campaign. Like Dukakis four years earlier, Clinton would wilt under the negative campaigning of the GOP. More serious in these months seemed to be the danger of a third-party candidate, Ross Perot.

A Texas billionaire who had made his name in the computer service industry, Perot was a feisty, hard-talking individual who had long disliked Bush and his family. During the winter, Perot announced his candidacy on a call-in show. A wave of enthusiasm lifted the Perot effort, and he soon had shot ahead of both Bush and Clinton in the polls. Bush's troubles continued. Racial rioting in Los Angeles over the acquittal of the police officers involved in the beating a black motorist highlighted an issue to which Bush responded with political slowness.

As the summer began, the political climate for the Republicans further worsened. Media scrutiny of Ross Perot revealed his personal quirks and brought his poll numbers down. On the eve of the Democratic convention, Perot dropped out. Clinton received his party's nomination and chose Senator Albert Gore, Jr., as his running mate. The impression of energy and dynamism lifted the Democratic ticket in the polls and gave Clinton a substantial lead over Bush as the Republican convention neared.

The GOP conclave renominated Bush and Quayle, despite some misgivings among the president's aides about the electoral value of the vice president. On the whole, the convention proved a public relations disaster for the party. To appease Buchanan, he was allowed to speak on the first night, and he had the most of his moment in the spotlight. "There is a religious war going on in this country. It is a cultural war as critical to the kind of nation we shall be as the

Cold War itself." He denounced the wife of the Democratic candidate, Hillary Rodham Clinton, and the liberal forces that supported her, and he spoke with particular asperity about homosexuals. The notes that Buchanan sounded would become part of standard Republican rhetoric for the next two decades, but for the Bush leaders Buchanan had gone off-message, even though at heart Republicans shared Buchanan's values. Since the Civil War Republicans had seen Democrats not just as political opponents but as a disloyal threat to the nation's existence. As a Bush aide put it, "We are America. These other people are not America."[12]

Bush regained some lost ground with his acceptance speech, and he got a small bounce in the polls. The Republicans entered the fall campaign with a dispirited candidate and an inept organization. Bush's reelection effort was one of the worst run in the party's history. Although James A. Baker left the State Department to manage the Bush campaign, even he could not save the president's collapsing candidacy. Angry at the way the press had treated his withdrawal, Perot reentered the race in October, which hurt Bush's chances even more. The president also did not perform well in several three-cornered debates with his two rivals.

As the election approached, some Republicans saw the polls narrowing and Bush closing the gap with Clinton. Then, five days before the voting, Lawrence Walsh, the independent counsel investigating the Iran-Contra affair, indicted Reagan's secretary of defense, Caspar Weinberger, for his role in the episode. The court documents filed with the charges indicated that Bush had known of the attempt to exchange arms for hostages, an allegation that Bush had long denied. Some Republicans became convinced that had the Walsh indictment not come down, Bush would have prevailed. Though that was not a likely scenario, the belief informed GOP opinion toward Bill Clinton and his right to hold office when he became president in January 1993.

The outcome of the 1992 election was a devastating personal defeat for Bush. He garnered only a little more than 37 percent of the popular vote to 43 percent for Clinton and nearly 19 percent for Ross Perot. Clinton won 370 electoral votes to 168 for Bush. Perot was shut out in that category. The GOP picked up one Senate seat and ten House seats, but still did not have control of either house of Congress.

The major cause of Bush's defeat was the economy, which had begun to turn around in the waning months of the year, but recovery did not arrive in time to push the Republican president into another term. A second administration for Bush might have been bereft of ideas in any case. The campaign against Clinton had been negative and had not offered a vision of where Bush

proposed to take the nation. After a dozen years of GOP presidency, the
Republican surge that began in the late 1970s seemed to have ebbed.

When the Clinton presidency got underway, the Republican Party
regrouped to examine its political future. The presence of a Democratic president in the White House allowed Republicans to concentrate on what they
were against in the 1990s without having to set out exactly what they were for.
In the process, the party moved ever rightward, convinced of its own recti-
tude and the validity of its core beliefs.

By 1992, the Republicans in electoral terms controlled two main geo-
graphical areas of the nation. In the Plains States and the Rocky Mountain
West, Democrats did not pose a significant challenge in presidential contests.
A newer area of dominance was the South, where George H. W. Bush still
carried seven states in his national loss to Clinton. In the region, white voters
went in large numbers for Bush while blacks gave the Democratic candidate
almost 90 percent of their support. However, the party was losing ground in
the Northeast and along the Pacific Coast, where the Democrats were establishing an ascendancy.

In economic terms, Republican polices won their greatest endorsement
from the business community, particularly small and middle-sized firms. Corporations provided a dependable source of campaign contributions that gave
the GOP a wide edge over the Democrats. Most Republican lawmakers
believed in the probusiness, antigovernment agenda that attracted such financial support. They asserted that their independence had not been compromised
because of their monetary links to lobbyists. In fact, when they took control
of Congress in 1995, Republican leaders punished firms that had donated
money to Democratic candidates in the past or dared to do so in the future.

The intimate relationship between the party and the lobbyists often influenced policy on such issues as gun control and the environment. The National
Rifle Association (NRA) found in the GOP an ardent backer of its efforts to
stymie gun legislation. The party's constituency among white males made the
link with the NRA a natural connection. Similarly, the Republican suspicion
of regulation often guaranteed support of industry attempts to hamper environmental legislation and block government efforts to implement such laws.
To warnings of the impending dangers of global warming, for example,
Republicans by and large denied the science behind it and mocked the proponents of remedial action.

The insurance industry found the GOP a congenial ally against national
health insurance and campaigns to put mental health problems on the same plane
as other diseases. Within the party's ideological core were those who wanted to

overturn the major programs of the New Deal and the Great Society: Social Security and Medicare. Others dreamed of abolishing the income tax in favor of a national sales tax or other consumption-based levies that would fall on the poor. Finally, an extreme fringe looked to ending the civil rights laws of the 1960s and returning minorities to a subordinate place in society.

While economics secured many votes and led interest groups into the GOP coalition, the party's stance on social issues attracted countless others. Antiabortion forces saw the Republicans endorse their goals in the 1980s and 1990s to the extent that supporters of abortion were an endangered minority within the party. Other goals that Christian voters sought from the Republicans included an amendment to permit prayer in the public schools, restrictions on the rights of homosexuals, and limits on illegal immigration. Another favorite cause of the religious right was opposition to the teaching of evolution as a scientific doctrine. Across the spectrum of social issues, Republicans dissented from the findings of science on matters ranging from research on embryonic stem cells to the impact of global warming.[13]

On foreign policy, Republicans in the 1990s disagreed on a number of problems relating to the nation's role in the world. Strains of isolationism and unilateralism persuaded a number of GOP members to oppose international organizations such as the United Nations, World Trade Organization, and International Court of Justice. Involvement of American military force overseas on behalf of "nation building" was another strategy that large numbers of Republicans disliked.

Yet the GOP also attacked the Democrats for an unwillingness to project national power around the world to safeguard American interests against terrorism and "rogue nations." For the Republicans one attractive feature of the strategic missile defense system meant to protect the United States against a surprise attack was that it maximized military power. At the same time it relied primarily on American technology and ingenuity, rather than foreign commitments or unreliable allies. The only problem with the system was that it was never made to work in practice.

Similar divisions existed on the issue of immigration. Many in the party, such as Patrick Buchanan, wanted to cut off the flow of legal and illegal immigrants into the country. In California, Proposition 187, which passed as a ballot initiative, prevented illegal immigrants from receiving state educational and health benefits. The Republican governor of the state, Pete Wilson, was at the forefront of advocates of the proposition's passage. His action identified the party with an anti-immigrant sentiment that in the years following moved California into the Democratic column in presidential elections. Republicans who sought a more inclusive, tolerant approach to immigration were an out-voted minority within the party.

Republicans became more and more the party of states' rights and dissatisfaction with the outcome of the Civil War. Senator Trent Lott, the party's leader in the upper house after 1996, and Senator John Ashcroft of Missouri praised neo-Confederate groups and at least hinted that the Civil War had been wrongly decided. Lott argued on several occasions that the nation would have been better off if the segregationist policies of Strom Thurmond in 1948 had been pursued instead of the civil rights revolution. The United States Supreme Court, under the leadership of William Rehnquist and Antonin Scalia, shifted power back to the states in an apparent effort to redress imbalances that in their minds the Civil War and its aftermath had created.

A major element in Republican cohesion during the 1990s was their shared distaste, sometimes verging on hatred, for President Bill Clinton and his wife, Hillary Clinton. Since the 1992 election had been, in the minds of Republicans, a shocking deviation from the natural order of American politics, it followed that Clinton's victory was not an authentic expression of the will of the American people. Clinton was president in fact, but not in legitimacy. He was a ruthless usurper and an incompetent at the same time.

Robert Dole said after the election that the Republicans in the Senate would represent the 57 percent of Americans who had not voted for Clinton. Dole argued that the opposition party had the right to determine the legitimacy of the president. Since Clinton had won on an electoral fluke, the Republicans were justified in withholding their votes and their cooperation from the new administration. This novel constitutional doctrine had long-term consequences. If a presidency was illegitimate and thus illegal, the Republicans faced a situation in which democratic norms only helped maintain a potential Democratic tyrant in power. Though Dole would later talk of adversaries rather than enemies among the Democrats, he had unleashed passions within his party that would shape the next two decades of partisan warfare.

In the opening days of the Clinton administration, Republicans made their views clear. Representative Richard "Dick" Armey told House Democrats that the incumbent was "your president." The Republicans were entering dangerous territory. Lockstep opposition to the policies of their political adversaries could result in the erosion of trust in democratic institutions and the malfunctioning of government. This process of legislative nullification, which came into full flower two decades later, started with the denial of Clinton's legitimacy.[14]

Since Clinton had run and won as a centrist Democrat, the extent of Republican animosity went beyond ideology. The first baby-boomer president represented all the elements of the 1960s that Republicans disliked: self-involvement, cultural looseness, and sexual promiscuity. Moreover, Clinton was a strong partisan infighter, something Republican had not seen in a Democratic president since Harry Truman. Hillary Clinton's apostasy in going from being a Goldwater Girl in 1964, with a stop to work on the Nixon impeachment with the House Judiciary Committee in 1974, to the Democratic champion of health care in 1993 made her an inviting target.

The loathing of Clinton sometimes unhinged the Republicans. Many on the far right of the party believed the president was a drug addict, murderer, and potential dictator with covert plans to perpetuate his tenure office and to end democracy in the United States. The American people had been deluded when they elected (and ultimately reelected) the man. Once the public learned the facts about Clinton's perfidy, they would come to their senses.

The first two years of the Clinton administration unfolded as if the Republicans had written the script. A tax-increase measure, which the Democrats had pushed through Congress in the summer of 1993, united the Republicans. Not a single member of the GOP voted for the law, which narrowly passed the House and then squeaked through the Senate with Albert Gore's tie-breaking vote. Designed to reduce the deficit and to assure the financial markets of the nation's fiscal integrity, the bill used hikes on upper-income taxpayers and spending reductions to achieve its goal.

The Republicans pounced. The law, they said, was the largest tax increase in the history of the world (Reagan's 1982 tax bill was higher in constant dollars). Moreover, none of the supposed benefits to the country that Clinton had promised would be realized. Instead, Republican speakers predicted, economic ruin impended. "It is a recipe for disaster," observed Dick Armey. "Taxes will go up. The economy will sputter along. Dreams will be put off, and all this for the hollow promise of deficit reduction and magical theories of lower interest rates." Newt Gingrich forecast "a job-killing recession" if the bill was enacted. Phil Gramm of Texas said that "hundreds of thousands of Americans will lose their jobs because of this bill."[15]

The tax fight energized the Republicans. The Democrats seemed listless and divided, with the Clinton White House beset with scandals and ineptitude. Republicans ran well in state races in 1993 and looked forward with anticipation to the congressional elections in 1994. A key element of the rising GOP morale was conservative talk radio, where charismatic figures such as Rush Limbaugh aroused a passionate audience for the Republican cause.

A former sportscaster turned conservative advocate, Limbaugh spoke to millions daily through his "Excellence in Broadcasting Network," where he taught "Advanced Conservative Studies" with "talent on loan from God."[16]

Despite his own personal foibles, which included multiple marriages and an addiction to painkillers, Limbaugh commanded a wide audience. Among those who listened to talk radio more than ten hours a week, a striking majority were Republicans. Limbaugh's hard-edged anti-Democratic, antifeminist, antiblack rhetoric appealed particularly to white males in the South who were unhappy with Clinton, affirmative action, gun control, and higher taxes. Democrats never found an answer to Limbaugh and the talk radio craze.

As Republican chances brightened, Newt Gingrich of Georgia saw a chance to achieve what had previously seemed politically impossible: winning a GOP majority in the House of Representatives and becoming Speaker. Fifty-one years old in 1994, the burly, rumpled Gingrich had been in Congress since 1979. From the outset he had wanted to be Speaker. Taking advantage of the newly televised proceedings of the House on C-SPAN to build an audience in nightly special order speeches, he and his like-minded colleagues harassed the House leadership. Gingrich's intention was to transform the House into a Republican stronghold. Passing legislation by cooperating with the Democrats was not one of his priorities. His biggest coup had been ousting Speaker Jim Wright of Texas in 1989 through an ethics investigation. Now Gingrich reached for power of his own.[17]

A former college history professor who thought in grand terms about national and world trends, Gingrich employed military metaphors (he had been an army brat) and the language of the new technology. In his mind, the Democrats in the House had been corrupted by having been in power since 1955. The majority party was identified with the overcentralization of the Great Society and was moving away from American values. Left unsaid amid all the moralistic language was any discussion of Gingrich's personal lifestyle, which included an abrupt divorce from his first (and older) wife while she was suffering from cancer and his clandestine affair with the congressional aide who ultimately became his third wife. A Republican associate in Georgia would later say of the future Speaker, "The important thing you have to understand about Newt Gingrich is that he is amoral. There isn't any right or wrong…only what will work best for Newt Gingrich."[18]

As a political strategist, Gingrich had a talent for organization and a good sense of the weaknesses of his opponents. In addition to his innovative use of television, he had taken over a political action committee, GOPAC, in 1987 to channel money to Republican House candidates. Gingrich used the group to train Republicans to be more effective politicians (if not legislators), and thus he built up a network of supporters in the House as his efforts brought more GOP members to the body. By late 1993, Gingrich concluded that his moment had arrived. The incumbent Republican leader announced that he would not run for reelection. The way was cleared for Gingrich.

Gingrich did extensive polling with focus groups to determine which issues resonated with those panels of voters. That process resulted in the Contract with America, which pledged to take action on a balanced budget, term limits for members of Congress, and laws to make Congress conform to the rules that they imposed on the rest of society. All these issues would be addressed within the first hundred days of the new Congress. If the public got the notion that they would be passed during the period, so much the better. Republican poll numbers were rising, and the Democrats saw their prospects for extending their control of the House eroding from week to week.

Newt Gingrich (right) brought the Republicans back into control of the House of Representatives in 1994, which earned him the right to negotiate with President Bill Clinton and Senator Robert Dole. Library of Congress, LC-USZ62-115908.

The GOP strategy was to nationalize the election and make it a referendum on the Clinton administration. Talk radio, advertising that rallied the GOP base, and Democratic mistakes all worked to Gingrich's advantage. By this time conservative animus against the administration had intensified. A complex and costly health care program, endorsed by Hillary Clinton, had become an albatross for the Democrats. They could not pass it, but neither would it go away as insurance companies funded negative ads against it. That millions of Americans suffered and died without health care did not affect the Republican calculus. A crime bill that included a ban on assault rifles aggravated the National Rifle Association and stoked the anger of conservative white males. Campaign contributions poured in to the Republicans, The party stood ready to implement the anti-Clinton, anti-Democratic agenda that Gingrich had formulated.

The climax of the Republican campaign occurred on September 27 when Gingrich and three hundred Republican representatives and congressional candidates made their appearance on the Capitol steps for their photo opportunity. The elections saw the Republicans pick up fifty-two seats in the House of Representatives and gain control for the first time in forty years. The GOP also won back the Senate, which they now controlled fifty-three to forty-seven. Republicans won gubernatorial races, including in Texas, where George W. Bush, the eldest son of the former president, ousted Ann Richards. Gingrich became Speaker of the House, and Robert Dole was Senate majority leader.[19]

The significance of the 1994 election was profound. The Republicans emerged as the dominant party in the House over the next two decades. More important was the attitude that the new GOP members brought to the legislative process. They did not contend with Democrats within a shared system of values about democratic governance. They were waging war on the very ideas of liberalism, consensus, and compromise. The Republicans divided society between its productive members, usually allied with the GOP, and the citizens who relied on government through a corrupt bargain with the Democrats. Legislation to nourish the former and punish the latter was a major Republican aim in Congress.

The House Republicans under Newt Gingrich set about implementing the Contract with America with great energy in the winter of 1995. The shift away from Democratic power introduced new GOP congressional leaders who reflected the disdain for the Democrats and any notion of meaningful arrangements with their adversaries. The new majority leader, Dick Armey, asserted that "the market is rational and the government is dumb." The new majority whip, Tom DeLay, also of Texas, believed that the Environmental

Protection Agency was "the Gestapo of government pure and simple." To offset the impact of liberal interest groups on Capitol Hill, DeLay and Armey pressured lobbyists not to contribute to Democratic candidates and brought in business executives to help draft legislation about the environment. While they denounced big government, the Republican congressional leadership directed federal appropriations away from Democratic districts and toward the districts that more affluent members of the GOP inhabited.[20]

The Republicans set a hurried pace through the spring of 1995. The balanced budget amendment that Gingrich's friends in the House proposed then failed by a single vote in the Senate. The law preventing Congress from imposing its mandates on the states without sufficient funding was adopted. A constitutional amendment to impose term limits on members of Congress did not pass. By April, Gingrich and his allies proclaimed that they had either enacted or brought to a vote most of the Contract and had thus fulfilled their one-hundred-day pledge.

The horrific terrorist bombing of the federal building in Oklahoma City on April 19, 1995, which killed more than 160 people, changed the political landscape. Dismissed as irrelevant a few days before this sad event, President Clinton regained his standing when he spoke eloquently at a memorial service for the victims. The bombing and his response shifted the political momentum toward the president.

One central battle in the budget fight was over Medicare. In their effort to secure a tax cut for affluent Americans and to halt the growth of federal spending, Republicans argued that the money allocated per patient would rise from $4,800 to $6,700 over the subsequent seven years. They bristled when Democrats described this policy as cutting Medicare and countered that their goal was protecting the program. Democrats responded that the government would have to spend $8,000 per year to maintain services at the 1995 level. The preexisting condition of Republican loathing of Medicare made it more difficult for them to make the case that the program would be safe in their hands.

By the end of 1995, the Republican Congress was itching for a showdown with the president. With no budget agreement in prospect, militant GOP members in the House thought that shutting down the government would pressure the president to agree to their terms. They would then have the satisfaction of humiliating their hated rival. If the American people suffered in the process, it was in the interest of a larger cause. Two government closures in November and December resulted in the Republicans getting the blame for the stalemate. As that perception sank in, the GOP leadership in Congress agreed to reopen the government in January 1996.

Clinton still seemed vulnerable as talk of financial scandals swirled around him and his wife. The Republicans were not able to connect the dots to make a compelling case against the president and the first lady. Meanwhile, the Democrats had raised ample sums of money, some of it from foreign corporations, and had begun a saturation advertising campaign to improve the president's poll ratings and drive down the numbers for his Republican rivals.

The Republican field was crowded, with Senator Dole the clear front runner after Colin Powell announced that he would not run. Dole lost an early race in New Hampshire and faced the ample war chest of millionaire publisher Steve Forbes. Despite these obstacles, Dole did well in the southern primaries and was within sight of the nomination. He was also out of money and unable to respond to Clinton's advertising. With his candidacy in the doldrums, Dole resigned his Senate seat in June 1996 and ran as a man without office or power in Washington. The poll numbers did not move.

With the election looming and control of the Republican House at stake, the GOP leadership in Congress decided to cooperate with Clinton in the adoption of welfare reform. Such legislation would bolster Clinton's credentials as an effective president and a "New Democrat" not tied to the failures of liberalism. By the end of July a compromise measure had cleared Capitol Hill. It terminated the Aid for Dependent Children program and replaced it with block grants for the states. The federal responsibility of dealing with impoverished Americans, established during the New Deal, was over. The law also cut back on benefits for undocumented immigrants during their first five years in the United States. During the remainder of the 103rd Congress, the minimum wage was raised over Republican objections. The GOP sought wording in appropriations bills that would deny public education to undocumented immigrants but lost that fight.

As the Republican convention neared, Senator Dole sprang two surprises. He promised a 15 percent cut in tax rates over a three-year period that would produce "a fairer, flatter tax." Many among the Republicans disliked the progressive income tax and had been advocating that the existing tax rate structure be replaced with a single, low tax rate on all Americans. The great beneficiaries of such a change would be the wealthy, with taxes on the poor rising in some instances. Since there would be a loss of federal revenues at the start of Dole's plan, Democrats claimed that what Dole proposed would "blow a hole in the deficit," but the Republican candidate promised to find spending reductions that would offset the revenue losses.

The second bold move was his selection of former congressman Jack Kemp as his running mate. A champion of tax cuts, Kemp was thought to be popular among African Americans, and he had the glamour of once played in the National

Football League. However, he brought little advantage to the ticket, since Dole had no chance of carrying Kemp's home state, New York, against Clinton. Kemp also turned out to be a mediocre campaigner. Dole got a modest bounce out of the convention, but Clinton's lead soon widened again.

In the campaign, Ross Perot once again launched a third-party effort, but without the enthusiasm of success of 1992. Dole and Clinton debated twice, with the Texan not present. In neither encounter did Dole inflict any serious damage. By mid-October, Clinton seemed far ahead, and the Democrats saw a chance to recapture the House and Senate. Then news reports surfaced about campaign contributions to the president from East Asia, with the possible involvement of Communist Chinese and Indonesian business interests. The revelations ate away at the Democratic lead, and the race tightened somewhat. Dole conducted a last-minute whirlwind tour of the country to show that his age was no bar to being president. Yet when his blitz was over, the result of the election still seemed predictable.

Clinton secured a second term with 379 electoral votes and 49 percent of the vote to 41 percent for Dole and 8 percent for Perot. Dole won 159 electoral votes from reliable GOP states. For the second presidential election, the Republican popular vote had been under 42 percent. The Republicans also lost some seats in the House of Representatives but held on to a ten-seat majority. In the Senate, the Republicans gained two seats but with fifty-five votes were still short of the sixty votes needed to halt a Democratic filibuster. A divided government remained in place.

The two parties worked together in 1997 to achieve a budget agreement to balance the government's books for the first time in decades. With a booming economy and a soaring stock market, the trend pointed to an end to the budget deficit. Clinton claimed that his policies, beginning with the 1993 tax bill, had produced that positive result. Republicans answered that their control of Congress had led to fiscal discipline and the brightening budget situation. Either way, by 1998, the nation could look forward to an unheard-of novelty: an annual budget surplus.

In the House, unhappiness with Speaker Gingrich culminated in an attempt by rebellious Republicans to oust him in the summer. Their perception was that Gingrich too often had failed to defeat Clinton on budget issues and other confrontations. An attempted coup against the Speaker collapsed in mid-July 1997 when the plotters could not agree on his successor. The episode left the House GOP in some disarray, but Gingrich had survived. Among his more intense supporters there was even talk of presidential candidacy in 2000, despite his weakened position in the House.

Then a dramatic development scrambled American politics and renewed Republican optimism about 2000: the revelation of President Clinton's affair with White House intern Monica Lewinsky and the possibility of his impeachment for perjury and other crimes in connection with this sordid episode. While Republicans had no doubts about Clinton's guilt, the situation presented delicate alternatives for the opposition. As the year unfolded and it became clear that the public did not want the president removed, the GOP was forced to reconcile its distaste for Clinton with political reality. In the end, the party decided to press forward with impeachment out of a genuine belief in the president's complicity in perjury and obstruction of justice.[21]

Having made that decision, however, Gingrich and his congressional allies then failed to develop a strategy that could achieve Clinton's conviction and removal from office. The legislative arithmetic was simple. A majority of the House could pass articles of impeachment. Since Republicans assumed that the 1998 election would increase their majority in the House, their capacity to place Clinton on trial was assured. The Senate was another matter. Assuming that all fifty-five Republicans voted to convict Clinton, the GOP needed to win over twelve Democratic senators to achieve the president's removal. Thus, the success of the impeachment campaign hinged on bipartisanship and conciliation of the Democrats in both houses. In a sign of their growing unwillingness to engage in constructive lawmaking, the Republicans adopted a confrontational approach that risked alienating the Democrats rather than seeking their support.

Gingrich and the House Republican leadership saw the autumn of 1998 as the chance to increase their slim majority, since the voters would punish the Democrats for their loyalty to Clinton. That did not happen. The partisanship of the GOP, including the release of a salacious report on Clinton's sexual misdeeds, backfired. The Democrats gained five seats in the House and cut the Republican majority to 221 over the Democrats' 211. The Senate alignment remained unchanged. The unexpected outcome of the election sealed the fate of Newt Gingrich. Restive Republicans now saw Gingrich as a liability. After a false start with one leading candidate, the majority settled on Dennis Hastert of Illinois as Gingrich's successor. Gingrich resigned his seat, ending one of the most fascinating legislative careers in American history. He was not done with American politics, however.

In spite of the election result, the Republicans pressed ahead with the impeachment of Clinton in December 1998. The writing of four articles of impeachment and the eventual adoption of two of them took place in a partisan atmosphere with only a handful of Democratic votes. By the time the trial opened in the Senate in January 1999, any chance of obtaining the dozen Democratic votes needed for conviction had long since disappeared. Republicans complained that Democrats had not displayed bipartisan statesmanship such as the GOP had shown during the Watergate controversy. Yet the Republicans in 1998 had forgotten to seek the votes of the Democrats if they really meant to oust Clinton. The Senate proceedings were anticlimactic and Clinton was acquitted on both counts. The Senate Republicans did not achieve a majority of senators voting for conviction on either count.

By mid-1999, Republican thoughts turned to 2000, when Clinton would not be on the ballot. The field was once again a crowded one for the GOP, but there were only two credible aspirants for the nomination, Senator John McCain of Arizona and Governor George W. Bush of Texas. In 1998, Bush had won a landslide victory over weak Democratic opposition in his race for a second term as governor of Texas. His triumph included strong Hispanic support, an evident plus for a party that was having difficulty attracting minority voters nationally. Under the leadership of his campaign manager, Karl Rove, Bush promised to pursue "compassionate conservatism" in social policy. That meant an emphasis on education, long a Democratic issue, and the standard Republican reduction in income taxes, especially for the well-off.

Bush soon established himself as the leader in the GOP race. His fund-raising was so successful that he did not accept federal matching funds. With his record as governor to run on, Bush promised to restore bipartisan harmony in Washington as he had done in Texas. Pledging to unite rather than divide the nation, he had found a reassuring message that played well with Republican audiences.

Bush also had vulnerabilities. Sober since the mid-1980s, he had been dogged by rumors of alcohol abuse and even some drug abuse as a young man. He brushed aside questions about these matters as only of historical interest. His military record in the National Guard in the early 1970s showed unexplained gaps in his service. Although he was intelligent, he had not shown an ability in his studies at Yale and Harvard Business School or in private business to frame an argument about public policy in an unscripted setting. His record in the oil industry and as a professional baseball executive indicated that he had not been an entrepreneur so much as a beneficiary of the largesse of Republican businessmen who were impressed by his name. The governorship of Texas, a constitutionally weak office, had not tested his leadership skills. The press, which had probed every aspect of the lives of the Clintons, largely accepted George W. Bush's self-evaluation and made only sporadic inquiries into his background and character.

The main challenge to Bush came from Senator John McCain of Arizona, who brought to the race a heroic war record, a reputation for plain speaking, and personal charisma. A conservative on most issues, McCain was nevertheless given to maverick moments when he worked with Democrats. The most notable such deviation from Republican loyalty was his alliance with Senator Russell Feingold, a Wisconsin Democrat, on behalf of campaign finance reform. Outraged by the corrupting flow of money into American politics, McCain attacked the trading of cash for access and votes. The perception, he told the Senate in 1998, was that "the more you give, the more effectively you can petition your government."[22]

McCain was an attractive candidate, especially to the media, who wanted to see a fight for the GOP nomination. Nonetheless, the senator had drawbacks of his own. Many of his fellow Republicans believed he was a loose cannon who was prone to excitable outbursts. In his personal life there were incidents of financial improprieties and romantic lapses that could hurt him in a general election. His brand of reformist Republicanism, which some of his adherents linked to Theodore Roosevelt, worried leaders of the GOP when they contemplated a McCain presidency.

McCain upset Bush in the initial primary test with a decisive victory in the New Hampshire primary. The Arizona senator did well in primaries where independents could vote. When the candidates headed south to territory where Democrats and independents played a smaller role, Bush's strong campaign organization, his deep pockets, and a hard-hitting, even vicious series of attacks on McCain from the right reestablished Bush as the front runner. In South Carolina, for example, Bush allies used McCain's adoption of a young Asian girl to tap into racial prejudices in that state by insinuating that she was actually the product of an affair with an African American women. Though McCain won some other primaries, Bush had the nomination locked up by the spring of 2000.

Vice President Gore had secured the Democratic nomination. With the prosperity of the Clinton years not yet faded, Gore seemed to have the advantage over Bush. Yet the vice president was not an appealing campaigner, and legacy of the Clinton scandals dogged him. So, too, did the national press corps, whose members displayed a visceral dislike of Gore and yearned to see him lose. The Bush campaign found reporters to be eager and credulous consumers of the anti-Gore materials that the GOP generated with its customary skill.

At the Republican convention in Philadelphia, Bush was nominated in a well-produced spectacle that emphasized his appealing qualities. His vice presidential running mate was Dick Cheney, who had selected himself for the post.

The Republican candidate made his proposal for a $1.6 trillion dollar tax cut, to take effect over a ten year period, the centerpiece of his campaign. Directed at upper-income taxpayers, the tax reduction would keep in people's hands the money that, in Bush's view, belonged to them and not the government. The fiscal health of the nation belonged to that segment of the population. The new Republican ticket got a good bounce from the convention, and Bush's lead over Gore was in double digits when the Democratic convention opened.

Gore, too, did well in his convention, and the Democrat again led in the polls in September. The elections seemed likely to turn on the three televised debates. In these confrontations, both candidates were mediocre. The press set low expectations for Bush, put their collective thumb on the scale against Gore, and named Bush the apparent winner.

In foreign policy matters, Bush attacked what he called the nation building of the Democrats overseas. He said in one of the debates, "I'm not so sure the role of the United States is to go around the world and say 'This is the way it's got to be.'" The Republicans made a strong appeal for the vote of American Muslims who were unhappy with the Clinton administration's intervention in the Balkans.[23]

The race tightened as Election Day neared, but the Bush camp was confident that their strategy would prevail. They predicted a Bush victory in the popular vote and a close contest for the electoral college. They were half right. The electoral count was indeed close, but Gore had a half-million-vote lead in the popular ballots. The Democrat had 266 electoral votes, Bush had 245 votes, and Florida was in doubt with 25 electoral votes. Basing their position on network television determinations of who had won Florida, the Bush people said that he was the winner. Democrats contested that judgment.

From the moment the controversy began, Republicans asserted that Bush had won Florida. The cohesion of the GOP and their refusal to lose gave them the upper hand over the Democrats, who never settled on a definitive strategy in the dispute. When vote counting in a Florida county seemed, in the minds of Republicans, slanted against their party, a vocal demonstration of angry GOP operatives shut down the process. Much as in 1876, the ingrained Republican sense of entitlement as the natural governing party proved useful, while the Democrats were depicted in the press as obstructionist, deceitful, and unpatriotic.[24]

The nation watched as lawsuits and court proceedings, along with recounts in various Florida counties, dominated television coverage through November and into December. The dispute reached the United States Supreme Court in December, and the justices ruled five to four in *Bush v. Gore* that the Florida vote count as recorded by state officials appointed by Jeb Bush, the brother of the Republican candidate, should be final. The recount in Florida ended. Gore accepted the decision and George W. Bush was the president-elect. He was inaugurated as the forty-third president on January 20, 2001, and became the eighteenth Republican chief executive since the party's founding in 1854.

The Republicans kept control of the House again by a narrow margin, and the Senate split into a fifty-fifty tie. For the third consecutive presidential race, the Republicans had not secured a plurality of the popular vote. While the party's base in the South and West was secure, the results indicated that the West Coast and Northeast were becoming more Democratic when it came to presidential elections. The Bush campaign in 2000 had achieved a victory by combining fragile elements that would require and receive constant management from the GOP and the White House in the years ahead. For the moment, however, Republicans celebrated a return to national power and the chance to enact their agenda. They could not know that events were shaping themselves among the nation's terrorist enemies that, in the first year of the Bush presidency, would challenge the Republican Party in the first decade of the new century.

13

Republicans and the George W. Bush Presidency, 2001–2009

THE REPUBLICANS RETURNED to the White House in January 2001 with a sense that the rightful political order had been restored after eight years of unwarranted Democratic usurpation. The catchphrase among the Republican-oriented Washington media was that the adults were again in charge. Bush might be a novice on the national scene, but Dick Cheney was an old Washington hand. So too were such Cabinet appointees as Colin Powell at the State Department and Donald Rumsfeld as Secretary of Defense. The echoes of the three previous Republican administrations were pervasive.[1]

With Republicans in control of both houses of Congress, albeit by a single vice presidential vote in the Senate, the way seemed clear to enact Republican priorities. The narrow election provided no constraint on their ambition. "A notion of a sort of restrained presidency because it was such a close election, that lasted maybe 30 seconds," Dick Cheney later observed. "We had an agenda, we ran on the agenda, we won the election-full speed ahead." The contrast with Robert Dole's observations about a minority president in 1993 were striking, especially since the Republicans had earned a minority of the popular vote.[2]

Republicans had also not informed the electorate of their larger policy goals. Conservatism did not mean preserving and building on the existing structure of social programs such Social Security and Medicare that previous Democratic administrations had enacted. Because these measures enjoyed widespread popularity, moving against them in a direct way was unwise for the moment. Rather, the Republicans would "fix" or "reform" these initiatives into a more privatized, scaled-back role while reassuring Americans that Social Security and Medicare had not really changed.[3]

Republican fortunes would, of course, turn on the performance of the new president. George W. Bush came to the office with the wind at his back as far as the media and Washington opinion was concerned. He had run as "a uniter, not a divider," and the press corps had concluded he was "someone you'd like to have a beer with." After Clinton's tawdriness and Gore's relentless focus on the deteriorating environment, Bush the open-handed campaigner would bring positive qualities to the White House to heal the nation. After all, the celebrity-minded media believed, campaigning and governing were essentially the same thing.[4]

In significant ways, Bush and the people around him approached the presidency in the manner of Richard Nixon. Creating the impression of executive strength and stage-managing the president's activities for the media took up large chunks of White House energy and time. References to "this president" in contrast to predecessors became a favored way of referring to whatever Bush said and did. These were signals that the Republicans had a strong leader at the head of their party.

The Republicans and the press had evaluated George W. Bush as a campaigner and not as a future president. He did not have a subtle mind and did not know where the boundaries of his lack of knowledge stood. For example, he was unaware of the historic difference between Shia and Sunni branches of Islam. Aides warned members of the administration: "Don't give the president a lot of long memos; he's not a big reader." Bravado and presidential authority would insure that he got the last word. When one government official told the president that a course he had decided upon constituted "bad policy." Bush retorted, "I don't ever want to hear you use those words in my presence again." The visitor asked, "What words, Mr. President?" Bush responded, "Bad policy. If I decide to do it, by definition it is good policy."[5]

The first eight months of the new presidency tested optimistic assumptions about the incumbent's qualifications and the nature of compassionate conservatism. The Republicans succeeded, with Democratic support, in enacting his large tax cut. Huge deficits returned to the nation's balance sheet. Vice President Cheney argued that "Reagan proved that deficits don't matter." The gains in fiscal credibility, hard won under the elder Bush and then Bill Clinton in the 1990s, soon disappeared.[6]

Tax cuts in every economic environment became Republican orthodoxy. Grover Norquist, an influential ideological voice within the party, insisted that Republicans sign binding pledges never to raise taxes under any circumstances. Stephen Moore and the Club for Growth sponsored the campaigns of conservatives and threatened moderate Republicans with primary challenges when they deviated from the accepted tax creed. As Moore put it, when he raised the prospect of a challenger before a moderate Republican, they would "start wetting their pants." Moore and the club, along with

George W. Bush and Dick Cheney made a powerful team in the White House during the first Bush term, but their partnership frayed after 2004. Author's collection.

Norquist and his forces, would be a potent element during the Bush years and beyond.[7]

Bush found similar bipartisan backing in Congress for his No Child Left Behind education reform measure. On other key topics, such as global warming and nuclear proliferation, the White House embraced a strict unilateral posture. Republican insistence on rolling back environmental regulations caused one Republican senator, Jim Jeffords of Vermont, to become an independent. Control of the Senate returned to the opposition. By the end of the summer of 2001, the new administration had run out of workable policy ideas, and the president's ratings slipped.

The general disdain for Democrats and especially Bill Clinton permeated the Bush White House and the Republicans. There was nothing for the new team to learn from what had been, in the minds of the Bush team, a feckless crew of reckless amateurs. When outgoing officials warned of the dangers of Osama bin Laden and al-Qaeda, the Bush officials refused to be distracted from what they saw as the real foreign policy threat, Saddam Hussein and an Iraq armed with weapons of mass destruction.

Bush's defenders contend that there was no way the attacks of September 11, 2001, could have been prevented, and that the intelligence failures that led to them should not be attributed to incompetence. At the same time, neither did the president nor his team strain every nerve to heed warnings, as a document from the Central Intelligence Agency put it, that bin Laden was "determined to strike in [the] US." On vacation in Texas, Bush brushed aside the briefer who conveyed the news and took no identifiable steps to alert the government of any impending danger.[8]

After the deadly attacks on New York and Washington, the Republican administration did not engage in soul-searching or express remorse for its lack of diligence and foresight. Instead, the thousands of dead Americans and foreigners provided both geopolitical and partisan opportunity. Unlike Franklin D. Roosevelt after Pearl Harbor, Bush commissioned no investigation into the causes of the disaster, discouraged congressional inquiries, and sacked no one for failures of command and execution. Bush later said: "I did not think it was appropriate to point fingers or fix blame in the middle of the crisis." Republicans took credit; Democrats faced accountability.[9]

In the hours and days after the September 11 attacks, the Bush White House reached several key decisions. Osama bin Laden had to be pursued and killed if possible, but the major military priority was Saddam Hussein and Iraq. The administration hoped and expected to locate a link between the dictator and the terrorist organization, and would find one whether or not any in fact existed.[10]

On a political level, the national outrage and trauma from 9/11 could serve the Republicans well in the 2002 elections and in the 2004 contest to reelect George W. Bush. The Republicans were back in a familiar mode of military aggressiveness and militant patriotism, which could make the Democrats appear wrong-footed as appeasers and even allies of the enemy. Their legitimacy as political opponents of the Republicans in the American system was an inviting target.[11]

Bush's popularity soared after his vigorous expressions of horror at the attacks and his stated resolve to seek vengeance for an America assaulted. He and Karl Rove viewed this endorsement from the nation not as a trust to be used with insight and caution; it was, rather, a political gift to be wielded in the service of seeking a national electoral majority. The presumption was that a powerful American military would prevail against what the president called the "axis of evil"—Iraq, Iran, and North Korea—and the Grand Old Party would reap the votes as the true protector of the nation.[12]

The armed forces failed to capture or kill bin Laden in Afghanistan but did defeat the Taliban, who had harbored the terrorist leader. A protracted American involvement began in that country that would last through the

Bush presidency and beyond. Soon the commitment in Afghanistan had to compete with preparations for regime change in Iraq.

There was a firm consensus among the president's team that Saddam Hussein represented the major threat to American goals in the Middle East, from the ending of terrorism to the settlement of the Arab-Israeli dispute. They interpreted the intelligence about Hussein and weapons of mass destruction in light of these convictions. Accepting only the data that justified intervention was seen as warranted because the guilt of the brutal Hussein was so self-evident.

With war in Iraq on the agenda (and Vice President Cheney sought such action in 2002), Republicans made the congressional elections of 2002 a referendum on patriotism. A Democratic candidate who expressed doubt about the wisdom of invading Iraq could be branded as soft on Saddam Hussein and stigmatized as unpatriotic. Unlike his father, who had scheduled a vote on liberating Kuwait after the 1990 elections, the younger Bush made a choice for or against war a central element in the canvass of 2002.

A campaign that turned on supporting the president and stressing patriotism motivated the Republicans. Attacking Democrats as covert or implicit allies of America's enemies fit with long-term GOP doubts about the allegiance of Democrats to the nation's true ideals. Saxby Chambliss, who had not served in the military during the Vietnam War, ran advertisements in Georgia criticizing Democratic incumbent Max Cleland, who had lost three limbs in that conflict. Cleland, said the Chambliss spots, had failed to vote for the president's department of Homeland Security and thus lacked "the courage to lead." The ads showed Cleland turning into Osama bin Laden and Saddam Hussein. In the voting, the Republicans gained two Senate seats to retake control of the upper house. The GOP majority in the House grew by eight seats. Bush and his party believed that they had gained a mandate for decisive action to secure regime change in Iraq.[13]

Having succumbed to one major intelligence failure with their lack of response to the threat that Osama bin Laden posed in 2001, the Republican administration now convinced itself that the Iraqi dictator possessed weapons of mass destruction and the means to deliver them, even against the American mainland. The presumption, later proved erroneous, of the existence of weapons of mass destruction underlay the attack on Iraq in the spring of 2003. As Paul Wolfowitz of the Defense Department put it, "We settled on the one issue that everyone could agree on, which was weapons of mass destruction as the core reason" to justify war.[14]

This self-adopted groupthink had the paradoxical effect of making Bush and his men vulnerable to faulty intelligence. When an Iraqi émigré named Ahmed Chalabi sounded like a plausible successor Hussein, the administration blinked away his shady past and shaky persona. An Iraqi defector named "Curveball" seemed to strengthen the case for the existence of weapons of mass destruction, and so his partisans ignored the factual errors in his story and the doubts of European intelligence services about his credibility. Vice President Cheney pressured the Central Intelligence Agency to endorse his dire conclusions. Condoleezza Rice, the national security adviser, warned of possible nuclear weapon attacks, while Secretary of State Colin Powell went before the United Nations to attest to the unquestioned worth of sources he knew to be weak and thin.

The actual invasion of Iraq produced the overwhelming victory that everyone anticipated. By May 1, 2003, the White House could stage a photo event on a carefully positioned aircraft carrier off the coast of California with Bush landing, dressed in a flight suit, and announcing success under a banner that read "Mission Accomplished." The media praised Bush's manly figure and aura of leadership.

The Republicans expected that the war would be short and the postwar period even shorter. American troops, they believed, would be greeted as liberators. More important, émigré Iraqis would form a pro-Western, pro-Israeli government that would transform the Middle East. Thus, the United States could bring its military home within a matter of months. Meanwhile, younger Republicans could gain valuable overseas experience in helping the Iraqis reboot their economy and start their democracy. Only loyal members of the party need apply. Potential candidates for positions in the American postwar administration were asked how they had voted in 2000 and where they stood on abortion.

The rosy scenario about reconstruction proved elusive as Iraq descended into political and military chaos. Worse yet, weapons of mass destruction did not surface to validate the Republican argument for war. Conservative pundits declared that such evidence was undeniable and that perhaps Saddam Hussein had moved the weapons to another country in advance of the American invasion. Eventually, with great reluctance and residual disbelief, Republicans had to concede that the main rationale for war had evaporated.

At the same time, Iraqis commenced an insurgency against the American occupation. This unwelcome development proved a political gain for Bush and the GOP as the 2004 presidential race neared. With American forces in harm's way, no Democratic candidate for the White House could make a plausible case for withdrawal. The Republican political apparatus geared up for another election that would feature spread-eagle nationalism and bashing Democrats for their innate betrayal of traditional national values.

To shore up Republican prospects on the domestic side, the Bush White House pressed Congress in late 2003 to enact changes in Medicare to cover prescription drugs. Costing $400 billion over ten years, the initiative would increase the deficit but would also resonate with senior citizens in key states such as Florida. Getting the measure through a conservative Congress required extraordinary tactics, including an almost three-hour roll call vote before the House went along, 220 to 215. The rollout of the new program encountered difficulties, but the law served Republican electoral purposes.[15]

The Democrats obliged Bush by selecting a weak ticket. John Kerry of Massachusetts was supposed to offset Republican assaults with his outstanding combat record in the Vietnam War. Kerry allowed that very aspect of his career to be assaulted by failing to respond in a timely and convincing fashion to charges that his service on US Navy Swift Boats was fraudulent. It wasn't, but the phrase "being swiftboated" became part of political lingo. As his running mate, Kerry selected John Edwards, a senator from North Carolina whose single term was ending. Edwards had been a successful trial lawyer, and seemed a handsome, charismatic vice presidential pick. Yet he did not really provide much of an electoral lift to Kerry's chances.

Kerry did well against Bush in three debates, but his success did not alter the nature of a close race. Kerry captured the 250 electoral votes that had become reliable for the Democrats but could not get over the top. Karl Rove and the Republican organization mobilized evangelicals in the key state of Ohio around opposition to gay marriage. While gay marriage would achieve greater social acceptance within a decade, in 2004 the practice evoked loathing among fearful evangelicals. Superior Republican turnout in the Buckeye State provided the twenty electoral votes necessary for Bush's ultimate victory, with 286 electoral votes to 251 for Kerry. The Republicans gained seats in the House and Senate. For the fourth consecutive election, however, the Republicans had not secured three hundred electoral votes. The president ran well among Latinos, a voting group that the Republicans would struggle to recapture after 2004. The main lesson of the campaign for Bush, however, was that he had sought and won political capital. "And now," he said, "I intend to spend it."[16]

To make a mark on the presidency that would eclipse what his father had done in a single term, George W. Bush turned to the volatile and controversial issue of Social Security. With favorable majorities in the House and

Senate, it seemed possible to address the centerpiece of the Democratic legacy and the New Deal and achieve "reform" as Republicans envisioned it. If he could dismantle the structure of the welfare state and reorient popular thinking toward what he called an opportunity society, he believed his greatness as a domestic president would equal his foreign policy triumphs after September 11.

A desire to remake Social Security was one of the few consistent policy priorities of George W. Bush's public career. When he ran for Congress in West Texas in 1978, he told an audience in Midland that "Americans should be given a chance to invest money the way they feel."[17] Coming from a family with a long history in investment banking, Bush saw the prospect of investing Social Security funds in the stock market (called "privatization") as a surefire winner for all concerned. His approach had the added appeal of reforming a program that took money from the successful to aid the improvident who could not support themselves. Since he acted from good motives, he expected the Democrats to embrace his scheme. On an even larger scale than his educational reform measure of 2001, Social Security privatization would illustrate how Bush could "transform the political and philosophical landscape of the country."[18]

To his surprise and lasting chagrin (in 2011 he was still puzzled why he failed), the president's campaign to alter Social Security flopped in the first half of 2005. Since Democrats believed the president had deceived them about Iraq and enabled the devastating criticism of their presidential candidate in 2004, they questioned Bush's credibility on a domestic topic. Moreover, for all of his infatuation with the Social Security issue, Bush never mastered the details of how the program worked or how his changes might affect the operation of the system for the average American.

In George Bush's world, the stock market always rose and his family's balance sheet always improved. He could not understand why his constituents might fear a social support system tied to the uncertain fortunes of the stock market. In the end the public did not buy what Bush was selling. He succeeded only in mobilizing the Democrats after their second presidential election defeat. The more the president talked about Social Security, the more his poll numbers dropped. By the end of the year the Bush initiative was dead.

The Social Security initiative might have worked had Bush been willing to talk substance with the Democrats and seek legislative success rather than political credit. That would have meant abandoning a hyperpartisan approach to governing. Since the ultimate end of the Bush plan was the surrender of the Democrats to a fundamental shift in one of their key social programs, the opposition, and in time the American people, deemed the Social Security plan a failure.

As the summer of 2005 wound down, Bush and the Republicans took another hit after the fiasco of their inept response to Hurricane Katrina and the damage it caused to New Orleans. The Bush administration had assumed that the federal government was a place where reliable Republicans could occupy sinecures with scant regard to the substantive requirements that the job involved. The Federal Emergency Management Agency (FEMA), which had been well administered during the Clinton years, was one such spot with a handsome salary. The appointment went first to a longtime Bush friend from Texas named Joe Allbritton and a few years later to a breeder of Arabian horses from Oklahoma named Michael Brown. Neither man kept FEMA running at operational efficiency. When Katrina happened neglect turned to disaster.

Bush's own apparent emotional detachment from the plight of the Katrina victims compounded the political fallout from the hurricane. Pictures of him with a guitar while the storm raged or staring out a plane window at damage on the ground became symbols of presidential indifference. He had appointed incompetents and had not hurried back to the capital to guide the federal disaster response. A friendly aide later recalled: "Katrina to me was the tipping point. The president broke his bond with the public. Once that bond was broken, he no longer had the capacity to talk to the American public."[19]

While George Bush and his team were grappling with the distance between their own reality and crises such as Hurricanes and Iraq, the Republican Party was developing an innovative approach to governance. One by one the unwritten and codified procedures of American democracy succumbed to the Republican aim not to achieve consensus but to impose their will on public opinion.

A leading proponent of disregarding political ground rules was Vice President Dick Cheney, who emerged as a major voice, and even, some thought, a copresident early in the administration. He was outspoken defending the proposition that the voters were entitled to one moment of accountability—when they voted for president and vice-president. Otherwise, neither press nor public should ask questions or pry into executive affairs.[20]

Cheney treated open government and full disclosure of administration procedures as intolerable burdens on the time of a busy executive. If he met with business leaders to shape an administration policy more favorable to their industry, it was nothing that the press or public needed to know. His disdain for the media knew few boundaries; he made no secret of his contempt for the reporters who disagreed with him.[21]

Wedded to the policy of invading Iraq, Cheney even bridled at good news if it might frustrate his military plans. The CIA selected a former ambassador, Joseph Wilson, to Niger to investigate reports that Hussein was attempting to buy yellowcake, a form of uranium, for his alleged nuclear program. Wilson's finding that the purported purchases had not happened weakened the case that Hussein had nuclear ambitions. Cheney disregarded the report. When Wilson went public, the vice president saw to it that Wilson's wife, Valerie Plame, was outed as an undercover CIA operative. A valuable intelligence asset was burned to demonstrate the dangers of crossing the vice president and his team.

On Capitol Hill, the Republicans played by one set of rules for themselves and another for the Democrats. The handling of judicial nominations stripped the Democrats of privileges the Republicans had insisted upon when they were in the minority. The House, under the nominal leadership of Speaker Dennis Hastert, but with Tom DeLay of Texas in actual control, brought up only legislation that commanded a majority of votes in the Republican caucus. Whatever the Democrats had done to excess in their four decades of legislative power, the Republicans emulated and transcended during their period of dominance. Meanwhile, ethical rules went unenforced. A lobbyist named Jack Abramoff hired former congressional staffers to gain influence over their legislative bosses.[22]

As the electoral balance between Republicans and Democrats tilted toward the Democrats, the Republicans recognized that demographic trends operated against their long-term interests. The black community was solid in its opposition to GOP priorities. More than 90 percent of African American voters voted Democratic in presidential contests. More worrying was the shift of Latino voters away from the Republicans. George W. Bush had been competitive among Hispanics in his Texas gubernatorial races and his two presidential contests. He knew that permanent alienation of this growing minority would doom Republicans chances in key states such as Florida, and even, over an extended time period, Texas.

The majority of Republicans did not want to vie for the votes of blacks. The programs that most African Americans wanted, such as civil rights enforcement and social welfare programs, were in direct conflict with Republican ideology. Especially in the South there was historically residual but intense reluctance to contemplate an approach that would diminish white dominance of politics and governance. With blacks and Hispanics voting in ever larger percentages relative to whites, a strategy of voter suppression based on a rationalization of voter fraud emerged as the preferred Republican response.

Republicans believed that Democrats and minorities participated in a grand conspiracy, dating back to the start of the New Deal, to pervert the electoral process with endemic fraud. As Richard Nixon said on black participation in his 1960 election defeat, it was "a bought vote, and it isn't bought by civil rights." One of his aides added, "The hell with them."[23] In 1982, Senator Christopher "Kit" Bond of Missouri told his colleagues that "a major criminal enterprise designed to defraud voters" was part of Democratic strategy. That widespread voter fraud existed was "an attitude of religious faith" for Republicans, a Texas party member said in 2007.[24]

How else could black voting preferences be explained when Republican policies were so tailored to African American ends compared to the cynical pandering of the Democrats? Republican appointments of prominent blacks to high posts—Colin Powell, Clarence Thomas, and Condoleezza Rice were the customary examples—attested to the purity of Republican motives. The alternative notion that what the Republicans proposed had little appeal to African Americans was rejected.

The difficulty with voter fraud as a rationale for measures to lower minority participation was that there was so little of it to root out. Mayor Richard M. Daley's Chicago was often cited as a notorious example of Democrats sending illegally registered voters to the polls on Election Day. Thorough probes, it was alleged, would reveal just how prevalent voter fraud was, and books were written to make the case. When reporters and legislative probes checked for specific fraud, however, the number of credible cases dwindled into insignificance.[25]

Meanwhile, the Republicans had for years practiced a number of techniques for reducing minority participation. The party sent out mass mailings to registered voters. Letters that came back as undeliverable because of an incorrect address provided an alleged basis for challenging a presumed illegal voter. Letters to voters in minority areas warned of criminal penalties if illegal voting took place. Aggressive poll watching, like that practiced by William Rehnquist in Arizona in the 1960s, was another Republican tactic. Misleading flyers urged black and Hispanic citizens not to vote at all or provided misleading information about how to vote or the precise date of the election.[26]

Despite the regular evaporation of a cause for action, Republican attorneys contended that all sorts of seemingly innocuous measures should be put in place to guard against fraud. When relaxed rules about absentee voting boosted turnout, especially among minorities, these lawyers recommended, and Republican legislatures concurred, that it should be cut back. College students who voted for Democratic candidates should be deprived of the franchise while away from home. Documentation of eligibility and residence should be made difficult to obtain and expensive for poorer voters. Southern states with their long history of ballot manipulation proved a fertile source of restrictive ideas. Election officials disclaimed any intention to discriminate but judged normality by the convenience of their white constituents. When the Voting Rights Act of 1965 blocked some of these initiatives, conservative attorneys looked to the Republican majority of the Supreme Court to eliminate that legislative protection. In 2013, the Supreme Court obliged, and southern states immediately began systematic efforts to roll back black voting.[27]

Republicans' relationship with Hispanics and immigrants mirrored their interaction with black Americans. On the one hand, the cultural values of Cuban, Mexican, and Puerto Rican newcomers to the United States seemed attuned with Republican conservatism. Many in the Republican base of white voters, however, believed that illegal immigrants deserved to be deported back to their native countries immediately. The Republicans favored strict and even militarized border security to keep unwanted immigrants out, strong efforts to compel undocumented migrants and their families to leave the United States, and measures to ensure that Hispanics, like blacks, played a minimal role in the electoral process. President Bush's attempt to enact immigration legislation failed in the face of unyielding opposition in Congress.[28]

One major asset that the Republicans enjoyed during the Bush presidency and beyond was a secure conservative majority on the United States Supreme Court. With the retirement of Justice Sandra Day O'Connor and the death of Chief Justice William H. Rehnquist, the Bush administration earned the chance to put its stamp on the high court. Chief Justice John Roberts and Justice Samuel Alito gained Senate confirmation when both men emphasized their deference to precedent and a limited view of their judicial role. "My job is to call balls and strikes and not to pitch or bat," Roberts told the lawmakers.[29]

Once seated, however, the two justices helped create a majority that limited the power of lawmakers to regulate campaign finance and invalidated the section of the Voting Rights Act of 1965 that called for enhanced scrutiny of elections in places with a history of voter discrimination. The justices also were disposed to uphold restrictions on abortion rights that came from the states. Only in the case of the Affordable Care Act and its constitutionality did Roberts decide to uphold the legislation in 2013, much to the disgust of Republican conservatives. For the most part, whatever their varying fortunes with the presidency and Congress, the Grand Old Party had a decisive check in the high court on the expansion of government power over the economy and cultural issues.

By 2006, both the Bush presidency and the Republican Party were in trouble. The conflict in Iraq seemed stalemated, with a grim tally of American casualties each month. At home the Democrats expressed optimism about retaking the House of Representatives from the GOP. The Senate seemed possible but likely out of reach. With the presidential campaign two years away, the consensus was that Hillary Clinton, now a senator from New York, was the likely nominee. There was some buzz about a first-term senator from Illinois, Barack Obama. Among the Republicans, Senator John McCain of Arizona seemed to have the edge over retiring Massachusetts governor Willard Mitt Romney.

The political tide ran against the Republicans in 2006. In Congress, a flurry of scandals within the House Republican ranks intensified the anti-Republican mood. As a result, the Democrats gained a decided victory. They picked up thirty-one seats in the House to return to majority status and installed Nancy Pelosi of California as the first woman Speaker. The opposition also did the improbable and won six Senate seats from the Republicans to establish a narrow 51–49 majority. Harry Reid of Nevada became the new majority leader.

In the aftermath of the voting, Bush dumped Secretary of Defense Donald Rumsfeld, the architect of the military result in Iraq. To stabilize the situation in that country, Bush proposed a "surge" of additional American troops. That policy, along with a dose of realism about what could be accomplished in Iraq, kept the American presence at a sustainable level through the 2008 presidential election. The ambition goal of a democratic, secular, pro-Western Iraq seemed part of a vanishing past.[30]

In the Republican tradition of having a clear line of succession from one presidential race to another, John McCain seemed the putative GOP nominee. His "maverick" tendencies of 2000, including support for campaign finance reform, were now only a memory. He had been a loyal foot soldier for the Bush agenda after 2004 and had embraced the hard-line conservative tactics that had defeated him in 2000. His timely conversion to party orthodoxy, while it did not convince everyone on the right, was enough, in a weak Republican field, to secure for McCain the nomination he had so long coveted.[31]

McCain then made one of the most controversial vice presidential selections in the party's history. His first choice was Senator Joseph Lieberman of Connecticut, a conservative Democrat alienated from his party over the Iraq war and his failure to secure the Democratic nomination in 2004. The Republican base would not accept Lieberman and threatened McCain with a floor fight the nominee would probably lose. McCain gave in.

John McCain won the Republican nomination in 2008; here he is greeted by the cheers of the delegates at the National Convention as he gives his acceptance speech. Library of Congress, LC-DIG-highsm-03808.

The party turned instead to Governor Sarah Palin of Alaska. Forty-four years old, Palin had been elected to the governorship two years earlier following stints as mayor of Wasilla, Alaska, and chair of the state's Oil and Gas Conservation Commission. Attractive and telegenic, Palin received the enthusiastic endorsement for second place on the GOP ticket from such pundits as William Kristol of the conservative *Weekly Standard*. Kristol had met her while on a conservative cruise to Alaska. Calling her "my heartthrob," he became her most enthusiastic backer. Another Republican said she was "a former beauty-pageant contestant and a real honey too." As the first female vice presidential candidate for the Grand Old Party, she would appeal to women. Moreover, Kristol suggested, Palin would bring the fresh ideas of a political outsider and an uncompromising conservatism to the Republican campaign.[32]

Once nominated, Palin did not live up to her advance billing. Her television appearances revealed no particular interest on her part in complex policy issues. Displaying talents more typical of a grifter than a guru, she dazzled Republican audiences in the fall of 2008. The political establishment wondered what had been going on in McCain's mind with her selection. In electoral terms, she added nothing to the ticket, since the Republicans were sure to carry Alaska against the Democrats.[33]

The Republican platform in 2008 spoke of many familiar issues—lowering taxes, rooting out voter fraud, reducing the size of government. In one controversial area, however, it offered language that would soon disappear from the party's official rhetoric. Speaking of global climate change, Republicans said that "the same human activity that has brought freedom and opportunity to billions has also increased the amount of carbon in the atmosphere." These words reflected John McCain's recognition at that time that climate change was a reality and a growing threat to humanity. At the same time, the platform writers hedged their language with a warning against "the doomsday climate change scenarios peddled by the aficionados of centralized command-and-control government."[34]

Within five years, such a recognition of climate change could no longer appear in the thinking of Republican policymakers. Mainstream Republicans believed that the earth had not warmed for the past decade and a half, that Democratic fears were a hoax, and that the warnings of imminent catastrophe if carbon in the atmosphere were not reduced were a fraud. Congressional hearings and statements of Republican pundits reinforced this position. By 2013, the Grand Old Party had made a historic wager regarding its beliefs about the future of the human species.[35]

To the surprise of political pundits who gave Senator Hillary Clinton the edge over Barack Obama in the race for the Democratic nomination, the Illinois senator displayed superior organization skills and a deft campaign style, ultimately garnering the nomination. Senator Joseph Biden of Delaware became his running mate. Democratic primary voters invested Obama in their minds with transformative qualities. His celebrated speech to the 2004 Democratic convention, for example, even though it could also have been given by George Bush, seemed to the senator's admirers a harbinger of change after eight years of Republican dominance.

Among Republicans, Obama's nomination produced a visceral negative reaction that shaped the next several years of American politics. The Grand Old Party had fulminated over the foibles, lapses, and excesses of Bill Clinton in the 1990s. That response was calm compared to the distemper that greeted Obama's emergence as a possible president. Some of the protesting harked back to currents of antiblack feeling, rooted in the Old South in the nineteenth century, that simply looked with horror at the prospect of a black man in the Oval Office.

In the world of political blogs, the right-wing response evoked echoes of the Democratic presidential campaign of 1868. Adding to the frenzy were the fears that Obama's Muslim first name stirred in a nation traumatized by September 11 and prone to regard all Muslims as potential terrorists.

The pathology had several elements. Obama's name, reflecting the Kenyan and Muslim background of his father, convinced many Americans that he must be a stealth terrorist who deserved the death penalty. Crowds at McCain rallies shouted, "Off with his head." Obama's membership in a black Christian church in Chicago did not deter Republican skepticism about his true faith and allegiance. When critics questioned the opinions of his pastor, Jeremiah Wright, for their alleged anti-American sentiments, Obama was doubly accused of being a radical Muslim and a radical deviant from Christian orthodoxy.[36]

The most virulent charge against Obama within the Republican Party turned on whether he met the constitutional requirement of being "a natural born citizen," which was necessary in order to be eligible to run for president and to serve in office. He was born in Hawaii in 1961, as his birth certificate said. Contemporary birth notices, placed in newspapers by a state agency, supported the conclusion that his birth had occurred in the United States. For those who questioned Obama's credentials, these documents were not enough. Doubters asserted that the birth certificate was not original. Hawaii had, like many other states, computerized all of its birth records. The short form "Certification of Live Birth" was the one that was digitized. Therefore, doubters were convinced that the long form "Certificate of Live Birth, "once released, would reveal that he was not a native-born American. As for the newspaper notices of the birth, the critics asserted that they had been planted by Obama conspirators in 1961 or inserted later to forge a credible paper trail. How the participants in this plot would have known in 1961 in what manner history would unfold over the next five decades was left to the conspiratorial imagination.[37]

Even if they failed to demonstrate that Obama was not a natural-born citizen within the meaning of the Constitution and the Fourteenth Amendment, Republicans saw in Obama's candidacy and election further proof of the essential lack of legitimacy among Democrats. Any victory for the opposition was in the minds of rank-and-file Republicans evidence of underlying fraud. The logical conclusion for Republicans to draw was that Democratic voter fraud had once again kicked in at peak efficiency for Obama. Minority votes had been bought or manipulated. White voters had been intimidated or stayed home in discouragement as the media fawned over a black presidential candidate.[38]

The 2008 election started out in Obama's favor, but the McCain-Palin ticket gained some ground in August. Some surveys put McCain in the lead with his post-convention bounce. At that point the most serious financial crisis since the Great Depression had engulfed the nation. The real prospect of the collapse of the world economy loomed as the financial system tottered and some markets buckled. The causes of what became known as the Great Recession were complex and are still being debated as the nation suffers through a prolonged slowdown. A housing boom that faltered; a banking system with unethical, sleazy, and sometimes criminal lending practices; speculative excesses; and the stripping away of regulatory legislation such as the Glass-Steagall Act of 1933 all contributed to the confluence of events that brought near disaster in 2008.[39]

The highly publicized failure of the banking firm of Lehman Brothers in 2008 sent a ripple effect through the economy that endangered the stability of the entire system. The atmosphere of crisis offered a chance for both presidential candidates to demonstrate their political skills and leadership qualities. For the Republicans, Senator McCain made a high-stakes gamble. He suspended his campaign and flew back to Washington in an effort to achieve a deal to address the financial situation. In the process he would show an ability to put his country ahead of political considerations.

The meeting at the White House on September 25 could not have gone worse for the Republican hopeful. The Democrats selected Senator Obama to make their case, and he did so with an authority that impressed Republicans in the meeting. McCain was not prepared with specific answers, added little to the discussion, and came out seeming to have failed to offer timely solutions to the crisis. He had no useful ideas to secure congressional action on a bailout plan and, indeed, only a modest comprehension of the issues at stake. McCain had raised expectations and then fallen well short of them.[40]

The polls turned in favor of Obama and the Democrats during the last month of the campaign. Palin's adventures as a running mate drew intense media attention, none of which helped the Republican ticket. The three debates saw Obama as the clear winner of the first encounter, and McCain's candidacy never recovered. When General Colin Powell endorsed Obama on October 19, it was a knockout blow to McCain's remaining chances.

It did not take long to call the winner on election night, as such traditionally Republican states as Indiana fell into the Democratic column early in the network coverage of the results. Obama secured 365 electoral votes to 173 for McCain. The Democrats picked up eight Senate seats to near the sixty seat mark that would enable them to withstand a Republican filibuster. In the House, the Democrats added twenty-one seats to lift their total to 257 seats. The new president, if ordinary political calculations operated, would have a reasonable chance to enact his priorities.

It was not to be. The Republicans conceded that Obama had been elected, but on the question of legitimacy their reservations persisted. Their congressional leaders declined to extend any customary political courtesies to the new Democratic president. Senate Minority Leader Mitch McConnell did not say until 2010 that his primary goal was to make Obama a one-term president, but that strategy was clear from the early days of the new administration. Using tactics that they would have denounced as unpatriotic had they been applied to a Republican chief executive, the opposition resolved to filibuster presidential nominations, require major legislation to meet the filibuster-proof sixty-vote threshold to achieve passage, and stymie efforts at cooperation with the White House as much as possible. As a former Republican staffer on Capitol Hill put it, the country now had "war minus the shooting."[41]

At the start of the decade that began in 2001, Republicans had credible claims that they were a party of mature adults who could govern the United States with an effectiveness and authority the Democrats could not match. Bush promised "a spirit of cooperation" once it was clear he had prevailed in 2000.[42] Eight years later they had on their record a devastating surprise terrorist attack, an unpopular war, a blundering response to a natural disaster, and governmental policies that had led to a near collapse of the national economy. An election defeat then followed.

The Republicans concluded that more of the same was the answer to Obama's election. Their opposition deserved no respect and no cooperation. All-out resistance to an illegitimate president and a traitorous party was the correct response to the mistake the voters had made. In a stance of unyielding negativity to the administration of the first black president, the Republicans turned to face the new alignment of national politics on January 20, 2009.

Conclusion

THE REPUBLICAN PARTY
AND ITS FUTURE

IN THE FIVE years after the inauguration of Barack Obama as President of the United States, the Republican Party devoted its formidable energies first to preventing his reelection in 2012. When that failed, the Grand Old Party sought to transform the routine procedures of democracy into extraconstitutional means of accomplishing his defeat and even ouster from office. As the revolutionary aims of the Republicans became clear, the nation faced a fundamental crisis about the future conduct of the political system.

The Republicans accomplished some elements of their obstructive agenda in 2009–2010. Pretending to cooperate with a Democratic president who believed his own rhetoric about working with the opposing party, they delayed action on what became the Affordable Care Act until that measure had gained such unpopularity that it became a debilitating electoral burden for the Democrats in 2010. The GOP also limited the effectiveness of Obama's stimulus package to get the economy rebounding while indicting him for failing to turn the economy around.

In 2010, the Republicans took back the House in a campaign that featured intense attacks on the Democratic administration for proposed cuts in Medicare funding arising from the Affordable Care Act. Embracing a program that they hated and intended to destroy, the Republicans targeted seniors with advertising that warned of coverage to be lost and deaths to come because of Democratic faithlessness to Medicare. The GOP did this while simultaneously relying on these same Medicare savings to produce their proposed budget reductions. They managed the improbable pose of seeming to be both for and against elements of the Affordable Care Act at the same time.

This political shift, coupled with Democratic voters staying home in 2010, put the Republicans back in control of the House and reduced Democratic power in the Senate. The new faction of the Republicans, known as the Tea

Party in homage to the American Revolution, intensified obstruction of the Democratic administration in preparation for the presidential election of 2012. Convinced that Obama was weak, illegitimate, and doomed to be deposed, the House Republicans displayed little interest in governance with their numerous votes to repeal the Affordable Care Act. They did so knowing that the Senate would not concur and, even if they did, a presidential veto would be sustained. Political theater filled up many a congressional day.

With the economy still in crisis and the president's poll ratings anemic, the Republicans thought that victory in 2012 was almost assured. They then proceeded to run a campaign that revealed their weaknesses and misapplied their strengths. They nominated Mitt Romney, who had ample financial resources for his campaign but never found a winning strategy. Although reputable polls forecast an Obama victory, Republicans persuaded themselves that Romney was heading for a decisive triumph. When he lost, members of his party once again concluded that the Democrats had purchased votes, concocted voter fraud schemes, and stolen an election that the Republicans should have won.[1]

In the wake of their defeat, the Grand Old Party contemplated for a few weeks reexamining their program, approach to the electorate, and overall strategy. That inward look soon gave way to a renewed confidence that an even more intense embrace of conservative thinking would remedy the party's ills. By the autumn of 2013, the House had shut down the government and threatened to use a vote to increase the nation's debt limit as leverage to achieve massive cuts in spending. Even after the shutdown failed, the GOP still planned to use the debt ceiling issue to extract spending cuts.[2]

For Republicans, scorched earth seemed the appropriate response to the presence of a pretender in the White House who pursued the collapse of the American republic. There no longer existed between Republicans and Democrats a rough consensus about the purpose of the United States. The rank and file of the Republican Party believed that Barack Obama was illegitimate and evil; that the fabric of society was being torn apart by gays, blacks, Hispanics, and liberals; and that meeting these threats by any means available was the urgent duty of all true patriots. In this worldview, global warming was a hoax, evolution was against God's will, government menaced freedom, and liberals and Democrats were instruments of evil. Reconciliation of these assumptions with the contrasting views of Democrats and independents seemed unlikely.[3]

How had it come to this? A long review of both political parties suggests that the experience of the Civil War introduced a flaw into American democracy that was never resolved or reconciled. The Republicans regarded the wartime flirtation of some Democrats with the Confederacy as evidence of treason. So it may have been at that time. What rendered that conclusion toxic was the perpetuation of the idea of Democratic illegitimacy and betrayal long after Appomattox. The theory ebbed and flowed with the unfolding of history, but it comes alive when circumstances warrant.

After the long years in the wilderness during the New Deal, the Republicans reasserted their dominance, with some Democratic interruptions, from 1952 to 2008. Had Kennedy not stolen the 1960 election from Nixon, Lyndon Johnson not lied about Barry Goldwater, Gerald Ford not lost to Jimmy Carter, and Ross Perot not enabled Bill Clinton to sneak into office, there might have been fifty-six years of uninterrupted Republican rule. Republicans thus saw in the ascendancy of Ronald Reagan and the two Bushes a return to the proper alignment of politics. Republicans were destined to be in charge and Democrats to occupy a position of perennial deference.

Then in 2008 the unthinkable occurred. Not just a Democrat but a black man won the White House. The southern-based Republican Party saw its worst fears coming true. Abraham Lincoln had been derided as a "black Republican," a Confederate parody of the truth. Now the black Democrat really was black, and with a foreign-sounding name, an equivocal religious background, and what the Republican rank and file presumed to be the most sinister goals. Under his administration, blacks became assertive, gays married, the poor got health care, and the wealthy faced both a lack of due respect and a claim on their income.

In this era of traditional values being shattered, the Republican allegiance to democratic practices wavered and then collapsed. Richard Nixon had viewed politics as war, and now his party saw the truth of his insight. Americans could not have really elected Barack Obama and put his party in control of the destiny of the nation. Such an outcome must be illegitimate. And what is the remedy for illegitimacy, treason, and godlessness? How the Republican Party answers that question over the coming decades will reveal whether the Republican conviction about Democratic illegitimacy, introduced into the American bloodstream so long ago, proves fatal to what Abraham Lincoln once called "the last best hope of earth."

Acknowledgments

I OWE THANKS to a number of people who helped me prepare this revised version of my treatment of the Republican Party and its history. Two old friends, Clarence Lasby and R. Hal Williams, listened to conversations about the nature of the Grand Old Party and stimulated my analysis of its history. The late Thomas K. McCraw was always a source of insightful comments as we exchanged email messages about the nature of American politics. Through her kindness and insights, and her valuable research assistance, Kristie Miller helped me better understand the role of Mark Hanna and the family of Theodore Roosevelt in the story of the Republicans. Heather Merrill was of great assistance in securing information about key Republicans in Massachusetts, and Hope Grebner performed with similar efficiency in providing information on party members in the Middle West.

Libby Miller Fitzgerald assisted me in achieving a fair judgment about the political career of her father, William Miller. John Rothmann and his colleagues enlightened me about the life and times of Harold Stassen.

While working on this book, personal circumstances caused me to relocate from Austin, Texas, to Monmouth, Illinois. Enabling me to make the transition and still engage with research and writing were such valued Austin friends as Emmett Sutton III, Ron Yam, Carl Brockman, Mary Robbins, Joy Sotille, and Elizabeth Sylvester. In Monmouth I owe a special debt to Glenn Brooks, Alan and Peggy Kulczewski, Mary Phillips, Rick Sayre, and Tom and Anne Sienkewicz. Mary Lou Pease assisted me with the obligations and challenges of daily living with great kindness and impressive energy. All these individuals rendered crucial personal assistance and should not be held responsible for any of the arguments or conclusions in the book itself.

My biggest obligation in Monmouth, however, extends to Stacy, Simon, and Gareth Cordery, who at a moment of intense personal grief on my part gave with great generosity and thoughtfulness of their time and energy to direct my life into new paths. This book would not exist without their affection and understanding.

This was far from an easy book for Susan Ferber of Oxford University Press to edit. She persevered through numerous distractions and outright obstacles to see it into a finished form. Her constructive influence is evident on every page.

I dedicated the first edition of my history of the Republicans to an old friend, Herbert F. Margulies of the University of Hawaii. The passage of a decade has only emphasized how much thirty years of correspondence with Herb about such figures as Irvine Lenroot and Robert M. La Follette shaped the way I thought about Republicans in general.

Karen Gould listened to me talk about Republicans for forty-one and a half years. I miss her every day.

Writing about American politics and especially about Republicans has become a contact sport in the world of blogs and social media. Therefore it is necessary to stress once again that I am responsible for any errors of fact or interpretation in this book. All of the opinions expressed are mine alone, and no one who helped me should be deemed to have shared the conclusions or judgments that I have reached.

Lewis L. Gould

Monmouth, Illinois
February 2014

Notes

INTRODUCTION

1. Republican National Committee, *Republican Campaign Text-Book 1920* (New York, 1920), 19.
2. Joe Scarborough, *The Right Path: From Ike to Reagan, How Republicans Once Mastered Politics-and Can Again* (New York, 2013), 10–11.

CHAPTER I. THE PARTY OF LINCOLN, 1854–1865

1. Benjamin P. Thomas, *Abraham Lincoln* (New York, 1952), 212.
2. William E. Gienapp, *The Origins of the Republican Party* (New York, 1983), 103.
3. Lewis L. Gould, *Alexander Watkins Terrell: Civil War Soldier, Texas Lawmaker, American Diplomat* (Austin, 2004), 29.
4. Gienapp, *Origins of the Republican Party*, 5, 6.
5. Democratic Party Platform of 1852, available online at the American Presidency Project, http://www.presidency.ucsb.edu/ws/?pid=29575.
6. Henry Steele Commager, ed., *Documents of American History* (Englewood Cliffs, N.J., 1973), 1:321.
7. Commager, *Documents of American History*, 1:332.
8. Gienapp, *Origins of the Republican Party*, 104–5.
9. Michael P. Johnson, ed., *Abraham Lincoln, Slavery and the Civil War: Selected Writings and Speeches* (Boston, 2001), 46, 49. This good brief introduction to Lincoln's political thought contains many of his key speeches and letters. For Lincoln's own writings in detail, see Roy P. Basler, ed., *The Collected Works of Abraham Lincoln*, 9 vols. (New Brunswick, N.J., 1953–1955).
10. Michael F. Holt, *The Political Crisis of the 1850s* (New York, 1978), 159.
11. Gienapp, *Origins of the Republican Party*, 95.

12. Gienapp, *Origins of the Republican Party*, 302.

13. Republican Party Platform of 1856, available online at the American Presidency Project, http://www.presidency.ucsb.edu/ws/?pid=29619; Beryl Frank, *Pictorial History of the Republican Party* (Secaucus, N.J., 1980), 14.

14. Richard H. Sewell, *Ballots for Freedom: Antislavery Politics in the United States, 1837–1860* (New York, 1976), 291.

15. Eric Foner, *Free Soil, Free Labor, Free Men: The Ideology of the Republican Party Before the Civil War* (New York, 1970), 266, 269; Johnson, *Abraham Lincoln*, 291.

16. Gienapp, *Origins of the Republican Party*, 359.

17. Don E. Fehrenbacher, *Prelude to Greatness: Lincoln in the 1850s* (Stanford, Calif., 1962), 106. Fehrenbacher's book remains one of the essential volumes for understanding Lincoln and his ties to the Republican Party.

18. Johnson, *Abraham Lincoln*, 90.

19. David Donald, *Lincoln* (New York, 1995), 165–67, deals with Lincoln's attitude toward colonization. Fehrenbacher, *Prelude to Greatness*, 74.

20. Fehrenbacher, *Prelude to Greatness*, 74.

21. Johnson, *Abraham Lincoln*, 72.

22. Republican Party Platform of 1860, available online at the American Presidency Project, http://www.presidency.ucsb.edu/ws/?pid=29620.

23. William Frank Zornow, *Lincoln and the Party Divided* (Norman, Okla., 1954), 153.

24. Zornow, *Lincoln and the Party Divided*, 161. Mark E. Neely, *The Union Divided: Party Conflict in the Civil War* (Cambridge, Mass., 2002), 158–72, discusses the Republican belief in the treasonous character of the Democrats in 1864.

25. Heather Cox Richardson, *The Greatest Nation on Earth: Republican Economic Policies during the Civil War* (Cambridge, Mass., 1997), 87, quotes Sherman. Richardson's book is crucial for understanding the governing philosophy of the Republicans in this period.

26. Richardson, *Greatest Nation on Earth*, 54.

27. Richardson, *Greatest Nation on Earth*, 101.

28. Richardson, *Greatest Nation on Earth*, 129.

29. Richardson, *Greatest Nation on Earth*, 143.

30. Johnson, *Abraham Lincoln*, 263.

CHAPTER 2. THE REPUBLICANS AND RECONSTRUCTION, 1865–1877

1. George Ticknor, quoted in Morton Keller, *Affairs of State: Public Life in Late Nineteenth Century America* (Cambridge, Mass., 1977), 9. 2.

2. Michael P. Johnson, ed., *Abraham Lincoln, Slavery, and the Civil War: Selected Writings and Speeches* (Boston, 2001), 332.

3. An important introduction to Andrew Johnson's life isEric L. McKitrick, *Andrew Johnson and Reconstruction* (Chicago, 1960).

4. Brooks Simpson, *The Reconstruction Presidents* (Lawrence, Kans., 1998), 76.

5. *Texas Republican* (Marshall, Tex.), June 30, 1865.

6. *New York Times*, August 17, 1865, quoted in Michael Les Benedict, *A Compromise of Principle: Congressional Republicans and Reconstruction, 1863–1869* (New York, 1973), 122.

7. Keller, *Affairs of State*, 65.

8. Edward L. Ayers, Lewis L. Gould, David M. Oshinsky, and Jean R. Soderlund, *American Passages: Brief Fourth Edition* (Boston, 2012), A-8.

9. Albert Castel, *The Presidency of Andrew Johnson* (Lawrence, Kans., 1979), 91.

10. Brooks Simpson, *The Reconstruction Presidents*, 112.

11. Jean Edward Smith, *Grant* (New York, 2001), 456.

12. Eric Foner, *Reconstruction: America's Unfinished Revolution, 1865–1877* (New York, 1988), 313, 316.

13. Joel H. Sibley, *A Respectable Minority: The Democratic Party in the Civil War Era* (New York, 1977), 199.

14. Democratic Party Platform of 1868, July 4, 1868, available online at the *American Presidency Project*, http://www.presidency.ucsb.edu/ws/index.php?pid=29579; Sibley, *A Respectable Minority*, 209.

15. Republican Party Platform of 1868 available online at the American Presidency Project, http://www.Presidency,ucsb.edu/ws/print.php?pid-29579.

16. William Dudley Foulke, *Life of Oliver P. Morton, Including His Important Speeches* (Indianapolis, 1899), 2:174–75.

17. *New York Tribune*, November 4, 1868.

18. Roger Alan Cohen, "The Lost Jubilee: New York Republicans and the Politics of Reconstruction and Reform, 1867–1878" (Ph.D. diss., Columbia University, 1970), 35.

19. David M. Jordan, *Roscoe Conkling of New York: Voice in the Senate* (Ithaca, N.Y., 1971), 80, gives Blaine's remark.

20. Foner, *Reconstruction*, p.449.

21. Foner, *Reconstruction*, 427; Smith, *Grant*, 545.

22. Foner, *Reconstruction*, 455; Charles W. Calhoun, *Conceiving a New Republic: The Republican Party and the Southern Question, 1869–1900* (Lawrence, Kans., 2006), 28.

23. Foner, *Reconstruction*, 458.

24. "The Cincinnati Convention," *The Nation*, March 21, 1872, 181.

25. Foner, *Reconstruction*, 503.

26. Smith, *Grant*, 550.

27. Keller, *Affairs of State*, 189.

28. Democratic Party Platform of 1876, available online at the American Presidency Project, http://www.presidency.ucsb.edu/ws/?pid=29581.

29. Jordan, *Roscoe Conkling*, 240.

30. Republican Party Platform of 1876, available online at the American Presidency Project, http://www.presidency.ucsb.edu/ws/?pid=29624 .

31. Donald A. Ritchie, "1876," in Arthur M. Schlesinger, Jr., ed., *Running for President: The Candidates and Their Images* (New York, 1994), 1:328; Michael E. McGerr, *The Decline of Popular Politics: The American North, 1865–1928* (New York, 1986), 27.

32. Cohen, "The Lost Jubilee," 669. The disputed election of 1876 has produced a large literature on how the sectional bargain was reached to settle the contest. The key works are C. Vann Woodward, *Reunion and Reaction: The Compromise of 1877 and the End of Reconstruction* (Garden City, N.Y., 1951), and Keith Ian Polakoff, *The Politics of Inertia: The Election of 1876 and the End of Reconstruction* (Baton Rouge, La., 1975). Michael F. Holt, *By One Vote: The Disputed Presidential Election of 1876* (Lawrence, Kans., 2011) is a good modern synthesis on the topic.

33. Foner, *Reconstruction*, 574.

34. Calhoun, *Conceiving a New Republic*, 123.

CHAPTER 3. REPUBLICANS IN THE GILDED AGE, 1877–1893

1. The turbulence of the 1884 presidential election is well captured in Mark Wahlgren Summers, *Rum, Romanism and Rebellion: The Making of a President, 1884* (Chapel Hill, N.C., 2000), xi. H. Wayne Morgan, *From Hayes to McKinley: National Party Politics, 1877–1896* (Syracuse, N.Y., 1969), 215 (first quotation).

2. James Bryce, *The American Commonwealth*, 3rd ed. (New York, 1909), 2:21.

3. Herbert Croly, *Progressive Democracy* (New York, 1915), 87.

4. Thomas Richard Ross, *Jonathan Prentiss Dolliver: A Study in Political Integrity and Independence* (Iowa City, 1958), 59.

5. *New York Tribune*, October 25, 1890.

6. Samuel J. Tilden, quoted in R. Hal Williams, "'Dry Bones and Dead Language': The Democratic Party," in H. Wayne Morgan, ed., *The Gilded Age*, rev. ed. (Syracuse, N.Y., 1970), 134; H. Wayne Morgan, *From Hayes to McKinley: National Party Politics, 1877–1896* (Syracuse, N.Y., 1969), 35.

7. Julia B. Foraker, *I Would Live It Again* (New York, 1932), 140; Brand Whitlock, *Forty Years of It* (New York, 1914), 27.

8. John S. Gilbert to "Cousin Samuel," November 21, 1884, author's collection.

9. Edward McPherson, *A Hand-Book of Politics for 1876* (Washington, D.C., 1876), 230–31.

10. *New York Tribune*, July 6, 1882, quoted in Summers, *Rum, Romanism, and Rebellion*, 108.

11. George Frisbie Hoar, "Are the Republicans In to Stay?" *North American Review* 149 (1889): 621.

12. Charles W. Calhoun, *From Bloody Shirt to Full Dinner Pail: The Transformation of Politics and Governance in the Gilded Age* (New York, 2010) is the best brief look at the tariff issue in the context of the political life of this period. For the quotation, see Henry L. West, "The Present Session of Congress," *The Forum*, 32 (December 1901): 428.

13. William McKinley, *Speeches and Addresses of William McKinley* (New York, 1893), 229.

14. McKinley, *Speeches and Addresses*, 194.

15. The *New York Tribune*, June 15, 1899, quotes sugar magnate H. O. Havemeyer as saying, "The mother of all trusts is the customs tariff bill."

16. Thomas Wolfe, *From Death to Mourning* (New York, 1953), 121.

17. The standard biography of Blaine is David S. Muzzey, *James G. Blaine: A Political Idol of Other Days* (New York, 1934). A more modern study of Blaine is very much needed.

18. James G. Blaine, *Twenty Years of Congress* (Norwich, Conn., 1884), 2:160.

19. The letter that contains the famous words "Burn this letter" is from Blaine to Warren Fisher, April 16, 1876, Autograph File, Houghton Library, Harvard University. I am indebted to R. Hal Williams for this reference.

20. Morton Keller, *Affairs of State: Public Life in Late Nineteenth-Century America* (Cambridge, Mass., 1977), 267.

21. Matthew Josephson, *The Politicos* (New York, 1938), 336.

22. Morgan, *From Hayes to McKinley*, 226.

23. Muzzey, *James G. Blaine*, 367.

24. Charles W. Calhoun, *Benjamin Harrison* (New York, 2005), is an intelligent, brief, well-informed study of Harrison.

25. *Tariff Texts of James G Blaine and Others* (New York, 1888) is a sample of Republican campaign literature.

26. Morgan, *From Hayes to McKinley*, 334; R. Hal Williams, *Years of Decision: American Politics in the 1890s* (Prospect Heights, Ill., 1993), 22.

27. Thomas B. Reed, "Rules of the House of Representatives," *Century Magazine*, March 1889, 795.

28. Williams, *Years of Decision*, 31.

29. Williams, *Years of Decision*, 45.

30. Morgan, *From Hayes to McKinley*, 383.

31. Morgan, *From Hayes to McKinley*, 355.

32. Williams, *Years of Decision*, 53.

33. Woodrow Wilson, "Mr. Cleveland's Cabinet," *American Monthly Review of Reviews* 7 (August 1893): 289.

CHAPTER 4. MCKINLEY TO ROOSEVELT, 1893–1904

1. Margaret Leech, *In the Days of McKinley* (New York, 1959), 93. Canton during the 1896 election is described in Edward Thornton Heald, *The William McKinley Story* (Canton, Ohio, 1964), 72–81.

2. Samuel T. McSeveney, *The Politics of Depression: Political Behavior in the Northeast, 1893–1896* (New York, 1972), 88; H. Wayne Morgan, *From Hayes to McKinley: National Party Politics, 1877–1896* (Syracuse, N.Y., 1969), 445.

3. Nelson Dingley, Jr., *The Democratic Tariff Outcome: A Most Instructive Speech by Hon. Nelson Dingley, Jr., of Maine, Delivered in the House of Representatives, August13, 1894* (Boston, 1896), 15.

4. Theodore Roosevelt to Henry Cabot Lodge, September 2, 1894, in Elting E. Morison, ed., *The Letters of Theodore Roosevelt*, vol. 1 (Cambridge, Mass., 1951), 398; Morgan, *From Hayes to McKinley*, 477.

5. William A. Robinson, *Thomas B. Reed, Parliamentarian* (New York, 1930), 321.

6. On the significance of the 1894 elections, see Richard J. Jensen, *The Winning of the Midwest: Social and Political Conflict, 1888–1896* (Chicago, 1971), 306; Charles W. Calhoun, *From Bloody Shirt to Full Dinner Pail: The Transformation of Politics and Governance in the Gilded Age* (New York, 2010), 153–55.

7. H. Wayne Morgan, *William McKinley and His America* (Kent, Ohio, 2003), is an updated version of a biography originally published in 1963.

8. Francis E. Warren to Henry L. West, April 4, 1896, Francis E. Warren Papers, American Heritage Center, University of Wyoming, Laramie.

9. These quotations appear in Lewis L. Gould, *The Presidency of William McKinley* (Lawrence, Kans., 1980), 10, 242.

10. R. Hal Williams, *Realigning America: McKinley, Bryan and the Remarkable Election of 1896* (Lawrence, Kans., 2010), 61.

11. Louis W. Koenig, *Bryan: A Political Biography of William Jennings Bryan* (New York, 1971), 197.

12. Williams, *Realigning America*, 136–39, has an excellent discussion of the role of money in the Republican campaign.

13. Jensen, *Winning of the Midwest*, 288.

14. Roosevelt to Cecil Spring Rice, October 8, 1896, in Morison, *Letters of Theodore Roosevelt*, 1:562.

15. Gould, *Presidency of William McKinley*, 78–90.

16. Gould, *Presidency of William McKinley*, 104, 130–31.

17. William McKinley, *Speeches and Addresses of William McKinley from March 1, 1897, to May 30, 1900* (New York, 1900), 84–156, provide a record of what the president said.

18. McKinley, *Speeches and Addresses*, 98.

19. Lewis L. Gould, *The Spanish-American War and President McKinley* (Lawrence, Kans., 1982, 1999), 112–14.

20. William R. Day to McKinley, November 18, 1899, William McKinley Papers, Manuscript Division, Library of Congress.

21. "Negroes Blame the President," *New York Tribune*, May 11, 1899.

22. Charles W. Calhoun, *Conceiving a New Republic: The Republican Party and the Southern Question, 1869–1900* (Lawrence, Kans., 2006), 282–84.

23. Andrew Van Bibber to Mark Hanna, April 6, 1899, McKinley Papers; Hanna to William E. Chandler, March 25, 1899, William E. Chandler Papers, Manuscript Division, Library of Congress.

24. Henry L. West, "The Republican and Democratic Platforms Compared," *The Forum* 30 (1900): 93.

25. For brief introductions to Roosevelt's life and times, see John Morton Blum, *The Republican Roosevelt* (Cambridge, Mass., 1954) and Lewis L. Gould, *Theodore Roosevelt* (New York, 2012).

26. *Taft and Roosevelt: The Intimate Letters of Archie Butt, Military Aid* (Garden City, N.Y., 1930), 2:441.

27. Lewis L. Gould, ed., "Charles Warren Fairbanks and the Republican National Convention of 1900: A Memoir," *Indiana Magazine of History* 77 (1981): 368; Leech, *In the Days of McKinley*, 357; Albert Shaw to W. T. Stead, June 25, 1900, Albert Shaw Papers, New York Public Library, Astor, Lenox, and Tilden Foundations.

28. Charles S. Olcott, *Life of William McKinley* (Boston, 1916), 2:296.

29. Gould, *Presidency of William McKinley*, 251.

30. Theodore Roosevelt, *Theodore Roosevelt: An Autobiography*, The Works of Theodore Roosevelt 20 (New York, 1926), 417.

31. Lyman Abbott, "A Review of President Roosevelt's Administration: Its Influence on Patriotism and Public Service," *Outlook*, February 27, 1909, 430.

32. Joseph Bucklin Bishop, *Theodore Roosevelt and His Time Shown in His Own Letters* (New York, 1920), 1:184–85.

33. John J. Jenkins to Theodore Roosevelt, October 6, 1902, Theodore Roosevelt Papers, Manuscript Division, Library of Congress. The Theodore Roosevelt Center at Dickinson State University in North Dakota is digitizing the Theodore Roosevelt Papers, and this letter, along with thousands of letters that the president wrote, is now available online for everyone to read at http://www.theodorerooseveltcenter.org/Research/Digital-Library.aspx.

34. Marcus A. Hanna to Nathan B. Scott, August 20, 1902, Hanna-McCormick Family Papers, Manuscript Division, Library of Congress.

35. Joseph B. Foraker, *Notes of a Busy Life* (Cincinnati, Ohio, 1916), 2:110.

36. *New York Tribune*, May 26, 1903; Orville H. Platt to Albert J. Beveridge, May 30, 1903, Orville H Platt Papers, Connecticut State Library, Hartford.

37. Theodore Roosevelt, *Addresses and Presidential Messages of Theodore Roosevelt* (New York, 1904), 121.

38. M. W. Blumenberg, comp., *Official Proceedings of the Thirteenth Republican National Convention Held in the City of Chicago, June 21, 22, 23, 1904* (Minneapolis, 1904), 137.

39. Jonathan Dolliver to S. W. Rathbun, September 6, 1904, Jonathan Dolliver Papers, State Historical Society of Iowa, Iowa City.

40. Roosevelt to Lodge, July 14, 1904, Roosevelt Papers.

41. William C. Beer to E. W. Lampton, November 4, 1904, Beer Family Papers, Yale University Library; *New York Tribune*, September 30, 1904; Linden Bates, *The Party of Facts* (New York, 1904).

42. Albert Shaw to W. T. Stead, October 7, 1904, Albert Shaw Papers, New York Public Library; New York *Herald*, October 9, 1904, clipping in Roosevelt Papers.

43. Oswald Garrison Villard, *Fighting Years: Memoirs of a Liberal Editor* (New York, 1939), 181; *New York World*, October 26, 1904.

44. William Howard Taft to Helen Taft, August 22, 1912, in Lewis L. Gould, ed., *My Dearest Nellie: The Letters of William Howard Taft to Helen Herron Taft, 1909–1912* (Lawrence, Kans., 2011), 284.

45. *Washington Post*, November 5, 1904.

46. " Joy at the White House," *New York Tribune*, November 9, 1904.

47. Roosevelt to Philander Knox, November 10, 1904, Roosevelt Papers.

CHAPTER 5. THE TAFT-ROOSEVELT SPLIT, 1905–1912

1. Charles D. Hilles to Mrs. S. A. Willis, June 17, 1912, author's collection. George W. Perkins to A. G. Hawes, June 29, 1912, George W. Perkins Papers, Box 23, Nicholas Murray Butler Library, Columbia University, New York.

2. William Allen White, *The Autobiography of William Allen White* (New York, 1946), 469; Daisy Borden Harriman, *From Pinafores to Politics* (New York, 1923), 99; Theodore Roosevelt, *Social Justice and Popular Rule: Essays, Addresses, and Public Statements Relating to the Progressive Movement*, The Works of Theodore Roosevelt 17 (New York, 1926) 231.

3. Orville H. Platt to Nelson Aldrich, November 12, 1904, Orville H. Platt Papers, Connecticut Historical Society, Hartford.

4. Platt to Roosevelt, November 21, 1904, Platt Papers; *American Economist*, January 27, 1905, 41.

5. Blair Bolles, *Tyrant from Illinois: Uncle Joe Cannon's Experiment with Personal Power* (New York, 1951), 5–6, 11 (quotation).

6. Richard L. McCormick, "The Discovery That Business Corrupts Politics: A Reappraisal of the Origins of Progressivism," *American Historical Review* 86 (1981): 242–74.

7. Quotation from Cummins: McCormick, "Business Corrupts Politics," 264; quotation from Roosevelt: *Washington Post*, January 31, 1905.

8. Roosevelt to Kermit Roosevelt, June 13, 1906, Theodore Roosevelt Papers, Manuscript Division, Library of Congress.

9. James Harvey Young, *Pure Food: Securing the Federal Food and Drugs Act of 1906* (Princeton, N.J., 1989); John Braeman, *Albert J. Beveridge: American Nationalist* (Chicago, 1971), 101–10.

10. Roosevelt to Lyman Abbott, July 1, 1906, Roosevelt Papers; Theodore Roosevelt, *American Problems*, The Works of Theodore Roosevelt 16 (New York, 1926), 421.

11. Theodore Roosevelt, *State Papers as Governor and President, 1899–1909*, The Works of Theodore Roosevelt 15 (New York, 1926), 416.

12. The best introduction to La Follette is *La Follette's Autobiography: A Personal Narrative of Political Experiences* (Madison, Wisc., 1913). Nancy Unger, *Fighting Bob*

La Follette: The Righteous Reformer (Chapel Hill, N.C., 2000), is a full, modern account of his life and times.

13. E. D. Crumpacker to Roosevelt, July 28, 1906, Roosevelt Papers; *Des Moines Register Leader*, August 17, 1906.

14. Roosevelt to William Allen White, July 30, 1907, Roosevelt Papers.

15. E. L. Scharf to William Boyd Allison, July 25, 1907, Box 366, William Boyd Allison Papers, Iowa State Department of History and Archives, Des Moines; George E. Dominick to Herbert Parsons, November 9, 1907, Box 6, Herbert Parsons Papers, Nicholas Murray Butler Library, Columbia University, New York.

16. James S. Clarkson to A. B. Humphrey, September 20, 1902, James S. Clarkson Papers, Manuscript Division, Library of Congress.

17. The main source for the historical reinterpretation of the Brownsville episode is John D. Weaver, *The Brownsville Raid* (New York, 1970), which led to the belated exoneration of the accused soldiers during the early 1970s.

18. Roosevelt to William Allen White, August 11, 1906, Roosevelt Papers.

19. Roosevelt to Albert Shaw, May 22, 1908, Roosevelt Papers.

20. Archibald Butt, *Taft and Roosevelt: The Intimate Letters of Archie Butt, Military Aid* (Garden City, N.Y., 1930), 2:551; Henry L. Stoddard, *As I Knew Them: Presidents and Politic from Grant to Coolidge* (New York, 1927), 386.

21. Roosevelt to Nicholas Longworth, September 21, 1908, Roosevelt Papers.

22. Mark Sullivan to Roosevelt, September 11, 1908, Roosevelt Papers.

23. Taft to Roosevelt, November 7, 1908, William Howard Taft Papers, Manuscript Division, Library of Congress; Lucius B. Swift to Ella Swift, July 8, 1910, Lucius B. Swift Papers, Indiana State Library, Indianapolis.

24. Oscar Straus Diary, January 23, 1909, Oscar Straus Papers, Manuscript Division, Library of Congress; Archibald Butt, *The Letters of Archie Butt, Personal Aide to President Roosevelt*, ed. Lawrence F. Abbott (Garden City, N.Y., 1924), 338.

25. George von Lengerke Meyer Diary, January 4, 1909, Manuscript Division, Library of Congress; Taft to Mabel Boardman, November 10, 1912, Taft Papers.

26. Henry F. Pringle, *The Life and Times of William Howard Taft* (New York, 1939), 1:394.

27. William Howard Taft, *Our Chief Magistrate and His Powers* (New York, 1916), 144.

28. Oscar King Davis, *Released for Publication* (Boston, 1925), 144.

29. William Howard Taft, *Presidential Addresses and State Papers* (New York, 1910), 222.

30. Taft to Otto Bannard, June 11, 1910, Taft Papers.

31. Roosevelt to Gifford Pinchot, January 17, 1910, Roosevelt to Henry Cabot Lodge, May 5, 1910, Roosevelt Papers.

32. Theodore Roosevelt, *The New Nationalism* (New York, 1910), 11–12.

33. Roosevelt, *The New Nationalism*, 18.

34. Robert S. La Forte, "Theodore Roosevelt's Osawatomie Speech," *Kansas Historical Quarterly* 32 (1966): 199.

35. Henry L. Stimson, "Personal Recollections of the Convention and Campaign of 1910," Henry L. Stimson Papers, Sterling Memorial Library, Yale University, New Haven, Connecticut.

36. Mark Sullivan to George S. Loftus, December 27, 1911, James Manahan Papers, Minnesota Historical Society, Saint Paul.

37. Roosevelt to William Allen White, January 24, 1911, Roosevelt Papers.

38. Roosevelt to James R. Garfield, October 31, 1911, Roosevelt Papers.

39. Roosevelt to Benjamin B. Lindsey, December 5, 1911, Roosevelt Papers.

40. *New York Tribune*, April 18, 30, 1912.

41. *New York Tribune*, April 26, 30, 1912; Francis L. Broderick, *Progressivism at Risk: Electing a President in 1912* (Westport, Conn., 1989), 50.

42. Roosevelt to James B. Reynolds, June 11, 1912, Roosevelt Papers.

43. Francis L. Broderick, *Progressivism at Risk: Electing a President in 1912*, 53. Victor Rosewater, *Back Stage in 1912: The Inside Story of the Split Republican Convention* (Philadelphia, 1932), 165, 174.

44. Roosevelt, *Social Justice and Popular Rule*, 204, 231.

45. "To the Republican National Convention, June 22, 1912," Roosevelt Papers; Republican National Committee, *Republican Campaign Text-Book, 1912* (Philadelphia, 1912), 271.

46. George W. Wickersham to Charles Nagel, September 19, 1912, Charles Nagel Papers, Sterling Memorial Library, Yale University.

47. Winthrop Murray Crane to Taft, November 12, 1912, Charles D. Hilles Papers, Sterling Memorial Library, Yale University.

CHAPTER 6. REPUBLICANS DURING THE WILSON YEARS, 1913–1921

1. Joseph G. Cannon to Mabel Boardman, November 18, 1912, Box 6, Mabel Boardman Papers, Manuscript Division, Library of Congress.

2. "President Wilson, the Democratic Party, and the 'New Competitive Tariff,'" *Independent*, October 9, 1913, 62.

3. Herbert F. Margulies, *Reconciliation and Revival: James R. Mann and the House Republicans in the Wilson Era* (Westport, Conn., 1996), 100.

4. Lewis L. Gould, *Reform and Regulation: American Politics from Roosevelt to Wilson*, 3rd ed. (Waveland, Ill., 1996), 176.

5. For Roosevelt's reaction, see Roosevelt to Archibald Roosevelt, May 19, 1915, Theodore Roosevelt Papers, Manuscript Division, Library of Congress. Wilson is quoted in Justus Doenecke, *Nothing Less Than War: A New History of America's Entry into World War I* (Lexington, Ky., 2011), 75.

6. Franklin K. Lane to Woodrow Wilson, June 8, 1916, Woodrow Wilson Papers, Manuscript Division, Library of Congress.

7. Henry L. Stoddard, *As I Knew Them: Presidents and Politics from Grant to Coolidge* (New York, 1927), 430. Roosevelt publicized his intentions through Stoddard.

8. Walter Prescott Webb and Terrell Webb, eds., *Washington Wife: Journal of Ellen Maury Slayden from 1897 to 1919* (New York, 1963), 279.

9. *Letters from Theodore Roosevelt to Anna Roosevelt Cowles, 1870–1918* (New York, 1924), 308.

10. Republican National Committee, *Republican Campaign Text-Book, 1916* (Washington, D.C., 1916), 48, 50.

11. Arthur Willert to Geoffrey Robinson [Dawson], October 14, 1916, archives of the *The Times*, London.

12. Gould, *Reform and Regulation*, 185.

13. "T. R. Arraigns Wilson as Failure in Crisis," *New York Tribune*, November 4, 1916.

14. Woodrow Wilson, *The New Democracy: Presidential Messages, Addresses and Other Papers (1913–1917)*, ed. Ray Stannard Baker and William E. Dodd (New York, 1926), 2:371.

15. *New York Times*, September 15, 1916.

16. William C. Widenor, *Henry Cabot Lodge and the Search for an American Foreign Policy* (Berkeley, Calif., 1980), 248.

17. Widenor, *Henry Cabot Lodge*, 274; Theodore Roosevelt to Kermit Roosevelt, June 8, 1917, Kermit Roosevelt Papers, Library of Congress.

18. Harold Ickes to James R. Garfield, February 18, 1918, Harold Ickes Papers, Manuscript Division, Library of Congress.

19. Will H. Hays, "The Republican Position," *The Forum* 60 (August 1918): 136.

20. Gould, *Reform and Regulation*, 203; Herbert F. Margulies, *Senator Lenroot of Wisconsin: A Political Biography, 1900–1929* (Columbia, Mo., 1977), 245.

21. "Start of the 1918 Political Drive," *Literary Digest*, April 13, 1918, 15; Hays, "The Republican Position," 152.

22. Seward W. Livermore, *Politics Is Adjourned: Woodrow Wilson and the War Congress, 1916–1918* (Wesleyan, Conn., 1966), 216.

23. "An Appeal for a Democratic Congress," in Arthur S. Link, ed., *The Papers of Woodrow Wilson, vol. 52: 1918* (Princeton, N.J., 1985), 382; Charles D. Hilles to William Howard Taft, October 28, 1918, William Howard Taft Papers, Library of Congress.

24. For the "round robin," see Ralph Stone, *The Irreconcilables: The Fight against the League of Nations* (Lexington, Ky., 1970), 70–75.

25. John Milton Cooper, *Breaking the Heart of the World: Woodrow Wilson and the Fight for the League of Nations* (New York, 2001), 353–75.

26. On the ultimate defeat of the treaty, see Herbert F. Margulies, *The Mild Reservationists and the League of Nations Controversy in the Senate* (Columbia, Mo., 1989), 215–60.

27. William E. Leuchtenburg, *The Perils of Prosperity, 1914–1932*, 2nd ed. (Chicago, 1993), 66.

28. William Allen White, *Masks in a Pageant* (New York, 1930), 390; Cooper, *Breaking the Heart of the World*, 390n25.

29. Cooper, *Breaking the Heart of the World*, 389.

30. White, *Masks in a Pageant*, 409. Robert H. Ferrell, *The Strange Deaths of President Harding* (Columbia, Mo., 1996), 153–59, discusses Harding's marital difficulties. He also calls into question the long-standing tale that Harding had an affair and a child with Nan Britton.

31. Republican Party Platform of 1920, available online at the American Presidency Project, http://www.presidency.ucsb.edu/ws/print.php?pid=29635.

32. Eugene Trani and David L. Wilson, *The Presidency of Warren G. Harding* (Lawrence, Kans., 1977), 22–23; Robert K. Murray, *The Harding Era: Warren G. Harding and His Administration* (Minneapolis, Minn., 1969), 37–39.

33. Leuchtenburg, *Perils of Prosperity*, 86.

34. Margulies, *Senator Lenroot of Wisconsin*, 328–31; Robert H. Ferrell, *The Presidency of Calvin Coolidge* (Lawrence, Kans., 1998), 15–16.

35. Melanie Susan Gustafson, *Women in the Republican Party, 1854–1924* (Urbana, Ill., 2001), 187–93.

36. Richard B. Sherman, *The Republican Party and Black America from McKinley to Hoover, 1896–1933* (Charlottesville, Va., 1973), 134–44.

37. Sherman, *The Republican Party and Black America*, 137, 140.

38. Murray, *The Harding Era*, 64.

39. Leuchtenburg, *The Perils of Prosperity*, 88.

CHAPTER 7. THE AGE OF REPUBLICAN DOMINANCE, 1921–1933

1. Katherine A. S. Sibley, *First Lady Florence Harding: Behind the Tragedy and the Controversy* (Lawrence, Kans., 2009), 76–77.

2. Robert K. Murray, *The Harding Era: Warren G. Harding and His Administration* (Minneapolis, Minn., 1969), 166–69, 397–403.

3. Roger Daniels, *Coming to America: History of Immigration and Ethnicity in American Life* (New York, 1990), 284.

4. Murray, *The Harding Era*, 418.

5. Robert H. Ferrell, *The Strange Deaths of President Harding* (Columbia, Mo., 1996), 5–9.

6. William Allen White, *The Autobiography of William Allen White* (New York, 1946), 619.

7. Murray, *The Harding Era*, 445.

8. Ferrell, *Strange Deaths*, 30–49, disposes of the conspiracy theories.

9. David H. Stratton, *Tempest over Teapot Dome: The Story of Albert B. Fall* (Norman, Okla., 1998), 229–300.

10. John L. Blair, "Coolidge the Image-Maker: The President and the Press, 1923–1929," *New England Quarterly* 46 (1973): 499–532; Daniel J. Leab, "Coolidge, Hays and 1920s Movies: Some Aspects of Image and Reality," in John Earl Haynes, ed., *Calvin Coolidge and the Coolidge Era* (Washington, D.C., 1998), 97–131.

11. Robert Sobel, *Coolidge: An American Enigma* (Washington, D.C., 1998), 191.

12. Sobel, *Coolidge*, 292.

13. Donald R. McCoy, *Calvin Coolidge: The Quiet President* (New York, 1967), 246.

14. H. L. Mencken, *A Carnival of Buncombe* (Baltimore, Md., 1956), 97.

15. McCoy, *Calvin Coolidge*, 255.

16. Address to the American Society of Newspaper Editors, January 17, 1925, available online at the American Presidency Project, http://www.presidency.ucsb.edu/ws/?pid=24180.

17. Historians have long known that American involvement in world affairs in the 1920s was extensive, but the perception of isolation in the decade has persisted as one of the legacies attributed to Republican rule. William Appleman Williams, "The Legend of Isolationism in the 1920s," *Science and Society* 18 (1954): 1–20, is the classic critique of this mistaken impression.

18. McCoy, *Calvin Coolidge*, 190, mentions the famous Coolidge quotation.

19. Paul Johnson, "Calvin Coolidge and the Lost Arcadia," in Haynes, *Calvin Coolidge and the Coolidge Era*, 11–12 (both quotations).

20. The copy of the original version of Coolidge's announcement is now in the Library of Congress.

21. Richard Hofstadter, "Could a Protestant Have Beaten Hoover in 1928?" *The Reporter* 22 (1960): 31–33; Allan J. Lichtman, *Prejudice and the Old Politics: The Presidential Election of 1928* (Chapel Hill, N.C., 1979).

22. There are two insightful biographies of Hoover: Joan Hoff Wilson, *Herbert Hoover: Forgotten Progressive* (Boston, 1975), and David Burner, *Herbert Hoover: A Public Life* (New York, 1979).

23. Republican Party Platform of 1928, available online at the American Presidency Project, http://www.presidency.ucsb.edu/ws/?pid=29637.

24. Herbert Hoover, *The New Day* (Stanford, Calif., 1928), 16.

25. Hoover, *The New Day*, 150–51.

26. Hoover, *The New Day*, 29.

27. David Burner, *The Politics of Provincialism: The Democratic Party in Transition, 1918–1932* (New York, 1968), 195 (quotation), 209–16, discusses Smith's limitations as a candidate.

28. On Hoover as a candidate, see Louis Liebovich, *Bylines in Despair: Herbert Hoover, the Great Depression and the U.S. News Media* (Westport, Conn., 1994), 126–27, and Martin L. Fausold, *The Presidency of Herbert C. Hoover* (Lawrence, Kans., 1977), 23–31.

29. Lichtman, *Prejudice and the Old Politics*, 154. See also, Donald J. Lisio, *Hoover, Blacks, and Lily-Whites: A Study of Southern Strategies* (Chapel Hill, N.C., 1985).

30. Hoover, *The New Day*, 217.

31. "Six Months of Hoover's Presidential Engineering," *Literary Digest*, September 21, 1939, 14.

32. Michael E. Parrish, *Anxious Decades: America in Prosperity and Depression, 1920–1941* (New York, 1992), 252.

33. Kermit Roosevelt to Theodore Roosevelt, Jr., October 30, 1929, Kermit Roosevelt Papers, Manuscript Division, Library of Congress.

34. The notion that Hoover stood idly by while the Depression worsened has long been discredited. An early statement of the continuity in policy between Hoover and Franklin D. Roosevelt can be found in Walter Lippmann, "The Permanent New Deal," *Yale Review* 24 (June 1935): 649–57. It contended that in the fall of 1929 Hoover did "something utterly unprecedented in American history. The national government undertook to make the whole economic order operate prosperously" (652).

35. Alfred E. Eckes, *Opening America's Market: U.S. Foreign Trade Policy Since 1776* (Chapel Hill, N.C., 1995), 100–139, argues that the Smoot-Hawley law did not have all the negative effects attributed to it. Fausold, *Presidency of Herbert C. Hoover*, 74.

36. William E. Leuchtenburg, *Franklin D. Roosevelt and the New Deal* (New York, 1963), 13 (rose comment). I first heard the Andrew Mellon story when I entered graduate school in 1961.

37. Fausold, *Presidency of Herbert C. Hoover*, 111.

38. Theodore Roosevelt, Jr., to Kermit Roosevelt, November 9, 1930, Kermit Roosevelt Papers.

39. Fausold, *Presidency of Herbert C. Hoover*, 142.

40. Wilson, *Herbert Hoover*, 155–56; Fausold, *Presidency of Herbert C. Hoover*, 154–55.

41. Wilson, *Herbert Hoover*, 157; Fausold, *Presidency of Herbert C. Hoover*, 157–62.

42. Republican Party Platform of 1932, available online at the American Presidency Project, http://www.presidency.ucsb.edu/ws/?pid=29638.

43. The Bonus March has been the subject of several studies. See, Roger Daniels, *The Bonus March: An Episode of the Great Depression* (Westport, Conn., 1971), and Donald J. Lisio, *The President and Protest: Hoover, Conspiracy and the Bonus Riot* (Columbia, Mo., 1974). Liebovich, *Bylines in Despair*, 155–77, argues that the administration's handling of the march did not hurt Hoover politically to the degree often assumed.

44. Robert S. McElvaine, *The Great Depression: America, 1929–1941* (New York, 1984), 131–32.

CHAPTER 8. THE REPUBLICANS AND THE NEW DEAL, 1933–1945

1. Donald Bruce Johnson, *The Republican Party and Wendell Willkie* (Urbana, Ill., 1960), 88.

2. Steve Neal, *Dark Horse: A Biography of Wendell Willkie* (Garden City, N.Y., 1984), 89, 121.

3. William E. Leuchtenburg, *Franklin D. Roosevelt and the New Deal, 1932–1940* (New York, 1963), 39.

4. For Roosevelt's start as president, see Jean Edward Smith, *FDR* (New York, 2007), 300–321.

5. Leuchtenburg, *Franklin D. Roosevelt*, 60.

6. Clyde Weed, *The Nemesis of Reform: The Republican Party During the New Deal* (New York, 1994), 37–43.

7. Weed, *The Nemesis of Reform*, 37, 39.

8. Smith, *FDR*, 350–59.

9. Weed, *Nemesis of Reform*, 162; Sheryl R. Tynes, *Turning Points in Social Security: From "Cruel Hoax" to "Sacred Entitlement"* (Stanford, Calif., 1996), 55.

10. Weed, *Nemesis of Reform*, 159.

11. Weed, *Nemesis of Reform*, 60.

12. William Allen White to E. Ben Johnson, August 19, 1935, in Walter Johnson, ed., *Selected Letters of William Allen White, 1899–1943* (New York, 1947), 358. Donald R. McCoy, *Landon of Kansas* (Lincoln, Neb., 1966), is a comprehensive and sympathetic study of Landon's public career.

13. Republican Party Platform of 1936, available online at the American Presidency Project, http://www.presidency.ucsb.edu/ws/index.php?pid=25836.

14. Peverill Squire, "Why the 1936 Literary Digest Poll Failed," *Public Opinion Quarterly* 52 (1988): 125–33. McCoy, *Landon of Kansas*, 300–301; Leuchtenburg, *Franklin D. Roosevelt*, 196.

15. McCoy, *Landon of Kansas*, 329.

16. Leuchtenburg, *Franklin D. Roosevelt*, 184.

17. Leuchtenburg, *Franklin D. Roosevelt*, 184–95, 189n72 (quotation) is excellent on the aspects of the New Deal coalition. Michael J. Webber, *New Deal Fat Cats: Business, Labor, and Campaign Finance in the 1936 Presidential Election* (New York, 2000), discusses the class basis of the Republican defeat.

18. The literature on the court-packing plan is vast and mostly focused on the Democrats and Roosevelt. A good, older source on the Republican strategy as the Democrats divided is Karl A. Lamb, "The Opposition Party as Secret Agent: Republicans and the Court Fight," *Papers of the Michigan Academy of Science, Arts and Letters* 46 (1961): 539–50.

19. Leuchtenburg, *Franklin D. Roosevelt*, 243 (quotation).

20. The effects of the 1937–1938 recession are discussed in Leuchtenburg, *Franklin D. Roosevelt*, 243–51 (Roosevelt Depression quotation, 250); Milton Plesur, "The Republican Congressional Comeback of 1938," *Review of Politics* 24 (1962): 540 (Roosevelt recession).

21. Plesur, "Republican Congressional Comeback," 535–36, 545.

22. James T. Patterson, *Mr. Republican: A Biography of Robert A. Taft* (Boston, 1972), 213 (first quotation); Richard Norton Smith, *Thomas E. Dewey and His Times* (New York, 1982), 311 (second quotation).

23. Smith, *Thomas E. Dewey*, 289.

24. Smith, *Thomas E. Dewey*, 299.

25. On the predicament of the Republicans, see Smith, *Thomas E. Dewey*, 302–9.

26. Neal, *Dark Horse*, is the best modern study of Willkie. James H. Madison, ed., *Wendell Willkie: Hoosier Internationalist* (Bloomington, Ind., 1992), is a collection of interesting essays about his public career.

27. Neal, *Dark Horse*, 38.

28. Neal, *Dark Horse*, 68.

29. Donald Bruce Johnson, *The Republican Party and Wendell Willkie* (Urbana, Ill., 1960), 84–85.

30. Republican Party Platform of 1940, available online at the American Presidency Project, http://www.presidency.ucsb.edu/ws/?pid=29640.

31. Johnson, *Republican Party and Wendell Willkie*, 102 (first quotation); Smith, *Thomas E. Dewey*, 328 (second quotation).

32. Neal, *Dark Horse*, 159.

33. On the passions that the campaign aroused, see the buttons displayed in Arthur M. Schlesinger, Jr., ed., *Running for President: The Candidates and Their Images* (New York, 1994), 2:210. Leuchtenburg, *Franklin D. Roosevelt*, 319.

34. The behind-the-scenes elements of the 1940 presidential race were first brought to the surface in R. J. C. Butow, "The FDR Tapes," *American Heritage* (February/March 1982): 10–15, 20–22.

35. Neal, *Dark Horse*, 167–68.

36. The results of the 1940 election are discussed in Leuchtenburg, *Franklin D. Roosevelt*, 321–22; Neal, *Dark Horse*, 176–79; and Johnson, *Republican Party and Wendell Willkie*, 160–67.

37. Taft to Scandrett, January 29, 1941, in Clarence E. Wunderlin, Jr., ed., *The Papers of Robert A. Taft*, vol. 2, *1939–1944* (Kent, Ohio, 2001), 218.

38. Neal, *Dark Horse*, 206.

39. Arthur H. Vandenberg, Jr., *The Private Papers of Senator Vandenberg*, ed. Joe Alex Morris (Boston, 1952), 10; Patterson, *Mr. Republican*, 244.

40. Neal, *Dark Horse*, 217; "Statement After the Bombing of Pearl Harbor, December 8, 1941," in Wunderlin, *Papers of Robert A. Taft*, 01.

41. Taft made these remarks in a Chicago speech on December 19, 1941. See Wunderlin, *Papers of Robert A. Taft*, 303.

42. Richard E. Darilek, *A Loyal Opposition in Time of War: The Republican Party and the Politics of Foreign Policy from Pearl Harbor to Yalta* (Westport, Conn., 1976), 53–57.

43. Smith, *Thomas E. Dewey*, 543–51 ("fat friend" quotation), 346. David M. Jordan, *FDR, Dewey, and the Election of 1944* (Bloomington, Ind., 2011), 22–41, surveys the Republican field in 1944.

44. Darilek, *A Loyal Opposition*, 106–12; Smith, *Dewey*, 385, 387.

45. Vandenberg, *Private Papers of Senator Vandenberg*, 58.

46. *New York Times*, April 28, 1944; Smith, *Dewey*, 397.

47. Smith, *Dewey*, 48.

48. Richard O. Davies, *Defender of the Old Guard: John Bricker and American Politics* (Columbus, Ohio, 1993), 82, 94.

49. Republican Party Platform of 1944, available online at the American Presidency Project, http://www.presidency.ucsb.edu/ws/index.php?pid=25835.

50. Jordan, *FDR, Dewey*, 46–48.

51. Smith, *Dewey*, 409–10, 433–34.

52. Jordan, *FDR, Dewey*, 5–6.

53. Davies, *Defender of the Old Guard*, 103–4; Jordan, *FDR, Dewey*, 307.

54. Smith, *Thomas E. Dewey*, 426–30; Jordan, *FDR*, 239–40.

55. Smith, *Dewey*, 436.

56. Joe Scarborough, *The Right Path: From Ike to Reagan, How Republicans Once Mastered Politics —And Can Again* (New York, 2013), 10–11. Diana West, *American Betrayal: The Secret Assault on our Nation's Character* (New York, 2013), depicts Roosevelt's government as being in thrall to the Soviet Union. For a more balanced view of the situation in the winter and spring of 1945, see Anne Applebaum, *Iron Curtain: The Crushing of Eastern Europe. 1944–1956* (New York, 2012), 19–22.

CHAPTER 9. FROM "HAD ENOUGH" TO MODERN REPUBLICANISM, 1945–1961

1. George L. Hart, reporter, *Official Report of the Proceedings of the Twenty-Fifth Republican National Convention Held in Chicago, Illinois, July 7, 8, 9, 10 and 11, 1952* (Washington, D.C., 1952), 178.

2. Richard Norton Smith, *Thomas E. Dewey and His Times* (New York, 1982), 594.

3. Earl Black and Merle Black, *The Rise of Southern Republicans* (Cambridge, Mass., 2002), 57–71.

4. Arthur Herman, *Joseph McCarthy: Reexamining the Life and Legacy of America's Most Hated Senator* (New York, 2000), offers a favorable assessment of the senator.

5. The opening of the Soviet archives after the end of the Cold War, along with evidence about American codebreaking, has allowed evidence about Soviet penetration of the American government to be disclosed. Katherine A. S. Sibley, *Red Spies in America: Stolen Secrets and the Dawn of the Cold War* (Lawrence, Kans., 2004).

6. James T. Patterson, *Mr. Republican: A Biography of Robert A. Taft* (Boston, 1972), 313.

7. Herman, *Joseph McCarthy* 30–32, 38–39, discusses McCarthy's war service and the 1946 election outcome. Irwin F. Gellman, *The Contender: Richard Nixon, the Congress Years, 1946–1952* (New York, 1999), 78–79; David W. Reinhard, *The Republican Right Since 1945* (Lexington, Ky., 1983), 15–16.

8. Patterson, *Mr. Republican*, 313; David M. Oshinsky, *A Conspiracy So Immense: The World of Joe McCarthy* (New York, 1983), 49.

9. Reinhard, *Republican Right*, 15.

10. George Steven Roukis, *American Labor and the Conservative Republicans, 1946–1948* (New York, 1988), 46.

11. For the enactment of the Taft-Hartley law, see Patterson, *Mr. Republican*, 352–66.

12. On Truman's credentials as a foe of Communism in 1947–1948, see Alonzo Hamby, *Man of the People: A Life of Harry S. Truman* (New York, 1995), 391–400, 427–29.

13. William B. Pickett, *Eisenhower Decides to Run: Presidential Politics and Cold War Strategy* (Chicago, 2000), 40.

14. Alec Kirby, David G. Dalin, and John F. Rothmann, *Harold E. Stassen: The Life and Perennial Candidacy of the Progressive Republican* (Jefferson, N.C., 2013), measures its subject's strengths and weaknesses in a lucid narrative.

15. Thomas E. Dewey, *Public Papers of Thomas E. Dewey, Fifty-First Governor of the State of New York 1948* (Albany, N.Y., 1949), 592.

16. Gary Donaldson, *Truman Defeats Dewey* (Lexington, Ky., 1999), 131.

17. Dewey, *Public Papers*, 636; Republican Party Platform of 1948, available online at the American Presidency Project, http://www.presidency.ucsb.edu/ws/print.php?pid=25836.

18. Herbert Brownell, with John Burke, *Advising Ike: The Memoirs of Attorney General Herbert Brownell* (Lawrence, Kans., 1993), 80. For Strom Thurmond and his presidential effort, Joseph Crespino, *Strom Thurmond's America* (New York, 2012), 74–84, is informative and insightful.

19. Andrew E. Busch, *Truman's Triumphs: The 1948 Election and the Making of Modern America* (Lawrence, Kans., 2012), 109–13.

20. Smith, *Dewey*, 512–13.

21. Dewey, *Public Papers*, 649, 654, 690.

22. Smith, *Dewey*, 535, 536.

23. Smith, *Dewey*, 51–512; Busch, *Truman's Triumphs*, 159–60, is less persuaded of the salience of the farm vote.

24. Smith, *Dewey*, 47, 48.

25. Clarence Budington Kelland, "Why the Republicans Lost," *American Mercury* 144 (February 1949): 181, 182.

26. Smith, *Dewey*, 547.

27. A recording of McCarthy's speech at Wheeling did not survive, and so a precise record of what he said does not exist. A copy was printed in the *Congressional Record*, 81st Cong., 2d Sess. (January 25, 1950): 1002–8. These quotations are from David M. Oshinsky, *A Conspiracy So Immense: The World of Joe McCarthy* (New York, 1983), 108–9. Herman, *Joseph McCarthy*, 98–99, quotes other excerpts.

28. Oshinsky, *A Conspiracy So Immense*, 133.

29. Ronald J. Caridi, *The Korean War and American Politics: The Republican Party as a Case Study* (Philadelphia, 1968), 145.

30. Caridi, *Korean War and American Politics*, 174.

31. Patterson, *Mr. Republican*, 499–516, traces the development of the Taft campaign.

32. Patterson, *Mr. Republican*, 514.

33. The main source for "Eisenhower revisionism" was Fred I. Greenstein, *The Hidden-Hand Presidency: Eisenhower as Leader* (Baltimore, Md., 1994). Greenstein's work was first published in 1982.

34. The bitter struggle for delegates in 1952 can be followed in Patterson, *Mr. Republican*, 535–36, and Smith, *Dewey*, 583–87.

35. Patterson, *Mr. Republican*, 569–78.

36. Nixon's own account of the fund controversy is in *RN: The Memoirs of Richard Nixon* (New York, 1978), 92–110.

37. Greenstein, *Hidden-Hand Presidency*, 50.

38. Nixon, *RN*, 376.

39. Republican Party Platform of 1956, available online at the American Presidency Project, http://www.presidency.ucsb.edu/ws/index.php?pid=25838.

40. Reinhard, *Republican Right*, 137. It was about this time that the Republicans, led by chairman of the National Committee, Leonard Hall, started the practice of referring to their opposition as "the Democrat party," on the grounds that there was nothing "dem-

ocratic" about their appeal. The practice annoys Democrats, which may explain why it persists, even though it has never caught on with the press or the public at large.

41. Barry Goldwater, "The Preservation of Our Basic Institutions: Effect of Governmental Spending and Taxation," *Vital Speeches of the Day*, May 18, 1957, 457, 458.

42. Crespino, *Strom Thurmond's America*, 10.

43. Jeffrey Frank, *Ike and Dick: Portrait of a Strange Political Marriage* (New York, 2013), 183–88, is excellent on the Adams case.

44. Geoffrey Kabaservice, *Rule and Ruin: The Downfall of Moderation and the Destruction of the Republican Party from Eisenhower to the Tea Party* (New York, 2012), 27–29, is perceptive on Rockefeller's strengths and weaknesses.

45. James T. Patterson, *Grand Expectations: The United States, 1945–1974* (New York, 1996), 424–27, 433–35.

46. Michael Kramer and Sam Roberts, *"I Never Wanted to Be Vice President of Anything!" An Investigative Biography of Nelson Rockefeller* (New York, 1976), 226–29.

47. Nixon did not discuss these events in his 1978 memoirs. Kabaservice, *Rule or Ruin*, 28–29.

48. Rick Perlstein, *Before the Storm: Barry Goldwater and the Unmaking of the American Consensus* (New York, 2001), 83–87; Robert Alan Goldberg, *Barry Goldwater* (New Haven, Conn., 1995), 144.

49. Perlstein, *Before the Storm*, 94–95; Lee Edwards, *Goldwater: The Man Who Made a Revolution* (Washington, D.C., 1995), 138–39.

50. Frank, *Ike and Dick*, 205.

51. Frank, *Ike and Dick*, 209.

52. Nixon chronicles some of the problems with his 1960 campaign in *RN*, 225–27. The quotation is from page 225.

53. Overturning the Kennedy win would have been difficult. Nixon and the Republicans would have had to shift the results in Texas and Illinois to change the outcome. The Republican inquiry in Illinois came up short, which made the issue in Texas moot. The best discussion of the case is Edmund F. Kallina, Jr., *Courthouse over White House: Chicago and the Presidential Election of 1960* (Orlando, Fla., 1988).

CHAPTER 10. FROM GOLDWATER TO WATERGATE, 1961–1974

1. Goldwater's acceptance speech is available online at http://www.washingtonpost.com/wp-srv/politics/daily/may98/goldwaterspeech.htm; C-SPAN also has a video available online at http://www.c-span.org/video/?4018-1/goldwater-1964-acceptance-speech.

2. Glenn Feldman, ed., *Painting Dixie Red: When, Where, Why, and How the South Became Republican* (Gainesville, Fla., 2011), is an interesting collection of essays about the rise of Republicanism in the South in the 1960s.

3. Barry Goldwater, *The Conscience of a Conservative* (New York, 1975), 21, 23, 27, 43, 64. L. Brent Bozell, brother-in-law of William F. Buckley, ghosted the work for Goldwater.

4. Goldwater, *Conscience of a Conservative*, 88–127.

5. Goldwater, *Conscience of a Conservative*, 32–38. For Goldwater's civil rights record, see Robert Alan Goldberg, *Barry Goldwater* (New Haven, Conn., 1995), 75, 88–90, 154–55.

6. Earl Black and Merle Black, *The Southern Republicans* (Cambridge, Mass., 2002), 90–91, 126–27.

7. On the political impact of Rockefeller's divorce, see Rick Perlstein, *Before the Storm: Barry Goldwater and the Unmaking of the American Consensus* (New York, 2001), 195–97.

8. F. Clifton White, with William Gill, *Suite 3505: The Story of the Draft Goldwater Movement* (New Rochelle, N.Y., 1967); Perlstein, *Before the Storm*, 191 (quotation).

9. For Goldwater's announcement, see, Goldberg, *Barry Goldwater*, 179 (Johnson quotation), 181.

10. Goldberg, *Barry Goldwater*, 177.

11. Lee Edwards, *Goldwater: The Man Who Made a Revolution* (Washington, D.C., 1995), 206.

12. David W. Reinhard, *The Republican Right Since 1945* (Lexington, Ky., 1983), 186.

13. Geoffrey Kabaservice, *Rule and Ruin: The Downfall of Moderation and the Destruction of the Republican Party from Eisenhower to the Tea Party* (New York, 2012), 107–11, examines Scranton's doomed campaign.

14. Byron Hulsey, *Everett Dirksen and His Presidents: How a Senate Giant Shaped American Politics* (Lawrence, Kans., 2000), 187–97, is excellent on Dirksen and the Republicans in the civil rights battle in the Senate.

15. Goldberg, *Barry Goldwater*, 197.

16. Robert Dallek, *Flawed Giant: Lyndon Johnson and His Times* (New York, 1998), 120.

17. The Goldwater forces and their dominance of the 1964 convention is discussed in Perlstein, *Before the Storm*, 366–70, 380–85; Goldberg, *Barry Goldwater*, 201–4.

18. Republican Party Platform of 1964, available online at the American Presidency Project, http://www.presidency.ucsb.edu/ws/?pid=25840.

19. Libby Miller Fitzgerald, *Bill Miller—Do You Know Me? A Daughter Remembers* (Lynchburg, Va., 2004), offers a strong defense of her father's qualifications. Perlstein, *Before the Storm*, 389.

20. Harry V. Jaffa, "Goldwater's Famous 'Gaffe': Extremism Twenty Years Later," *National Review*, August 10, 1984, 36, makes an academic rather than a political argument for the phrase. Edwards, *Goldwater*, 267 (Goldwater quotation).

21. Richard Nixon, *RN: The Memoirs of Richard Nixon* (New York, 1978), 260; Goldberg, *Barry Goldwater*, 206.

22. The internal problems of the Goldwater campaign are discussed in Stephen Shadegg, *What Happened to Goldwater: The Inside Story of the Republican Campaign* (New York, 1965), 171–75, 198–209, and Perlstein, *Before the Storm*, 415–48.

23. The story of the Daisy Field commercial is outlined in Edwin Diamond and Stephen Bates, *The Spot: The Rise of Political Advertising on Television*, 3rd ed. (Cambridge, Mass., 1993), 122–33. The anger of the Goldwater campaign with Johnson's tactics can be followed in Edwards, *Goldwater*, 305–12 and Goldberg, *Barry Goldwater*, 225–27.

24. For Reagan's speech and its impact, see Perlstein, *Before the Storm*, 503.

25. For the enactment of the Voting Rights Act and Republican support for the measure, see Hulsey, *Everett Dirksen and his Presidents*, 210–12, 215–16.

26. Lewis L. Gould, "Never a Deep Partisan: Lyndon Johnson and the Democratic Party, 1963–1969," in Robert A. Divine, ed., *The Johnson Years*, vol. 3: *LBJ at Home and Abroad* (Lawrence, Kans., 1994), 30.

27. Alan L. Otten and Charles B. Seib, "The Minor Masterpiece of Ray C. Bliss," *Reporter*, February 10, 1966; Lewis L. Gould, *1968: The Election That Changed America* (Chicago, 2010), 24–25.

28. Stephen E. Ambrose, *Nixon*, vol. 2: *The Triumph of a Politician, 1962–1972* (New York, 1989), 100.

29. Nixon, *RN*, 273–77, describes his encounter with Johnson.

30. Kabaservice, *Rule and Ruin*, 221, gives Romney's brainwashing quotation.

31. Nixon, in *RN*, 298, denies that he had a secret plan for Vietnam. Gould, *1968*, 30.

32. Gould, *1968*, 40.

33. Gould, *1968*, 68.

34. Gould, *1968*, 102.

35. Tom Wicker, *One of Us: Richard Nixon and the American Dream* (New York, 1991), 343.

36. Jules Witcover, *Very Strange Bedfellows: The Short and Unhappy Marriage of Richard Nixon and Spiro Agnew* (New York, 2008), considers the decision to choose Agnew.

37. Nixon, *RN*, 314–15.

38. Gould, *1968*, 112.

39. Sam Tanenhaus, "Original Sin: Why the GOP Is and Will Continue to Be the Party of White People," *New Republic*, February 25, 2013, 24–31.

40. The best book on Nixon in the White House is Melvin Small, *The Presidency of Richard Nixon* (Lawrence, Kans., 1999).

41. Stanley I. Kutler, *Abuse of Power: The New Nixon Tapes* (New York, 1997), 31.

42. Small, *Presidency of Richard Nixon*, 250.

43. Nixon, *RN*, 770.

44. For a thorough and sympathetic treatment of Nixon's civil rights successes and failures, see Dean J. Kotlowski, *Nixon's Civil Rights: Politics, Principle and Policy* (Cambridge, Mass., 2001).

45. Nixon, *RN*, 495, 500.

46. On the various aspects of Nixon's criminal activities in the White House, see John A. Andrew III, *Power to Destroy: The Political Use of the IRS from Kennedy to Nixon* (Chicago, 2002), 179–224, and Stanley Kutler, *The Wars of Watergate: The Last Crisis of Richard Nixon* (New York, 1990), 78–125; Small, *Presidency*, 254.

47. Kabaservice, *Rule and Ruin*, 330–32.

48. Nixon, *RN*, 669.

49. Small, *Presidency of Richard Nixon*, 273.

50. Goldberg, *Barry Goldwater*, 145, 274.

51. Herbert S. Parmet, *George Bush: The Life of a Lone Star Yankee* (New York, 1997), 161; Lou Cannon, *President Reagan: The Role of a Lifetime* (New York, 1991), 76.

52. Kutler, *Wars of Watergate*, 451, 454. The papers of Thomas Railsback, an Illinois Republican, at Western Illinois University document how one moderate Republican representative decided to vote for Nixon's impeachment.

53. John Robert Greene, *The Presidency of Gerald Ford* (Lawrence, Kans., 1995), 17.

CHAPTER 11. REPUBLICANS IN THE REAGAN ERA, 1974–1988

1. Jack W. Germond and Jules Witcover, *Blue Smoke and Mirrors: How Reagan Won and Why Carter Lost the Election of 1980* (New York, 1981), 280.

2. Lou Cannon, *President Reagan: The Role of a Lifetime* (New York, 1991), 141.

3. Fred Sperapani, comp., *Official Report of the Proceedings of the Thirtieth Republican National Convention Held in Miami Beach, Florida, August 21, 22, 23, 1972* (Washington, D.C., 1972), 235.

4. Laura Kalman, *Right Star Rising: A New Politics. 1974–1980* (New York, 2010), 71–75.

5. Kalman, *Right Star Rising*, 228–32, is a good treatment of the supply-side movement.

6. Allen J. Matusow, *Nixon's Economy: Booms, Busts, Dollars, and Votes* (Lawrence, Kans., 1998), 281–89.

7. Kalman, *Right Star Rising*, 76–77.

8. Steven F. Hayward, *The Age of Reagan: The Fall of the Old Liberal Order, 1964–1980* (Roseville, Calif., 2001), 384.

9. Hayward, *Age of Reagan*, 384.

10. Jeremy D. Mayer, *Running on Race: Racial Politics in Presidential Campaigns, 1960–2000* (New York, 2002), 152–55, and Kenneth O'Reilly, *Nixon's Piano: Presidents and Racial Politics from Washington to Clinton* (New York, 1995), look at Reagan's racial views as they relate to his stance on states' rights.

11. Kalman, *Right Star Rising*, 166–67.

12. John Robert Greene, *The Presidency of Gerald R. Ford* (Lawrence, Kans., 1995), 157–58.

13. Hayward, *Age of Reagan*, 466.

14. Raleigh E. Milton, reporter, *Official Report of the Proceedings of the Thirty-First Republican National Convention Held in Kansas City, Missouri, August 16, 17, 18, 19, 1976* (Washington, D.C., 1977), 332–33, 347.

15. Milton, *Official Report*, 479.

16. Greene, *Presidency of Gerald Ford*, 178–79.

17. Max Frankel, *The Times of My Life and My Life with the Times* (New York, 1999), 229.

18. Kalman, *Right Star Rising*, 232–35, is excellent on the tax revolt in California and its national implications.

19. Kalman, *Right Star Rising*, 227–32.

20. Germond and Witcover, *Blue Smoke and Mirrors*, 170; Herbert S. Parmet, *George Bush: The Life of a Lone Star Yankee* (New York, 1997), 134, 246 (Reagan quotation).

21. Raleigh E. Milton, reporter, *Official Report of the Proceedings of the Thirty-Second Republican National Convention Held in Detroit, Michigan* (Washington, D.C., 1981), 245–46, 250 (blacks), 252 (Equal Rights Amendment), 255 (abortion), and 270 (tariffs).

22. Milton, *Official Report*, 294, 297.

23. William E. Pemberton, *Exit with Honor: The Life and Presidency of Ronald Reagan* (Armonk, N.Y., 1997), 191.

24. Mayer, *Running on Race*, 168; Hayward, *Age of Reagan*, 696 (quotation).

25. Robert Shogan, *War Without End: Cultural Conflict and the Struggle for America's Political Future* (Cambridge, Mass., 2002), 179–91.

26. Reagan's first inaugural address can be found online at The American Presidency Project, http://www.Presidency.ucsb.edu/ws/index.php?pid=43130.

27. Raleigh E. Milton, reporter, *Official Report of the Proceedings of the Thirty-third Republican National Convention, Held in Dallas, Texas* (Washington, 1984), 416, 418.

28. Pemberton, *Exit with Honor*, 413.

29. Asher & Associates, reporters, *Official Report of the Proceedings of the Thirty-Fourth Republican National Convention Held in New Orleans, Louisiana, August 15, 16, 17, 18, 1988* (Washington, D.C., 1989), 105.

30. Ethan Bronner, *Battle for Justice* (New York, 1989), is a detailed look at the Bork fight.

31. Cannon, *President Reagan*, 807.

CHAPTER 12. BUSH TO GINGRICH TO BUSH, 1988–2000

1. Elizabeth Drew, *Showdown: The Struggle between the Gingrich Congress and the Clinton White House* (New York, 1996), 25–35, 26 (quotation), gives the background for the September 27, 1994, event.

2. The most complete biography of the elder Bush is Herbert Parmet, *George Bush: The Life of a Lone Star Yankee* (New York, 1997).

3. Jack W. Germond and Jules Witcover, *Blue Smoke and Mirrors: How Reagan Won and Why Carter Lost the Election of 1980* (New York, 1981), 170.

4. John Brady, *Bad Boy: The Life and Politics of Lee Atwater* (Reading, Mass., 1997), 162.

5. Ed Rollins with Tom DeFrank, *Bare Knuckles and Back Rooms* (New York, 1996), 191.

6. Asher & Associates, reporters, *Official Report of the Proceedings of the Thirty-Fourth Republican National Convention Held in New Orleans, Louisiana, August 15, 16, 17, 18, 1988* (Washington, D.C., 1989), 554–55, 558.

7. Asher & Associates, *Official Report*, 554.

8. Jeremy D. Mayer, *Running on Race: Racial Politics in Presidential Campaigns, 1960–2000* (New York, 2002), 201–28.

9. Parmet, *George Bush*, 336–37.

10. Parmet, *George Bush*, 361.

11. Richard Darman, *Who's in Control? Polar Politics and the Sensible Center* (New York, 1996), 251, 263.

12. Peter Goldman, Thomas M. DeFrank, Mark Miller, Andrew Murr, and Tom Mathews, *Quest for the Presidency, 1992* (College Station, Tex., 1994), 404; Parmet, *George Bush*, 503.

13. Chris Mooney, *The Republican War on Science* (New York, 2005).

14. Joe Klein, *The Natural: The Misunderstood Presidency of Bill Clinton* (New York, 2002), 54.

15. *Congressional Quarterly Almanac, 103d Cong., 1st sess., 1993* (Washington, D.C., 1994), 122 (Armey and Gingrich); *New York Times*, June 24, 1993 (Gramm).

16. Rush Limbaugh, *The Way Things Ought to Be* (New York, 1993), outlines his views on issues.

17. Mel Steely, *The Gentleman from Georgia: A Biography of Newt Gingrich* (Macon, Ga., 2000) is a friendly biography of the Speaker that discusses the 1994 campaign.

18. Jason W. Gilliland, "The Calculus of Realignment: The Rise of Republicanism in Georgia, 1964–1992," *Georgia Historical Quarterly* 96 (Winter 2012): 439.

19. Jeffrey M. Stonecash and Mark D. Mariani, "Republican Gains in the House in the 1994 Elections: Class Polarization in American Politics," *Political Science Quarterly* 115 (2000): 95–113.

20. Drew, *Showdown*, 56; Michael Schaller and George Rising, *The Republican Ascendancy: American Politics, 1968–2001* (Wheeling, Ill., 2002), 132–33.

21. Jeffrey Toobin, *A Vast Conspiracy: The Real Story of the Scandal that Nearly Brought Down a President* (New York, 1999), and Joe Conason and Gene Lyons, *The Hunting of the President: The Ten-Year Campaign to Destroy Bill and Hillary Clinton* (New York, 2000), provide narratives of the impeachment story in 1998–1999.

22. Elizabeth Drew, *The Corruption of American Politics: What Went Wrong and Why* (Woodstock, N.Y., 1999), 172–73.

23. Terry M. Neal, "Bush Backs into Nation Building," *Washington Post*, February 26, 2003.

24. Jake Tapper, *Down and Dirty: The Plot to Steal the Presidency* (Boston, 2001), 3–53, 259–75; Jeffrey Toobin, *To Close to Call: The Thirty-Six Day Battle to Decide the 2000 Election* (New York, 2001), 3–25. It is interesting that more than a dozen years after the 2000 election there are few scholarly treatments of the contest.

CHAPTER 13. REPUBLICANS AND THE GEORGE W. BUSH PRESIDENCY, 2001–2009

1. Peter Baker, *Days of Fire: Bush and Cheney in the White House* (New York, 2013), 80–83.

2. Terry H. Anderson, *Bush's Wars* (New York, 2012), 57.

3. Both Bush and Cheney saw a major domestic task of a Republican running for president in 2000 as altering the nature of Social Security. See Baker, *Days of Fire*, 44, 49.

4. Jacob Weisberg, *The Bush Tragedy* (New York, 2008), is a good survey of Bush's political rise. Baker, *Days of Fire*, 30–64, is less probing.

5. Ron Suskind, "What Bush Meant," *Esquire*, September 19, 2008. Jacob Weisberg, "The Enigma in Chief," *Slate*, January 10, 2009.

6. Ron Suskind, *The Price of Loyalty: George W. Bush, the White House, and the Education of Paul O'Neil* (New York, 2004), 291.

7. Geoffrey Kabaservice, *Rule and Ruin: The Downfall of Moderation and the Destruction of the Republican Party from Eisenhower to the Tea Party* (New York, 2012), 385.

8. George W. Bush, *Decision Points* (New York, 2010), 135, omits the title of the warning memo and says that the document "could not confirm any concrete plans." The clear intent of the CIA warning was to ask the president to intensify security preparations in general. That he did not do. Baker, *Days of Fire*, 113, conducts an exculpatory exegesis of the CIA memo and calls the document "maddeningly unspecific." In July 2001, Attorney General Ashcroft took a similarly dismissive attitude toward the potential of al-Qaeda, saying "there was nothing he could do about that." Kurt Eichenwald, *500 Days; Secrets and Lies in the Terror Wars* (New York, 2012), 9. See also, the comments of Mark Danner, "Donald Rumsfeld Revealed," *New York Review of Books,* January 9, 2014, 68, about the administration's failure to react to intelligence warnings during the summer of 2001.

9. Bush, *Decision Points*, 135.

10. Anderson, *Bush's Wars*, 71–76, is excellent on the early focus on Iraq after September 11th.

11. James Moore and Wayne Slater, *Bush's Brain: How Karl Rove Made George W. Bush President* (Hoboken, N.J., 2003), 288–90.

12. Anderson, *Bush's Wars*, 95.

13. Mike Lofgren, *The Party Is Over: How Republicans Went Crazy, Democrats Became Useless, and the Middle Class Got Shafted* (New York, 2012), 33; Baker, *Days of Fire*, 220.

14. Anderson, *Bush's Wars*, 148.

15. Julie Rovner, "Messy Rollout of Health Law Echoes Medicare Drug Expansion," *Shots* (NPR blog), July 12, 2013, http://www.npr.org/blogs/health/2013/07/12/200401757/ACA-VERSUS-PART-D; Baker, *Days of Fire*, 292–95.

16. Baker, *Days of Fire*, 360.

17. Richard W. Stevenson, "For Bush a Long Embrace of Social Security Plan," *New York Times*, February 27, 2005.

18. Baker, *Days of Fire*, 81, quoting a White House aide.

19. "Farewell to All That: An Oral History of the Bush White House," *Vanity Fair*, February 2009, 35.

20. Baker, *Days of Fire*, 79–80, 101–2.

21. Barton Gellman, *Angler: The Cheney Vice Presidency* (New York, 2008), is informative on Cheney's role in the administration.

22. Lofgren, *The Party Is Over*, 37; Thomas E. Mann and Norman J. Ornstein, *It's Even Worse Than It Looks: How the American Constitutional System Collided with the New Politics of Extremism* (New York, 2012), 68.

23. Jeffrey Frank, *Ike and Dick: Portrait of a Strange Political Marriage* (New York, 2013), 220.

24. Lorraine C. Minnite, *The Myth of Voter Fraud* (Ithaca, N.Y., 2010), 135; Andrea Wang, *The Politics of Voter Suppression: Defending and Expanding Americans' Right to Vote* (Ithaca, N.Y., 2012), 79.

25. Wang, *Politics of Voter Suppression*, 42–59, is a useful survey of the persistence of Republican efforts to constrict the electorate to the disadvantage of minorities. Jason Noble, "Iowa voter Fraud Probe Nets Few Cases, No Trials since July 2012," *Des Moines Register*, December 16, 2013.

26. Timothy N. Thurber, *Republicans and Race: The GOP's Frayed Relationship with African Americans, 1945–1974* (Lawrence, Kans., 2013), 386–88.

27. The assurances from Chief Justice John Roberts that the Voting Rights Act was no longer necessary because the South accepted the legislation proved hollow within minutes of the decision, as southern states such as Texas and Florida moved with all deliberate speed to institute new, tighter measures on who could vote and under what circumstances.

28. Baker, *Days of Fire*, 394–95.

29. "Roberts: 'My Job Is to Call Balls and Strikes and Not to Pitch or Bat,'" CNN.com, September 12, 2005, http://www.cnn.com/2005/POLITICS/09/12/roberts. statement .

30. Anderson, *Bush's Wars*, 201–6, and Thomas E. Ricks, *The Generals: American Military Command from World War II to Today* (New York, 2012), 436–38, both deal with the surge.

31. David Grann, "The Fall: John McCain's Choices," *New Yorker*, November 17, 2008, available online at http://www.newyorker.com/reporting/2008/11/17/081117fa_fact_grann.

32. Jane Mayer, "The Insiders: How John McCain Came to Pick Sarah Palin," *New Yorker*, October 27, 2008, available online at http://www.newyorker.com/reporting/2008/10/27/081027fa_fact_mayer. John Heilemann and Mark Halperin, *Game Change: Obama and the Clintons, McCain and Palin, and the Race of a Lifetime* (New York, 2010), 359–64.

33. Heilemann and Halperin, *Game Change*, 369–76, is interesting on the Palin phenomenon in the summer and fall of 2008.

34. 2008 Republican Party Platform, available online at the American Presidency Project, http://www.presidency.uscb.edu/ws/?pid=78545.

35. Carolyn Lochhead, "How GOP Became Party of Denial on Global Warming," *San Francisco Chronicle*, April 28, 2013.

36. David Grann, "The Fall."

37. Ben Smith and Byron Tau, "Birtherism: Where It All Began," *Politico*, April 22, 2011, http://www.politico.com/news/stories/0411/53563.html; J. F., "To the Nation Born," *Democracy in America* (*Economist* blog), February 7, 2012, http://www.economist.com/blogs/democracyinamerica/2012/02/birtherism-2012.

38. Eric Kleefeld, "Poll: Majority of Republicans Think Obama Didn't Actually Win 2008 Election—ACORN Stole It," *TPM*, November 19, 2009, http://talking-pointsmemo.com/dc/poll-majority-of-republicans-think-obama-didn-t-actually-win-2008-election-acorn-stole-it. ACORN stands for Association of Community Organizations for Reform Now, which closed down in 2010 after attacks on its methods from right-wing blogs. Republicans attributed to ACORN extraordinary power in the political process, which most objective observers concluded never existed.

39. For McCain's lead, see James E. Campbell, "The Exceptional Election of 2008: Performance, Values, and Crises," *Presidential Studies Quarterly* 40 (June 2010): 235–36. Baker, *Days of Fire*, 607–9.

40. Heilemann and Halperin, *Game Change*, 382–90, reconstructs the origins and ultimate failure of the McCain initiative.

41. Lofgren, *The Party Is Over*, 26; Mann and Ornstein, *It's Even Worse Than It Looks*, 8–26.

42. Baker, *Days of Fire*, 78.

CONCLUSION: THE REPUBLICAN PARTY AND ITS FUTURE

1. Michael Kranish, "Mitt Romney Was Hesitant to Reveal Himself," *Boston Globe*, December 23, 2012; Timothy N. Thurber, *Republicans and Race: The GOP's Frayed Relationship with African Americans, 1945–1974* (Lawrence, Kans.: 2013), 387–88.

2. "Mitch McConnell: Don't Expect GOP to Raise Debt Ceiling In 2014 Without New Conditions," December 17, 2013, http://www.huffingtonpost.com/2013/12/17/mitch-mcconnell-gop_n_4461180.html.

3. Juliet Eilperin and Scott Clement, "Tea Party Republicans Are Biggest Climate Change Deniers, New Pew Poll Finds," *The Fix* (*Washington Post* blog), November 1, 2013, http://www.washingtonpost.com/blogs/the-fix/wp/2013/11/01/only-tea-party-members; Aaron Blake, "Republicans Growing More Skeptical about Evolution," *Post Politics* (*Washington Post* blog), December 30, 2013, http://www.washingtonpost.com/blogs/post-politics/wp/2013/12/30/republicans-growing-more-skeptical-about-evolution/; Mike Lofgren, *The Party Is Over: How Republicans Went Crazy, Democrats Became Useless, and the Middle Class Got Shafted* (New York, 2012), 157–59, summarizes Republican skepticism about evolution and global warming.

Suggestions for Further Reading

HERE ARE EIGHTEEN books, presented in chronological order of their topics, that seem to me essential works for understanding the history of the Republicans. No doubt others would have different lists. That's what makes history interesting.

David Herbert Donald, *Lincoln* (New York, 1995). The best one-volume study of the president and his party.

Heather Cox Richardson, *The Greatest Nation of the Earth: Republican Economic Policies during the Civil War* (Cambridge, Mass., 1997), shows how the Republicans wielded government power to win the Civil War.

Eric Foner, *Reconstruction: America's Unfinished Revolution, 1863–1877* (New York, 1988). Reconstruction was a formative experience in the shaping of Republican attitudes on race at the time and later. Foner's work repays close reading.

H. Wayne Morgan, *From Hayes to McKinley: National Party Politics, 1877–1896* (Syracuse, N.Y., 1969). An older study, but still the best narrative treatment of Gilded Age politics.

R. Hal Williams, *Realigning America: McKinley, Bryan, and the Remarkable Election of 1896* (Lawrence, Kans., 2010). The best book on this crucial election that brought the Republicans to power for a generation.

John Morton Blum, *The Republican Roosevelt* (Cambridge, Mass., 1954). This masterwork by one of the great historians of the twentieth century is essential to comprehending what made Theodore Roosevelt second only to Lincoln among important Republicans.

Lewis L. Gould, *Four Hats in the Ring: The 1912 Election and the Birth of Modern American Politics* (Lawrence, Kans., 2008). The election of 1912 was crucial for the history of the party. This volume covers the essentials in fewer than two hundred pages of text.

Herbert F. Margulies, *Reconciliation and Revival: James R. Mann and the House Republicans in the Wilson Era* (Westport, Conn., 1996). One of those biographies of a forgotten politician that tells a great deal about the Republicans and how they worked in a key period of their history.

John Milton Cooper, *Breaking the Heart of the World: Woodrow Wilson and the Fight for the League of Nations* (Cambridge, U.K., 2001). Cooper's superb study provides many insights about the Republican response to Wilson that are important for understanding the GOP.

Allan Lichtman, *Prejudice and the Old Politics: The Presidential Election of 1928* (Chapel Hill, N.C., 1979). This is an excellent study of an election that climaxed the 1920s and foreshadowed the turbulent New Deal decade to come.

Richard Norton Smith, *Thomas E. Dewey and His Times* (New York, 1982). Smith's is one of the most informative and best written American biographies of a twentieth-century politician, period.

Jeffrey Frank, *Ike and Dick: Portrait of a Strange Political Marriage* (New York, 2013). This joint biography is fair to its main characters, illuminates the Republican Party, and has an abundance of funny quotations and even better anecdotes.

Byron C. Hulsey, *Everett Dirksen and His Presidents: How a Senate Giant Shaped American Politics* (Lawrence, Kans., 2000). Dirksen was an influential Republican leader in the two decades after 1950, and this fine book shows how he did what he did.

Rick Perlstein, *Before the Storm: Barry Goldwater and the Unmaking of the American Consensus* (New York, 2001), provides rich detail on Goldwater and the election of 1964.

Stanley Kutler, *The Wars of Watergate: The Last Crisis of Richard Nixon* (New York, 1990), is a thorough account of the entire Watergate process with many insights into the relationship between Richard Nixon and his party.

Laura Kalman, *Right Star Rising: A New Politics, 1974–1980* (New York, 2010). A deft and perceptive account of how the Republicans embraced Ronald Reagan and his conservative ethos.

Geoffrey Kabaservice, *Rule and Ruin: The Downfall of Moderation and the Destruction of the Republican Party from Eisenhower to the Tea Party* (New York, 2012). Kabaservice shows why moderate Republicans lost out in a sprightly account. There is no better quick source for locating relevant manuscript collections on Republicans over the past half century.

Mike Lofgren, *The Party Is Over: How Republicans Went Crazy, Democrats Became Useless, and the Middle Class Got Shafted* (New York, 2012). A Republican defector seeks and finds intellectual asylum. Lofgren is tough on everyone and is therefore illuminating.

Index